D0960436

Bottom Feeders

Also by John Hubner
MONKEY ON A STICK

John Hubner

BOTTOM FEEDERS

From Free Love to Hard Core

THE RISE AND FALL
OF COUNTERCULTURE HEROES
JIM AND ARTIE MITCHELL

DOUBLEDAY
New York   London   Toronto   Sydney   Auckland

PUBLISHED BY DOUBLEDAY
a division of Bantam Doubleday Dell Publishing Group, Inc.
666 Fifth Avenue, New York, New York 10103

DOUBLEDAY and the portrayal of an anchor with a dolphin are
trademarks of Doubleday, a division of Bantam Doubleday Dell
Publishing Group, Inc.

Library of Congress Cataloging-in-Publication Data

Hubner, John.
Bottom feeders: from free love to hard core—the rise and fall
of counterculture heroes Jim and Artie Mitchell/John Hubner.
p.   cm.
1. Pornography—California—San Francisco—Case studies.
2. Mitchell, Jim. 3. Mitchell, Artie. 4. United States—Social
conditions—1960–1980.   I. Title.
HQ472.U6H83   1993
364.1'74'092279461—dc20
[B]   92-26091
CIP

FOR JILL,
WHO BAILED ME OUT AGAIN

Virtue is a mean between two extremes determined by reason.
—ARISTOTLE

Said, "Hey Babe, take a walk on the wild side."
—LOU REED

Acknowledgments

MY AGENT, Robert Gottlieb, called one afternoon in March 1991 to say he had received a call from Andy Finley, a former employee of the Mitchell Brothers. Now a writer-producer in Santa Monica, California, Finley was interested in writing a book about the brothers.

Jim had recently shot Artie, their friends were in the papers and on television trying to explain why, and I was as curious as anyone. Robert put Andy in touch with me, and I flew to Los Angeles to meet with him. We agreed that Andy would arrange interviews with friends of the Mitchell Brothers and former employees, and that I would write the book. Andy and I soon discovered that getting people to talk to us was not going to be an easy task. A number of writers were also interested in writing books about Jim and Artie and, in an attempt to protect Jim, the tight inner circle had grown even tighter.

Andy arranged a meeting with Meredith Bradford, Artie's widow, and we had a long talk about the kind of book I wanted to write. We agreed that a percentage of any royalties or money would be paid to Meredith, which she would then distribute to Artie's children. Meredith agreed to review parts of the book dealing with family life for accuracy, but she was to have no say in editorial content.

Andy and Meredith turned out to be fine partners. Andy proved himself adept at beating the bushes to locate old friends and former employees. He also contributed the title of the book. Meredith was thoughtful and honest all the way through, even when it was painful for her.

I am indebted to Robert Gottlieb, who became more than an agent, for bringing us all together, and for making it possible for me to write this book.

I would also like to thank George McDonald, who spent many

hours with me and made sure I got a copy of every word about the Mitchell Brothers that appeared in local papers. I came to enjoy George's offbeat sense of humor.

Mike Bradford gave me hours of his time, as did Joanne Scott, who helped me understand both her relationship with Artie and what life was like for a performer at the O'Farrell Theatre. Missy Manners was a gracious hostess during the many hours of interviewing, and she took me through her walk on the wild side with Artie in a way that was direct and heartfelt.

I got an education from Marilyn Chambers, who was candid and willing to answer any question. I listened to Bob Callahan talk about the Mitchell Brothers for hours; I'd listen to Callahan talk about anything. He's an Irish sage with a great sense of loyalty to and appreciation for his friends. I am grateful to Bob for taking a chance and talking to me at a time when few others in the inner circle would.

Two of my most productive interviews were with Liberty Bradford and Dave Patrick. I found Liberty to be strong and insightful, and I went away realizing that although I had thought I understood her father, I hadn't until I had talked to her. Dave Patrick is one of those rare individuals whom journalists are always looking for, a born truth-teller. What appeared to be an exotic and confusing world focused for me after I began talking to Dave.

Rev. Ted McIlvenna gave me his time and allowed me to roam through the Mitchell Brothers' files at the Institute for the Advanced Study of Human Sexuality. Particularly helpful were videotapes of two long interviews Jim and Artie gave to students at the Institute in 1978 and 1984. The account of a raid by Lillian Wright, a former dancer at the O'Farrell, comes from the 1984 interview.

Free-lance journalist Rusty Weston did much research for a piece on the Mitchell Brothers called "Fatal Split" that ran in *West*, the Sunday magazine of the San Jose *Mercury News*, on August 11, 1991. I purchased Weston's notes. Particularly helpful was a long telephone interview Weston had with Karen Mitchell.

Some information about Michael Kennedy came from a February 18, 1991, cover story in *New York* magazine called "Ivana's Avenger" by Michael Gross.

The History of Sex in the Cinema was serialized in *Playboy* magazine in 1967.

My researchers, Katrina Jonholt and Rob Neil, did a thorough job combing the libraries for magazine articles and the courts for documents relating to the Mitchell Brothers.

Writing on pornography tends to be highly polemical, as one writer after another leaps to condemn or defend it. The most scholarly, unbiased, and helpful book I read on the subject was Walter Kendrick's *The Secret Museum: Pornography in Modern Culture*. I am indebted to Kendrick's book, and to Gay Talese's *Thy Neighbor's Wife* for explanations of the legal battles that have been waged over pornography.

Maitland "Sandy" Zane, the veteran San Francisco *Chronicle* reporter, helped me to understand what it was like to live in San Francisco during the 1960s. I am grateful to Iris Frost of the San Francisco *Chronicle* for helping with research and to Dave Talbot, the editor of *Image*, the Sunday magazine of the *Chronicle and Examiner*, for doing the same. The co-author of *Burning Desires: Sex in America*, Dave provided insight into the Mitchell Brothers' world at a time when I needed it. Joan Smith was a perceptive reader.

Whatever its faults, this book is countless times better because, Jill Wolfson, my wife, edited it and helped me think it through. Whenever I met our friends, their first question wasn't "How's the book coming?" It was "How's Jill doing with the book?" Meaning, of course, how is she putting up with that awful subject matter you have inflicted upon her? Jill handled it beautifully, and although I have thanked her 50,000 times for her help, I haven't thanked her enough.

Joel E. Fishman was my editor at Doubleday. I knew from the first time we spoke that Joel and I saw the book the same way. Joel has been an intelligent and sensitive editor—the two do not always go together—whose work on the book has been most helpful. I consider myself lucky to have had him.

I'd like to thank my parents, Rev. John and Elaine Hubner, and my in-laws, Gil and Lil Wolfson, for their support; Jon Krim and Joyce Gemperlein for their friendship and the use of their home in the Santa Cruz Mountains when I was working long hours; Jeffrey Klein, my great friend and longtime editor at *West* magazine, for helping arrange my leave from the San Jose *Mercury News*; Bob Ingle, the executive editor of the *Mercury* and a longtime friend, for granting me that leave; David Gelber, who periodically held my hand; Cindy Dyer for her excellent child care and for copying a number of Mitchell Brothers movies (she says she watched only *Green Door*).

Dave O'Brian, a friend and colleague dating back to my days at the Boston *Phoenix* in the late 1970s, died while I was writing this book. His death made me realize how much I admired him, and how much I have adopted his standards for truth and accuracy as my own.

Six-year-old Alexander Sam and three-year-old Gwendolyn Sarah put up with their father not being home as much as he usually is. I've promised to make it up to them; they've promised to stay away from places like the O'Farrell Theatre.

Contents

PROLOGUE: "Uncle Jim Took All Our Fun Away"
1

CHAPTER 1: Mill Fodder
15

CHAPTER 2: The Best Bad Things in America
37

CHAPTER 3: Nudies, Beavers, and Horn Dick Daddies
64

CHAPTER 4: Might As Well Show It All, Bob
101

CHAPTER 5: A Stud Is Born
127

CHAPTER 6: Behind *Behind the Green Door*
162

CHAPTER 7: The Boys Hit It Big
193

CHAPTER 8: Real-Life Theater
225

CHAPTER 9: The Theater of Sex
255

CHAPTER 10: Family Affairs
288

CHAPTER 11: Artie Ups the Ante
314

CHAPTER 12: "A Possible Multiple Drowning off Ocean Beach"
340

CHAPTER 13: Guns and Threats
353

CHAPTER 14: Death in the Family
368

EPILOGUE: The Trial
381

INDEX
401

Author's Note

SOME OF THE DIALOGUE in this book is taken from court transcripts, newspaper stories, and interviews with Jim and Artie Mitchell that are in the archives of the Institute for the Advanced Study of Human Sexuality in San Francisco. The bulk of the information comes from hundreds of hours of interviews with scores of people who grew up with, worked for, or were close friends of the Mitchell Brothers. Because few people can remember exactly what was said at a distance of more than twenty years, the author has on numerous instances reconstructed dialogue based on the best recollections of relevant individuals. The author took pains to discover what key individuals were thinking and feeling at the time the events were unfolding.

No names have been changed. Identities have not been disguised; nor have composite characters been created.

Bottom Feeders

Prologue

"Uncle Jim Took All Our Fun Away"

WALKING DOWN POLK STREET to the Mitchell Brothers' O'Farrell Theatre one typically chilly San Francisco summer afternoon, Herb Gold—novelist, essayist, world traveler, and something of a rake—was wondering if the nude dancers would be there. He was, after all, on his way to a wake, and it was incredible to think of dancers at a wake. But this was going to be Artie Mitchell's wake. It was being held at the O'Farrell, where sex was theater, and nobody had appreciated the theater of sex more than Artie. Yes, Gold decided, there was sure to be exotic dancing.

Gold had been dropping by the O'Farrell to say hello to Jim and Artie Mitchell for twenty years. It would never be the same, now that Artie was gone. Cocaine-skinny and razor-tongued, Artie had been the host and clown prince of the boys' club upstairs at the O'Farrell. Gold was sorry that Artie was gone, but he was also a connoisseur of the strange, the offbeat, the utterly different, and he could not help but savor the approaching encounter with the bizarre.

Gold took an envelope out of his pocket and studied the invitation. It was engraved and oddly formal for anything connected with the Mitchell Brothers: "Please join us for a bereavement ceremony in memory of Artie Mitchell on Sunday, June 23, 1991, 1–4 P.M. RSVP."

With the invitation had come an eight-by-ten black-and-white glossy of Artie leaning against a split-rail fence with a raven perched only a few feet away. Artie had a mischievous "Can you believe this shit?" look in his eyes, a look he got whenever something unbelievable happened.

Gold couldn't figure out why the picture had been included, and had asked around and found out it had sentimental value. The picture had been taken in May 1990 in Aspen, the site of what had turned out to be the Mitchell Brothers' last hurrah.

The brothers had set out on a gonzo road trip to visit the lair of their real good buddy Hunter S. Thompson. Years earlier, Thompson had signed a contract to write a book about being the night manager of the O'Farrell Theatre. The dean of gonzo journalism had never delivered the book—there's nothing gonzo about fulfilling a contract—but he had become insider number one upstairs at the O'Farrell, living proof that the boys in the clubhouse were absolutely the wildest and coolest substance abusers on the planet.

Since Thompson's idea of romance combines weapons and explosives with drugs and alcohol, he has, from time to time, attracted the attention of the authorities. After sheriff's deputies had spent eleven hours searching Thompson's house, the Pitkin County, Colorado, district attorney had hit him with a sexual assault charge, plus four felony counts of possession of illegal drugs and dynamite.

"There couldn't have been any drugs in Hunter's house!" Jim and Artie had said in mock outrage when news of the arrest reached them. "Hunter does drugs too fast to leave any lying around."

Set up or not, Hunter's troubles were an excuse for the Mitchell Brothers to have some fun and tweak the authorities. To upstage the DA, the brothers had held a rally on the courthouse steps prior to the preliminary hearing, and had presented Hunter with a huge buffalo head (to acknowledge the movie *Where the Buffalo Roam*) and the keys to a classic Chrysler convertible.

Stunts like that had endeared the Mitchell Brothers to Herb Gold. In an era when everybody wanted to be an MBA, they were the last of the hippie pranksters. In 1983, when Queen Elizabeth II visited San Francisco, they had formed the "Irish Republican Navy" and fed hundreds of pounds of mackerel to the sea gulls in the hope that one bloated bird, and *it would only take one,* would get through and splatter the queen as she stood on the deck of the *Britannia.*

Thinking back, Gold decided that his all-time favorite was the stunt they had pulled on Dianne Feinstein when she was mayor. Feinstein was an old nemesis who had begun her career as the sole antiporn crusader on the San Francisco Board of Supervisors. "Di-Fi" wore power suits and blouses with a big bow and she was a professional prude, no fun at all. She had barely settled into the ornate mayor's office in city hall when the cops began raiding the live shows at the O'Farrell. The Mitchell Brothers figured Mrs. Grundy had to be behind the raids, so up on the marquee, below the movie title and the list of featured performers, they put "For show times call Mayor Feinstein" followed by the mayor's office number. Every time the mayor changed it, the new one went up.

Obviously, the Mitchell Brothers were great copy, and whenever Gold had dropped by the theater, journalists were usually hanging out upstairs. Gold had been around journalists all his life and could almost read their minds: I may not be making much money, I'll probably never write my novel, I might as well forget a job that carries clout at the New York *Times* or the Washington *Post,* but look where I am! Beautiful naked women are walking around nonchalant as all hell. There's beer in the refrigerator and booze behind the bar, Jimmy Reed and the Stones are on the big Wurlitzer jukebox, Artie's rolling another joint, and the guy next to me just cracked the funniest one-liner I've heard in months. If Kerouac was alive, he'd be here! Man, this is cool!

Gold liked the O'Farrell because it reminded him of his years in Paris. The place had *louche,* a French word that he translates roughly as an ease with explicit sexuality. The O'Farrell didn't have a sense of sleaze. It had a risqué, offbeat craziness, a bohemian sense of play that, with the possible exception of New Orleans, was not to be found elsewhere in America.

Or elsewhere in San Francisco, for that matter. Especially on Polk Street, the street Gold considered the most depressing in town. Polk Street was a flesh market where teenage boys, runaways and throwaways from all over the country, hard-eyed, sallow-skinned kids wearing baseball caps backward and amateur tattoos, wandered up and down, searching for the next trick. They were there at 7 A.M., hustling businessmen on their way to work, and they were there at 1 A.M., waiting for the bars to close.

Gold had heard somewhere that Jim had been arrested 190 times and Artie 186. Why had the cops pounded the Mitchell Brothers while ignoring what was happening a few blocks from the theater on Polk Street? Perhaps because explicit sex did not offend the authorities as much as turning a profit on sex did? The Mitchell Brothers made big money on sex; these poor street kids did not.

Gold caught sight of the blinking lights on the O'Farrell marquee down the street and stopped thinking about kids whose career path led to the morgue. The O'Farrell was *sui generis,* as cheerful as a street carnival. A huge undersea mural, painted in exquisite detail and at great expense to Jim and Artie, covered the back of the building. Humpback whales swam majestically and dolphins cavorted above octopuses, salmon, and colorful reef fish. On the Polk Street side, an even bigger mural depicted life in a tropical rain forest filled with tigers, gorillas, pythons, toucans, and exotic orchids.

Gold waited for the light and then crossed O'Farrell Street. He went up to the glass doors, where a sign warned people to stay out if they were offended by the explicit display of sex.

Once inside the theater, Gold was again struck by the uniqueness of the place. The tourist traps in North Beach used yards of tacky red velvet and overstuffed Victorian recliners to create a New Orleans whorehouse–neo-Mafia look. You risked getting crabs just looking at the furniture. In contrast, upon entering the O'Farrell a customer was met by assistant managers in starched white shirts and black bow ties and exotic fish gliding through a large saltwater aquarium that formed an L behind the cash register.

If the average sex club was a Kmart, the O'Farrell was Bloomingdale's. Gold had long considered the theater a major San Francisco cultural artifact, a fine way to illustrate the difference between San Francisco and other cities. When an old friend from Cleveland, Gold's hometown, came to visit, Gold would take him by the O'Farrell to show him that a sex club could be out-front and fun, not creepy, silent, meanspirited, and deadening like the nasty places back home that stayed open by paying off the cops.

Whenever a culturally hip, sophisticated New York editor flew out to visit, Gold would take him to the O'Farrell and explain how two Okies from a town called Antioch had ridden the sexual revolution to fortune and notoriety and, in some circles, cult status as sexual libertarians and defenders of the First Amendment. It was the best kind of lecture, delivered impromptu and on-site, with plenty of visual aids.

Before Jim and Artie had come along, Gold would explain, most American pornography had been cranked out in New York. It had a hard, cold Forty-second Street feel because the lizards who made it figured if it wasn't dirty, it wouldn't turn on the raincoat trade.

Jim and Artie were the pornographers of the flower children. They had brought the central idea of the sexual revolution to the screen: sex is not shameful or dirty, it is healthy, it is fun. Instead of tattooed hookers who went through the motions so they could score a fix, the Mitchell Brothers had used hippie "chicks" they recruited in Haight-Ashbury, fresh, guileless kids who had an "It's my body, I can damn well do what I want with it" attitude.

Gold's kicker to his little lecture was always the same: No actress had embodied that idea better than Marilyn Chambers. That's why *Behind the Green Door* was one of the first pornographic films to break into the mainstream.

"These guys made *Green Door?*" more than one Ivy League-educated editor had exclaimed with sudden respect. "That was the first porn film I ever saw!"

A framed *Green Door* poster, with Marilyn Chambers gazing at the camera with a naughty expression that only emphasized her wholesomeness, hung in the O'Farrell lobby, prominent as an icon. The lobby itself was now packed to the rafters, but Gold immediately spotted Jim Mitchell and walked over to say hello.

It was strange to see Jim without Artie. Business partners, best friends, closer than any married couple, the Mitchells were everyone's idea of brotherly love. When one of them had walked into a room where his brother was, he would always go over and drop a hand on his brother's shoulder, even if only an hour had elapsed since the two had last seen each other. Jim and Artie had resembled each other so closely, especially when both had beards, they had seemed more like identical twins than brothers with a two-year difference in age.

Jim, the older brother, had always looked more like a no-bullshit high school principal than a stereotypic pornographer. No thick, well-oiled hair, no gold chains or heavy gold watch, no $300 tasseled loafers. Like Artie, Jim was about five-eight and 160 pounds, and, also like Artie, a classic example of pattern baldness, with a broad forehead that rounded into a dome bordered on the sides by a band of blondish hair. At forty-seven, Jim was lean and energetic-looking, a man whose metabolism was still hot enough to burn off the love handles that form when most men hit middle age.

The brothers had differed primarily in temperament. Artie had been a puppy dog who did everything but jump into old friends' arms when they visited the O'Farrell. Jim was serious and subdued. His thin lips were often locked together, giving him a resolute, almost grim appearance.

Jim had been under considerable stress lately, but on this day of his brother's wake, he did not show it. He was tan and healthy and looked disarmingly preppie in slacks, a V-neck sweater, and button-down shirt.

"Where's Michael Kennedy?" Gold asked after they had exchanged greetings.

"No lawyers, only friends here today," Jim replied.

That's odd, Gold thought. Kennedy, a brilliant, radical attorney, had been defending the Mitchell Brothers on obscenity charges since the late 1960s. Despite the hundreds of arrests, neither Jim nor Artie had ever spent a night in jail, thanks in large part to Michael Kennedy. And now, more than ever, Jim needed Kennedy.

People kept coming up to greet Jim and give him a hug. Gold looked around the room and was amazed at how Jim and Artie had managed to cut through the San Francisco social strata. It was not an easy thing to do. San Francisco might have a reputation for being open and friendly, everybody's favorite city, but it was closed and snobbish, with old families (history in San Francisco begins in 1849) that were as smug and self-satisfied as European nobility.

Gold spotted State Senator Quentin Kopp, one of the most powerful politicians in San Francisco, smack-dab in the center of the lobby, pressing the flesh. Only in San Francisco would a man who was floating rumors about running for the U.S. Senate attend a wake for a porn king in a porn palace. And there was San Francisco Supervisor Terence Hallinan, a friend of Jim and Artie's since 1972, when the brothers had held a fund raiser for Hallinan's father, Vincent, who was campaigning for a judgeship. Vincent was a San Francisco legend, a courageous, two-fisted attorney who had defended Harry Bridges, the leader of the International Longshoremen's Association, who in 1934 had led the largest general strike in American history.

Gold got a drink at an open bar and watched while the owners of some of the best restaurants and most popular saloons in San Francisco milled about the room. George McDonald, who had once billed himself as San Francisco's first male porn star, showed up wearing his trademark Giants baseball hat and black T-shirt. George hovered around until he saw an opening, and finally went up and shook hands with Jim.

A petite, pretty woman with the tiny waist of a dancer walked into the lobby from the back of the theater, and Jim immediately went over and put his arm around his mother. Georgia Mae Mitchell looked bright and cheerful, as if this was just one more of the parties her sons were legendary for throwing.

Gold wondered how the mother must have felt when she got the phone call. He saw her smiling and shaking hands and laughing at something someone had said, and suddenly realized he would never find out by watching her. Apparently, Georgia Mae Mitchell was one tough lady.

Gold walked by the Kopenhagen Intimate Lounge, which was closed that day. On an ordinary day, customers would be in there sitting on soft cushions, shining long, red, phallic flashlights, the kind used at airports to direct planes, on women doing a "girl-girl," or lesbian act. Gold continued on past the entrance to the Cine Stage, a small theater where XXX films are shown continuously and dancers wearing male fantasy Frederick's of Hollywood or Victoria's Secret lingerie roam the aisles, asking the same two questions:

"Hi. Do you want some company?"

"Hi. Do you want to play?"

If the answer was yes, the woman would then sit on a customer's lap and perform a "lap dance." She would rock back and forth rhythmically and forcefully grind her scantily clad buttocks into the customer's groin until, in all probability, the guy had an orgasm. The rate fluctuates, but the usual, tacitly agreed-upon charge for lap dancing is $1.00 a minute.

The hallway Gold was walking up ended in the Green Door Room, a large oval room built to resemble a nightclub. There was a curved stage, an array of small round tables, big curved booths, and elaborate paintings of nymphs and satyrs on the walls. Every seat had been taken and a crowd was hovering around a bountiful seafood buffet. Jim and Artie had flirted with a second career as commercial fishermen and knew where to buy the freshest salmon and plumpest oysters. With typical self-disparaging humor, the brothers had named their first fishing boat the *Bottom Feeder.*

"Would all you narcs move away from the buffet table and come visit the show?"

The voice had come booming out of the New York Live, a small arena with a large stage equipped with state-of-the-art sound and light systems. Gold walked in and found Sharon McKnight, an exciting cabaret performer who had directed several movies for the Mitchell Brothers, emceeing a show that had been dedicated to Artie.

Now this is truly bizarre, Gold thought as he eased into a space against the back wall. A dancer was performing a "love dance for Artie" nude on the floor, slowly spreading her legs to form a large V while the crystal-clear sound system delivered the Supremes' "Someday We'll Be Together." Then a woman who identified herself as Artie Mitchell's lover for seventeen years came out and read a long poem she had written about Artie, the last truly free spirit in America. When another dancer took the stage to perform yet another "love dance for Artie," this one to Led Zeppelin's "Stairway to Heaven," Gold had had enough.

Heading back to the Green Door Room, Gold was thinking about hitting the buffet when conversations suddenly ceased and the room fell silent. A man who had just lifted an oyster off a bed of ice stopped with his hand in midair and looked over his shoulder at the entrance.

Missy Manners was standing there, looking very pregnant and very elegant with her blond hair stacked high. She was wearing a hand-beaded white dress and holding Mr. T, the teacup poodle Artie had given her. Missy took Mr. T everywhere.

The memories came flooding back so fast Missy felt faint. She grabbed her husband Robert's arm, steadied herself, and walked farther into the room. Missy had just come from the memorial show in the New York Live and it had made her feel ill. Artie had fucked those girls once or maybe twice, that was all. They hadn't meant anything to him. Missy had meant something to him. She and Artie had been soul mates. They had had a spiritual marriage.

Missy looked around the Green Door Room and remembered the

sixteen-hour day she had spent here filming *Green Door: The Sequel*. Missy had starred in the movie, the first and still the only big-budget safe-sex porn film. The film had alienated her family and had bombed at the box office, but Missy was proud she had done it.

Missy stared at the stage and remembered the night she and some friends had come down from upstairs to watch the dancers. Missy was wearing street clothes and was wildly drunk, and on a whim she had seized the stage and done a nasty strip, popping buttons and tearing clothes. She had picked up a bullwhip, a prop a dancer had left behind, and was snapping it at ringsiders when Artie had leapt onto the stage and immediately dropped his pants. Missy had lashed Artie across the ass and the audience had gone nuts. Dancers and employees who had run in to see what was happening were laughing so hard they had tears in their eyes.

The O'Farrell had been Missy's stage, the setting for a play she had lived, a real-life drama where she had destroyed the person she once was and had created herself anew. One night, she and Artie had dropped acid and, as they often did, had ended up upstairs, bundling themselves in the pool-table cover and lying under the table, talking for hours before they fell asleep.

"You know what the O'Farrell is, Missy?" Artie had asked. "It's a giant fuck-you to the establishment!"

Missy had loved that. That was what her career in porn had been: a giant fuck-you to her family and the Republican world she had left behind. Missy Manners had been an outlaw who had ridden with Artie Mitchell. God, the fun they'd had!

Missy hadn't seen Jim yet. She hadn't spoken to him since Artie's death. There were times she had wanted to and she had written him several letters, but now that she was here, she wasn't sure she could handle seeing him.

But she had to see Jim sometime and it might as well be now. Missy screwed up her courage, took her husband by the hand, and went to find Jim. She spotted him down the hall, talking to a group of people. Jim saw her coming, detached himself, and moved toward her.

"Hi, Miss," Jim said softly when they met.

Hi, Miss. That was how Jim had always greeted her, when she walked into the office to talk business or when they were all living together. Jim would come home and put his hat on the table and say, "Hi, Miss."

Missy tried, but she choked up before she could say hello. She put her arms around Jim and Jim wrapped his arms around her and Missy started to cry. Jim held her for a moment and then backed away.

Missy composed herself and introduced her husband to Jim and Lisa Adams, a former dancer who was Jim's live-in girlfriend.

"How are the kids?" Missy asked.

Artie had left six children. Jim had four. They had spent so many weekends together, Jim and Artie and Missy and the ten kids. All day long, there was at least one kid yelling, "Dad!!!" or "Uncle Jim!!!" or "Uncle Artie!!!"

"They're fine, just fine," Lisa Adams replied.

"Good, that's good," Missy said, and turned and walked back to the Green Door Room, wiping away the tears.

Missy looked up at the murals and, suddenly, her magic kingdom evaporated. The theater of sex where she had acted in scenes few women would dare to appear in, the stage where she had felt so intense and *so alive,* where she had brought her parents' worst nightmare to life, suddenly seemed cheap and tawdry, as manipulative as a tourist trap in North Beach. The dancers looked like shit, freaks from a German expressionist film. People Artie had known only casually were talking about how much Artie had meant to them. It was all phony, and Artie had hated phonies as much as he despised the hypocrites who denounced pornography in public and consumed it in private.

Artie was gone. The O'Farrell had lost its heart. Missy Manners started to cry again.

Missy placed Mr. T on the ground, accepted a handkerchief from her husband, and dried her eyes. Mr. T usually didn't leave her side, but now he wandered up the hall, looking around for Artie. That hit Missy really hard and she began to sob.

"What's wrong? Is something wrong with Mr. T?" asked an old friend who had come up to say hello.

Between sobs, Missy blurted out, "Uncle Jim took all our fun away!"

Exotic dancers at a wake was indeed strange, but they were not what made this event so bizarre. It was Jim, the genial host, the guy collecting all the hugs. Jim had killed his brother.

It had happened almost four months earlier, on the rainy night of

February 27. Jim had driven across the Golden Gate Bridge to Corte Madera, a middle-class bedroom community in Marin. He had parked his Ford Explorer three blocks away from his brother's house and slashed the tires on Artie's car. Armed with a .22 rifle and a .38 in a shoulder holster, he had walked through an unlocked door and fired eight shots from the lever-action Winchester .22, hitting Artie three times.

Chances are Jim might have made a clean escape if Julie Bajo, a former O'Farrell dancer and Artie's live-in lover at the moment, had not had the presence of mind to grab a phone, dive into a closet, and dial 911. A police officer just happened to be a block away, writing a traffic ticket. He arrested Jim, a dark figure walking with a stiff-legged gait—the .22 was jammed down his pant leg—approximately a hundred yards from Artie's front door.

At the wake, there were people in the crowd, politically hip, worldly-wise people, who still refused to believe Jim had killed Artie. Impossible! *Jim loved Artie!*

"We can't talk now, but I really need to talk to you," Jim said when Meredith Bradford came through the door.

"I need to talk to *you*, that's for sure," Meredith replied.

It was the first time Meredith had spoken to Jim since he had summarily fired her as the Mitchell Brothers' in-house attorney, almost ten years ago to the day.

Meredith was Artie Mitchell's first wife, the mother of his three oldest children. She had helped find the building that became the O'Farrell Theatre and had sewn curtains for the lobby. She had added sound to the Mitchell Brothers' loops and had shot many of their early featurettes. She had sat in courtrooms watching Michael Kennedy defend the brothers, and had finally decided: Hey, I can do what Kennedy does. She had gone to law school, passed the bar, and become the Mitchell Brothers' attorney.

Meredith and Artie had divorced in 1976 after seven years of marriage. She had remained on good terms with Artie and his brother, but then they had had a falling-out. And then she and Artie had become friends again. Sometimes it seemed to Meredith that her whole adult life could be neatly divided into periods when she was in the Mitchell Brothers' inner circle or out of it.

And now, Jim had killed Art. Until it happened, Meredith had not realized how much she had counted on Jim. Despite their feud, she knew that if something happened to Art, Jim would hold the family together. Jim was fair, he would make sure that Artie's three oldest children got everything that was coming to them.

Meredith walked around the O'Farrell, deeply troubled. She understood the wake. It was a Mitchell Brothers funeral for a Mitchell Brother, a way to show the community that Jim Mitchell was not a criminal in hiding, a way of saying, "I've got nothing to be ashamed of. I'm doing this because this is what my brother would have wanted. If I didn't love my brother and if I didn't have friends who understood that, they wouldn't be here."

It was also a fuck-you to the smug and self-righteous who think in black-and-white terms, and that was fine with Meredith. She had always been happy to stick it in the eye of people who think they can decide what's right and what's wrong for others.

What bothered Meredith were the bullet holes.

Meredith had spent several days after the killing cleaning out Art's house. The bullet holes Jim had left behind were tightly grouped and chest high.

People kept saying that Jim had gone over there to try to force Art to enter a hospital that had a drug and alcohol treatment program. Artie was so out of control, the only way to get him to go was to point a gun at him. Jim hadn't meant to kill him. The shot that had killed Artie had ricocheted off his wrist and gone through his right eye.

But Meredith kept coming back to those bullet holes. Jim had fired eight shots, and all but one were chest high. It looked to Meredith like Jim had gone into that house at 23 Mohawk in Corte Madera to kill his brother. It looked like first-degree, premeditated murder.

Jim shot up our family, Meredith thought as she walked into the Green Door Room. But why had he done it? Nobody had loved Artie more than Jim. Even she hadn't. That was the real reason Meredith had divorced Art. Jim had always come first.

But Jim had killed Art! It was inconceivable. Absolutely inconceivable. The one thing you could not do in front of one brother was criticize the other. Do that more than once or twice and you were gone, ostracized. Loyalty meant more to Jim and Art than anything.

But Jim had killed his brother!

There had to be a reason, Meredith told herself. Something had happened between them, something had caused Jim to snap. It had to be something buried deep in their relationship, something that had been boiling away inside both Jim and Art, something that went back a long time. Back to the days when they were boys, growing up in Antioch.

1

Mill Fodder

"A.J., WHAT GRADE are you starting today?" his mother asked.

"That's easy! First grade!" replied Artie, a cute little boy with a blond crew cut and an eager-to-please attitude.

"Jim, that means you got a very important job today, don't it?" his father said, laying a hand on Jim's shoulder.

"I know, Dad. You already told me about a million times," replied Jim, a third-grader with buzz-cut light brown hair and dark brown eyes. Artie was lighthearted, a born comedian; Jim was a serious little boy who insisted that things be explained.

"And I'm gonna tell you again," Jim's father said. "You take care of your little brother. It's his first day of school. You look after him, hear?"

Jim furrowed his brow and nodded. Artie was shifting his weight from one foot to the other, eager to get started.

"Off you go, then," Georgia Mae Mitchell said, handing them each a brand-new lunchbox.

"I'll be waiting for a full report when you get home," said James Robert Mitchell, "J.R." to his friends, "Rob" to his wife.

Jim took Artie's hand and didn't let go until they reached the mazelike, single-story elementary school a few blocks from their home.

When the final bell rang that day, Artie's first-grade teacher opened the classroom door and found a small boy in the hallway. It was Jim Mitchell, waiting to walk his little brother home. Every day the teacher opened the door and every day Jim was there, solemn and dedicated to the task at hand.

One Saturday morning, Jim cautiously approached his father. When he caught his eye, Jim launched into a speech he had been rehearsing for several days.

"Dad, can I get a new bike?" Jim asked. "My old one's pretty wrecked. There's this new one in a window downtown and it's really neat. It's red. I'll take good care of it, Dad, honest I will. It'll last a real long time. Till I'm grown, practically."

"How much is it?" J.R. asked.

"Sixty dollars," Jim said, and it was all he could do to keep from gasping at the amount.

J.R., a bald, homely man with coarse features, reached into his "bank," his right front pocket, peeled off three twenties, and handed them to Jim.

"Dad! Gee! Thanks, Dad!" Jim cried.

J.R. then peeled off three more twenties. Jim looked confused.

"Buy one for Artie too."

"Dad!" Jim cried.

"Take your brother and buy him one too," J.R. insisted.

"But, Dad! I'm two years older! Why should he get everything I get?"

"He's your brother, that's why. In this house, everything's equal."

The "share and share alike, all for one and one for all" mind-set that J. R. and Georgia Mae Mitchell hammered into their boys extended to distant kin. During the holidays, relatives from all over converged upon the small, two-bedroom, one-bath stucco bungalow with a joke for a front porch at 405 Gragnelli Avenue in Antioch, California. Mae cooked for days—the house was filled with the smells of rolls and roast turkey and pumpkin pies—and cousins chased each other in one door and out another.

It wasn't just a matter of hospitality. It was a matter of *taking care of your own.* Kin were especially important to a poor white like J. R. Mitchell, who never got on the great American escalator to the middle class. Kin were allies in a world that had a way of turning hostile with no warning. When it came down to us against them, a man could always rely on his own.

And he could rely on his friends. The poor whites who settled in Antioch were "Okies" who had come to work in mills that turned out low-tech products like corrugated boxes. Wages were low, but a man working in a mill made more than he, his wife, and their children did working in what California historian Carey McWilliams called "factories in the fields."

Unlike their parents, who had been run off the land by dust and bankers, these Okies did not have to follow the crops, north in the fall to pick apples, south to the Imperial Valley in the winter to harvest melons. They did not have to get up at dawn and stand in line, hoping to get a day's work. The mills worked year-round and provided medical benefits.

But the Okies did not forget that when the kids were hungry, when there was no money for gas and the closest grower who was hiring was two hundred miles away, a man could always count on his friends to help. Everyone had been in a situation like that at one time or another.

"We are proud of being Okies, but our parents didn't view the term very kindly," says Richard Lackey, Jim Mitchell's best friend in high school. "Okies in the thirties were what illegal Mexicans are today, migrants who would take any work they could get. Those of us who grew up in Antioch were half-breed Okies. We'd pretty much all been born in California, but there was still a strong Okie influence: there were no locked doors, the refrigerators were open, and you expected friends to sleep on the couch."

Thousands and thousands of tiny houses identical to the one that Jim and Artie Mitchell grew up in were built in California before, during, and after World War II faster than bees can construct hives. J. R. Mitchell could eventually have owned his house but chose not to. Like a lot of Okies, whether instinctively or as a result of clashes with the law, J.R. did not trust bankers or cops. He was fond of bragging that he did his banking out of his right front pocket. Owning something as substantial as a house was foreign to him.

When Jim and Artie were boys in the early 1950s, Antioch was solidly blue-collar, an industrial, farming, and river town of about

15,000. Forty-five miles east of San Francisco at the north end of the vast San Joaquin Valley, Antioch sits on the San Joaquin River, not far from its confluence with the Sacramento River. Though only an hour or so from San Francisco, the town was a world away from the sophisticated city by the sea.

Antioch was in the wrong part of Contra Costa County, which is divided by foothills that are crowned by Mount Diablo, a Bay Area landmark 3,850 feet high. West of Mount Diablo, places like Lafayette were Bay Area outposts, sophisticated, comfortable middle-class towns composed largely of white-collar workers and college-educated professionals. But if you drove east over Willow Pass, you were in the tules, a backwater full of redneck Okies.

"We all grew up fairly poor," says Bill Boyer, a friendly, straightforward man who owns a bar and a comedy club today and was Artie's best friend when they were kids in school. "If you didn't work in the mills, you were probably pumping gas or working in the bars."

It was an abundant supply of fresh water and a deep-water channel in the big, powerful Sacramento that had brought industry to the California delta in the 1930s. South of town, there were still farms and cattle ranches in the lovely brown foothills. Almond and walnut orchards flourished along the river, as did vineyards where table grapes grew until California wines became fashionable and wine grapes like zinfandel replaced Thompson Seedless.

Farmers and ranchers came to Antioch to shop on Saturdays. The people who lived in town worked in the mills. The fathers of Jim and Artie's friends punched the clock at Dow Chemical, Du Pont, Crown Zellerbach, Fibreboard, or Continental Can. Four miles away, the blue-collar town of Pittsburg had U.S. Steel, Shell, and Union Oil. A giant Pacific Gas & Electric steam-generating plant sat between the two towns.

For most people who lived there in the 1950s and 1960s, Antioch was the center of the universe. The threshold of expectations was as low as the visibility on days when tule fog blanketed the valley. Few people bothered to read a newspaper. Anybody in a management position, anybody who wore a shirt and tie, was suspect. Life was good if you had a soft job in a mill. Life was bad if you had to bust your ass.

"We were mill fodder," says Richard Lackey, an intense, intelligent man who is bald on top and has long hair stringing over his ears. "We were all going to work in a mill, it was only a question of which mill. The hierarchy was determined by how hard you had to work. U.S. Steel was up near the top. They had programs where you could learn to be an engineer. Fibreboard was the lowest. It was hot, dirty, physical work."

The drive to excel that was missing in the classrooms and in the mills found its expression on the football field. As in the steel, rubber, and coal towns of Ohio and western Pennsylvania, Antioch's sense of worth rose and fell with the fortunes of the high school football team. On the gridiron, a boy established his manhood and earned himself a ticket to a good job in a good mill. A winning team confirmed the superiority of the community over surrounding towns, especially archrival Pittsburg.

There wasn't much that was pretty or charming about Antioch. Long freight trains rumbled through on the tracks that divide downtown from the river. There were no broad grassy banks for picnics along the river, no quiet shady paths for walks. The waterfront was dominated by a huge cannery. A dozen bars and their adjacent cardrooms were clustered on Second Street, tough, smoky places where the music was country and western and a mixed drink was bourbon and water.

J. R. Mitchell did not come to Antioch to sweat over a machine that stirred cardboard mash in the Fiberboard mill. He came to play cards in Jack's, Blu's, the Nevada Club, the Santa Fe, and the Rendezvous. Most of the clubs have disappeared, but Blu's, J.R.'s home base, is still there, even if it is only a shadow of the jumping place J.R. knew.

Dirty and drafty, Blu's serves people who drink too much, talk too loud, and have bad teeth. The cardroom is padlocked and covered with dust. All that remains is one lonely green felt table at the end of the bar. Today, if people in Antioch get the urge to gamble, they can get on an interstate and be in Reno or Lake Tahoe in a few hours.

In J.R.'s day, there were no interstates. A workingman who had cashed his paycheck and was looking to have a few drinks and a few laughs and play some cards headed downtown to Second Street. He played lowball, in which the object is to get the lowest hand possible.

J. R. Mitchell was a professional gambler, a real-life expression of the character Jim and Artie watched James Garner play every week in *Maverick*. When the other dads were going to bed, J.R. was going to work. When they were punching the clock at the mill, J.R. was under the covers.

The professional sportsman who runs a high-stake card game in a private room in a casino in Monte Carlo is nothing more than the sophisticated second cousin of the redneck cardshark who scratches out a living in "Minimum Bet $1" games in beery card-rooms. Both must be accomplished actors. Both must be charming, or no one will want to join them at the table. Both must be able to read character at a glance. Both must be able to project what is going to happen from what has already happened.

The character J.R. played was a good ole boy who had joined the game simply because he enjoyed everyone's company. J.R. always wore a straw or felt hat with a wide band and loose-fitting clothes. If he was playing with strangers or in a cardroom out of town, J.R. introduced himself as "Manteca," a pear farmer from the small farming town in the San Joaquin Valley. No sense letting them know he was a pro.

In a voice that was as lazy as a summer afternoon and twangy as a guitar, J.R. told funny stories that went on and on. If the players just happened to get so wrapped up in a story and only half concen-trated on the cards they were holding, so much the better.

"I played cards now and then with J.R. and I always had a good time," says Micheal Sweeney, a retired Antioch schoolteacher who had both Jim and Artie in his classes. "He was charismatic. You had to like J.R. He had a good sense of humor and got along well with everybody."

J.R. was smarter than most of the mill workers sitting around a table in Blu's. He knew more about cards than they did, and al-though he was a heavy smoker who liked a drink as much as the next man, J.R. did not touch a drop when he was gambling. Gam-bling was his business, his family's livelihood, and he was able to spin a story and appear nonchalant at the same time he was com-pletely focused on the game.

J.R. cared more about his family than he did himself. He did not disappear for days at a time and lie about where he had been. Once a night, he called home to let Mae know how he was doing. He did not go on wild drunks, and he did not chase women.

"Go to Blu's, talk to the people there. They'll tell you J.R. had character," Georgia Mae pleads. "To understand anything about us at all, you've got to understand that *a professional gambler can have character.*"

This is not to say that J. R. Mitchell was Ward Cleaver with a deck of cards. Ward was the perfect suburban dad, tame as meat loaf. J.R. grew up in Oklahoma when it was still on the frontier and was the product of a family that did not dream of sending its children to Harvard because they had never heard of Harvard. The goal of J.R.'s family was survival.

One of the few traits J. R. Mitchell appears to have shared with his father was a predilection for strong-willed, younger women. Georgia Mae Guynn was sweet seventeen and still in saddle shoes when she and J.R. said "I do" in 1941. J.R. was thirty-four, a gambler who had dealt thousands of hands, smoked countless cigarettes, and been in serious trouble with the law.

J.R.'s parents, James Samuel and Minnie Lee, were married in 1893. James Samuel was twenty-eight, Minnie Lee was fourteen.

James and Minnie were sharecroppers who worked a number of farms in south-central Oklahoma, outside of towns like Mannsville and Wapanucka. Typically, they farmed corn and cotton and kept a vegetable garden, a cow, and some chickens for themselves.

In those days, James would have been described as shiftless, a bounder, or just plain no good. He was around enough to father eleven children—J.R., the seventh, was born in 1907—but most of the time James was off somewhere. Exactly where, no one ever knew.

"Father would leave without telling the family where he was going and we would not hear from him again until one day he would reappear, which could be as long as three or four years," Charles, J.R.'s older brother by two years, told Georgia Mae when she interviewed him for a family history in 1984. "As we grew older, we marveled at Mother's courage and pioneer spirit, that she was brave enough to uproot the family for such an adventure as moving to a new farm."

Through Charles's rambling narrative, a portrait emerges of the Mitchells as a family similar to John Steinbeck's Joad family when the Joads were still farming in Oklahoma. When things got tough on one farm, Minnie Lee loaded her family and everything they owned into a couple of wagons and moved to a new farm. In 1912, with the help of her older children and a couple of sons-in-law (her older daughters married almost as early as she had), the family traveled fifty miles over dirt roads to a farm on the Choctaw Indian Reservation in Oklahoma. The farmhouse was larger than any they had lived in and there was an apple orchard out back. The barn was in good repair, the soil was better than what they were used to, and the Clear Boggy Creek was nearby for fishing and swimming. The weather was good that year and the family worked hard and brought in a fine crop of corn and cotton.

The children got their reward on Christmas Day. When they came out of their bedrooms, they found their names written on stockings that were hanging all over the living room. Inside, the children found apples, oranges, candy, and a quarter. It was the first spending money they had ever had.

J.R. and his brothers and sisters were as wild as the wilderness at the edge of the farms they sharecropped. Minnie Lee didn't have much time for discipline; she had her hands full running the farm and taking care of the younger children. The two brothers-in-law weren't much good as father figures. They were kids themselves, as undisciplined as the wind.

"You want to see something the likes of which you never seen before?" one of the brothers-in-law asked J.R., Charles, and their sister Bessie one afternoon.

" 'Course we do! You go ahead and show us," J.R. replied.

It was a hot day, and the three children, whose proximity in age had made them close friends, had gone down to the Clear Boggy to fish for catfish. It was so still even the mosquitoes weren't flying and they hadn't had a bite.

"Okay, just you watch this, then," the brother-in-law said.

He reached around and took a stick of dynamite out of his back pocket. The summer doldrums vanished as the children scrambled to their feet, poised to run. The brother-in-law lit the stick, held it at arm's length, and studied the sizzling fuse. The children raced behind a cottonwood tree.

At the last second, the brother-in-law threw the dynamite into the creek. BOOM!!! A waterspout fifteen feet high erupted in the middle of the creek and the sound ricocheted off the trees.

"Was that ever somethun!" the brother-in-law shouted, slapping his knees. "Didn't I tell you I'd show you somethun?"

"Look! Look here!" Bessie shouted.

She had run to the bank and was pointing to a large catfish that was floating on the surface, belly-up. Another catfish popped to the surface. And another and another.

"The whole creek is white with them! Who'd-a thought there'd be that many? We hadn't even had a bite!" Charles yelled.

"Don't stand there! Get in there and get after them!" the brother-in-law cried as his hands flew over the buttons on his shirt. "We got days of good eatin' lookin' at us here!"

The children waded into the creek and were soon scooping up fish and throwing them on the bank. They cleaned and filleted the fish and carried them home, where the older girls rolled them in cornmeal and fried them in lard.

Train tracks ran through the fields near the farm. Charles and J.R. were out hunting one day when the train came through and killed their favorite dog.

"Bastard! Bastard!" J.R. said, fighting back tears as he picked up the mangled carcass.

"We'll fix 'em for this," Charles vowed.

The two brothers buried their dog, and the next day they hid in the woods near the tracks and waited. As the engine passed and J.R. gave the signal, Charles leaned against a tree trunk, took careful aim, and squeezed off a shot at the engineer.

"Did you get him? Did you get him?" J.R. asked.

"I don't think so," Charles said. "He's still sittin' there and the train's still rollin'."

The engineer never knew a shot had been fired at him and the boys did not try again. Their anger, and their primitive sense of frontier justice, had been satisfied. They'd gotten even.

In March 1917, J.R.'s father was found dead under a fence. Minnie Lee got the kids scrubbed and dressed in their best and the family boarded a train for the forty-mile trip to Ardmore, Oklahoma, where the family claimed the body and brought it home for burial.

"He took his gun and had started out hunting that evening," Charles recalled. "He was found the next morning at a place where he was crawling through a fence. It was not determined how or why Dad was shot. It's been a question in our minds over the years."

The Mitchell family did not miss their father much because he had not been around enough to miss. They kept on sharecropping and in 1923 had their best year. Charles and J.R. "got so rich" they did what red-blooded American boys with money in their pockets have been doing before and since: Charles, eighteen, and J.R., sixteen, bought a car.

The boys took the train up to Oklahoma City and walked into the first dealership they passed. They had studied car ads and knew exactly what they wanted.

"We'll take this one right here," Charles said, pointing to a Model T.

"Well, fine, boys, just fine. And how will you be paying for it?" the salesman asked, amused at the cocky farm boys.

"With this," J.R. said, pulling a wad of bills out of his right front pocket.

"Well! It's a pleasure doing business with young men who are so well prepared," the salesman said. "Step right over here and we'll take care of the transaction and then you can drive her away."

"We got to talk about that," Charles said.

"We do?" the salesman asked.

"Neither of us knows how to drive," J.R. said.

"I can't sell you a car you don't know how to drive!" the salesman said, throwing up his hands.

"We figured you could teach us," J.R. said. "We figured if you didn't want to, we'd buy our car from somebody who did."

For J.R., buying the car was an initiation into manhood. It wasn't the car itself; it was the look on the salesman's face when he pulled out the wad of bills, and the salesman agreeing to teach him and Charles to drive because of that same wad. J.R. never forgot that money made people do things, and from then on, unless he was broke, he always had a roll of bills ready in his pocket.

J.R. was a smart country boy whose schooling had been skimpy at best. Instinctively, he knew that life is more challenging if you use your wits instead of your hands. So instead of picking up the reins of a mule, J.R. started shuffling a deck of cards.

How J.R. ended up holding a number and facing a police photographer is shrouded in the myth his adoring sons created around him. Over the years, Jim and Artie gave different accounts of how their father had ended up behind bars.

In one rendering, J.R. did ten years in a federal penitentiary for armed robbery. But neither the Federal Inmate Locator Service nor a federal penitentiary archivist in Washington, D.C., could find prison records for a James Robert Mitchell born in or around 1907.

In another version, J.R. and a partner worked a card scam in windblown Texas towns. J.R.'s partner would pretend to get blind drunk and J.R. would wink at the rubes and subtly encourage them to fleece the drunk. The drunk would lose hand after hand. And then, suddenly, he'd go on an astonishing run—the only hands he lost, J.R. would win—and before the rubes knew it, they were cleaned out and the drunk was weaving toward the door.

Another story had J.R. and two good-looking girls working a check-kiting scam in small towns across the Southwest. They'd stick around long enough to establish an account and gain the trust of the local bankers. On a Friday afternoon, they would write over-drafts on their accounts and tell the bank managers the business they had come to town to conduct was coming to fruition. They'd promise that the first thing Monday morning they would be in to make a handsome deposit that would more than make up for this small inconvenience.

On Monday, the trio would be miles down the road.

Georgia Mae has heard all the stories, and even she isn't sure which one is accurate.

"It happened before Rob and I married and I honestly don't re-member what he went to prison for," Mae says. "When you've got something like that in the family, you put it behind you and go on. All I know is, he was in Huntsville, Texas. Whatever prison is there."

A thorough check of the Texas State Penitentiary records in Huntsville, Texas, failed to produce a James Robert Mitchell. The Oklahoma State Penitentiary had a James Robert Mitchell, but he was black and born in 1911. The Arkansas State Penitentiary had never incarcerated a J. R. Mitchell.

When the teenage Georgia Mae Guynn fell in love with J. R. Mitchell, he may have been a fugitive who had come to California on the run. If he was, it doesn't seem to have mattered to Mae. Once she decided she wanted to be with Rob, no one, not her mother, her father, or anyone else could keep her from him.

Georgia Mae is the product of the Arkansas version of Oklahoma Mitchells. She was born in a small town in Saline County, west of Little Rock, Arkansas, the daughter of a logger. Her father and mother were believing Baptists. It was hellfire and brimstone and woe unto him who lets his guard down for the instant it takes Satan to set up a base camp in the human heart. When Mae was a girl growing up, her parents would not allow a deck of cards in the house, for fear of the temptation. And she went off and married a professional gambler!

Arkansas had not pulled out of the Great Depression in 1938, when Mae's family migrated to California, looking for work. Mae's father and older brothers found jobs in the forests of Northern California; her mother and older sister went to work in a factory in the San Joaquin Valley.

Mae and J.R. met in 1940. J.R. was gambling in and around Lodi, California, and was introduced to Mae by friends of Mae's mother. He was such a gentleman, so thoughtful and so much fun to be with, and Mae, a slim girl with a tiny waist, was so flattered by all the attention he paid her, she was soon living for his visits.

By 1941, Mae's family had saved enough money to move back to Arkansas, where her father planned to open a sawmill. After giving it some thought, Mae decided to do what Rob had asked her to do: marry him and stay in California.

J.R. and Georgia Mae Mitchell began life together on a ranch in the San Joaquin Valley. Every night, J.R. drove into towns like Lodi and Stockton to gamble in drab cardrooms. Cardrooms could be found in every working-class community in California in the 1930s and 1940s. In the mid-1950s, stiff local ordinances in cities and towns across the state reduced their number.

J.R. managed to get a stake together and with a partner opened the Black Cat, a bar, restaurant, and cardroom in Stratford, a dot on the map (pop. 800) in the middle of the San Joaquin Valley. The clientele was Mexican farm workers who had spent all week cutting lettuce under an inescapable sun and who figured they had some fun coming to them on Friday and Saturday nights.

Financially, the Black Cat was touch and go. It was a shabby little place that limped through the week on the weekend receipts. But Mae and J.R. were both used to hard times. Both worked long hours and neither complained. If J.R. passed a rabbit lying dead in the road, he stopped. If the road kill was fresh, he brought it home for Mae to cook.

For J.R. and Mae, financial hardship was no impediment to having children. Both wanted children, both were confident they would make excellent parents. They didn't worry about providing for their children or what schools they would attend or how they would ever be able to put money away for college. It was enough to want children and to know that, no matter what, you would take care of them.

A healthy baby boy, James Lowell Mitchell, was born to J.R. and Georgia Mae in Stockton on November 30, 1943. Another healthy boy, Artie Jay, was born in Lodi on December 12, 1945. A third son, Robert Lewis, was born on June 8, 1947, but lived only four months before succumbing to pneumonia.

Jim was eight and Artie six when J.R. threw in the towel on the Black Cat and moved the family north to Antioch, where the mills provided a steady stream of "clients" for a cardshark. But earning a living playing cards is as difficult as earning a living playing the horses. J.R. had his ups and downs.

"He did well, but let's face it, you don't always put bread on the table playing poker," Georgia Mae says.

There are two sides to Georgia Mae Mitchell. On one side, she was J.R.'s little lady, the cute wife who was J.R.'s pride and joy. Bill Boyer can remember going to Artie's house and finding Mae in slacks and a blouse, looking as fresh as a college coed. Mae had what the 1950s called "a great build"—and today is often described as "a dancer's body."

"Well, Bill," Mae would say with a smile, "it's nice to see you again. You haven't been here since this morning."

J.R. would watch his wife leave the room and shake his head.

"It's some kind of miracle, don't you think, boys?" J.R. would ask in his slow country drawl. "What would a sweet little thing like that be doin' with a worn-out old mess like myself? Could it be that I'm a younger man than I appear to be?"

J.R. would wink and go back to his paper.

Mae was a wonderful mother, a mom a guy could be proud of. Besides being younger and prettier than the other Antioch moms, she was sweet and gracious and very accommodating. Artie and his friends would burst into the house after playing baseball in the park and Artie would shout, "Hey, Mom, we're hungry!" and Mae would reply, "Well, I just figured," and go into the kitchen and fry hamburgers for everyone.

Beneath the sweet mommy, there was another woman. Mae never directly challenged J.R. She hadn't been brought up that way. She always thought of Rob and herself as a team, and he was the captain. But she was a tough, resilient woman. She had stayed in California to marry Rob. She had skinned rabbits when there was nothing else to eat. And now, when Jim and Artie were off in school all day, Mae decided that she too was going to go to school.

It was a remarkable decision in a working-class, white-bread conservative town like Antioch, where most women took off night-gowns to put on aprons. Mae went back to school in part to supplement her husband's uneven income. But there was also a deeper reason.

"I felt like there was no me left," Mae says. "Teaching gave me a purpose in life."

Mae earned a two-year degree at Diablo Valley College and began substituting in elementary schools in Antioch. She continued her education by making the long commute to San Francisco to take night classes at San Francisco State College. She eventually earned her BA and a teaching certificate and began teaching full-time.

When Artie was in the fourth grade, his teacher read an announcement that caught his attention. After school the next day there was going to be a meeting for students who were interested in being crossing guards. Doughnuts and milk would be served.

Crossing guards got to wear white belts across their chests. Artie liked that. He liked the idea of the doughnuts too, so he decided to go to the meeting. But when he walked into the room, the teacher who was in charge of the crossing guards looked up and said, *"What are you doing here, Mitchell?"*

"I, I wanted a doughnut," Artie stammered. His legs suddenly felt weak and he was afraid he might urinate.

"Well, you won't get one here!" the teacher said, and stared Artie out of the room.

"Why'd the teacher do that?" Artie asked his father when he got home. "I didn't do anything wrong."

"You didn't do anything wrong. The teacher thinks I did something wrong," J.R. said.

"You? You did something wrong and the teacher found out about it?"

"No. He thinks what I do for a living is wrong," J.R. said. "People been looking down their noses at gamblers since a caveman carved a pair of dice out of mastodon tusks and beat somebody out of the bearskin he was wearin'."

"What's wrong with gamblers?" Artie asked.

"Nothing!" J.R. snapped. "Your daddy makes his living usin' his head and that's a damn sight better than makin' little kids feel bad about themselves!"

It would be years before either Artie or Jim adopted that point of view. When they were in elementary school, neither boy talked about his father's occupation. Richard Lackey, Jim's best friend, didn't know Jim's father was a gambler until they were in high school. When Artie's friends asked what his dad did for a living, he usually told them J.R. drove a cab at night.

Because J.R. didn't leave for Blu's or Jack's until ten or ten-thirty, he minded the boys on nights when Mae was away in San Francisco attending classes. They watched TV, and J.R. cracked jokes Artie and Jim thought were wildly funny. He'd start a story about growing up in Oklahoma, only to stop it at a point of high excitement and send the boys off to bed. He'd tease them the next morning—"You sure you want to hear the rest of that old story?"—before telling the rest.

When Jim and Artie got a little older, J.R. taught them to hunt and fish. Because he didn't have to punch a time clock at a mill, he could meet them at the river after school and spend an afternoon fishing off the bank for catfish. During the summer, J.R. was often the only dad in the stands at Jim and Artie's Little League games. In the fall, he took them hunting for geese in marshes near the river. They stalked doves in the orchards and rabbits in the foothills.

But the things J.R. passed on to his sons went far beyond the traditional masculine pursuits of hunting and fishing. As time went on, Jim and Artie realized their dad not only had the prettiest wife in town, he was the *most different* dad in town.

J. R. Mitchell had always been a Nash man. Every two years, he traded the old Rambler in for a new one. A man with a fine car likes to take it out for a spin, and with Georgia Mae beside him and Jim and Artie in the back seat, J.R. was rolling down a road outside Antioch when he glanced in the rearview mirror and saw a sheriff's car coming up fast. The cruiser perched on the Rambler's tail, anxious to pass.

"Boys, there's a cop fixin' to pass us," J.R. told his sons. "When he goes by, give him the finger."

Jim and Artie, who were around ten and twelve at the time, whirled around to face the cop. Moments later, they entered a straight stretch of highway and the cop pulled out to pass. He was almost even with the Rambler when Jim and Artie flipped him the bird. The cop slammed on the brakes, swerved back behind the Rambler, and hit the flashing red light. J.R. pulled over and got out of the car.

"I can't believe those boys would do something like that, Officer," J.R. told the cop, perplexed as could be. "I'm certainly glad you brought it to my attention. Believe me, when we get home, I'm gonna bring it to the attention of those two boys sittin' back there!"

The deputy got into the cruiser and sped away. J.R. climbed back in the Rambler and narrated his conversation with the cop. Mae shook her head but did not say anything. Jim and Artie laughed and laughed.

"Rob didn't like the police," Georgia Mae says. "He handed that distrust down to the family, and it rubbed off more on the boys than it did on me. I always tried to look on police as individuals."

J.R. was always doing something fun like that. Other dads were dull; J.R. was full of life. He told Jim and Artie things they would never learn in school, things like "Boys, you can't con an honest man, because if you offer him a scam, he won't take it." And "Always think in terms of an angle. Everybody's got one. If you can figure out what it is, you can figure out the man that's working it."

It was cool to have an angle and it was cool to escape the mills. If you had to choose, who would you rather be? The guy who slogged through a miserable week in a mill and then went downtown and lost his money at Blu's? Or a gambler in Blu's who had the angles figured and took the working guy's money?

Jim and Artie may have been wary of telling their friends what their father did for a living. They may only have received a token present for Christmas—other fathers had stayed home and saved for gifts for their own children instead of gambling in Blu's—but Jim and Artie didn't care. Their dad was their very own version of the Wizard of Oz, a magical figure who could turn life into a game. They were the good guys; the cops and other authority figures who happened to cross their path were the bad guys. And nothing was more fun than putting one over on the bad guys.

"Jim and Artie loved their dad. He gave them the cockiness that they had," says Bob Cecchini. "They were the sons of a *real* con man. They felt they were real clever, and in fact, they were. No one was going to outcon them."

By the time they were in high school, Jim and Artie had become, once and for all, their father's sons. Both were 'Tioch-style cool guys who wore their blond hair in flattops. Acceptable dress was T-shirts with the sleeves rolled up, blue denim or black Levi's, boots or black tennis shoes. Jim and Artie were tough kids but not thugs; smart kids who did not do particularly well in school. And both were examples of that essential teenage paradox: self-styled individualists who ran with a tight pack of buddies.

"They weren't bad students, but they could have been better, if they'd applied themselves," says Mike Sweeney, the retired teacher who had both Jim and Artie in his classes. "They were more Huck Finn and Tom Sawyer types, all-American, mischievous kids. Especially Artie. He was a mischievous little dickens."

Jim and Artie were both five-eight or five-nine, 150 to 155 pounds. Both, particularly Artie, had strong upper bodies. Artie could have been a competitive swimmer or wrestler, but he wasn't interested. There were too many other things to do.

Jim was tough enough to play football, but too small to play first string. "If he couldn't be first string, he wasn't going to play. That's just the way he was," Richard Lackey says.

It turned out that Jim and Artie's true sport was pool. And their second home was a juvenile version of Blu's, a pool hall called Jimmy's Billiards a few doors down Second Street from J.R.'s home base.

Jimmy's was an old-fashioned smoke-filled pool hall with a shoeshine stand and a snooker table in front, six or eight full-size pool tables in the center, and two or three snooker tables in the back. Like Blu's, Jimmy's was an all-male world. The only woman who ever set foot inside was Gladys, the stern, wrinkled, sharp-tongued lady who ran the place during the day. The game of choice was straight, or rack, pool. You called your shot before attempting it and the first player to sink 100 balls won.

Jimmy's had become Jim and Artie's second home after Artie's friend Bill Boyer got a job there and let them play free when they were out of money and there were tables open. There were always two games going on at Jimmy's: pool and verbal aggressiveness masquerading as wit. At the second game, Artie Mitchell was an acknowledged master. When he was happy and loose, Artie could be very funny. But if he got irritated, if, for instance, some guy Artie thought he should beat got lucky and beat him, his tongue turned nasty.

"If there was one thing that was original with Art, it was that his barbs cut to the bone more than others," says Bill Boyer. "Art was always ready to return fire with a bit more venom, a bit more acid than other people had."

"Artie was a punk as a kid, a skinny smart-ass, more quick-witted than any normal human had a right to be," says Richard Lackey. "I kept my distance because I didn't want him firing on me. If he did and I got pissed off, then Jim and I aren't friends anymore."

Jim had developed into a natural leader, the one other kids want to be like without ever quite knowing why. Jim was a solid guy with a lot of self-confidence. He was energetic and a good organizer who was always making things happen. He was generous to a fault. One day at the Tastee-Freez, Jim bought two cones, one for himself and one for a buddy. On his way back to his buddy's car, he stopped at a water fountain to get a drink. A little kid rushed up to turn on the fountain. Jim took a drink, handed the kid one of the cones, and went back and bought another one.

"You know how you can pick up that some people are soft in the middle and some are hard?" asks Bill Boyer. "You could tell that Jim had a solid core. He had steely eyes and a determined look. There was a tenacity about him; if he really wanted to do something, he'd do it. Also, he was very persuasive. If he wanted you to believe something, he'd talk all night until you thought the way he did. He was hard-nosed that way."

Jim was the leader of a group of guys who called themselves the Studs. They all felt the same way about Artie that Richard Lackey did, and did their best to exclude Artie from their parties and keep him out of the cars they went cruising in. That frustrated Artie and made him feel jealous, and every once in a while in Jimmy's he'd turn his razor tongue on one of the Studs.

On occasion, Artie would go too far and the Stud would come around a pool table after him. Artie would take off and the Stud would pause for the split second it took to decide whether to chase him. The Stud knew that if he laid a hand on Artie, he would probably have to fight Jim. He didn't want to fight Jim, even if he could take him. He wanted to stay friends with Jim.

So the Stud would shrug or throw up his hands and go back to his game. And Bill Boyer, who would be watching from behind the counter, would yell, "Johnny Concho!"

"Johnny Concho!" Artie would echo, and he and Boyer would both laugh.

Johnny Concho is an obscure Frank Sinatra film that was Artie and Boyer's private joke. Sinatra plays Johnny, a punk in a western town who can get away with anything because his big brother is Red Concho, the feared gunfighter. He sasses the marshal and the marshal takes a deep breath and walks away. In a poker game, Johnny lays his cards face down on the table and says he has won. No one has the courage to demand that Johnny show his hand, and he laughs as he rakes in the pot.

Then comes word Red Concho has been killed in a gunfight. And the town turns on Johnny.

"I'd kid Art all the time about being Johnny Concho," Boyer recalls. "I'd tell him if it wasn't for Jim, he'd get run out of town."

Next to football and perhaps pool, the two most popular sports in Antioch were cruising and drinking. Jim was too poor to own a car and Artie was too young, so unless Jim hooked up with a Stud who had wheels, he and Artie spent Saturday night in front of Jimmy's, leaning on their cues and drinking Sundrops, watching the cruisers roll by.

By the time Jim and Artie were old enough to argue with friends over who was going to ride shotgun, taking a detour to Pittsburg for some head bashing was pretty much a thing of the past. By the early 1960s, it was no longer cool to be a thug. *The Wild One* and *The Blackboard Jungle* looked dated and true hard rockers like Gene Vincent and Eddie Cochran had been exiled to England. Pop music belonged to the original wimps, the "Bobbys," Bobby Vinton, Bobby Vee, Bobby Rydell. It was a year or two before the Beatles arrived, but even blue-collar kids in Antioch were more interested in making love than war.

"We'd get a six-pack, go to a drive-in or up in the hills, and get drunk," Boyer says. "We'd drive around looking for that perfect blonde who'd want to go with you and you'd get laid. Of course, it never, ever happened. But the dream, the myth, was always there."

The boys would cruise until they got bored looking for that fantasy girl or ran out of gas money. Then it was time to score some beer, a sport they liked almost as much as cruising or pool.

The first thing Artie did when he turned sixteen and got his driver's permit was to alter the birth date to make himself five years older. Faking an ID was a rite of passage in Antioch. The artistry of forgery was a point of great pride among the cool guys, but in some places around Antioch the quality of the forgery was irrelevant. There were small bars, little out-of-the-way places, where you could hand the bartender a paper you wrote in English class and he would draw you a beer.

Artie and a friend would go in, flash a fake ID, and order a draft, polish it off and order another, and then, almost as an afterthought, say, "Oh yeah, and bring us a case to go." They'd lug the case out to the car and head for the river or the foothills, where they'd chug the beers and talk about girls.

Jim and Artie both spent much more time hanging out with the guys and talking about girls than they did with girls. A number of girls developed crushes on Jim and for a time he went steady with a girl named Judy, but after a while he got tired of her and went back to the Studs. Lots of girls liked witty, high-energy Artie, but he was too kinetic, too busy fooling around with his friends or hanging out in the pool hall to get involved with any of them.

It is probable that the closest either of the future porn merchants came to actual sexual intercourse in high school was a film Bill Boyer showed.

It was in Bill Boyer's house (actually, in his room; Bill had that teenager's dream, a room with an outside entrance) that Artie Mitchell first encountered commercial sex. Boyer's older brother had gotten a copy of *The Nun,* a black-and-white 8mm film that was distributed by salesmen who looked both ways before opening the trunks of their cars. Typically, the film was screened at smokers in places like an American Legion Hall or an Elks Club.

Like mainstream films, pornography reflects the society that produces it. In every corny old Western, there is always the same tired scene. John Wayne wraps his arms around a feisty, independent young lady and tries to kiss her. The young lady beats his chest with her fists and struggles to break free. Then she melts, closes her eyes, and passionately returns the kiss.

The pornography of that time was that scene over and over again. Only instead of a kiss, the girl ends up eagerly submitting to sex.

Basically, pornography was a male's adolescent version of the romance of sex. Boy meets girl; girl fulfills boy's every carnal desire. Life isn't like that (and therein lies pornography's appeal), particularly in a conservative, working-class town like Antioch, where a girl was likely to put a death grip on a young man's wrist, look him in the eye, and say, "I'm saving *that* for my husband."

In *The Nun,* things happened the way young men thought they were supposed to happen. A woman dressed as a nun walks into a room and a Peeping Tom watches through a window as she disrobes. He finally goes through the window. She, of course, resists, but like the leading ladies in the old John Wayne films, she quickly submits.

For years, magazine and newspaper feature writers repeated the myth that Jim and Artie were both in Boyer's room that night and that one turned to the other and said, "Hey, bub. An ole boy could make himself a lot of money with these movies." In that moment, their careers in pornography were supposedly born.

In fact, neither Jim nor Artie had any idea what he was going to do when he got out of high school. The only thing they were certain of was that, one way or another, they were going to get out of Antioch.

The summer after Jim graduated in 1961, the Studs got together to drink beer down by the river. The mood turned nostalgic as they remembered the good times.

"Remember the time we got juiced up and climbed to the top of that stanchion?" someone asked, pointing to the huge tower that supported high-tension wires as they crossed the river.

"Yeah," Jim said, "we got to the top and—"

"No hands!" Richard Lackey interjected.

"Remember the Ranchero out on Highway 4?" Jim asked.

"Yeah," Lackey said. "We're in the back, we're going a hundred twenty miles an hour, we stand up, and—"

"No hands!" Jim said, laughing.

"How 'bout the time we climbed that bastard and dove into the river?" one of the Studs asked, pointing at the stanchion again. "How far up did we get before we jumped?"

"Too far up," Lackey said. "I'm more scared now looking at it than I was when we did it."

"The Studs, man," someone said, "the Studs."

"This town has never seen the likes of us. Won't again either," someone said.

"Let's show 'em we were here!" Jim said. "Let's say goodbye the Studs' way."

The next morning, a custodian at Antioch High arrived to find

THE STUDS and CLASS OF 61 painted all over the building. Two days later, Lackey walked over to Jim's house and told him the bad news. The cops had picked up a Stud and he'd confessed. The other guys were turning themselves in.

"Jimmy and I were in a jam," Lackey concludes. "I couldn't afford the fine and I don't think he could either. It was pay the fine, go to jail, or join the Army."

Richard and Jim did what 95 of the 125 boys they graduated with had already done: they joined the Army. Jim's problem of how to get out of Antioch and what to do with his life had been solved, at least temporarily.

Two years later, in 1963, Artie faced the same problem. Artie's grades were mediocre, and about the only thing he had earned in high school was a letter suspending him for drinking. He found himself envying Bill Boyer, the president of their senior class, who was on his way to Diablo Valley College. Boyer was determined to work hard and get good grades, and then transfer to a state college and major in journalism.

"I've got to get out of this goddamn town!" Artie told Boyer one night over a hamburger in Hazel's. "Can you imagine spending your life working in a mill? Or flippin' burgers in this goddamn place? The body snatchers have been through here, man. These people are the livin' dead."

"Nobody's saying you have to live here, Art," Boyer replied.

"I know," Artie said. "I just don't know how the hell I'm going to get out."

2

The Best Bad Things in America

"AMERICA IS PISSING AWAY its moral capital!" an anguished longhair was saying in a political science class at Diablo Valley College in 1966. "We're sending marines into the jungle to kill and be killed and lying about why they're there! There's one good thing you can say about the whole sorry mess, though. It's makin' people wake up to the fact that this country is run by moral lepers!"

"That's bullshit!" Jim Mitchell said, quietly but firmly, looking at the longhair from a seat across the classroom.

Everything about the freak offended Jim, from his politics to his ratty T-shirt and worn-out sandals. The guy had no respect.

Prematurely balding and deadly serious, Jim looked like someone you would expect to find behind a desk in an H & R Block office. But there was a fire burning under that nondescript appearance. After taking things cool when he was in the Army, Jim was surprised to find himself feeling more militant at DVC than he ever did when he was wearing olive drab.

"Complete and utter bullshit!" echoed his friend Richard Lackey, who was as deadly earnest as Jim.

"If you'd been in the service, you'd know this is all about keeping the Communists from taking over the world," Jim said.

"Oh, sure! The North Vietnamese are going to attack California in sampans!" the longhair fired back.

"First Vietnam, then Thailand, then India, then who knows?" Richard said, ignoring the kid. "I say level North Vietnam. We won't have to worry about them coming south then."

"Flatten Hanoi," Jim agreed. "They'll have to stay home to rebuild it."

Teachers at DVC relished the stormy debates, and there were times when Jim and Richard would come out of class with their hands shaking in anger. Merle Haggard had defined Jim and Richard's politics in "Okie from Muskogee." They were not right-wing ideologues, nor were they ex-grunts who had seen their best friends blown to bits by land mines in Vietnam. Richard had done soft duty in France. Jim had served as an intelligence officer in Okinawa before the Army transferred him back to a security installation near Petaluma, California.

Jim had not been the kind of security officer who worked with secret codes or processed information on troop or tank movements. He drove the bus that ferried soldiers around the base in Marin County, and that was fine with him. He had no interest in becoming a hotshot intelligence officer or doing whatever it was you had to do to get promoted.

Jim had a typically blue-collar view of the way the world worked. He thought we needed a strong Army to keep the Commies at bay, but he also thought the Army was stupid, a bad joke that lasted three or four years. Sloughing off and trying to have a good time with a few good buddies was about the only option open to a guy with a head on his shoulders.

But now, with the Army behind him, Jim had turned serious about school in the same intense way he had once been serious about winning an argument or being the leader of the Studs. Jim had returned to Antioch and come face to face with the problem that had haunted him through high school. His friends were stuck in dead-end jobs and passionate about nothing but the cars and the good old days. What was he going to do to get the hell out of there?

Jim had decided to use the GI Bill to follow the route his mother had taken before him: Diablo Valley College and then San Francisco State. To an Okie like Jim, San Francisco was a magic land where people had interesting jobs, lived in wonderful houses, and led exciting lives. Jim was determined to join them. He wasn't sure what kind of work he wanted to do in San Francisco, but he knew the ticket of admission was a college degree, and he knew a degree would open up all kinds of choices he did not have now.

Jim had expected to find students at DVC who were as committed to getting ahead as he was. Instead, the classes were cluttered with pimply hippies. Jim had also assumed that his time in the service would give him an edge. He had been around and seen a few things, he'd paid some dues. Instead, the hippies assumed he was a moron or a fascist tool, or both.

What the hippies thought bothered Jim less than their extreme self-righteousness. They were such moralizers, so absolutely convinced they had the far-out truth on everything. If they really thought that college was shit, business was shit, the government was shit, then why were they taking classes at a junior college?

Jim had asked hippies that a couple of times during classroom debates and their answers had always been the same: We're working for change within the system. Well, how are you going to change things? Jim had asked. By being me, more than one hippie had replied.

The hippies were bullshit, and Jim didn't have time for bullshit.

Diablo Valley College is in Pleasant Hill, fifteen miles from Antioch, in the sophisticated eastern half of Contra Costa County. DVC drew students from all over the county, and its modern classrooms and green grass were quite a contrast to Antioch High, which was as stripped down and charmless as a building on an Army base.

The students at DVC were different too. Girls in high school had chewed gum and worn their hair in beehives. DVC girls from nearby Orinda, an affluent commuter suburb, were slim, tanned blondes who all looked as if they were on the swim team. At first, Jim couldn't figure out why they smiled at him when passing in a hallway. Did they like him or something?

Then he realized they were simply being nice. Unlike the girls in high school, who generally regarded boys with suspicious glances because boys only wanted one thing, girls from Orinda smiled at everybody.

At Antioch High, flattop cats showed up for school wearing Levi's and white socks. At DVC, boys from upper-middle-class Lafayette and Danville looked like they could be members of the Beach Boys.

Their longish hair was always carefully combed, the short sleeves of their striped sport shirts were always rolled up, and they usually wore nicely pressed chinos and penny loafers, often without socks.

But working-class kids from the tules felt intimidated by kids from the western half of the county, and the more socially sophisticated students from towns like Lafayette avoided the rubes from Antioch. Students from Antioch sat at the self-proclaimed Antioch table in the cafeteria. Students from commuter towns like Concord and Walnut Creek kept to the tables they had staked out.

"What teacher's good? Who do the Antioch guys take?" Jim had asked Bill Boyer, Artie's best friend, on the day he went to DVC to register for classes.

Bill was starting his last semester at DVC and had already been accepted at Chico State College, where he was going to major in journalism. Artie had followed Bill to DVC, but his heart had not been in it. He had screwed around and cut classes, dropped a few courses and failed a couple of others, and had finally fallen below the minimum number of credits the draft board required students to carry to qualify for a 2-S deferment. To avoid being drafted and sent to Vietnam, Artie had enlisted.

"Gerald Hurley," Bill had replied. "All the Antioch guys take Hurley. I've had him three times. He's great."

Gerald Hurley believed that great writers reach a deep level of truth and have something to say to all people at all times, and he taught students to read actively rather than passively, to dig for meaning. Jay Gatsby wasn't just a bootlegger who went nuts over a rich, skinny bitch named Daisy, Hurley told his students. Gatsby was a larger version of a kid from Antioch, a poor boy from nowhere who was determined to make reality conform to his dreams.

Jim and Bill Boyer also enrolled in a film appreciation class Hurley was offering that semester. It was the first film course offered at DVC and it was a triumph for Hurley, who had finally convinced the administration to take the radical step of adding to the curriculum a class that examined the twentieth century's most powerful medium.

Jim loved Hurley's English class, but it had nowhere near the effect on him the film class did. In English class, Hurley made his students do a lot of textual analysis. It was hard work to find the paragraphs that unlocked the character of Jay Gatsby. Kids from

Lafayette who had had better English classes in high school always seemed to find them first. It left Jim feeling frustrated and inferior.

But in film class, you could sit back and watch the story unfold in front of you. Jim and Artie had always been great movie fans. When they were kids, they had loved staying up to watch *The Late Show*. But Jim had never seen films like *The Birth of a Nation; The Battleship Potemkin; Hiroshima, Mon Amour; The Virgin Spring*; or *Jules and Jim*. He had had no idea that movies could be so serious—not serious and dull, like Hawthorne or some other dead writer, but serious and alive!

The comfortable, better-educated kids from Lafayette had no advantage over Jim in film class. If anything, he had the edge on them. When Hurley broke a film down and explained how a story is told in pictures; when he talked about establishing conflict, developing characters, and telling a story, Jim knew exactly what he meant. His father had been doing that for years.

J.R. wasn't a great storyteller because he was a born comedian or could mimic voices. J.R. told stories that had real characters and a beginning, a middle, and an end.

Hurley stressed that, more than anything, a director strives for control over his material. He took *Jules and Jim* apart and showed how Truffaut had used every scene to create an effect. Jim didn't say so in class, but it seemed to him that making a film wasn't all that different from playing cards.

A director tried to control what happened in front of a camera; Jim's father tried to control what happened during a poker game. J.R. had painstakingly taught Jim and Artie how to play cards, had spent hours showing them over and over again how to use cards to control a game. Jim had learned that if you held the right cards and knew how to use them, you could script a card game.

And now Jim was learning that directors did the same thing. It might even be easier to be a director than it was to be a gambler because a director had more control over a film than a gambler did over a card game.

Jim and Richard Lackey earned much higher grades at DVC than either had in high school. When they graduated, the two agreed that although the hippies had been a huge pain in the ass, the political free-for-alls they had fought in class had probably done more to prepare them for the big world of San Francisco State than anything they had absorbed from a book. The guys from Antioch had taken the best shots the hippie-dippy Commie-pinkos could fire and had emerged with their belief systems unaltered.

That would soon change.

The Bay Area in the late 1960s was the center of a widening gyre. Hippies had turned the Haight, a neighborhood of run-down Victorians bordering Golden Gate Park, into an international mecca. Hippies were a crazy quilt of innocents, convinced that life was a trip and eager to take it. Some were dedicated hedonists— "What's good? Sex and drugs and rock 'n' roll. What's better? More sex, more drugs, more rock 'n' roll." Others were romantics—"We can change the world"—and still others were civil libertarians— "We the people shall determine our own destiny." They were united by a hatred for the Vietnam War and the draft and, most of all, by a strong desire not to repeat the lives their parents had led.

During a short halcyon period, the world really did seem different in the Bay Area. Young men and women hitchhiked everywhere without incident. People met in the park and invited each other home for dinner. They formed communes and studied Zen and yoga. They dropped acid to explore everything from the hairs on a caterpillar to the true nature of love.

The Movement found its cultural expression in music, wonderfully smart, blues-based rock 'n' roll. The Grateful Dead, Big Brother and the Holding Company, the Jefferson Airplane, Santana, and Quicksilver Messenger Service were playing gigs in clubs all over San Francisco. Allen Ginsberg and Ken Kesey were organizing love-ins and be-ins and happenings in Golden Gate Park, events which a majority of both the performers and the audience experienced with perceptions that had been altered by marijuana and LSD. Bill Graham, the fiery leader of the San Francisco Mime Troupe, was sneaking past the guard at the San Francisco *Chronicle,* elbowing his friend the columnist John Wasserman away from his desk, and spending hours on the phone calling long-distance, piecing together the network that would make him rock's great impresario.

Over at *Ramparts* magazine, editor Warren Hinckle and the leftists on his staff were rubbing their hands in glee. Ronald Reagan had been elected governor of California, just as they had hoped. Reagan was a dolt, a ham actor whose political scripts were written by Neanderthal right-wingers. Hinckle and his friends in the New

Left were certain that Reagan's ascension to power would trigger the revolution they so eagerly anticipated.

Across the bay at the University of California, Berkeley, the Free Speech Movement had mushroomed into mass rallies against the war and the school's bureaucratized, factorylike approach to education. On Telegraph Avenue, students and street people were fighting rock and tear-gas street battles with the police over "People's Park," a small open space the University of California wanted to build on and political activists and hippies wanted turned into a park. In front of the Armed Services Induction Center over in Oakland, police were hauling away scores of antidraft protesters. Their bodies limp in passive resistance, the protesters sprang magically to life to smile and flash the peace sign before disappearing in paddy wagons.

In the Oakland ghetto, the Black Panther Party was taking it to the streets in a way that brought a ton of cachet to opposing the Man. The Panthers had Eldridge Cleaver, the eloquent author of the best-seller *Soul on Ice,* and Huey P. Newton, a martyr supposedly framed by the cops, a black revolutionary with a beautiful face and fine skin, a sex symbol in a black beret and leather jacket.

Although not as well known nationally as Cal/Berkeley, that infamous breeding ground of student radicals, the drab campus at San Francisco State was also producing socially active students. If Berkeley radicals identified with the proletariat, SFS students *were* the proletariat. Most of them didn't have the grades to get into Berkeley or parents who could afford the tuition. Most had part-time jobs and commuted to the school on Nineteenth Avenue, on the edge of solidly middle-class neighborhoods and Lake Merced.

The protest politics of the 1960s had begun earlier in San Francisco than they had in other cities. In 1960, a routine meeting of the House Un-American Activities Committee was scheduled to be held in San Francisco's city hall. Joe McCarthy was dead and in disgrace by then, but HUAC was still active. Beats, radicals, and students from Berkeley and SFS showed up to oppose the hearings and the police overreacted. Somebody turned on a fire hose and tried to wash the protesters down the marble steps of San Francisco's ostentatious city hall; motorcycle cops beat college kids with nightsticks.

The riot helped awaken what had been a somnambulant, low-profile school. In the early 1960s, SFS students picketed car showrooms on Van Ness Avenue, carrying signs that accused dealers of being racist because they employed no black salespeople. By the mid-1960s, the school had one of the most powerful Black Student Unions in the country. Articulate, street-smart black leaders confronted the administration at every opportunity and staged rallies to issue demands for a black studies program and an end to the war in Vietnam. The rallies attracted wide attention and a school that had always lived in the shadow of Berkeley and Stanford suddenly had political cachet as one of the truly radical campuses in America.

Say no to fascist Amerika! SFS activists shouted at students. Burn your draft card! Boycott classes! Don't study history, make history! Take the battle to the streets!

"Jimmy, there's a big event scheduled for noon today that sounds interesting," Richard Lackey mentioned to Jim a few weeks after they had arrived at SFS. "The radicals are going to debate some profs and people from the administration. Wanna go?"

"Why not? It'll be a scene, just like everything else around here," Jim replied.

DVC had *not* prepared Jim and Richard for San Francisco State. San Francisco had always been like a foreign country to the boys from Antioch, a place you visited, had a look around, maybe went to a Giants game or saw a movie, and then returned to your own turf. Now Jim and Richard were in San Francisco every day, and they were overwhelmed by what they had found.

Their classes seemed irrelevant, the least important thing that was happening. The real action was outside the classrooms, where two students with wild looks in their eyes would begin arguing and other students would gather to listen. Pretty soon, the spectators would start taking sides, and before long everybody would be arguing. The louder your voice, the more extreme your views, the more attention you attracted.

Jim and Richard had joined the fray at DVC; at SFS they kept their mouths shut. It was one thing to take on a hippie from an East Bay suburb; it was quite another to take on a black activist from a tough street in the Mission who wore his hair in a do-rag and had mastered the art of ridicule.

At noon that day, Jim and Richard went to the debate between campus radicals and conservative representatives of the faculty and administration. Like many before and many after it, the attempt to conduct a "rational discussion of the issues" turned into a travesty.

A radical opened with the usual denunciations of U.S. imperialism. A professor stepped to the microphone and was reading from notes when the radical jumped up and interrupted him. The professor waited for the radical to stop talking, and when he didn't, the professor asked him to sit down. The radical demanded that the professor answer the questions he had posed. The professor went back to reading his notes and the radical interrupted again.

"This is intolerable!" the professor finally shouted. "Until you recognize the rules of debate, until you learn common decency, *until you grow up,* reasonable discourse on this campus is impossible!"

With that, the delegation from the faculty and the administration marched off the stage to the sound of loud boos.

In the back row, Jim and Richard were shaking their heads, more in humor than in disgust. It was exciting to see passions run so high. But faculty members stomping off the stage like that struck them as arrogant.

Jim and Richard prided themselves on being "fair guys" who wanted to hear what everybody had to say. They were two of the very few people in the audience who had come to the debate prepared to side with the conservatives from the faculty and the administration. So why hadn't the professors stuck around and slugged it out? Couldn't they take a punch? Did they think they were above mixing it up with the radicals? If they didn't have the guts to fight it out, why the hell had they climbed into the ring?

Richard Lackey commuted to SFS from Antioch, where he had a part-time job in a Lucky supermarket. Jim had moved into an apartment over a bar on Diamond Street with Bob Cecchini, another old friend from Antioch High. It was a nice San Francisco apartment— large rooms with high ceilings and hardwood floors—in a lower-middle-class neighborhood.

Jim was majoring in political science and minoring in film, and in time he became friends with other film students who shared his passion for the medium. They often stayed up late, discussing the differences between Jean-Luc Godard and François Truffaut.

Many of Jim's new friends were radicals and would-be revolutionaries who had come to San Francisco to fight the good fight. Jim accompanied them to hear the Grateful Dead in Golden Gate Park and to informal be-ins where Allen Ginsberg, Lawrence Ferlinghetti, and Ken Kesey read from their works. The film students got Jim stoned and took him on long walks through the Haight to check out the hippies. A couple of times, they dropped acid together.

In only a few months, Jim had entered a world he had never imagined existed, a world that was farther away from Antioch than he had ever expected to travel. Jim watched and listened and kept his political views pretty much to himself. By osmosis as much as anything else, he absorbed the left-wing rhetoric that was as omnipresent in those days as marijuana smoke. In time, Jim realized he had been on the wrong side.

The radicals were right about the way things worked. Why hadn't he seen it before? They weren't really saying anything different from what J.R. had been saying for years. The fat cats dealing the cards in America had stacked the deck against guys like Jim Mitchell. He was white trash, an Okie who was supposed to stay in Antioch and be mill fodder. Meanwhile, the people who did nothing but invest in the corporations that owned the mills were getting rich.

In his own unique way, J.R. had rebelled against that power structure. And look what had happened to him. Because he had not played by the power structure's rules, the smartest man Jim had ever known had been exiled to the purgatory of small-stakes card games in Blu's. Jim got angry every time he thought about it.

But it wasn't just rhetoric that turned Jim Mitchell's political views around. It was violence.

J.R. had passed on his dislike and distrust of the police to Jim, and every time Jim went on campus he saw more cops. The Black Student Union's demands for courses in black history had not been met and radical students had begun storming buildings and taking over classes. That had led to the appearance of young men with mustaches, short hair, and windbreakers, who roamed through the crowds, detached and seemingly unconcerned. And then suddenly two of the windbreakers would wade into the crowd. One of them would say, "Police! You're under arrest!" and grab a kid and handcuff him while the other cop read him his rights. Then they'd drag him through the crowd.

Naturally, the arrest would incite the students and there was always somebody who would try to stop it. That would lead to more arrests for interfering with an arrest.

On a Tuesday in 1968, Lackey and Jim were on their way to an antiwar rally when Richard grabbed Jim's arm and said, "Look. Up on that roof there. Look at those guys."

Jim looked up and saw men standing at the edge of a roof that overlooked the rally site. One of the men was saying something into a walkie-talkie.

"Cops," Jim said.

"They're everywhere. Look over there, and over there, at that building there," Richard said, pointing around.

The rally started and tactical officers marched in and formed a ring on the outer edge of the crowd. The tac squad had been on campus before, so no one in the crowd paid much attention, even though today the cops were out in force.

The rally started and the same old scenario played out. Plainclothes officers waded into the crowd and made an arrest. Students intervened and more plainclothes officers appeared. And then all hell broke loose.

"Jimmy! The tac squad is charging the crowd!" Lackey cried. "Look! Their badges are off! The bastards have taken their badges off!"

The tactical squad cops had drawn riot batons and were carrying them raised in both hands. Some of the cops had ax handles. Slowly, steadily, they waded into the crowd. There were shouts and screams and the sickening sound of clubs hitting flesh and bone. People ran in every direction. Everywhere they headed, they ran into cops. The police had sealed off every escape route.

"Lackey! Up there on the roof!" Jim shouted. "Those fuckers are using walkie-talkies to tell the cops which way to go!"

"Jimmy! This way!" Richard yelled.

Lackey had spotted a break in the police lines. He and Jim broke through, ran between a couple of buildings, and separated. Lackey ran up Nineteenth Avenue and kept running until he reached his car. He jumped in and drove straight home to Antioch. That evening, he went to his part-time job at the supermarket.

"Hey, Lackey, what happened over there today?" one of his co-workers asked when he walked in. "I saw the whole thing on TV. They're calling it Bloody Tuesday."

Three or four workers, people Lackey had known all his life, gathered around him.

"You guys wouldn't believe it!" Lackey said. "The cops caused it! It was a police riot!"

"Bullshit it was a police riot! Radicals and outside agitators started it just like they always do," one of the workers said.

"That's right," another worker added. "I saw it on TV. That's exactly what happened."

"Wait a minute, wait a minute," Lackey said, waving his hands in the air. "I was there and you guys are telling me what I saw didn't happen?"

"You were too close, Lackey. You can't tell what's happening when things are going crazy like that," one of the workers said.

"Bullshit! It was a police riot!" Lackey said, raising his voice.

"You know something, Lackey? The more time you spend at that school, the more you sound like one of those fuckin' hippies."

"You know something? Maybe you're right!" Lackey said, turning to face the guy. "And I'll tell you something else: I'd rather be a hippie who sees what's going on with his own eyes than a dumb Okie who believes everything he sees on TV!"

Lackey did, in fact, join the counterculture, leaving SFS to hitch-hike across the United States again and again, staying with Jim whenever he wandered back to the Bay Area. Eventually, he settled in Alaska, where he became a commercial fisherman.

Jim's passion for film proved to be the anchor that helped him ride out the radical tide that swept away his old Antioch buddy. At this early point in his career, whether Jim was able to conceptualize visually or was any good with a camera was not nearly as important as the fact that Jim was a natural leader.

Film, being a machine-based art, requires money and people. A novelist needs time, a place to work, a pen, paper, and envelopes in which to send his work into the world on a wing and a prayer. A filmmaker needs a camera and a crew to help with the lights, sound, and editing equipment. If the members of a film crew like each other and enjoy working together, they will do more work in less time and produce a better product than a crew that spends time bitching and bickering.

Jim, who had grown up surrounded by kin and evolved into the leader of the Studs, had turned out to be a terrific line producer. The tight group of student filmmakers Jim belonged to were very good about helping each other develop ideas for films. Jim was their take-charge guy, a balding elder who figured out how they could share equipment and help each other on projects without leaving anyone feeling angry or slighted.

Through film, Jim had found a way to approach the world. He could never be a hippie; they didn't have any ambition. He wasn't really a radical either. A little political theory was interesting, but large doses were boring, and Jim was not fueled by a drive to change the world.

A filmmaker did not have to change the world. He only had to find the drama in what was going on. A filmmaker can be detached behind a camera, he can observe, and Jim liked that. He was far more comfortable recording an event than he was participating in it.

Academically, Jim found it was easier and a lot more fun to make a film than to write a paper. He didn't have to figure out a thesis or do research. With film, he was free to do whatever he wanted. It didn't matter if the events he recorded happened in the world or inside his head.

SFS in the 1960s epitomized the new laissez-faire approach to education, which, depending on your philosophy, was a freshening wind blowing down the cobwebbed halls of academe or a mindless trashing of educational standards. In the creative writing program, students were working on senior projects like William Blake as a comic book. In the film school, students were encouraged to make experimental films that documented their dreams and fantasies, no matter how erotic they might be.

"There was no prior restraint with students' work," says James Goldner, who taught Jim filmmaking and is still teaching at SFS. "As film people, we felt there were no no-no's."

Incipient filmmakers typically think of themselves as the second coming of Fellini or Truffaut, prattling on about the uniqueness of their vision and the courage it takes to approach the medium on your terms, not Hollywood's. Jim emerged as the star of his class, perhaps because he was more mature and took a pragmatic rather than a sophistic approach to the medium.

"Jim was a very diligent guy," says James Goldner. "He stood out. He seemed to have that energy, he was going to do it. I'd remember him even if he hadn't become so notorious later on."

"I think I got it. I think I figured out how we get the money we need to make our films," Jim announced one evening over a spaghetti dinner in Earl Shagley's apartment. Shagley had developed into Jim's best friend among the SFS filmmakers.

"One of your rich Oklahoma uncles died and left you a fortune, right?" joked Annie, another film student.

"No, no, let's hear this, Annie," Shagley said. "Let's find out if this is Jim or the joint talking."

"What's the difference?" Annie cracked, and everyone laughed.

Earl was blond, bearded, and long-haired, an amateur folksinger from Indiana who had come to San Francisco because he "was certain there was going to be a revolution" and wanted to help make it happen. He left the Movement "when it came to guns and blowing up PG&E towers."

Annie, a twenty-year-old filmmaker from Los Angeles, was small and very smart. She had a better technical grasp of film equipment than either of her two male friends, and she was driven to become a serious filmmaker. Annie had dated Earl; now, she and twenty-two-year-old Jim were a couple. Earl had begun seeing a woman named Maureen, and everyone had remained friends.

Earl relit the joint and tried to think of another one-liner. He didn't want to appear too eager to hear what Jim had to say. The fact was, Earl considered Jim Mitchell the most impressive man he knew.

Jim was always loose, always funny, very kind, and very generous. If he owned something, anything from a shirt to a camera, you could consider it yours. Earl had a big German shepherd, and one day Jim had reached down and used his thumb and forefinger to wipe mucus away from the dog's eyes. That had really impressed Earl. Not many people would do that for their own dog, let alone someone else's.

More than anything else, Earl admired Jim's courage. The guy was absolutely fearless. To pay the rent and his tuition, Jim had taken a job as a summons server. Earl knew other guys who had tried that job and quit after a week or two of threats and abuse. Jim was unbelievable. Not only had he hung on to the job with the tenacity of a pit bull, he banged on doors and stuck subpoenas in people's hands in the Mission and Fillmore districts *in the middle of the night*. If people gave him shit, Jim gave them shit back.

That's why Earl was eager to hear what Jim had to say. Film students were always bullshitting about ways to raise money to finance films. Jim didn't bullshit. Earl knew that if Jim had an idea, he would stick with it and make it work.

"What I'm thinking is, Earl and I are in the business in a half-ass way," Jim said. "Why not get all the way in?"

"What business?" Annie asked. "The film business?"

"No," Jim replied, "the skin trade."

For the better part of a year, Earl had been working part-time as a night manager at the Roxie Theatre on Sixteenth and Valencia in the Mission. The Roxie had been showing foreign films without subtitles when Earl first started. For obvious financial reasons, Harold Greenland, the principal owner of the theater, had changed the format and begun showing "nudies."

Greenland was pure show biz, a fabled character in the world of burlesque who was under five feet high, lived in Jayne Mansfield's old house in Hollywood, and owned theaters all over the country. Everybody loved Greenland because he was colorful and funny as hell, but he was a treacherous man to do business with. The word was, if Harold Greenland gave you a cashier's check, it was not necessarily money in the bank.

When Earl learned that a part-time job as a doorman had opened up at the New Follies, an old-time burlesque house on Sixteenth near Mission that Greenland had also converted into a nudies house, he convinced Jim to quit delivering subpoenas and take the $1.25-an-hour job.

"I've been at the Follies a few months now and I can't believe the number of guys who go to see nudies. It's amazing, isn't it, Earl?" Jim asked.

"Business sure picked up at the Roxie when we went to nudies, I'll tell you that," Earl replied.

"What I'm thinking is, we could make a nudie or two ourselves. Maybe not right away. We could start with stills. You know, take some pictures of girls with their tops off and try to sell them to the bookstores on Market Street."

"I don't think so," Annie said.

"Why not?" Jim asked.

"Because it's the slave trade, that's why!" Annie said. "You're selling flesh. I don't want to do it."

"Bullshit we're selling flesh!" Jim replied. "We find a hippie chick and ask her if she'll take her top off and let us take her picture. If she says no, we walk away. If she says yes, we give her ten dollars. Who gets hurt, Annie? Who gets hurt?"

"It doesn't feel right," Annie said.

"It doesn't feel right to take a picture of some girl with a great set of tits and sell it to a sailor over on Treasure Island so he's got something to stroke to when he's on board a ship a thousand miles out in the Pacific and the nearest thing to a woman is some fucking female whale? What doesn't feel right about that?"

"I don't know," Annie sighed. "It's like you're turning a woman into an object. She isn't a human being, she's a set of tits."

"Look, I'm not saying we should get in the business and stay in it," Jim countered. "What I'm saying is, we want to make our own films, right? We want to do what John Cassavetes is doing, right? So how can we do that?"

Jim held up an index finger. "One: we can go to Hollywood and pay our dues. We already decided fuck that, right?

"Two," Jim said, holding up a second finger, "we can go to New York and try to break into commercial. Fuck that too, right? Three: we can try to find some company that wants a film made of its assembly line. That doesn't turn anybody on. Or, four, we can stay right here, make a few nudies, and use the money to finance our own films."

The three were quiet for a while. Finally, Earl said, "I can dig it from a political angle."

"Oh yeah?" Jim asked.

"Yeah. We like to think of ourselves as iconoclasts, right? We want to make films that will wake people up and make them think about what they are seeing, right? Well, why not do that with sex? Why not make sex films that take the shock value out of sex? Why not show sex like you'd show anything else?"

"That's it, man!" Jim said, turning on his light-bulb smile.

"I mean, what's more dishonest than the way Hollywood handles sex?" Earl continued, encouraged by Jim's response. "Doris Day and Rock Hudson chasing each other around a bed? Come on, man! And TV! It's even worse on TV! What couple do you know besides Ozzie and Harriet that sleeps in single beds?"

Annie laughed.

"It'll be a kick, Annie," Jim said, encouraged by her laugh. "We'll do it together. We'll form our own company and do things exactly the way we've always done them. It'll be share and share alike."

"I'll think about it," Annie said.

"It's a means to an end, Annie," Jim said. "The beauty is, we can stay independent and keep learning about film."

Several weeks later, Jim and Earl were walking up Ocean Beach with cameras dangling from their necks.

"That one over there. How about her? She's got her top unhooked," Earl said, pointing to a woman who was sunbathing on a beach towel.

"Go ask her," Jim said.

"You go ask her. It was your idea," Earl replied.

"Let's wait a while," Jim said.

A girl in a bikini ran past. She was tall, slender, and large-breasted, with long sandy-blond hair. A piece of rawhide with a bell dangling from it was tied around one ankle.

"Hey! Wait!" Jim yelled, and ran after her.

The girl stopped and turned around.

"How about taking your top off?" Jim asked when he caught up with her.

The girl looked confused, like she was trying to decide whether to laugh or be angry.

"We're photographers. Filmmakers, actually," Jim explained. "We're looking for models, topless models. We couldn't pay you much, ten dollars maybe, but it wouldn't take very long. We could go over by the cliffs and take your picture right there. You'd be making lots of sailors real happy."

The girl thought for a moment.

"Okay, why not," she said finally. "I go to a nude beach every time I go down to see my boyfriend in San Diego. What's the difference?"

An hour and two rolls of film later, Jim and Earl paid their first model and thanked her profusely. Jim took the film back to the apartment on Diamond Street, where he had built a darkroom. When his roommate, Bob Cecchini, walked in that evening, the walls and the floor, everywhere Cecchini looked, were covered with photos of a beautiful young woman with a great smile and attractive breasts.

"They're almost dry," Jim said when he saw Cecchini. "What do you think?"

"She's really cute. It looks like someone just told her a joke," Cecchini replied.

"I did," Jim said.

"What was it?" Cecchini asked.

"I told her to watch my head when she took her top off 'cause my hair was gonna come back."

"Good one," Cecchini said.

The store owners on Market Street loved the girl. They bought every picture Jim had of her and every picture he brought in after that. And then Jim discovered that the store owners would pay more for the pictures they sold under the counter in plain brown paper.

One afternoon, Cecchini came home and the walls and floors were covered with pictures of a couple having sex. Jim had found that, incredibly enough, if you looked for them, some people were as willing to be photographed having sex as some women were to take off their bras.

"They were doing it doggie-style," Cecchini recalls. "The guy was looking at the camera and laughing. All over the apartment, every-where I looked, the guy was looking at me and laughing."

Business was good, but Jim was not satisfied. He was a film-maker, not a still photographer. Besides, there was more money in making a nudie than there was in selling stills, even sexually explicit stills. The Roxie and the New Follies constantly needed new films to feed to their ravenous audiences. It was time to take the plunge and make a nudie.

Jim borrowed a Bolex, the film student's camera of that era, a crude 16mm camera that ran for three or four minutes before it had to be reloaded, and shot his first nudie. He found the model in the Haight. It was an easy sell—$25 for spending ten minutes topless in front of a camera—and the girl seemed flattered by the attention. Jim took the raw film down to the Roxie and sold it to the manager, sight unseen.

"It seemed incredible to us," Earl Shagley recalls. "The Roxie was paying a hundred dollars for a loop, plus they gave you the film and paid for the processing. We could shoot two or three loops a week, easily. It was like free money. Whatever you made, they slapped up on the screen. You couldn't do anything wrong."

The sex film industry did not originate in San Francisco, but it was in San Francisco that the sex film emerged from the under-ground, from smokers in Elks Clubs and peep shows in arcades located on some of the meanest streets in town.

Beginning with the gold rush, San Francisco has always been a city of men without women. Miners back from the mother lode roamed the streets, looking to celebrate their return to civilization. Sailors off tall ships bound for the Orient for Chinese laborers or for Oregon for a cargo of timber flooded the saloons of the Barbary Coast.

In *Land of Gold,* published in 1855, Hinton Helper wrote: "I have seen purer liquors, better seegars, finer tobacco, truer guns and pistols, larger dirks and bowie knives, and prettier cortezans here in San Francisco than in any place I have ever visited; and it is my unbiased opinion that California can and does furnish the best bad things that are obtainable in America."

During World War II, soldiers and sailors who thought they would never again see America went on one last drunk and saw one last burlesque show before sailing under the Golden Gate for the Pacific theater. In the 1960s, lonely, frightened young men on their way to Vietnam sat in North Beach bars and silently downed beer after overpriced beer while topless dancers worked to Motown and Beatles songs. Today, Japanese tourists and conventioneers who have left their wives behind do things in San Francisco they would never do at home.

The market for "dirty pictures" that Jim had tapped into began with the development of still photography in 1827. Edison developed the first commercially successful motion-picture camera in 1889, and by 1904 pornographic films recording the sex act from disrobing to insertion to male orgasm were being cranked out in Buenos Aires and shipped to buyers who could afford their high price in England, France, Russia, and the Balkans. The hoi polloi got their first look at people copulating on celluloid in French whorehouses, where it cost around $20, a steep price in those days, to view a film.

Customs in European countries cracked down in 1907 and 1908, resulting in the inevitable—nascent pornographic film industries in France and Germany, particularly France, which was to become synonymous with the blue movie. Despite their reputation for being dirty, French films emphasized story line, often at the expense of raw sex.

An emphasis on plot over sex was also the hallmark of the early American sex films, most of which were made in New York City after World War I. The plots were as hackneyed and the characters as wooden as those in a Harlequin Romance. A traveling salesman rings a doorbell and a housewife invites him inside; a doctor ushers a female patient into his office; something stimulates the women (women in blue movies are like light bulbs, they turn on at the flick of a switch; something as innocuous as an ad for nylons in a magazine can send them into a frenzy), and the next thing you know, clothing is being removed and erogenous zones are being explored.

The American sex film declined from this low point. "Particularly pronounced by the 1930s is a pervasive anti-woman theme, with the female treated as a sex object rather than as a sex partner," Arthur Knight and Hollis Alpert wrote in *The History of Sex in the Cinema*. "Also in keeping with the mores and taboos of the time, many of the performers in both decades [the 1920s and 1930s] were relatively unattractive and close to middle age. The males were usually lower socioeconomic types—pimps, drifters and the like— the females generally prostitutes."

The genre went further downhill in the 1940s and early 1950s. Knight and Alpert write that "the performers continued to be chosen from the lower socioeconomic levels of society. In this period, especially, many of the male and some of the female performers wore masks or otherwise attempted to conceal their identities by the use of often rather bizarre disguises. This is the period, too, when many of the male performers made a habit of removing everything but their black socks for their 'performances'; thus did the masked man in stocking feet become a classic symbol of the U.S. stag film."

The masks and black socks were a reflection of a society that was still in the grips of the Puritan values it had been founded upon. In America, men put on a mask to rob a bank or have sex in public. Sex was dirty, something to be ashamed of.

There was an occasional exception to these ludicrous films. The Los Angeles stripper Candy Barr took a boyfriend to a cheap motel in Bakersfield, California, in the early 1950s and made *Smart Aleck*, a film as straight-on and unabashedly sexual as any the Mitchell Brothers would go on to make. But 99 times out of 100, a stag film is of lasting interest only to those who are enthralled watching couples perform sex acts.

In the 1920s and 1930s, some men made a living traveling from town to town providing both films and projection equipment for private parties or smokers in fraternal lodges and veterans halls. In the late 1940s and early 1950s, when 8mm equipment became available and affordable, the stag show men became distributors, selling and renting films from the trunk of a car. The same projector that was used to show grandparents movies of baby's first bath could be hauled down to the Elks Club every fourth Friday and threaded with an equally crude but very different kind of home movie.

There were statutes against showing and viewing obscene material in all fifty states, but rarely, if ever, did the police raid a smoker. The audience at a stag film were members of the Elks, Lions, and Eagles, the Kiwanis or the Rotary Club, the same organizations that the local chief of police belonged to. The chief wasn't about to authorize a raid that would result in the arrest of a couple of dozen pillars of the community.

If the audience at a smoker was more or less immune from prosecution, the producers and distributors of stag films were at serious risk of ending up behind bars. The federal government had laws against sending obscene material over state lines, and under J. Edgar Hoover the FBI went after stag film distributors who were foolish enough to use the mails. And the same chief of police who overlooked smokers in local fraternal organizations was eager to arrest the people who made or appeared in stag films or who came into town to sell the films.

Why the traditional stag film was such a travesty of sex, acting, storytelling, and everything else connected with film is a matter of some debate. On one side are those who argue from the religious or spiritual premise that sex is sacrosanct. To turn it into a spectator sport is vile and degrading because it strips sex of the romance, intimacy, and passion that flow from the heart and head as well as the loins, from all the things that distinguish humans from donkeys copulating in a farmer's field.

Defenders of the traditional stag film argued that it never developed into a legitimate genre because of the presence of fear and the absence of money. They point out that the stag films of the 1940s and 1950s were seldom, if ever, perverse. Bestiality, child pornography, violent S&M, or films featuring teenagers were—and are—rare or nonexistent for the simple reason that the men who went to smokers and stag parties were husbands and fathers who would be sickened by animals having sex with humans. More to the point, the men in the audience had daughters of their own. Rare is the father who could watch a prepubescent girl having sex on the screen without thinking: This is terrible! That could be my Betty!

The traditional stag film is a bad joke, say those who believe there is nothing inherently wrong in the explicit display of sex, because the stag film is a perfect expression of how sexually repressed America was in the middle of the twentieth century. The films are bad because the people who made them were inept and had only a vague idea of what they were doing. If sex was open and considered healthy, if no moral or legal penalties were incurred for making a stag film, people who knew what they were doing would have made genuinely erotic films and the genre would eventually have been legitimized. But because you could end up doing time in a penitentiary for making or distributing a stag film, no filmmaker with any talent, no producer with any money, would ever risk making one.

The people who brought the stag film up from the underground in the 1960s were not fronting for the local mob, as has so often been claimed. Typically, they were people on the fringes of retailing or show business. Some were the owners of newsstands who had kept copies of the nudist publication *Sunshine & Health* in plain brown wrappers under the counter for years. Others were men who had owned burlesque strip joints, like Harold Greenland. They started by renting vacant storefronts in run-down parts of town and installing arcades where men could step into a small booth, pull a curtain, drop a quarter in a slot, and see a film.

The films shown in arcades were called "loops" because they were ten to twelve minutes long and played over and over again. In some cities, police raided and padlocked the arcades. In others, the authorities left them alone, in large part because the early loops, or "nudies," as they were called, were innocuous by all standards but fundamentalists'. In the typical nudie, women bared their breasts, but not for long. You got a better, longer look in a topless bar.

The topless phenomenon began in San Francisco about the same time the stag film began working its way up from the arcades to movie houses with big screens. In 1964, when a man's bulk came from pasta, not steroids, a 360-pound press agent named Davey Rosenberg was hustling for a struggling nightclub at the corner of Broadway and Columbus called the Condor Club. The Condor featured tired burlesque acts that were boring even to tourists from the heartland. Rosenberg came up with the idea of having a dancer take off her top—no tease, just take it off—and dance bare-chested.

Soon, there was a line down the block waiting to see Carol Doda, America's first topless dancer, one of the first women to have silicone implanted in her breasts, and the subject of some of history's most tiresome ad copy ("Carol Doda: San Francisco's New Twin Peaks!"). Before long, North Beach was wall-to-wall topless joints and "go-go" girls in white boots were dancing topless in bars all over the country.

Topless dancing was a significant step away from the burlesque that had preceded it. Backed by bands that featured drummers with a deadened snare, gorgeously dressed strippers like Sally Rand and Gypsy Rose Lee had danced a fine line between sex and tease, between dance for dance's sake and the display of female flesh. The art was to give 'em a peek and leave 'em intrigued (as opposed to exploited) and wanting more.

Topless, on the other hand, had little or nothing to do with the art of dancing. Few topless dancers moved well enough to get paid to dance. They were there to show their breasts.

Much was written at the time about what a "cultural revolution" topless dancing was—this was in the days when early feminists were burning their bras—but topless was actually more a commercial than a cultural phenomenon. Davey Rosenberg had come up with yet another way to make visiting squares open their wallets.

The stag film's rise from the underground was also, on one level, a matter of economics. The arcades around the Transbay Bus Terminal were doing a steady business. A theater owner like Harold Greenland figured that if men were willing to stand in a dirty booth and shove quarters into a slot to see grainy nudies, they would be willing to pay a couple of bucks to sit in a nice dark theater and see the same films.

"In the mid-1960s, a theater like the Roxie was showing two hours of loops that were strung together and set to music that was totally unrelated to what was happening on the screen," says Lowell Pickett, who, with his partner Arlene Elster, became one of San Francisco's leading pornographers in the late 1960s and early 1970s. "Can you imagine anything worse? I've often thought that if there is a hell, I'm going to be condemned to watching those films throughout eternity."

But there are other than economic reasons why San Francisco was destined to become "the Porn Capital of America." At the same time Jim Mitchell was making his first crude loops, there were changes taking place in San Francisco that were deeper than the marquees in North Beach could reflect.

For some people in and on the fringes of the Movement, sex had become a political issue. Years before the word "swinger" was coined, they were experimenting with sex as freely as they were with psychedelic drugs.

"The sex parties were different here than they were anyplace else; that's one of the things that distinguished San Francisco," says Lowell Pickett, who was the genial host of many such parties in his rambling Victorian on Hayes Street. Pickett's rules were few but firm. Partygoers had to arrive before a certain time or be locked out. They took off their clothes upon entering the house and were given pieces of fabric and told to make a costume. There was no pairing off and going to bedrooms. Everybody had sex in one room where the furniture had been cleared away.

The food had to be bountiful and excellent.

"At other sex parties, people stood around waiting to see who was going to be the first to take off their clothes," Pickett says. "Then it was 'I'll fuck your wife, you fuck mine' and couples would split up and go to different rooms. Our parties were very much in the spirit of 'Let's everybody have a good time, let's use our imagination, let's go exploring.'

"People were finding out that you didn't go blind if you masturbated—they were still afraid it might be true," Pickett continues. "They were finding out if you smoked pot you didn't turn into a dope fiend as portrayed in *Reefer Madness*. They were finding out that nice girls—and nice boys—liked sex."

Jim was emboldened when he discovered that instead of condemning his foray into pornography, his political friends praised it. They thought Jim was helping to free America from its emotionally crippling puritanical past. Free love was as important in breaking the society's mind-forged manacles as free speech—maybe even more so.

The political justification for free love was an almost tantric belief that liberating the senses led to a higher plane of consciousness. The thinking was that because of its puritanical past, America was as hypocritical about sex as it was in its foreign policy. Sex was life-affirming and therefore could not be evil. Gays and lesbians and those consenting adults who ventured beyond the missionary position weren't the ones with psychological problems. It was the generals in the Pentagon who ordered bombs dropped on villages in Vietnam. They were the ultimate sexually repressed sickos. They got their rocks off by blowing things up.

The Movement was full of weirdos by the score—crazies, after all, are the ultimate counterculture figures—but none were quite as colorful as those who took up the cause of sexual liberation, especially in San Francisco.

The sexual liberation point man in San Francisco was Jefferson Poland, the founder of the Sexual Freedom League. When Jim was a student at SFS, Poland was taking off all his clothes and sitting in the center of the campus to publicize his cause. He had founded his own church, the Psychedelic Venus Church, and later he changed his name to Jefferson Fuck. Then he changed it to Jefferson Clitlick.

"The thing about Jefferson was, he had grave sexual problems he was trying to overcome by staging elaborate orgies," says Maitland "Sandy" Zane, a San Francisco *Chronicle* reporter who covered the sexual revolution for his paper in the 1960s. "It was rather pathetic, having a sexually disabled person pressing to lead the sex liberation movement, but in a way, it's typical of revolutionaries throughout history who work out private problems by becoming political exhibitionists."

Up to now, the people who made sex films had done it for money. The game was played by setting up a dummy corporation, cranking out as many films as you could in as short a time as possible—three or four in an afternoon was standard practice—selling the product to a distributor, and getting out before the authorities knew you were in. In San Francisco, for the first time, filmmakers like Jim Mitchell and Lowell Pickett started claiming that they were making pornographic films for political as well as economic reasons.

"Pornography was antiestablishment, another way of changing things," says Lowell Pickett. "We were very conscious of trying to break down barriers. In the late 1960s, my partner Arlene and I went to the first meeting of the Adult Film Association in Kansas City. We took along a projector and ran some San Francisco loops and people were dumbfounded! They'd been showing movies of nudists playing volleyball."

Leftists and countercultural types were attracted to pornography because there is something deeply subversive about the explicit display of sex. It brings into the open the most private act, an act that traditionally is supposed to occur only in the bedrooms of married couples, and then only in the missionary position. Sex strips away identities it takes a lifetime to build. A naked aroused man is not a brain surgeon or a university president or a Methodist bishop. He is an animal with an erection.

"Sex is the one area that is innately subversive to the rules and regulations of society, and pornography is the celebration of the subversive side of sex," says Dr. Martin Blinder, a prominent Bay Area psychiatrist who has testified in dozens of obscenity cases. "Pornography revels in all of sex's deliberately subversive permutations. It shows sex in a convent or a schoolroom, all the most unlikely places. We all have fantasies about our ninth-grade English teacher, and in pornography you can indeed subvert her dignity. There she is with her butt in the air, getting it in both holes. That's very subversive."

Jim had it made: he had found a way to be subversive *and* to make money. The money he was starting to make was important because it meant that he had escaped Antioch. Jim went back often, to emphasize to his old friends, as well as to himself, that he had indeed broken free of the dismal town.

"Jimmy liked to come back to Antioch and flash a wad," says Richard Lackey. "The guys in town were dirt poor, even if they had a job. Jim was an Okie with a pocketful of money. He was showing a wad, and he was cocky."

But for Jim, there was a kick in pornography that transcended money or radical politics. Jim Mitchell had inherited his father's outlaw-gambler ethic. It was cool to work a con. It was cool to get over on the law, as J.R. had done on the day that he had coaxed Jim and Artie into giving that cop the finger.

To Jim, pornography was a glorious con. It was fun, the money was good, and you didn't have to work hard. Best of all, pornography was a way to stick your thumbs in your ears and wiggle your fingers at authority figures like cops and all the smug tight-asses who automatically dismissed people like J.R. and Jim Mitchell as white trash.

"The outsider-outlaw feeling was very much alive in Jim and Artie. They were unremittingly in opposition to central authority," says Martin Blinder. "Their outlaw bent may have sprung from the same anti-authoritarian, slightly sociopathic drive that formed Bonnie and Clyde, but it took a benign and even therapeutic form in the

1960s, rather than the malignant form that we see in the gangsters of the 1930s.

"That was what was so special about the 1960s," Blinder concludes. "Being an outlaw blended effortlessly and seamlessly with the best of the civil libertarianism ethos. I like to think Ralph Nader was an outlaw when he took on GM."

Clearly, Jim was on to a good thing. The Roxie and the New Follies had bought every film he produced. His girlfriend Annie was still uncomfortable about shooting nudies, but she was coming around. Jim really liked working with Annie and Earl, and they were talking about forming a company and dividing the shares evenly.

But Jim had decided that as soon as Artie came out of the Army, he was going to bring him in. Pornography was a chance for Jim and his brother to be outlaws together. Artie would understand the con. And Jim needed Artie. When it was us against them, a man needed someone he could trust.

3

Nudies, Beavers, and Horn Dick Daddies

WHILE JIM was watching his first foreign films at Diablo Valley College, Artie was trapped in Fort Holabird, an Army base tucked in the southeastern corner of Baltimore. The Army was supposed to be training the balding twenty-year-old to be an intelligence officer, but Artie had even less interest in what the Army instructors were saying than he'd had in the courses he had dragged his ass through at DVC. High school, college, training in the Army, it was all bullshit. You never learned anything worth knowing.

Artie came fully alive only when he and his two Army buddies, Jerry Ward and John Rowe, had weekend passes. Jerry and John were a throwback to Artie's Antioch buddies, witty guys who loved a good time and delighted in coming up with a one-liner that made everybody double up with laughter. The trio had hitchhiked up and down the eastern seaboard and thrown some outrageous drunks, but somehow had always managed to avoid the MPs and make it back to the base before curfew.

Now it was the summer of 1966 and the three were close to shipping out. They decided to use their last three-day pass to take a road trip to visit John Rowe's parents in the upscale town of Bath, New York. Jerry Ward, who was from Plainfield, New Jersey, had borrowed his parents' Chevrolet for the trip.

"If you get back early enough Sunday afternoon, we'll have a barbecue for you guys," Jerry's father had said as he handed him the keys.

High on a few beers and their temporary freedom, the soldiers had driven four hours to Ithaca, New York, where they stopped to visit a friend of Jerry's. The friend had gotten them seriously plastered on gin and tonics. They got back on the road and somehow made it to Bath. Jerry was in the back, leaning forward with both arms on the front seat. Artie was in front, swirling the ice in his gin and tonic. John Rowe was driving.

"So where's this house that's supposed to belong to Peter Sellers?" Artie asked. "We want to see the *actual* house."

"It's up there on the hill," John said. "I think it's the one with the deep red shutters."

"You think those shutters are red? I'd say they're puce," Artie teased, trying to imitate a finicky interior decorator.

"Definitely puce," Jerry agreed.

"Red, puce, I don't even know if it's Sellers's house!" Rowe laughed.

Good-looking and blessed with a sweet disposition that came from being completely comfortable with himself, John Rowe was a talented musician. Name a song, any song, and not only could Rowe sing it, he could sound like Dylan or Donovan or any of the folk-rockers who were on the charts at the time.

Only a year earlier, Jerry Ward had been a senior with solid grades in the engineering program at Cornell. He had abruptly changed his major to hotel management, and the eagle-eyed minions at his draft board had decided he was trying to dodge the draft by becoming a professional student. The draft board took away his student deferment and classified him 1-A, and Jerry had been promptly drafted.

"We're almost there," John said. "It's just up this hill here."

As John was making the turn up the hill to his house, he oversteered and drove off the road. He gunned the engine to power out of a small gully and ran the car up the guy wire of a telephone pole. The car flipped and landed on its roof.

Artie and John were dangling from their seat belts. Jerry was sprawled on the roof of the car. Artie reached over, pulled a tray out of the dash, and let a stream of coins flow into his hand.

"Here," Artie said, handing the coins to Jerry, "you may need this for the bus."

They crawled out of the car and scrambled to their feet. Ignoring the crowd that was forming and the pitcher, paper cups, and limes that were lying on the road, Artie sidled up to Jerry, who was looking at the crunched tin can with the windows blown out that only moments earlier had been the family sedan.

"I guess this means the barbecue is off," Artie whispered, and Jerry surprised the crowd by roaring with laughter.

The cop who arrived to handle the accident turned out to be an old friend of John's, and he ignored the obvious intoxication of the driver. A tow truck used a cable to flip the car over and then hauled it to a garage, where a mechanic offered Jerry $15 for the wreck. Jerry refused and he and his buddies hammered the roof up and poured fresh oil in the crankcase. Next day, the trio made the five-hour return trip to Plainfield, New Jersey, wearing sunglasses to keep the bugs out of their eyes, eating peanuts and releasing the shells to the jet stream that flowed through the car.

A few weeks later, Artie, who had volunteered in order to avoid being drafted, shipped out for Heidelberg, Germany, where he worked as a clerk, filling out an endless stream of mind-numbing forms.

Jerry Ward, the draftee, went to Vietnam.

John Rowe decided to go Regular Army and become a helicopter pilot. Jerry and Artie did everything they could to dissuade him, including throwing a wild drunk in a noncommissioned officers' club for the express purpose of earning John a dishonorable discharge—but it didn't work. John went to Vietnam, where he was killed in action.

Two years later, Jerry Ward completed his tour of duty and made his way back home to Plainfield. He had been there for all of ten minutes when the phone rang.

"Jerry!" his mother cried. "You'll never guess who it is! Artie Mitchell!"

Jerry picked up the phone. "What's the difference between a Jewish American Princess and a Mexican American Princess?" he asked.

"Hit me," said the twangy voice on the other end.

"With the Mexican American Princess, the jewels are false—"

"And the orgasms are real!"

"Artie! It's really Artie!" Jerry cried. "Nobody else has ever been able to complete one of my jokes. Where the hell are you?"

"Fort Dix, man! All I gotta do is sign a few more papers and my days as a warrior are over! Hey, can you get up here and pick me up?"

"Absolutely," Jerry replied.

"You got a job yet?"

"Jesus, no, I just walked in the door myself."

"Good. 'Cause I got a job for you."

"You do?"

"Yeah. How 'bout helpin' me drive a Porsche across the country?"

"A Porsche? You got a Porsche??"

"I do, but it ain't here yet," Artie said. "I saved my pennies and got a little help from the folks and bought it in Germany. It's being shipped over; it should be here any day. Are you ready to see the good old U.S.A. in the style to which we are soon to become accustomed?"

"I'm ready!" Jerry cried.

Artie spent two weeks at Jerry's house, waiting for the Porsche. It finally arrived and they took off, winding their way through the South, stopping to see the sights during the day, hitting bars at night, laughing at and completing each other's jokes, wishing the trip could go on forever.

"When we get to Vegas, we can stay with my aunt and uncle," Jerry said one night in a motel along Interstate 40. "You'll love 'em, they're great people. My uncle says, if I want, he can set me up with interviews at a couple of casinos."

"A job. Sooner or later that dreaded word had to appear," Artie said, suddenly glum.

"Which way are you leaning, jobwise?" Jerry asked.

"I don't know," Artie sighed. "I got a letter from Bill Boyer when I was still in Germany. He's back home working for the Antioch *Ledger*. He says if I want to be a journalist, he'll sell me his typewriter and corduroy jacket. I hear from Jim that he's making dirty movies. He wants me to work with him, but I figure that's got to be bullshit. Mom says I should live at home and go back to school. She says I could get a job working nights as a security officer at a mall they're puttin' in. I don't know. I hate fucking school."

"Something could happen in Vegas," Jerry suggested.

Two nights later, the Porsche crested a hill and there in the distance were millions of white lights, twinkling in the clear desert air.

The Vegas lights were the most exciting thing Artie had ever seen. They were proof that the world wasn't all nine to five. They promised fun, excitement, nonstop action. If the straights were in charge everywhere else in America, Vegas was for guys who understood angles.

Artie had emerged as a better card player than his brother. Jim was cool and had a classic poker face that nobody could read. But Artie was an actor who could use mood and expression to mislead people. Cards were one of the few things Artie was serious about—he always felt that he was representing J.R. at the table—and when he played, he played for keeps.

Artie had done pretty well hustling pool and playing poker in the Army. Now he was going to find out how good he really was, playing with the big boys in Vegas. He was as jittery as a college senior who was about to take the LSAT.

Artie played a little blackjack in casinos up and down the Vegas Strip and a lot of poker in the crowded, smoky cardroom at the Dunes. He didn't win money, but he didn't lose any, and he took that as a complete victory. All he needed to come out ahead was a little more time and a few more moves.

Artie loved walking into a casino as the sun was setting, sitting down to a poker game, and having cocktail waitresses bring him drink after complimentary drink as long as he stayed there. He loved finishing the night with a $1.19 steak-and-eggs breakfast in the casino and walking out the door to see the sun inching its way above the mountains to the east. This, Artie thought as he walked through the huge casino parking lot to his Porsche, was living.

"Morning, Jerry," Artie said when Jerry walked into the bedroom they were sharing at Jerry's aunt and uncle's.

It wasn't morning. It was late afternoon and Artie was just waking up.

"The name is no longer Jerry," Jerry said in a haughty voice.

"So what is it?" Artie asked.

"Mr. Junior Executive."

Artie sat up in bed.

"You got a job!" he cried.

"As of this afternoon, that is correct. You are looking at the newest junior executive at the one and only Flamingo Hotel."

"Hey, that's great, man!" Artie said.

Artie thought about it and later that night said to Jerry, "Tell you what. You find a nice apartment. I'll take the Porsche up home and say hi to Jim and Mom and Dad. Then I'll come back, move in with you, and find a job. I might give dealer's school a try."

"You're on!" Jerry said.

Artie left for California a day or two later and Jerry found an apartment in a brand-new complex. He dropped Artie a note with his new address and phone number, but weeks went by without word from Artie. Jerry was considering calling Artie in Antioch, when he came home from work one evening and found a letter in his mailbox. It was postmarked April 4, 1968, and Jerry knew it was from Artie because in the upper left-hand corner, instead of a return address, Artie had written: "Are you kiddin? I'll tell you nuthin!!"

Jerry opened the envelope and discovered Artie would not be joining him in Vegas.

Jim, Artie wrote, had been on the level about making sex films. The market was booming and Jim had offered to cut Artie in on half the profits, which, Artie bragged to his Army buddy, could bring him $15,000 that summer.

Needless to say, Artie would be staying in San Francisco. Teasingly, he added that he hoped Jerry had rented an expensive apartment. Eating the rent would teach Jerry not to depend on Artie Mitchell.

Jerry was doing well at the Flamingo. He had discovered that the internal politics at the hotel were savage, but so far he had managed to float above them. Jerry was tall and handsome, with thick black hair and a healthy mustache. He was competent and a lot of fun to work with.

Jerry was very curious about Artie's new occupation and often wondered what he was doing up there in San Francisco. Jerry had been raised Catholic and had been indoctrinated to believe that sex was the nitroglycerin of the human spirit, to be handled with extreme caution or, better yet, not handled at all. The girl he dated all through high school had a priest who had told her, "Never touch your breasts with your hand. Always use a washcloth." Jerry liked to joke that by the time he got to Cornell he had balls the size of church bells.

And now his Army buddy Artie was in the sex business. Artie liked women and was very relaxed around them. Artie had always been the one who approached girls in bars. But thinking back on it, Jerry decided that Artie had always been more interested in getting drunk and having a good time than in getting laid. And now, good old Artie was a . . . pornographer. Somehow, the word and the connotations it raised of Mafia types paying beaten-down women to do dirty things just did not apply to Artie.

A few weeks after Jerry got the letter, Artie called.

"We've made seven films so far and sold every damn one!" Artie said in an excited voice. "And guess what. We're branching out."

"To where?" Jerry asked.

"To Vegas!" Artie replied. "You just got a new title to go with Mr. Junior Executive. You are now the official Las Vegas distributor for the Mitchell Brothers. I'm gonna mail the films to the Vegas post office. I'd send them to your place but you gotta be kind of careful because there's some legal bullshit about shipping 'obscene' material over state lines."

"Artie, I don't know," Jerry said.

"Forget it!" Artie said, cutting Jerry off. "Nobody cares about this shit anymore. Things are going crazy, we can do whatever we want!"

Jerry spent the next few days wondering how he was going to distribute blue movies. Finally, he approached a bell captain—bell captains seemed to know everything. The bell captain was interested, so Jerry rented a projector and invited him over to his apartment.

"This is a full-service hotel, sir. Should you be interested in viewing an exciting film in the privacy of your room, just let me know," the bell captain said in the deep, soothing voice that FM disc jockeys use. Then, in his real voice, he grunted, "This could develop into a nice little market."

The bell captain and his girlfriend settled into the couch in Jerry's apartment and Jerry went to the kitchen and brought back a couple of beers. Jerry was excited; it was fun, doing things you shouldn't be doing. Coming back with the beers, he glanced at the bell captain's girlfriend, trying to figure out how she was going to take this. She looked curious, but had yet to say anything.

"Well, here's hopin' they're as hot as Artie claims," Jerry said, raising his glass. Then he turned off the lights and switched on the projector.

"What'd they do, wait for the fog to come in before they started to shoot?" the bell captain asked after a few minutes.

"They must have. There's supposed to be a girl in there somewhere. Do you see a girl?" Jerry asked.

"I see gray and dark gray," the girlfriend said.

Jerry stopped the projector.

"Let's try the next one," he said.

Jerry ran three more films through the projector. The exposure on each was as bad as the first. Jerry was so embarrassed he wanted to call Artie and yell, "What're you trying to do, put me on?"

"How much did you say you could get paid to be in one of these?" the girlfriend asked. "I think I'd like to do it. As long as nobody can see anything, what's the difference?"

Jerry and the bell captain laughed.

"Well, let's try one more. What have we got to lose besides our vision?" Jerry said, and threaded another film through the projector.

This time, the film was visible, but there wasn't much to see. A girl ran down to a small lake in a park and tested the water. She looked around and then ran behind a tree. The camera followed her. Slowly, she removed her shirt. Then she reached around and unhooked her bra. She spent an inordinate amount of time fondling her breasts. Finally, she struggled out of her bell-bottoms and, wearing only panties, raced back to the water. The film ended before she went in.

"So that's a nudie," Jerry said when the film ended. "I must say, it doesn't match my fantasies about what my old buddy is doing. Let's see if the other two are any better."

The other two films were more of the same, women taking off their tops and fondling their breasts. Jerry turned off the projector and turned on the identical lamps that were sitting on coffee tables at either end of the couch.

"I'll give you fifteen dollars for the last three," the bell captain said in a take-it-or-leave-it tone of voice.

The films were supposed to be Jerry's samples. He was supposed to use them to get orders for dozens more, not to sell them outright. But he was stunned to discover how bad Jim and Artie were as filmmakers. Maybe it was different in a theater, where there was music and you could see nine or ten films in a row. Maybe audiences in San Francisco were so sex-starved they would *pay* to watch films that were this bad, but Jerry knew he couldn't sell stuff this amateurish in Vegas—not when every hotel on the Strip had a revue that featured leggy showgirls with incredible bodies that burst through the sequins.

"It's a deal," Jerry told the bell captain. "Hell, take the other four too. You can rent them to people who can't sleep and don't want to take Sominex."

For the next few weeks, Jerry dreaded Artie's call. Should he tell him the truth? Or should he just say that he had approached several people but they had all found the films too hot to handle?

Jerry didn't want to offend Artie. After seeing the films, he didn't think Artie would be in the porn business much longer, and it would be great to have Artie come back to Vegas and move into the apartment.

Time passed and Artie didn't call. Jerry wondered if Jim and Artie had gone under, or if Artie was so busy he had forgotten about sending the films. Gradually, Jerry forgot about the films himself. He was on the fast track at the Flamingo, leapfrogging over employees who had been there for years. Before long, he was running the Flamingo's in-house travel agency.

The money was good and the perks were spectacular—offers for free trips and tickets to shows poured in daily. When Jerry was offered a block of tickets to *Hair,* which was about to open its 1968 run in Los Angeles, he snapped them up. A half dozen of his friends from Cornell lived in L.A., sharing a house in Topanga Canyon. Jerry called to tell them to reserve the next weekend and then called Artie and told him to get on a plane to L.A., there were good times ahead.

Jerry was really excited. It would be great to see Artie again, and he had a date in mind for him. After he had described her to Artie, Artie said, almost as an afterthought, "Hey, what ever happened to those films I sent you?"

"To tell you the truth, Artie, they were so badly done I couldn't sell them," Jerry said. He bit his lower lip and waited for a reply.

"Yeah, weren't they!" Artie said cheerfully. "But wait'll you see the next few! We're getting better all the time!"

"Where did you find that asshole?"
"Who? What? Artie?" Jerry asked.

Jerry had gone into the kitchen of the house in Topanga Canyon to fix another pitcher of gin and tonics, and Sharon, the twenty-three-year-old Cornell graduate he had set Artie up with, had followed him in.

"Yeah, Artie," Sharon said sarcastically. "What a jerk. There's no way you can talk to that guy. It's nonstop one-liners."

"He's a little tense, maybe," Jerry said.

"Tense! He's smoked three joints!" Sharon said. "And that voice! There's so much twine in it, you could use it to bale hay."

"So he flunked speech class," Jerry said, mildly irritated.

"Meredith digs him," Sharon said, ignoring Jerry. "That's what I don't get. She's out there laughing at everything he says."

"So let her have him," Jerry said.

"Done!" Sharon said, and held out her glass, which Jerry promptly refilled.

Meredith Bradford did indeed dig Artie Mitchell. Art kept her laughing all weekend, and more than anything, Meredith loved to laugh. Art had the nebbish charm of a natural clown. At the same time, there was a sweetness about him, an openhearted honesty. Art was wearing leather pants and a white shirt with a couple of buttons open, and Meredith thought he was sexy and virile without trying to be macho. That Sunday evening, Meredith drove Art to the airport and they hugged for a long time before he got on the plane to San Francisco.

Two days later, Art called. They made small talk for a while and then Art said shyly, "Hey, I guess we fell in love."

"I guess we did," Meredith said. "I've been really, really hoping you'd call."

Art paused for a moment.

"Why don't you come up this weekend?" he asked. "I'll show you San Francisco and you can meet my brother."

"That'd be great!" Meredith said. "I'll drive up."

"Call me from the road and I'll give you directions and meet you at the apartment," Art said.

Meredith was a Yankee blue blood, about as far removed from Artie's Okie roots as it is possible to be and still be an American. Her family didn't just come over on the *Mayflower*; William Bradford, her eleventh-great-grandfather, was in charge of the expedition. The author of the Mayflower Compact and oft-elected governor of Plymouth Colony, Bradford packed a tiny band of fanatics in an overloaded ship and led them over terrifying seas to an unknown land, where he helped lay the civil and religious foundations for a great nation.

Before she met Artie, Meredith's life was heading in a direction her mighty ancestor would no doubt have approved. An all-American girl, Meredith grew up in a small town south of Boston, one of five children of a prominent surgeon who taught medicine at Boston University. The family summered on Cape Cod, swimming and playing on the very beach where William Bradford himself had once walked.

Meredith was famous in her family for being absolutely fearless. One time she and her brother Mark were in Provincetown, walking on a dock long after dark. They looked down and saw thousands and thousands of squid schooling. "What would it feel like to be in there with all those squid?" Meredith wondered aloud. "You'll never know, you're too chicken," her younger brother said. The next thing Mark knew, there was a splash and Meredith, in her new summer dress, was swimming with the squid.

That daring, playful spirit made the pretty, athletic strawberry blonde a big favorite with her peers. In high school, Meredith had been *both* the homecoming queen and the head cheerleader, the one the squad threw up in the air and caught with locked arms. A photo in one of Meredith's yearbooks shows her floating in the air above the one-word caption "Win!"

An excellent student, Meredith was premed at Cornell. She had the grades to get into medical school but, much to the surprise and disappointment of her father, decided not to go.

"It drove him crazy that, in his eyes, I threw that away," Meredith says. "But I hated Type A medical students, I didn't want to go to school anymore, I just didn't want to be a doctor. I wanted to get as far away from the East Coast as possible. I wanted to screw around in California."

In that, Meredith was very much a product of her times. Life was a trip. The one sure way to fail was not to take the trip.

The trip was a journey out of the middle class, away from the lives your parents had led, whether you loved them or not. The idea was, you would end up a happy, fully realized human being only if you took some risks. Taking a risk could mean joining the Peace Corps or hitchhiking across Europe, dropping acid or dating a black guy, becoming a vegetarian or chanting "Hare Krishna," or quitting a job to go to New Hampshire to campaign for Gene McCarthy.

For some women, the trip was to become a doctor instead of marrying and having kids. But Meredith had been bred to go into medicine, and for her, taking a risk was getting off that path, saying goodbye to the East Coast and traditions that went back to the Puritans, and heading to California, where she could create herself anew.

When Meredith met Artie, she was living in a small apartment in funky Hermosa Beach, a downscale beach town tucked between Manhattan Beach and Redondo Beach, which were both going condo in a big way. Meredith lived a half block from the water and was running around L.A. on a 250cc BSA motorcycle. Every weekend, she went to an antiwar rally or rode up to Venice to hang out with the hippies.

The slogan "Banned in Boston" had more or less begun with Meredith's great ancestor, but instead of finding her new boyfriend's career morally reprehensible, Meredith was intrigued.

There were few, if any, feminists in those days who condemned pornography as degrading and exploitive of women. Pornography might have come out of the closet in San Francisco and a few other big cities, but in most places it was still considered dark, dirty, and largely irrelevant.

For many liberated young women in the 1960s, extracting as much pleasure from sex as a male partner was central to the trip. It was a valid way for a woman to free herself from a confining past. Artie had told Meredith that he considered pornography a public expression of women's new freedom, a way for a woman to say, "This is my body, I'm proud of it, I'll do with it as I please!"

Meredith had liked that. She also liked the fact that pornography was dangerous. She considered the cops pigs, mindless enforcers of a corrupt social order. If the cops found something threatening in pornography, there had to be something good in it.

But the best part was that although Artie's business was dangerous, there was nothing dangerous or threatening about him. Artie was a sweetheart, polite, sensitive, and cuddly. Meredith knew a bastard when she met one. If she thought Artie looked at women as pieces of meat, Meredith would not have spent more than five minutes with him.

Friday finally came, and at the end of a 400-mile drive, Meredith picked her way through the Haight, casting glances at the hippies, street people, and musicians who were clustered on almost every corner. She located Art's apartment at Haight and Broderick, found a parking place, and knocked on the door, but Art, contrary to his promise, wasn't home. Meredith went for a walk to stretch her legs, but it was after dark and she didn't know the neighborhood, so she went back to her car and spent the next two hours staring at the rubber chicken that was hanging in Art's window. Whatever anger she'd built up vanished as soon as she spotted Art running up the street.

"We were shooting a film. I couldn't get away," Art said, raising his eyebrows mischievously. "If you could stay over Monday, you could help work on it. It's really fun working on a film."

"Work on a sex film? I've never even *seen* one," Meredith replied.

"We'll fix that!" Art said. "Come on up, I'll show you the place."

There was only one chair in what could have been, with a little effort, a comfortable apartment in a nondescript building. When Artie ducked into the bathroom, Meredith looked around the kitchen and opened the refrigerator. Except for a jar of pepperoncinis and a pack of Rolaids, it was empty.

Meredith walked into the bedroom and saw that Artie had put her small suitcase down by the bed. She had really done it. She had driven to San Francisco to spend the weekend with this guy with the bald head and quick laugh. She looked at the bed—actually it was just a mattress on the floor—and suddenly felt uncomfortable. Artie must have picked up on that or felt a bit ill at ease himself, because he suggested they go to a great little Mexican place nearby for dinner.

The new couple went to the restaurant, a small room that adjoined the bar, and had a wonderful time, laughing and getting to know each other better. They put away a couple of pitchers of margaritas, and then went back to Artie's place and went to bed.

The next day, they smoked a joint or two and wandered through the Haight and Golden Gate Park. It was so much fun being with Art that Meredith was surprised to discover that the light was fading and it was time to go to Jim's apartment for dinner.

"Soon as we get the money to buy the equipment, we'll make better films than anybody else is making," Jim told Meredith that night.

"That's not saying much," Annie, Jim's girlfriend, said from the kitchen. "A chimp could make better films than they show in beaver houses."

"Beaver houses?" Meredith asked.

"One of pornography's many charms is the elegance of the adjectives used to describe female genitalia," Annie said as she came into the room.

"Beaver houses show beaver films," Artie explained as he rolled a joint. "In a nudie, you get tit shots. They're old hat. Nobody would pay to see a nudie today. Beavers are the happening thing. In a beaver, you get muff shots."

"It's the same damn film over and over," Annie said as she returned to the living room. "Girl appears in a bedroom. Girl looks at herself in the mirror. Girl takes off blouse and removes bra. Girl fondles breasts and lies down on the bed. Girl slowly removes panties and writhes away. Film ends. The only thing creative about them is the titles."

"How Deep Is My Beaver," Artie said.

"Valley of the Beavers," Jim said.

"The Beaver Cleaver," Jim and Artie said together, and laughed at the reference to the television show they and every other young adult in America had grown up with.

"I actually kind of feel sorry for the guys who go to see these films," Jim said, remembering his days as a doorman at the New Follies. "The films change once a week but the audience never does. Horn dick daddies, I call them. Lonely, sad guys. You'd think they were deaf-mutes, the way they walk in and out with their heads down."

"They're harmless," Artie said. "They go in, sit as far from each other as they can, choke the chicken, and go home."

"That's right," Jim agreed. "The assholes who are against pornos make it out that perverts see these films and then go rape Catholic girls in plaid skirts. That's total bullshit."

"We're providing a sexual outlet for people who otherwise would have none," Annie said, sighing and rolling her eyes at Meredith.

Meredith wondered why Annie seemed so weary. Was it because she had had this conversation too many times? Were Jim and Artie trying to convince her that what they were doing was all right at the same time they were describing it for Meredith?

"It's true, Mouse," Artie said. "What would the daddies be doin' if they took away beaver movies? Peeking in the window of the lady across the street, that's my guess."

Meredith noticed Annie's shoulders tighten. Apparently, she did not like being called Mouse.

"The people against us say they're against filth," Jim said, warming to the subject. "But what they're really against is sex. They think sex is filthy. It's as simple as that."

"This society is so fucked," Artie added. "You can blow ninety-nine people away ninety-nine different ways in a Hollywood movie and nobody says a thing. But show a little pubic hair and you're a leper. It's like you're selling speed to sixth-graders."

"Over and over again in film school they told us, 'Make films that have an effect,'" Jim said. "So you make a film and the audience cries and you're a genius. But make a film that gets a guy up and you're a pervert."

"I don't mind being a pervert as long as there's money in it." Artie grinned.

"To make any real money in porn, you have to have your own theater," Jim said, looking at Meredith. "Otherwise, you sell a film and the guy you sold it to copies it and sells it to someone else. That guy copies it and sells it to someone else and you never see a dime. There's no copyright laws in porno."

"That's right, Bob," Artie said quickly. "We got to do what de Renzy's done."

"We got to do what de Renzy's done, Bob," Jim agreed.

"Who's Bob?" Meredith asked.

"Our nickname for each other," Artie said, smiling at Jim. "Robert is our father's name. It's kind of an Okie thing."

"And who's de Renzy?"

"A guy who's a step or two ahead of us," Jim said. "We're gonna catch him."

Alex de Renzy was one of the pioneers of the sex film in San Francisco. In 1968, he was thirty-three, a former photographer for the Gordon News Service in San Francisco and craps dealer in Reno, Nevada. Handsome, with long blond hair pulled back into a ponytail and a Fu Manchu mustache, de Renzy had a deeply scarred face and he walked with a limp, the legacy of a motorcycle race up a steep hill in San Francisco that ended when he slammed into a car that had stopped in an intersection.

Earlier on the day of his crash, de Renzy had seen a prostitute knife a man across the street from the Screening Room, the theater he owned in the Tenderloin, the San Francisco version of Skid Row. When he came to in the emergency room, his face was torn away and his leg was shattered, and he found himself lying next to the man the prostitute had carved up.

The doctor who was going to operate on his leg stopped by de Renzy's bed and introduced the plastic surgeon who was going to work on his face. "Well, Doc, impress your friends," de Renzy said. Later, he told friends that he liked the scars because before the accident he was too pretty. De Renzy lived with two women and several of his children from a previous marriage in his hillside estate in Marin. From the beginning, he was a loner who kept his distance from other San Francisco pornographers.

When Meredith woke up the next morning, she found herself alone in bed. She smelled fresh coffee, got up and put on a robe, and walked into the living room. Artie was in the kitchen, putting rolls on a plate. Two pillows had been placed on the floor beside a 16mm projector that was aimed at a blank white wall.

"What's all this?" Meredith asked.

Artie looked up and grinned.

"Oh, hi!" he said. "Hey, have one of these Danish pastries. I had to stand in line twenty minutes to get 'em but they're worth it. I got apple and cheese."

"And the projector?"

"From the closet. I thought I'd get your porn cherry." Artie grinned.

"The first thing in the morning?" Meredith asked, incredulous.

"Hey, you might as well get used to it," Artie said, flashing his mischievous grin. Then he turned serious. "I haven't seen this one yet myself. It's supposed to be really hot. It's a split beaver."

"Oh God, I think I know what that means," Meredith said.

Artie pulled the shades and turned on the projector. A skinny woman with very short blond hair who reminded Meredith of the model Twiggy walked into a bedroom and disrobed. Wearing a bra and panties, she went over to the bed, lay down, and took off her underwear. Then she brought her knees up and spread her legs.

The camera entered the spread and focused on her vagina. The colors were reminiscent of early 1950s CinemaScope. What should have been pink was red. Meredith felt a bit nauseous.

"Jesus, Art, it's like going to a gynecologist," Meredith said.

"Yeah, isn't it," Art replied without taking his eyes off the screen.

The woman rubbed two fingers slowly across her stomach and then let them slip between her legs. Apparently she found her clitoris, for she stuck her tongue out and began to vibrate, as if the bed was equipped with Magic Fingers.

"Whoa! Can you really get away with this? Can you really show that film and not get busted?" Meredith asked when the film ended.

"Yep," Artie said. "Nobody's had the balls to show a split beaver in an aboveground theater yet, but they will. And when it happens, it'll happen here first. The competition in this town is incredible. Every time somebody takes it an inch further, somebody else goes an inch further than that."

"You really think people will pay to see this?"

"I think they'll be standing in line."

"But it's so crude," Meredith said.

"Hey, crude is good, crude is what they want," Artie replied. "As Jim likes to say, 'The only Art in this business is my brother.' "

They both laughed, and then Artie frowned and looked Meredith in the eye.

"You haven't told me what you thought of it," Artie said.

William Bradford's eleventh-great-granddaughter was silent for a moment.

"I don't care if I ever see another one," she said.

"Okay," Artie said, obviously disappointed.

"But if other people want to, I don't see why they can't. Where's the harm?"

"Right! That's right!" Artie said.

"I mean, the same government that is saying these films are obscene is napalming children in Vietnam. If they're against it, I'm for it!"

Artie crawled around the projector and threw his arms around Meredith.

"I knew you were one of the boys!" he said.

By early 1969, when Jim and Artie were producing crude films and selling them to theaters like the Roxie and the New Follies, pornography had become a thriving cottage industry in San Francisco. The *Chronicle* and the New York *Times* counted between 20 and 25 theaters showing beaver films and 100 filmmakers and performers who were making or appearing regularly in the films. Some theaters were small-time operations, saloons where you could get a drink and watch a film on a screen behind the bar. (Sign over the door of Expo 69 on Kearny Street: "Pornography for the price of cocktails—Why pay more?") Other beaver houses were fine old theaters like the Sutter near Union Square.

Pornography had come out of the closet and joined the 1960s party, and Jehovah in His wrath had not caused the sea to open and swallow the city. Except for Dianne Feinstein, a candidate for the San Francisco Board of Supervisors and leader of a band of anti-porn crusaders, few people in town seemed to care one way or the other.

"What distinguishes San Francisco from any place else is the style with which porn is marketed, its practitioners' attitude toward it and the tolerance most square citizens display concerning the whole question," said *The New York Times Magazine* in a January 1971 story called "The Porn Capital of America." "The flourishing underground press in San Francisco all share the idea that porn, even at its sleaziest and most bizarre, is an important and healthily revolutionary ingredient of the new culture. The basic assumption [among the square citizens], even on the part of Mrs. Feinstein and some of her fellow crusaders, is that a 'mature adult' is entitled to get his kicks any way he can, provided decent citizens don't have to witness the process and nobody gets hurt."

Sex had been for sale in San Francisco since the days of newspaper ads for Irish "washerwomen," a turn-of-the century euphemism for prostitutes. Whores had knifed and been knifed, drunk themselves to death and overdosed on laudanum in San Francisco, as they had in every city on the American frontier. But in San Francisco, the sordid death of a young prostitute or the cribs in Chinatown were overlooked because, as Curt Gentry wrote in *The Madams of San Francisco*, "[San Francisco is] a city which takes uncommon pride in its past sins, real or imagined." The early entrepreneurs of sex, madams like Ah Toy, Belle Cora, Jessie Hayman, and Tessie Wall, were celebrated as tough, bawdy ladies, part of the city's colorful past. And next to physical splendor and great food, nothing is as important to San Francisco as local color.

The San Francisco pornographers of the late 1960s inherited that tradition and turned it into a major asset. Aging beatniks like Lowell Pickett and borderline hippies like Jim and Artie Mitchell weren't *really* in the sex business. They and others like them thought of themselves as being in the fun business.

"We knew we might have to take a bust, but we also knew we'd never have to go to jail in San Francisco," Lowell Pickett explains. "No San Francisco jury wanted to put a pornographer away, even if they didn't like pornography. We'd have been hung in Alabama, but in San Francisco, people generally felt that adults should be free to decide whether they wanted to see a pornographic film. The courts shouldn't make that decision for them."

Mayor Joseph Alioto, district attorney John J. Ferdon, and San Francisco police chief Thomas Cahill generally took a live-and-let-live attitude toward the city's newest local industry. No one in city hall had paid much attention to the sex trade before Dianne Feinstein was elected to the Board of Supervisors. And inside the police department, the vice squad was considered largely irrelevant.

"In some cities, vice squad officers are considered heroes. "In San Francisco, they're the so-called pussy posse," explains Captain Dennis Martel of the San Francisco Police Department, who as a lieutenant in the mid-1980s would head the vice squad. (The SFPD somewhat euphemistically calls the vice squad the Bureau of Special Services.) "Vice has never been a popular or sought-after position in the department, and a lot of that is due to the fact that the vice squad was never supported. We'd go in and make legitimate arrests and the DA would fail to prosecute and it would look like we had made bad or illegal arrests. So we approached cases with less than total enthusiasm."

In the late 1960s, when San Francisco was buried under the onslaught of hippies, drifters, and flakes looking to be in on the action, the DA's office was overwhelmed with cases. The Haight had quickly degenerated into a behavior sink as methamphetamine replaced marijuana as the drug of choice and the hippies' doctrine of love gave way to the drug dealers' code of violence. Antiwar rallies were turning ugly, SFPD intelligence officers were hearing from the FBI and their own sources that the Weathermen were manufacturing bombs, and the number of muggings and murders in the city kept rising.

So if the DA and the cops overlooked the flourishing pornography industry, it was because they had plenty of other things to do and because few citizens seemed overly concerned with the proliferation of beaver houses.

While Jennifer, Meredith's older sister, was doing everything "right"—getting engaged to a wonderful young man, planning the perfect wedding, and looking forward to membership in the Junior League—Jennifer's little sister Meredith, the former prom queen and perky head cheerleader, the A student her father thought would make an excellent physician, was plunging into the pornography industry.

After that first weekend with Artie, Meredith flew to San Francisco almost every weekend. She soon became a charter member of the Mitchell Brothers' inner circle, a player in the decision-making process.

Decision-making Bob-style was a hippie parody of what went on in a corporate boardroom, with joints and beer instead of cigarettes and coffee and slapped hands instead of handshakes. Jim and Artie loved those "meetings." A hot cliché in those days was "Live your own movie," and the brothers felt they were doing exactly that. They were J.R.'s boys. They hadn't ended up working in a mill or selling insurance. They were living life on their own terms.

"They couldn't make a decision without six people in the room," Meredith says. "We'd brainstorm ideas and it'd be 'That's great, Bob!' 'We gotta do that, Bob!' Then either Jim or Art would change his mind and the next day it would be 'Naw, we're not going to do that,' and we'd start all over again.

"But it was great," Meredith continues. "The world was in front of us, everything was a challenge. Could we get our own theater? Could we make better movies than anybody else? Would we ever actually make any real money doing this?"

Meredith's parents had shot through the stratosphere when she told them about Artie and the kind of work she and her boyfriend were doing. Their reaction had upset her—she might have moved 3,000 miles away, but she loved and respected them—and had caused her to reexamine her feelings about pornography. She had once again reached the conclusion that pornography was innocuous —no one, neither the women who appeared in the films nor the men who watched them—seemed harmed by the explicit display of sex.

Since the encounter with her parents and the soul-searching that followed it, Meredith had not given much thought to the issues surrounding pornography. She was too immersed in the process of making the films. Annie was teaching her to handle a camera and that, as Artie had promised, was very exciting. Filmmaking is far more seductive than pornography. The more Meredith learned about filmmaking, the more she wanted to learn.

Jim, meanwhile, was concentrating on making as much money as possible. He was determined to open a theater, and to do that he had to have a stake. Securing a loan was impossible because the banks were not eager to loan money to an entrepreneur who wanted to open a beaver house.

But there was money to be made by giving the horn dick daddies what they wanted. Jim knew they wanted rank sex, and he knew that if he didn't give it to them, somebody else would. So it might as well be him.

Bob Cecchini, Jim's roommate, came home from work hungry and opened the refrigerator. Cecchini sighed. It was empty as usual except—what's this?—for a small salami.

It must be Jim's, Cecchini thought as he took the salami out of the refrigerator. Well, it's mine now.

Cecchini made himself a sandwich and half an hour later, Jim came bursting through the door.

"I was hopin' you'd be here!" Jim said. "I got something to show you! Come on!"

Cecchini followed Jim into the room that served as his studio.

"I just got this back from the lab," Jim said, holding up a film. "It's hotter than anything we've done!"

Jim threaded the 16mm projector and turned off the lights. The words *Sacramento Salami* appeared on the screen and Cecchini suddenly felt queasy.

"Can you believe it? Can you believe what she's doin'?" Jim asked.

Cecchini forced himself to look. A woman was masturbating with a small salami, plunging it in and out of her vagina.

"I just ate that salami!" Cecchini blurted out.

"You what?" Jim asked.

"I came home, I was hungry, the salami was in the refrigerator, I ate it!" Cecchini said in agony.

Jim turned off the camera, saw the look on his friend's face, and started laughing so hard he collapsed in a chair.

"I skinned it first!" Cecchini screamed.

Jim laughed even harder.

"You better not tell anybody about this," Cecchini threatened.

"Never! Well, maybe only Artie," Jim said, laughing.

"That'd be like putting it in Herb Caen!" Cecchini said, referring to the *Chronicle's* popular columnist.

Six months after meeting Artie, Meredith quit her computer job in Los Angeles and moved to San Francisco. She and Artie lived in the apartment in the Haight for a while, and then moved to a larger place at Fillmore and Pacific in Pacific Heights. In time, they acquired six cats, a rooster they called Poultry Groceries, and an iguana. The iguana had played the role of a dinosaur in a Mitchell Brothers' movie called *2001 B.C.*

Meredith was happier than she had been since the summer days when she was a kid running down a beach on Cape Cod. It was all a lark. Working with Jim and Artie was like belonging to a great commune, only instead of raising organic vegetables, they were making sex films. Every job was interchangeable; everybody was each other's best friend.

The most fun was sitting around and smoking up and brainstorming titles. Artie was the best at coming up with titles. Meredith thought *Rampaging Nurses* was his greatest. Who could resist a film with that title? Oftentimes they came up with a title and then thought up a film to go with it. Like *The ABCs of Sex*. Of course, they had gone to the zoo and shot a beaver for B.

"It was a joke!" Meredith says. "There we were laughing about getting a beaver in a film and later the DA accuses us of bestiality, of making films with animals! Jeez!"

Z turned out to be a killer. Nobody could think of anything, so they went back to the zoo. Meredith stood next to the zebra cage. While Annie shot from long range, Meredith lifted her skirt and flashed the camera. It was her first and last appearance in a film.

Meredith or Annie or Maureen, the woman Earl Shagley had recently married, did not even *think* about appearing in a film in a sex role. They were professionals who prided themselves on the distance they put between themselves and what went on in front of the camera. Let the right-wing fanatics fantasize that their lives were nonstop indiscriminate sex. It only showed how sick and twisted the reactionaries were when it came to sex.

Jim and Annie, Artie and Meredith, and Earl and Maureen were no different than any of a thousand other young couples in San Francisco in the late 1960s. They were interested in having a good time and hanging out with their friends. The men were loyal to the women they were living with and did not try to hustle the actresses who appeared in their films. A true sensualist like Lowell Pickett might throw an orgy on the weekend. But Jim and Artie's idea of a good time was a picnic in Golden Gate Park with softball and lots of good stuff to eat, drink, and smoke.

"It's time we found a theater," Jim said over dinner one night. "We've saved every dime we could and borrowed from everybody we could."

"Not that anybody did us any favors," Artie added as he rolled a joint. "Ten percent interest. That comes pretty close to usury, don't you think?"

"If the theater goes, we can pay everybody off within a year," Jim said firmly. "I'm not real worried about how much money we'll need. I just think we should figure out exactly what kind of place we want before we start lookin'."

"I think it should be classy," Annie said. "There's enough sleaze in this business."

"That's what I think!" Jim agreed. "I don't even want to look in the Mission or the Tenderloin or North Beach. There's no reason why the horn dick daddies should have to risk getting mugged to see a film. And I don't want to run a joint that charges tourists from Iowa six dollars admission plus a two-drink minimum at three-fifty a pop. We're gonna show straight-ahead sex films and charge an honest price."

"We're gonna put our names on the theater and our names on the films so people will know we're not in business to rip them off," Artie said. "Nobody else in porn has ever done that."

"It's something we learned from our father," Jim explained. "Porn's a con, but it's a good con. When you're on to a good thing, you don't mess it up."

The Mitchell Brothers' inner circle spent weeks scouring the city, looking for the right building in the right location. Some buildings were too expensive; some landlords refused to rent to people who wanted to open a beaver house. Some of the places they looked at were too disgusting even to think about renovating; others were located in far corners of the city.

Finally, they found a vacant building at the corner of Polk and O'Farrell that had once housed a Pontiac dealership. The location was perfect, in Polk Gulch, only a block west of Van Ness, the artery that carried traffic through the city to the Golden Gate Bridge.

The building turned out to be owned by Beatrice Presant, a woman who appeared to be in her late fifties or early sixties. Jim and Artie put on clean shirts and did a "Shucks, ma'am, we're just country boys from Antioch trying to make it in the big city" routine. Like most people, Presant immediately took to the two brothers. She found them charming and courteous, virtues that were sadly lacking in so many of today's young people. And it was so nice to see brothers working so closely together.

Of course, it helped that it had been a long time since anyone had wanted to rent the building. In the end, Presant agreed to defer rent for the first few months, and was glad to sign a long-term lease.

Meredith bought a sewing machine and made curtains out of the cheapest muslin she could find. The curtains looked fine when they were hung, but the former showroom had ceiling-to-floor windows and the curtains didn't shut out enough light. They ended up painting the windows black.

The brothers got a deal on indoor-outdoor carpet for the lobby and found two hundred used theater seats in a wholesale supply store. Mark, Meredith's younger brother, flew out for a visit over the Memorial Day weekend. Mark had gone to the "right" blue-blood schools, Exeter and Denison, and, much like his older sister, had passed up the "right" jobs to work as a tuna fisherman on Cape Cod.

Mark ended up spending the holiday using a converted .22 pistol to drive in the bolts that anchored the theater seats to the floor. Upstairs in the back of the theater, the crew hammered together a crude studio. The idea was to do everything under one roof: the films that were to be shown downstairs would be shot upstairs. That way, if an attractive woman showed up in the lobby and said she was interested in appearing in a film, they could have her upstairs and in front of a camera before she had time to change her mind.

"Look! Here he comes again! I know he's coming in this time!" Meredith cried.

"Bet you a dollar he doesn't," Earl Shagley said.

"You're on!" Meredith said.

"He's already walked around the block twice," Artie said.

"If he doesn't do it now, he won't do it," said Maureen, the friendly, fun-loving woman who had recently married Earl Shagley.

"Come on, mister, do it! Do it this time!" Meredith pleaded.

"He's gonna go right past," Earl said.

"He did it! He's buying a ticket! You owe me a dollar, Earl!" Meredith cried.

"Here comes another!" Artie exclaimed.

"And another!" said Maureen.

"This is better than waiting for trick-or-treaters!" Meredith said.

"If this keeps up, we could break a thousand dollars at the box office the first week!" Jim said.

It was the Fourth of July 1969, the day the O'Farrell, "The Adult Theatre," opened its doors. There was free coffee and sandwiches and even a suggestion box in the lobby. Tickets were $4.00, a relatively steep price in 1969, when it cost $1.75 to $2.25 to see a Hollywood film. The box office took in $600 that first week and moved inexorably toward the $1,000 barrier during the next two weeks.

On the evening of July 25, three weeks to the day from when the theater opened, Jim and Artie were upstairs, working on a shift schedule.

"RAID! COPS!" somebody shouted up the stairs.

"What's that?" Jim asked, jumping up.

"RAID! The cops kicked the door in!"

"That's Robert, the kid we got at the window!" Artie cried. "What do we do? We're holding!"

"Run! The attic!" Jim yelled, grabbing a lid of marijuana.

The brothers ran for the attic and closed the door behind them. Jim buried the lid under some pink fiberglass insulation. They tiptoed behind some empty boxes, crouched, and waited.

It was not a polite raid. Nine cops, seven uniforms and two vice detectives, hit the O'Farrell hard. One of them made Vince Stanich, the projectionist, turn off the projector and remove the film. When Stanich didn't do it fast enough, the cop ripped the film—an L.A. loop called *Lessons in Love*—out of the projector. Other officers kicked over filing cabinets and charged into the rest room, terrifying a patron at the urinal.

"They'll be coming back for you guys," an employee said when Jim and Artie appeared.

"I'll go over and turn myself in," Jim said, trying to appear calm.

"I'll go with you," Artie said.

"No sense both of us going," Jim said, opening the floor safe and cleaning out the cash. "The theater was my idea. I'll take the bust."

"The fuck you will," Artie said, suddenly angry. "We're partners. We got in this together and we'll take the heat together."

"That's stupid, Art," Jim said. "All it means is, we'll both get fined."

"It's not your decision to make," Artie said, stepping in front of Jim.

"The fuck it isn't," Jim said. "Get out of the way!"

Jim pushed Artie, and Artie stumbled a few steps back and then rushed at Jim. He pushed Jim, and Jim pushed back extra hard.

"All you wanna be is the boss!" Artie screamed.

"Fuck you, Art," Jim said, and walked out the door.

"Fuck you too!" Artie yelled after him.

Jim walked up the street to Northern Station, where he was arrested and released after posting $500 bail.

"Hard-core obscenity! They busted us for hard-core obscenity and the woman in the film had her panties on!" Jim raged when he returned from the police station.

"I know," Artie said. "And we started out extra-soft so we *wouldn't* get busted."

Neither brother gave any indication they had just gotten into a fight. The anger, the hostility, and the resentment had vanished, a shower on a summer day that is forgotten as soon as the pavement dries.

"Bra and panties, Art! Hard-core obscenity and the woman didn't even get naked!"

"What'd we do? Why'd they pick us?" Artie asked.

"I'm thinking maybe we're supposed to pay off," Jim said. "Nobody's approached us, but maybe they raided us to soften us up. I'm gonna make some calls."

Jim called the owners of two or three other theaters, and if they were leveling with him, and he had no reason to think otherwise, nobody was paying off the cops.

The Mitchell Brothers' inner circle met that night and decided the cops had hit because they were the new kids on the block. Or because they had located outside of the Mission and the Tenderloin, the unofficially designated porn areas.

That was part of it, but there were a half dozen other reasons why the San Francisco police suddenly became enthusiastic about busting porn houses, and none of them had anything to do specifically with Jim and Artie Mitchell.

The peace and love revolution was starting to wear thin by the summer of 1969, despite the monumental Woodstock concert. In San Francisco, the original hippie movement had degenerated into filthy street people who shoplifted and panhandled incessantly, stayed stoned on increasingly dangerous drugs, and often had to be rushed to an emergency room because they had OD'd or were suffering from acute drug toxicity. The panhandlers slept in ratty vans or in the parks, and they littered the Haight and Golden Gate Park with garbage.

Generally, the feeling around city hall and the police department was: enough is enough. Officials had had enough of the hippies and they were tired of watching beaver houses pop up everywhere. Solid citizens were complaining that their children were walking past theaters that had titles like *Pink Beaver* on the marquee. The Mission Coalition Organization, a grass-roots group of homeowners and parents, was picketing the Crown Theatre, a beaver house at 2555 Mission, handing out leaflets proclaiming that "pornography advertising is not good for the neighborhood," and demanding the Crown revert back to the "family" theater it once was.

And one theater owner showed a film that went so far beyond beavers it crossed every line of decency.

"Some jerk in the Tenderloin showed a man-pig bestiality film. The DA and the brass in the police department were so sickened by it they decided to go after everybody," says Arlene Elster, a beautiful brunette who was Lowell Pickett's partner at the Sutter Cinema. Elster and Pickett met when they were working as volunteers at the Haight-Ashbury Free Medical Clinic and arranged an abortion for Elster's high school girlfriend, Janis Joplin.

Deputy DAs in San Francisco had traditionally been reluctant to prosecute pornographers. DAs tend to be crime fighters who feel their work is worthwhile when they are prosecuting violent criminals or working on complex fraud cases.

Ambitious young attorneys, looking ahead to a private practice specializing in criminal law, saw no gain in spending months on a low-profile obscenity case. They also knew that pornographers could afford good attorneys, which meant delays, hassles over legal technicalities, and reduced chances of winning.

But all that changed when Jerome Benson became an assistant district attorney. Benson found pornography offensive. He was eager to take the cases, and aggressively pursued them in court.

Three weeks after they raided the O'Farrell, the police hit the Peerless Theatre. This raid really sent tremors through the San Francisco sex industry. Not only did the cops haul away the owner of the Peerless; they also arrested nine patrons and booked them on charges of viewing obscene material.

The O'Farrell had 341 paying customers the day the cops raided the Peerless. The next day, it had 70. That whole day, managers and owners of other theaters kept calling to say they had heard the cops were going to take down the O'Farrell that night.

Jim and Artie talked it over and finally decided to refund the admission charge. That way, if the cops came, they couldn't arrest anyone in the audience because technically they were not paying customers.

The rumors turned out to be half right. The cops were indeed planning another raid, but not at the O'Farrell. They hit Alex de Renzy's Screening Room and hauled away 10 more mortified film buffs.

Clearly, this was war. The Mitchell Brothers couldn't just sit back and watch their audience shrink. They had to do something besides refund money. But what?

"Go talk to my brother Michael," said Biff Kennedy, an amiable employee at the theater whom Artie and Meredith liked so much they eventually named a cat after him. "Michael will find a way to make the cops stop this shit."

A radical young attorney, Michael Kennedy wore his blond hair in a pageboy puff and had a Fu Manchu mustache. He liked shirts that were in solid colors—purple was a favorite—ties that were fat and wild with psychedelic colors, and suits that had extra-wide lapels. Thirty-three at the time, Kennedy had practiced law in San Francisco before going to New York, where he worked with radical lawyers like William Kunstler.

Kennedy was one of the attorneys in the celebrated trial of the Chicago Seven that followed the riots at the 1968 Democratic convention. Kennedy had returned to San Francisco a hero in radical circles. He and his partner, Joe Rhine, opened an office in a Victorian in the Western Addition and had everything, from the walls to the typewriters, painted black and red.

Outrageous! Kennedy declared after Jim and Artie told him about the raids. The cops are arresting patrons for watching a film? How can they do that when the patrons had no prior knowledge of what they were going to see? They're trampling all over the First Amendment! The next thing you know, they'll be breaking into homes to confiscate *Playboy*!

"Here's my advice," Kennedy said. "If you roll over and play dead, they'll roll over you. Hit back. Hit back hard."

Jim and Artie left Kennedy's office elated. "Wait till you meet Michael!" Artie told Meredith when he got home. "He'll change the way you think about lawyers forever!"

It was a match made in leftist-outlaw heaven. The Mitchell Brothers needed a weapon to take on the establishment. Michael Kennedy was the perfect weapon. They were outlaws who wanted to beat the system. Kennedy was a radical who wanted to tear the system down. Deeply antiestablishment, Kennedy thought of prosecutors as representatives of "the forces of darkness" and "the proctologists of the body juris."

As Jim and Artie got deeper into their roles as pornographers, they began to see life more and more as theater. To Michael Kennedy, the courtroom was a theater and a trial "a play with the highest conceivable stakes; sometimes life, always liberty." The Mitchell Brothers paid Kennedy a retainer that freed him to concentrate on the pro bono cases of high-profile clients like George Jackson, author of *Soledad Brother,* and Huey Newton. Kennedy gave the Mitchell Brothers a raison d'être that went far beyond making a buck and rationalizing it with a lot of left-wing rhetoric.

There would be no more hiding from the cops. With Kennedy beside them, Jim and Artie were going to be fighting in the trenches in the never-ending war for individual freedom and the First Amendment. Jim, in particular, was fired up. Kennedy fascinated him. Going to court with Kennedy was going to be exhilarating!

On August 15, two days after the police had raided Alex de Renzy's Screening Room, Michael Kennedy marched into federal court to file a series of legal motions on behalf of Jim Mitchell.

Kennedy charged that California's obscenity law violated the First, Fifth, and Fourteenth amendments. The constitutional issues were important because they gave Kennedy grounds for appeal if he lost the case. He also asked the court for "a temporary ten-day injunction against the mayor and others to prevent them from driving Mr. Mitchell out of business."

The mayor? What did Joseph Alioto have to do with an Okie pornographer who had been in business for only six weeks?

Kennedy's strategy went something like this: The power structure by definition was corrupt. They all work together, which meant that the mayor, not the DA or the chief of police, was behind the raids. And why was Alioto orchestrating the raids?

Because Alioto was a competitor! According to the lawsuit Kennedy filed, the mayor had a financial interest in Syufy Enterprises, a nationwide chain of motion-picture houses that owned several theaters in San Francisco.

It was an outrageous, grandstanding charge, but Kennedy didn't care. It worked.

"Listen to this, listen to this," Artie shouted the next morning. He was reading a story (on page seven of the *Chronicle*) about the suit Kennedy had filed and seemed oblivious to the fact that everybody upstairs at the O'Farrell had a *Chronicle*, and everybody had turned to page seven.

Artie cleared his voice and read, " 'The mayor did have a theater interest here but he divested himself of it when he took office to avoid a conflict of interest,' Hadley Roff, an Alioto aide, told the *Chronicle*. 'Mayor Alioto, in any case, does not dictate tactics of the police department, which acts under its own directives to enforce the law.' "

"We're nobodies and yet here the mayor is, reacting defensively to our charges! Amazing!" Meredith said.

"It's really true, what the freaks say," Earl Shagley said. "You really can write your own movie."

"Artie, one of us has gotta call home," Jim said. "J.R. is gonna love this!"

"I'll call 'em, Bob," Artie said.

A preliminary hearing on the charges was held in federal court a week later. Kennedy opened by asking Judge Alfonso J. Zirpoli, on behalf of Jim Mitchell and the owners of the other adult theaters in San Francisco, to issue a temporary restraining order that would halt police raids on the theaters. Zirpoli, a highly respected jurist with a liberal reputation, said that he had already gone into several cases involving obscene films in depth and was prepared to grant a full hearing on the matter of police raids in one week.

"Will the city agree to halt the raids until that hearing can be held?" Judge Zirpoli asked H. Leroy Cannon, a deputy city attorney.

"No, sir," Cannon responded quickly. "We will agree to no stipulations."

Paul Halvonik, an attorney for the American Civil Liberties Union, whom Kennedy had asked to appear in a "friend of the court" capacity, rose to suggest a compromise. Perhaps the city would agree to a more limited restraining order, one that did not stop the raids but prohibited the police from arresting patrons?

"Without such an order, until the hearing a week away, people will be afraid to go to theaters, including *Hair,* because they will not know what is obscene and what is not," Halvonik told the court. "If they were afraid to go to a political meeting for fear of arrest, your honor would issue such an order."

Halvonik's was a classic example of the kind of inference that drives law-and-order conservatives crazy about the ACLU—watching a sexually explicit film is like going to see *Hair* is like attending a meeting of Young Republicans. Judge Zirpoli, however, took the point.

"Would the city agree to leave the patrons of adult theaters alone until a hearing can be held?" the judge asked city attorney Cannon.

"No!" Cannon snapped. "There are statutes that prohibit viewing obscene material and the duty of the police is to enforce those—"

"All right," Judge Zirpoli said, cutting Cannon off. "I will issue a temporary restraining order limited exclusively to patrons."

"We won! We won!" Artie yelled as he and Jim raced up the stairs at the O'Farrell. "You should have been there! That judge was pissed at the cops!"

"No more raids?" Meredith asked.

"We got a temporary restraining order that protects the patrons from being arrested, but they can still come for us," Jim explained. "I don't think they will, though. Not after the way that city attorney got slapped around today."

That afternoon, Alex de Renzy jumped on the bandwagon, filing a suit similar to Jim Mitchell's, charging conspiracy between city hall and the police department. De Renzy upped the ante by demanding $250,000 in damages.

The next day, the cops raided both the Mitchell Brothers' O'Farrell Theatre and Alex de Renzy's Screening Room.

The first thing the cops did at the O'Farrell was to stop the movie and bring up the lights in the theater.

"You gentlemen should be ashamed! Ashamed!" a policeman shouted as he walked down the center aisle. "It's a beautiful day outside and you pasty-faced perverts are in here abusing yourselves! Don't you care about your health?"

"Stand up, all of you," another officer said.

The film buffs did as they were told.

"Just as I thought," said the cop in the center aisle. "Nobody in here is in shape. You guys have definitely got to start exercising more than your elbows."

The cops patrolled the aisles for forty-five minutes. When they left, they took Artie Mitchell with them.

Early the next morning, Meredith and Artie hauled ten copies of the *Chronicle* into the O'Farrell.

"Not bad, Bob, not bad," Jim said, bending the paper so he could look across the room at his brother. Artie didn't look up. He was engrossed in the story.

"Listen to this," Artie said. " 'We were the ones that filed the suit in federal court. It's significant that we were the ones that got busted,' said Artie Mitchell. 'I don't know why they had to use nine policemen. It was an indiscriminate waste of police manpower.' I sound pretty good, don't I, Bob?"

"Not to the cops, I'll bet," Meredith said, laughing. "I'm sure they don't appreciate a twenty-four-year-old pornographer telling them their priorities are wrong."

"Somebody's gotta," Artie said.

The police raids had turned the porn industry and the Mitchell Brothers into a major story. Two different reporters had already described Jim as "personable," an adjective not often used to describe pornographers. The *Chronicle* assigned Sandy Zane, a reporter with ten years' experience on the streets, to do a series on the porn business. When Zane interviewed Jim and Artie, they asked him almost as many questions as he asked them.

"Tell us about the vice cops," Jim said. "Who's Shaughnessy?"

"Gerald Shaughnessy, captain of the squad," Zane replied. "They call him 'the Pope' in the police department because he's such a prude. He's had as much to do with the crackdown as any police-man."

"And Sol Weiner? What's he like?" Artie asked.

The reporter laughed.

"They call him 'the Green Weenie,' " Zane said. "I assume it's an ironic reference to the Green Hornet. Weiner and a partner busted Allen Ginsberg for *Howl* in 1956."

"And Pete Maloney?" Jim asked.

"He's worked vice for thirteen years," Zane said. "By all accounts, he's a good guy."

Zane became one of the first of dozens of journalists to become friendly with the Mitchell Brothers and to hang out at the O'Farrell. The lure of sex and meeting women who took their clothes off for money was part of the appeal. But not all of it.

"Reporters weren't interested in seeing the films," Zane says. "The people who patronized the theater were squares, tourists, guys who couldn't live out their sexual fantasies. It was such an open time in the Bay Area you *could* live out your fantasies. We'd go up there to drink their tequila and smoke their dope. The Mitchell Brothers corrupted a generation of reporters—assuming, that is, that we could be more corrupted than we already were."

There are reasons that go deeper than fun and tequila. A large number of reporters are uneasy spirits, would-be rebels. Journalism provides them with a wonderful outlet. They can write investigative pieces that expose chicanery in high places and take the pants off the arrogant. But deep down, journalists know that they are as wed-ded to the establishment as congressmen and real estate agents. Without them, journalists would have no role to play.

Few journalists who bothered to watch the crude loops Jim and Artie cranked out admired them for their work. They liked them because the brothers had defied the moral code, had told society, "You don't like what we're doing? So what? We're going to do it anyway." Jim and Artie were *real* rebels.

"The Mitchell Brothers weren't stultified by normal middle-class inhibitions like I was," says Sandy Zane. "They were direct, impu-dent, unapologetic. They didn't give a shit what anybody thought. They had an instinctive grasp on the fact that they would come out ahead if they didn't apologize for what they were doing, if they stood up and said, 'It's a waste of city money to arrest us. If you don't want to go to these movies, don't go.' "

The stories that Zane and other reporters wrote taught the Mitchell Brothers a fundamental truth about their business: In pornography, there is no such thing as bad publicity. The more ink the brothers got, the larger the audiences at the O'Farrell became. The brothers knew the horn dick daddies weren't coming to the theater because of the free coffee or because Jim had been described as "personable." The customers were coming because they figured that if the cops were picking on the Mitchell Brothers, it must be because the O'Farrell was showing the hottest films in town.

Weeks passed before Judge Zirpoli released his written ruling on Jim's lawsuit. When he did, the judge's decision was a smashing victory for San Francisco's pornographers. The judge not only ordered the police to stop arresting patrons in sex cinemas; he also handed down a ruling that was to have long-lasting consequences in the battle between the police and the owners of adult theaters.

The cops had been going into theaters and carrying away the film that was on the screen. Judge Zirpoli said they had to stop doing that. Prior restraint, the judge ruled, was censorship. Before the police could seize a film, there had to be an adversary hearing and the district attorney had to get a warrant.

Zirpoli's ruling led to one of the curiosities of the pornographic theater: the plainclothes cop with the infrared camera. The program at the O'Farrell changed once a week, on Tuesday. The usual program consisted of two loops made by the Mitchell Brothers' film crew, plus four L.A. loops that Meredith Bradford set to music. Every Tuesday, Sol Weiner or Pete Maloney, or both, would show up at the theater and buy a ticket.

"Pete! Our biggest fan!" an employee would shout when Maloney walked into the lobby. "Opening day would be nothing without you! We've saved your favorite seat!"

"Sol! I gotta know, baby: how many stars did you give it?" someone would yell when Weiner came out.

The cops would smile and go about their business.

"I became friendly with Sol Weiner and Pete Maloney," recalls Lowell Pickett. "This was the days of the Zebra killer and the Black Panthers, and one day I asked them what they thought of their work. They smiled and one of them said, 'No policeman has ever been shot in a movie theater.' And then they went in and saw the film."

The vice cops would aim the infrared cameras at the screen and take pictures every few seconds. They would take the film back to the station to be developed, and then they would walk the developed pictures over to the DA's office. The cops would show the pictures to a deputy DA—usually Jerome Benson—who would take them into court.

A judge would preside over an adversary hearing and then decide whether to issue a search warrant. If he did, the cops would go back to the O'Farrell, seize a copy of the offensive film, and arrest Jim and Artie. The boys would make bail, and the next week it would happen all over again. The arrests eventually became so routine the cops stopped coming by the O'Farrell to arrest the brothers.

"Pete Maloney was pretty easy to deal with," Meredith recalls. "He'd call Art to tell him he was going to be arrested, and Art would say, 'Okay, Pete, I'll be down.' We got an acquittal because of that once. One of the jurors said after the trial he'd voted to acquit because anybody who would tell a cop, 'Okay, Pete, I'll be right down,' had to be a good guy."

One evening when the arrests had been coming one after another, the Mitchell Brothers' inner circle gathered at Meredith and Artie's for dinner. Jim brought along suggestions he had culled from the box that was located in the lobby of the theater.

"This one is a riot!" Meredith squealed. "'Bring back Martha Raye. Let's see that mouth in action.'"

"Here's one," said Artie. "'How about a film called *Sex on Mars*? The cast could wear far-out costumes. Each man could have about fifteen penises and each woman about fifteen pussies.'"

"There's a lot of that kind of stuff, but if you take these things as a whole, they're really telling us something," Jim said.

"It's true," Meredith said. "They don't want to see S and M."

"They don't want to see rape," Annie said.

"They don't want to see children," Artie said.

"They don't want us to get cute either," Jim said. "Listen to this: 'Last week's film had the camera hidden behind a rubber plant in one scene. The leaves blocked out some of the action!'"

"It's pretty clear what they want," Meredith said.

"They want to see pussy," Jim said. "Listen to this: 'Turn the lights up, get bright, keep it in focus, let me see it.'"

"How nice it is to work in porno, where the only true superstar is the vagina," Annie sighed.

"I think we ought to put the superstar in action, Mouse," Artie said. "I think we ought to show fucking."

The room fell quiet as everyone pondered Artie's suggestion.

The DA had been setting up Maginot Lines and pornographers had been running through them since the nudie emerged from the underground in San Francisco. First it was pubic hair. Show pubic hair and we'll bust you, the cops had warned theater operators.

They made arrests but the charges had no effect. Women in the films began removing their panties.

Then it was masturbation. If we come in here and see a finger in a vagina, you're under arrest, the cops had vowed.

Filmmakers chopped frames where fingers entered the forbidden zone for a while and then left them in. Arrests were made but it didn't matter. Soon every theater in town was showing films with digital insertion.

Then it was men. Women can do whatever they want in these films, the vice cops told theater owners, but if you have a man in a film and there is physical contact, we'll bust you.

The dreary old stag films had men in them, even if they were wearing masks and black socks. But so far the prohibition against having men in the films was holding up. No one had dared put a man in a film since the stags had emerged from the arcades in San Francisco.

Artie was proposing to break two taboos. He not only wanted to put a man in the film; he wanted to show that man in action.

"We're getting busted anyway," Artie pointed out.

"I don't know, Bob," Jim said. "We've got something like fifteen cases pending. Maybe we should wait and see what happens when we get to court."

"Let's do it," Artie argued. "There'll be lines around the block. We can use the money to pay Kennedy."

The group argued on into the night, and Jim finally came around to seeing things Artie's way. When they finally broke up, everyone was turned on by the risk they were about to take. The next film they made would have *actual insertion*.

The next morning, Meredith woke up and was surprised to see that Art wasn't in bed. She walked into the kitchen and was again surprised to find Artie on the phone.

"Who are you calling?" Meredith asked.

"Jim," Artie replied.

"Why? He only left here about six hours ago."

"Jim?" Artie asked, raising an index finger for Meredith to see. "I changed my mind. We can't do it. We can't show it all. It's like asking to be sent to jail. Let's just keep doin' what we're doin' and see what breaks."

4

Might As Well
Show It All,
Bob

THE MITCHELL BROTHERS' inner circle had gathered upstairs at the O'Farrell to brainstorm ideas for the following week's loop. Good marijuana contributed to the giddy atmosphere, but the true fun came from getting their ideas on celluloid. The people in the room could come up with an idea for a film on a Monday, and no matter how half-baked or harebrained it might be, that film would be up on the screen at the O'Farrell the next Tuesday. They were *really doing it.*

"I know! Let's shoot in a cemetery!" Artie cried.

"Sex and death! What a trip!" Meredith said.

"We'll go to Colma," Jim said.

"Colma! Now that is a trip," said Earl Shagley.

Colma is a Bay Area oddity, a town that has lived on death since San Francisco curtailed burials early in the century. In downtown Colma, eight miles south of downtown San Francisco, Italian restaurants sit across the street from mortuaries and small businesses where stonecutters chisel polished marble tombstones. The brown hills above the town are lined with row after row of tombstones.

"We could have her be a widow," Artie said. "She could be grieving at her husband's grave."

"That's good, Bob," Jim said. "Let's go with that. Got anybody in
mind for the part?"

Jim looked around the room and everybody shrugged.

"We got the usual 'Now casting for a motion picture. Nudity
required' ads in the *Chron* and all the underground rags—the *Barb*
and the *Guardian* and the *Oracle*," Artie said. "Somebody will turn
up. They always do."

Meredith and Artie got home late that night, and early the next
morning Meredith was back in the theater working on a sound track
for a loop.

"We were all committed to better production values because we
could see that better-quality films were drawing patrons from the
seedy establishments around town," Meredith says. "Other places
showed films without titles. We titled every film we showed, even
the L.A. loops."

Sound was a matter of personal pride to Meredith. The sound
track on the average L.A. loop was as mind-numbing as propa-
ganda, ten minutes of a woman continuously going "oooohhhh" and
"aaaahhhh" while wretched and preposterous music—it could be
anything from a Sousa march to "Yes! We Have No Bananas"—
played in the background.

Before they could afford the Nagra tape recorder needed to make
sound films, Meredith did the heavy breathing and added the
"ooohhs" and "aaahhs" to dozens of Mitchell Brothers' loops. She
combed record stores, buying whatever albums she thought might
enhance a beaver film. She spent hours up in the projection room
with headphones on, trying to time the sound track to what was
happening on the screen. When a film ended in other San Francisco beaver houses, the music kept right on playing. When a film
ended at the O'Farrell, the music stopped too.

One morning, Meredith carried a stack of albums she had just
purchased up the stairs at the O'Farrell and walked into the studio.
She stopped in her tracks when she saw Artie aiming a Polaroid
camera at a nude woman standing against a white wall.

Shooting a Polaroid was standard operating procedure. When a
woman came in and said she wanted to be in a film, the first thing
they did was have her strip and Jim or Artie or one of the crew

would shoot a Polaroid. What had stunned Meredith was the woman's lush, incredibly beautiful body.

Meredith had been in the porn business for over a year and it still amazed her how many women were willing to appear in a beaver film for the paltry sums they were paid—the going rate was $25 to $50. Every week the O'Farrell put a new film on the screen, and every week the film featured a woman—some of them girls in their late teens—who had never before appeared in a film.

The women were always pretty too. Jim and Artie liked to tell people that the only place they asked their actresses to use makeup was on the soles of their feet, which had become permanently dirty from traipsing around barefoot in the Haight and Golden Gate Park.

"We didn't use whores—they could make a lot more money hooking—and we didn't use professional dancers from North Beach—they were too Forty-second Street," says Bill Boyer, the former newspaperman from Antioch. Journalism had turned out to be fun, but the pay was abysmal, so Boyer had taken a PR job in Reno. That had turned out to be boring, and it had not taken Artie long to convince his old friend to become part of the Mitchell Brothers' team.

"A lot of the girls were college kids who needed the money," Boyer continues. "Our ads always said nudity, and in a lot of cases that's all the women thought it was going to be. But Jim and Artie were so charming and the rest of us on the crew looked like we could be students, so when Jim or Artie said, 'Hey, let's do this, it's no big deal,' they'd go ahead and do it."

Meredith gazed at the woman Artie was photographing, who seemed to have stepped out of a Pre-Raphaelite painting. She had an Afro of beautiful red hair, hazel eyes, creamy white skin, and long dancer's legs.

"Who's she?" Meredith whispered to a crew member.

"The girl who's going to do the Colma movie," a crew member replied. "We're gonna call it *Requiem*. Soon as she's done here, Jim wants you to take her out and buy her a black dress. You know, widow's weeds."

Meredith and Annie shot the grave scene later that day in Colma. Dressed in black, the woman stood over her husband's tombstone, lost in a grief she conveyed by staring at the stone, dropping her head to her chest, and then summoning all her energy and lifting her head again. Meredith found herself strangely moved.

"You know what? She can act! She can really act!" Meredith said sotto voce to Annie.

"I know!" Annie said. "Isn't it great!"

The film cut from the cemetery to the woman's bedroom—actually, the studio upstairs at the O'Farrell—where the woman took off her black dress, lay down on the bed, and masturbated. Meredith used a full Gregorian choir performing fifteenth-century liturgical chants for the sound track. The somber elegance of the sound track gave dignity to a physical act moralists were still denouncing as "self-abuse."

"I never bothered to see our films, but I really wanted to see *Requiem*," Meredith recalls. "That film was as close as I ever came to liking a masturbation film. She was so good, so beautiful, and so striking at the cemetery it was painful to watch. And when she went home and got into bed, it turned into an erotic movie with a message. When a lover dies, sex doesn't."

Requiem, a 15-minute film, is a significant departure in the dreary annals of American sex films. The lizards in sharkskin suits in New York who were making beavers that featured lifeless, tattooed hookers would never have used a Gregorian choir in a film. The smooth operators in L.A. who cranked out loop after loop that were as devoid of feeling as an industrial film that follows a can of soup from the vat to the shipping crate would never have come up with a story line that involved a grieving widow.

Requiem was the result of the "hang loose, what the hell, let's do it" atmosphere at the O'Farrell, a milieu that mirrored the "we are all living our own movies" mentality of the 1960s. Jim and Artie were like Lenny Bruce when Lenny was emceeing strip shows in Los Angeles. Lenny knew he could say anything and be as outrageous as he wanted and the audience wouldn't care, as long as he kept bringing out the girls. Jim and Artie knew they could concoct the wildest plots and craziest characters imaginable and the horn dick daddies wouldn't care, as long as a woman climbed out of her panties.

The "anything goes, porn is a goof, let's have fun" atmosphere that Jim and Artie created at the O'Farrell is what made the Mitchell Brothers different from other San Francisco pornographers, or, for that matter, pornographers anywhere else in the world. That atmosphere attracted actresses like the redhead in *Requiem,* who made one film as a lark and, as far as anyone knows, never made another. She brought an openness and an innocence to pornography that had not been seen before. Through actresses like her, the Mitchell Brothers carried the central idea of the sexual revolution to the screen: sex is not dirty and perverse; sex is normal and healthy.

"Acting is believing, and the New Age people who acted in those films believed in what they were doing," says Lowell Pickett. "It could only have happened in San Francisco in the 1960s. Arlene [Elster] and I would go up Haight Street and Arlene would stop girls and say, 'We're making sex films. Beaver films. Want to be in one?' We got probably eighty percent of the women we wanted and no one ever got angry, even though in the beginning we were only paying twenty-five dollars a film.

"It wasn't about money, it was about freedom," Pickett concludes. "Women felt they were free to use their bodies in any way they chose."

"I was just down on Jones Street, Bob. There's a line around the corner waiting to get in the Screening Room," Jim told Artie.

"Oh, man, de Renzy has really scored!" Artie replied.

"There's more, Bob. Couples are standing in that line. Lots of couples."

"They want to see it, Bob," Artie said. "They all want to see it."

"That's why this film is such a brilliant move on de Renzy's part. It gives couples *an excuse* to see a sex film."

In 1967, Denmark became the first Western country to abolish all laws governing pornography. The repeal made international news that year, and was even bigger news the next when the Danish government released statistics that showed there had been a substantial decline in sex offenses like voyeurism in Copenhagen.

De Renzy and a partner went to Copenhagen to film Denmark's first sex fair and in 1969 released a documentary called *Pornography in Denmark.* The film cost de Renzy $15,000 to produce and did $25,000 at the box office during its first week at the Screening Room. *Pornography* eventually grossed more than $2 million. Its boffo run was not due to riveting material; *Pornography* was a clumsy, simpleminded film that succeeded because it was about sex in a Scandinavian country and Scandinavian sex films like *I Am*

Curious (Yellow) were considered hot stuff in the late 1960s and early 1970s.

Pornography in Denmark also attracted a wide audience simply because it was a documentary. A Berkeley couple could tell their friends, "We went over to the Tenderloin and saw *Pornography in Denmark* the other night. It's a documentary about an interesting social experiment the Danes are conducting." *Serious* people went to see documentaries. They were educational and elicited images of the great Robert Flaherty and films like *Nanook of the North* and *Man of Aran*.

The Mitchell Brothers' crew went down to the Screening Room to see *Pornography in Denmark* for purely commercial reasons. If another theater had a hot film, they wanted to see it.

"Word traveled fast in those circles," Meredith says. "If we heard there was a particularly graphic scene in another movie, we'd go see it, because Jim and Artie always wanted to be ahead of the crowd."

To be the best in pornography means to be the most notorious, and the question before the Mitchell Brothers was "How can we get out in front of de Renzy?" They had the usual marijuana, wine, and beer meetings, and finally decided to take the step they had spent so much time debating.

The Mitchell Brothers were going to break the barrier. They were going to be the first to put a man in an aboveground porn film. The man turned out to be Artie.

"It's for you," Meredith's mother said.

Meredith was back home in Massachusetts for her sister Jennifer's wedding. She knew it must be Artie on the phone because her mother had the "I'm upset but I will not show it" tone in her voice and was holding the receiver like it was a dead rat.

"I told your mother to send you home," Artie said when Meredith got on the line.

"The sooner the better for all concerned," Meredith said. "I miss you."

"I miss you too. And you missed my acting debut!" Artie said, his voice rising with excitement.

"YOU! IN A FILM?" Meredith shouted, quickly looking around to make sure she was alone.

"Yep. In our bedroom. In our bed!"

"ART! You didn't—"

"Of course I didn't. What do you think, we've gone hard-core since you left? We decided to make a soft-core couple film, remember?"

"Right. But how'd you end up in it?"

"Simple. The guy didn't show up," Artie said.

"So what happened?" Meredith asked.

"I'd been toiling away for hours, working on the script for *Summer of Laura*. We decided to use our place because we wanted the look of a full bedroom and it's easier than dragging dressers and mirrors and all that stuff up to the studio. We were all set up, we'd paid the girl twenty-five dollars and she's all ready to go, and then the guy didn't show. I had no choice but to get into it."

"How soft was it, Art? Tell me what you did."

"I kissed her. That was about all. I just kissed her," Artie said. "In our bed!"

"Hey, the world's a stage," Artie said merrily.

The soft-core films the Mitchell Brothers pioneered were an immediate hit at the O'Farrell box office. It wasn't so much what the man did or did not do on the screen. It was having a man in the films that made the difference. Men in the audience could fantasize that *they* were up there on the screen, about to do things to a beautiful young lady.

Soft-core films mirrored the rapid evolution of millions of couples who were burning with what Bob Seger called "the fire down below." Artie's demure kiss in *Summer of Laura* was followed by hot tongue kissing in later films. As the weeks went by, hot kissing led to rubbing and grinding and heavy groaning. Then came heavy petting, with hands disappearing under skirts and inching up thighs. And then came simulated intercourse, what high school kids call "dry humping."

Watching the films, Artie and Jim found themselves asking: What is, and exactly what is not, intercourse?

"Jim and Artie didn't like getting busted, they didn't want to go to jail," Meredith says. "We'd screen a film one week and Jim would say, 'Oh, man, this is definitely intercourse! We can't use this, we'll get busted!' Art would argue the other way. The next week, it would be Art who'd be saying, 'This one has gone too far! It's sure to get us busted!' and Jim would be arguing the other way.

"It finally evolved to the point where there was no discernible difference between what we were showing and fucking," Meredith says. "One day, they just decided to go ahead and show penetration. They were getting busted anyway, so what was the difference? It was 'What the hell, we might as well show it all, Bob.'"

"I don't know, Jim. I don't feel right about it," Earl Shagley was saying as he and Jim drove across the Bay Bridge.

"About what?" Jim asked.

"Shooting hard-core, for one thing. Where we're gonna shoot it, for another," Shagley said.

"Hey, it's not like it's a church," Jim said.

"It's a seminary! That's almost like a church," Shagley said.

Jim shrugged. He had enough on his mind without being bothered with Earl's qualms. He had to find the place, get in and set up the equipment, shoot the film, and get out before anyone discovered they were there.

The leading man had recommended the location. His brother was studying to be a minister at a seminary over in Berkeley. His brother was out of town and he and his girlfriend often stayed in his brother's room when he was gone. She had always felt comfortable there. It would make things easier for her.

"Annie isn't real happy about this and I'm not either, Jim," Shagley said. "We got into this to get money to make serious films and before we turn around we've got a theater and we're cranking out film after film, one raunchier than another. And now we're gonna go hard-core. It might not be just you and Artie who get busted this time. They could put us all away for this."

"We *are* doing what we said we'd do, Earl," Jim said. "We got into this to become filmmakers and that's what we've become. Where else could you have shot so much film? Where else could you have learned so much? You're really getting good, man. I can't wait to see what you'll do when we get some decent equipment."

They turned off Interstate 80 at University Avenue in Berkeley and headed east toward the campus. The seminary was located above the campus on "Holy Hill," a collection of churches, temples, and seminaries clustered around the Graduate Theological Union. They found the dormitory, located the room, and knocked on the door.

The leading man opened it. Earl walked in, took one look at the leading lady, and placed the Bolex camera on the floor because he was afraid he was going to drop it.

The girlfriend was the perfect image of Annette, Earl's favorite Mouseketeer, the favorite of every boy who grew up watching *The Mickey Mouse Club* in the 1950s, probably because she was the first to develop breasts. She saw Earl staring at her, and when she smiled at him, she looked even more like Annette.

Earl was heartbroken. What happened to you? he wanted to ask. How did you end up here? Why are you doing this?

Earl didn't say a word. As soon as the door closed, the leading man went to a dresser near where Earl was standing and jerked open the top drawer. Earl glanced over and saw bottles filled with red pills and a pistol.

"Anybody tries to interfere with what's comin' down here tonight is gonna have to answer to this," the leading man said as he pulled the gun out of the drawer and waved it around for everybody to see. "Anybody goes through that door and it's 'Nam all over again," he said, staring at the gun.

Earl would have bolted for the door if he hadn't been too afraid to move.

"Hey, nothing to worry about, everything's cool. Put that back and let's start the action," Jim said with a relaxed smile.

While Jim explained what was going to happen, the couple got in bed, the crew set up the lights, and Earl got the Bolex ready. They turned on the lights and the room was immediately flooded with a hot, brilliant glare.

The couple were kissing and taking each other's clothes off when somebody knocked on the door.

"Goddamn!" hissed the leading man. He popped out of bed, dashed to the dresser, and pulled out the gun. Earl turned off the Bolex and was debating whether to hit the floor when the knock came again.

"Yeah?" Jim asked.

"I was just wondering what all those lights were about," said a voice on the other side of the door.

"We're shooting wedding pictures," Jim said quickly, watching his leading man.

"Oh, okay," the voice said. "I was just curious."

A few minutes later, there was another knock on the door. Again, the leading man jumped out of bed and grabbed his gun.

"We're shooting wedding pictures," Jim said in response to the same question.

"But this is James's room and James doesn't even have a girlfriend," the voice said.

"It's his brother," Jim said, letting his irritation show. "His brother is getting married. Is that all right with you? Now please, you are taking valuable time."

The couple had sex, and the crew packed up and got out of the room as quickly as possible.

"I was afraid that guy was going to kill us all," Earl said as they were crossing the Bay Bridge back to San Francisco.

"Yeah, I was scared too," Jim said. "He's nuts."

The shoot had left them both exhausted and they drove on in silence. Finally Earl said, "What are you going to call it?"

"*Redball*," Jim said matter-of-factly.

By the early 1970s, only three of the scores of filmmakers who were cranking out sex films in San Francisco really mattered. The "Big Three" were Alex de Renzy, who made and showed films at the Screening Room; Arlene Elster and Lowell Pickett, who did the same at the Sutter Cinema; and Jim and Artie at the O'Farrell.

When the Mitchell Brothers went hard-core, they emerged as the clear leaders of the pack, the vanguard of the subculture, the hustlers, sleazoids, iconoclasts, and sensualists who were turning what had been a dirty underground secret into an aboveground commercial endeavor.

"It took Jim and Artie to go all the way. They were our leaders," Arlene Elster would say later, with genuine admiration. "The old-school pornographers were really very conservative. If Jim and Artie hadn't broken through, magazines like *Playboy* and old-school types like Hugh Hefner would have kept sex a tease forever."

Redball and the hard-core films that followed played to near-capacity crowds almost every night at the O'Farrell. The horn dick daddies finally had a home of their own. A $4.00 ticket bought them complimentary coffee in a lobby that was decorated with interesting erotic art. If it was a slow night, they could linger on a couch and listen to Claire, the woman who ran the candy counter, play Brahms beautifully on her violin. Inside the theater, the horn dick daddies sat in big rocking-chair loge seats. Best of all, they got to see the event they found more fascinating than any other: people *doing it* in living color.

Every theater in San Francisco was soon showing hard-core films, and the national media were arriving to do stories about "the Copenhagen of America." Every reporter got the royal treatment at the O'Farrell. "This gentleman is from *Time* magazine," Jim or Artie would tell an employee. "Anything he needs, make sure he gets." In interview after interview, Jim came across as a solid young businessman who had found a market niche.

"People want to see these movies," Jim told reporters from the *Examiner.* "They're not flashy. We're clean-cut, all-American boys. We're going to stick with clean-cut little f—— movies."

Arlene Elster and Lowell Pickett took a more highbrow approach, hosting the First International Erotic Film Festival in December 1970. Don Simpson, who went on to become famous as half of the notorious film production team of Bruckheimer and Simpson, handled the publicity; Annie Leibovitz took the pictures for the advertisements; Arthur Knight, the esteemed *Saturday Review* film critic, was one of the judges.

The winning entry was a three-minute film made by a woman of a woman peeling an orange.

"The Dick Cavett Show wanted to show the film, so I flew to New York," Elster remembers. "I hate doing talk shows, I'm no good at it, but I figured I'd be okay because the film would take up most of the time.

"At the last minute, the censors at ABC said we couldn't show the film. They thought it was too suggestive, even though only her hands were visible. Cavett hadn't done his homework and the whole thing was a disaster."

The networks may have been too timid to show even the most abstract of the San Francisco sex films, but the owners of the adult theaters that had begun popping up all over the country were eager for the product. Because there were federal laws against shipping obscene material across state lines, the filmmakers avoided the postal system and took the films to the airport and shipped them air freight. Or, like drug dealers, they paid a courier to fly across the country and deliver the product in person.

"We'd shoot two versions, a hard-core for here and a soft-core for elsewhere," Lowell Pickett remembers. "The places we shipped hard-core versions always surprised me—San Diego, Indianapolis, and small towns all over the country where, I presume, the authorities were being paid off."

Jim had supposedly gotten into pornography to finance the legitimate films that he, Annie, and Earl wanted to make. Artie would get stoned and occasionally fantasize about making a million dollars, selling out, and retiring before he was thirty to a condominium on Maui with a lifetime supply of pungent, powerful "Maui-Wowie."

Jim was no longer talking about making mainstream films and Artie was probably just blowing smoke, albeit marijuana smoke. But Mark Bradford, Meredith's brother, who had become a member of the film crew, often wondered if there were times when Jim and Artie questioned what they were doing. They never showed it, but the arrests had to be a heavy weight to carry around. A conviction or two and the party was over.

Mark also wondered if the brothers ever thought ahead, if they ever asked themselves, "What's it going to be like to be making fuck films when we're forty?" A born observer who was fascinated by the men and women he met making pornographic films, Mark had become deeply interested in Jim and Artie. He suspected that, in their heart of hearts, the brothers were Okies with inferiority complexes. Some of the films they made were shoddy and second-rate, even by the "throw it together and slap it up on the screen" standards that governed the O'Farrell. Mark sometimes wondered if those shoddy films were an expression of how Jim and Artie felt about themselves.

If Jim and Artie did stop to ponder what they were doing, they didn't do it often. They were doers who were not inclined to self-analysis. They were too busy and making too much money to spend much time contemplating who they were and what they were doing. The next guy through the door at the theater could be a cop and it was likely the next phone call would be from an attorney, but Jim and Artie never seriously considered folding the game and cashing in. Their father had been run out of Texas. No one, *absolutely no one*, was going to run them out of the porn business.

Besides, Jim and Artie's whole identities were tied up in being pornographers. To the press, they were throwbacks to the Barbary Coast, characters in a town that loved characters. To Michael Kennedy's radical friends, they were true iconoclasts, a refreshing change from pallid academic Marxists who only talked a good game.

Jim and Artie had the guts to thumb their noses at the establishment. They were willing, even eager, to take the battle against *the man* to the courtroom.

The Mitchell Brothers' first test in San Francisco Municipal Court (actually, it was Jim's first test; Artie was not a defendant in the initial case) came at a jury trial that began on November 25, 1970. From the dozen or more films that had been seized in raids, assistant district attorney Jerome Benson had chosen three films to show to the jury: *Soft*, *Seduction*, and *Up Against the Wall*.

Michael Kennedy, the Mitchell Brothers' big gun, was fresh from the explosive Los Siete trial, in which he had helped defend seven young Chicano men who had been charged with murdering a police officer in San Francisco's Mission District. His wife, Eleanore, was assisting him in analyzing the jury.

Like a good cardplayer, Kennedy was able to think three or four moves ahead during a trial. He tailored his courtroom demeanor to win points with the jurors, and for this trial he was ready to turn on the jets and burn with righteous indignation or turn abrasive and try to grind a prosecution witness into cornmeal—to do whatever it took to convince a few or even *one* member of the jury that the films Jim Mitchell showed at the O'Farrell were not obscene. Kennedy didn't think an acquittal was in the cards. He was hoping to hang the jury and force a retrial.

The first thing assistant DA Benson did was to turn the courtroom into a pornographic theater. A projector was wheeled in, a screen set up, and the lights turned off. Every seat in the courtroom was taken and the curious were standing in the hallway, peering through the circular windows in the doors.

The cops had made a grainy black-and-white copy of a color film, but nobody in the courtroom took their eyes off the screen. In fact, as she looked around, Meredith didn't see anyone blink. She studied the six men and six women who were sitting in the jury box. One man was yawning—Meredith was sure it was to relieve tension. Another man had his handkerchief out and was mopping his brow.

"Oh God, that's a definite insertion shot!" Meredith said softly to Artie, who was sitting beside her in the first row. "Damn, I wish we hadn't left that in this movie. That's no doubt the line we can't cross."

"Here comes the blow job," Artie groaned. "Yep, there she goes. Oh Jesus, we're guilty!"

Until this moment, Meredith had not realized how immersed in sex she was and how blasé about sex she had become. If the Mitchell Brothers made a film that had oral, anal, and lesbian sex in it, if couples switched in midstream, Meredith's attitude was: So what? That's what people *do* when they have sex.

The patrons who occupied the loge seats at the O'Farrell thought the same way, and now, sitting in the hard wooden seat in the courtroom, Meredith realized that she had more in common with the horn dick daddies than she did with the straight citizens in the audience and the jurors' box. They were flabbergasted by what she had come to take for granted. This obviously was their first encounter with explicit sex on film.

But rather than feeling like some sort of slimy creature that had crawled out from under a rock, Meredith felt proud. She had done it. She had liberated herself from the middle class. The people around her were stiffs, straights who had no right to pass judgment on the Mitchell Brothers. They didn't get it; they'd never get it. Meredith longed to be back upstairs at the O'Farrell, smoking a joint with others who had broken free from the hypocritical, guilt-ridden middle class.

Meredith thought of J.R. and Georgia Mae. They had recently moved to a suburb of Sacramento, and she, Jim, Artie, and whoever else wanted to go often drove up there on a Saturday or a Sunday for a visit. It was hard to imagine two families that were more different than the Mitchells and the Bradfords, but when it came to the things that really mattered, Meredith often found herself feeling as close to Artie's family as her own.

J.R. and Georgia Mae understood how things worked. J.R. had told his boys from the beginning that they were going to be arrested. It was the price you paid for going against society. He never moralized or questioned his sons' profession. Instead, he spent hours with them, plotting legal strategies and ways to increase the O'Farrell box office.

Georgia Mae could not have been more proud of her sons if they were running a major Hollywood studio. Personally, she didn't like pornography, but then, she didn't like to play cards either. Did that mean she was supposed to condemn the people who did? Georgia Mae did not regard her sons' frequent arrests as a blot on the family name, and she did not worry about Jim and Artie ending up in jail. Her boys were standing up for people's right to see any kind of a movie they wanted to see. In a world where it was us against them, the side of freedom was the right side to be on.

Meredith wished J.R. and Georgia were there for moral support. She glanced at Jim, who was sitting at the defense table. His longish hair had been carefully trimmed and he was wearing a new suit and tinted glasses. His face showed no trace of embarrassment or worry. He could have been an insurance agent watching a training film at a seminar. Meredith admired him for that. She knew that Jim knew he was in trouble.

"Did you see a sign outside the theater near the box office?" Kennedy asked when he cross-examined Ben Luttinger, the cop who had surreptitiously copied the films.

"Yes, I did," Luttinger replied.

"What did it say?"

"It warned people that the films shown inside contained explicit acts of sex and said that if they were offended by such acts, they should not come in."

"Then who filed the complaints that resulted in the raids? Did any customers file complaints with the police department?" Kennedy asked.

"I don't know," Luttinger replied. "I work in the photo lab."

"You answered 'Yes' when the DA asked you if the film *Soft* goes substantially beyond community standards, did you not, Sergeant?" Kennedy asked when he cross-examined Sergeant Sol Weiner, the friendly "Green Weenie."

"That's correct," Weiner answered.

"Would you say that community standards regarding candor about sex have changed in recent years?"

"That's correct," Weiner replied, and under further questioning testified that in 1968 there were no theaters in California showing hard-core films. By 1970 there were 125, and 22 to 24 were in San Francisco.

"Then what are community standards?" Kennedy asked. "Isn't it true that what may be offensive to one person might not be to another? Isn't the fact that there are twenty-two to twenty-four adult theaters in town proof that in San Francisco the sex film has entered mainstream culture?"

"Yes," Weiner answered, and under further questioning, Kennedy got the vice officer to concede that a film could be "arousing" without being "obscene."

"Have you read the recent *Report of the Presidential Commission on Obscenity and Pornography?*" Kennedy asked Sergeant Weiner.

"Not all of it," Weiner answered.

"Are you aware that that distinguished panel reached the conclusion that the explicit display of sex *does not* lead to antisocial behavior?"

"I know that dissenters filed a report claiming that pornography does have harmful consequences."

"Are you aware that the *majority* of the panel recommended abolishing all laws governing 'obscene' material? Are you aware they want to put you out of business, Sergeant?"

The audience laughed, and Kennedy continued to use his cross-examination of Sergeant Weiner as a vehicle to educate the jury about the findings of the so-called Johnson Commission report.

In 1968, the eighteen-member commission had been appointed by a lame-duck President to determine what effect the spread of sexual material was having on American society. Since law enforcement officials from J. Edgar Hoover to county sheriffs for years had been linking pornography with acts of violence, the commission was charged with recommending what legal steps should be taken to stop the spread of the poison.

In 1969, one of the commissioners resigned to take a diplomatic assignment overseas and President Nixon appointed America's number one antipornography crusader to take his place. Known in his hometown of Cincinnati as "Mr. Clean," Charles Keating was the founder of Citizens for Decent Literature.

Twenty-three years later, after the Lincoln Savings and Loan debacle, Keating is known as "Mr. Swindler."

The commission had a $2 million budget and two years to do its work. Staffers interviewed postal inspectors, organized crime experts, and inmates who had been convicted of sex crimes. Commissioners toured the immense collection of erotica and watched films at the Kinsey Institute for Sex Research in Bloomington, Indiana. They even sent a team of researchers to Denmark to study the effects of decriminalizing pornography.

In the end, a majority of the commission members made the same discovery that Knight and Alpert had made when they were researching *Sex in the Cinema*. While the mob might own a few theaters in places like New York or Chicago, pornography was not a mob-run industry. The commission also discovered that the people who bought skin mags and tickets to adult films were not perverts looking for a stimulus to commit rape. Rapists were less likely to be consumers of pornography than men who were "predominantly white, middle-class, middle-aged, married, dressed in a business suit or neat casual attire." These men had come out of "conservative, repressed, sexually deprived backgrounds."

The majority of the commissioners recommended that the United States do what Denmark had done: abolish all laws and let the marketplace regulate the industry.

"The Commission believes that there is no warrant for continued Government interference with the full freedom of adults because extensive empirical investigation, both by the Commission and others, provides no evidence that exposure to or use of explicit sexual materials plays a significant role in the causation of social or individual harms such as crime, delinquency, sexual or nonsexual deviancy or severe emotional disturbances."

Charles Keating, defender of the high moral ground, was incensed by the majority report. With Father Morton Hill and several other commissioners, he blasted the majority's conclusion and alerted the White House to the moral damage the report could cause the country. Richard Nixon, who was known to appear on the beach at San Clemente in a business suit with all three buttons buttoned, issued a statement "totally rejecting" the majority's recommendations. A Democratic President had appointed the commission; the Democrats were as soft on smut as they were on Communism. A Republican President would never relax "the national effort to control and eliminate smut from our national life."

Michael Kennedy picked up a copy of the Johnson Commission's report and walked up to the witness stand. "The majority report says that the people most concerned about pornography are the 'over-zealous and the religiously active' and citizens who believe 'that newspapers should not have the right to print articles which criticize the police, that people should not be allowed to publish books which attack our system of government, and that people should not be allowed to make speeches against God,' " Kennedy read. "Now tell us," Kennedy said, looking up at Sergeant Weiner, "exactly how many complaints has the police department received about pornographic films?"

"Very few," Sergeant Weiner replied.

"Can you recall the last one?"

"It was about two weeks ago."

"Who made this complaint?"

"It was anonymous."

The next day the obligatory expert witnesses paraded to the stand. Dr. Louis Noltimier, a psychiatrist and conservative Republican who was president of Physicians for Good Government and a member of Governor Ronald Reagan's Advisory Committee on Mental Health, testified that there was indeed a connection between pornography and antisocial behavior. However, under cross-examination, Dr. Noltimier acknowledged that no studies had been done which presented "absolute" evidence that such a link in fact existed.

To retaliate, the defense called Dr. John Davies Black, a San Francisco psychiatrist who was the head of the Counseling Center at Stanford University. Dr. Black testified that the three Mitchell Brothers' films that were the subject of the trial had "redeeming social value." Far from leading to sex crimes, the films actually had a therapeutic value for thousands of lonely, frustrated men who have been unable to develop fulfilling sexual relationships.

"Without these films, their sex pattern would get out of whack," Dr. Black told the jury.

Taking the stand next was Bay Area psychiatrist Martin Blinder, who taught courses at Hastings College of the Law at the University of California and at the University of California Medical Center. Dr. Blinder carried the ideas Dr. Davis had presented several steps further.

A man does not commit a rape because he saw a sex film, Dr. Blinder testified. A man rapes a woman because he has a deep hatred or fear of women.

"A man becomes a rapist because he chose the wrong mother, not the wrong movie," Dr. Blinder told the jury. Asked by Kennedy what constituted "normal" and "abnormal sex," Dr. Blinder testified that the spectrum of normal sexual behavior is far broader than moralists or the repressed would have society believe. There is nothing morbid or prurient about oral, anal, or any other kind of nonviolent sexual activity.

"God gave us this extra erogenous zone," Dr. Blinder testified about anal sex. "I see nothing unhealthy or abnormal in such activity."

Assistant DA Benson spent twenty minutes making his final argument. The issue isn't whether pornography produces harmful effects, Benson said. It doesn't matter how many dirty movie houses there are in San Francisco. What matters is that showing obscene films is against the law.

"Crime is not to be accepted, no matter how much it burgeons," Benson told the jury.

In his summation, Kennedy addressed the jury for two hours, insisting that the police should be out arresting muggers rather than "trying to tell people what they can see."

The jury went out and the agonizing wait—the first of many for the Mitchell Brothers—began. Ten hours and ten votes later, the jury came in, hopelessly deadlocked. The vote was seven to five for conviction on two films and eleven to one for acquittal on *Up Against the Wall*.

"The law is too vague," Ralph Lockett, the exasperated jury foreman, told the *Chronicle* after the judge had dismissed the jury. "We were unable to determine what 'community standards' are. I don't believe there is such a thing as community standards so far as this kind of thing is concerned."

Asked about socially redeeming values, the jury foreman threw up his hands and said, "That's in the realm of psychiatry."

Lockett then gave a clue to how frustrating things must have been in the jury room. After seeing the films, he said, "a couple of people on the jury were in such a state of shock, they wouldn't even discuss them."

It is impossible to reach a unanimous decision if some members of a jury refuse to discuss the case, a fact the elated Mitchell Brothers and their friends did not fail to notice. Jim was free to go home while the DA decided whether he wanted to bring another obscenity case to trial. Trials cost time and money. Perhaps the DA would think twice before going to court again.

However, to the Mitchell Brothers' consternation, Jim was back in court three months later, on March 3, 1971. This time, Artie was beside him at the defense table. The brothers were charged with showing an obscene film called *Glowy Flesh*. *Glowy* was not one of their films. It was an L.A. loop they had added to fill out a 90-minute program.

"The film contained an act of sixty-nine," vice cop Gerald Shaughnessy testified.

"Could you explain to the jury what sixty-nine is?" asked assistant DA Jerome Benson.

"It's a homosexual act," Shaughnessy replied.

Meredith was acting as a researcher for Michael Kennedy and in that capacity was sitting at the defense table, next to Artie. Artie leaned over and whispered, "Oh no! This guy is the police expert and he's never had a blow job!"

It took everything Meredith and Jim had not to laugh out loud. But as the cliché says, it's who laughs last that matters, and there was nothing for Jim, Artie, or Meredith to laugh at when the jury came in with the verdict. Kennedy had presented essentially the same case he did during the first trial, but this time not one member of the jury bought it. The jury of nine men and three women came in with a guilty verdict after deliberating for ten and a half hours.

Six weeks later, Judge Frank E. Hart sentenced Jim to six months in jail and fined him $1,000. Artie got four months and a $1,000 fine. Kennedy immediately appealed the verdict on the grounds that Judge Hart's "instructions to the jury amounted to a directed verdict."

"Art was furious, he blamed Kennedy," Meredith recalls. "I remember him saying, 'It was Kennedy's fault. He had us dress up so we looked like pimps.'

"It was serious stuff," Meredith continues. "The first offense is a misdemeanor. The second is a felony that carries a five- to fifteen-year sentence. We could go to court a hundred times and win ninety-nine. All they needed was that one win and Jim and Art were gone."

The sentences were later overturned on appeal and Jim and Artie did not have to go to jail. But the loss did lead to an important evolution in the Mitchell Brothers' films, and in pornography.

In the late 1960s and early 1970s, a porn film like *Requiem* that had a plot was a rarity. The typical loop, like *Glowy Flesh*, had no plot and no dialogue. In *Glowy*, two women have sex with each other and then both have sex with a man. It had been relatively easy for the jury to come in with a guilty verdict because *Glowy* was "utterly without redeeming social importance."

The phrase "redeeming social importance" had come from the landmark *Roth* v. *The United States of America*, a case the Supreme Court heard in 1957. Samuel Roth was sixty-seven at the time, a serious man, a true iconoclast whose long rap sheet included arrests for selling *Lady Chatterley's Lover* and smuggling the printing plates of *Ulysses* into the country from Paris. This time, Roth had been sentenced to five years in prison for mailing circulars advertising sexual material, including Aubrey Beardsley's *The Story of Venus and Tannhäuser.*

The law governing obscenity in the United States in 1957 had been modeled after the *Hicklin* decision that had been handed down in England in 1868. *Hicklin* said that a book could be banned if as much as one paragraph on one page was deemed to be lewd. The intent was to protect the most vulnerable members of the Victorian public, innocent juveniles whose morals might be forever sullied if they happened to stumble across the offensive paragraph.

Unfortunately for Samuel Roth, the Supreme Court let his conviction stand, but, at the same time, the court rewrote the U.S. obscenity law.

In a majority decision written by Justice William J. Brennan, Brennan defined obscenity as material that was "utterly without redeeming social importance." A book could no longer be banned on the basis of an offensive passage. Now, "the dominant theme of a book had to be judged obscene for it to be banned." A book could no longer be banned if it introduced a naïve adolescent to a wider world than she—for the judge in *Hicklin* surely had in mind a she—was ready to accept. Now, the "average person" had to find a book offensive before it could be banned.

But the key phrase in the *Roth* decision was "utterly without redeeming social importance." Justice Brennan seemed to be saying that if a book or a film dealt with some kind of serious social issue in addition to portraying sex, it could not be judged obscene.

At the Mitchell Brothers' first trial, the jury had voted seven to five for conviction on *Soft* and *Seduction* and eleven to one for acquittal on *Up Against the Wall.* All three were blatant sex films. The difference was, *Up Against the Wall* had a plot, the other two films did not.

A sex film that told a story gave a jury *a reason* to come in with a not-guilty verdict. In thrashing out a decision, it seemed inevitable that at least one fair-minded juror would say, "Well, I don't think we can say the film was *utterly* without redeeming social importance, because it did have characters and a story." And all the pornographers needed to hang a jury was one vote.

In the past, when a pornographer bothered to throw in a plot, the plot was so simplistic, it boiled down to "Hi. Let's fuck." After the

Glowy trial, the Mitchell Brothers began to crank out "featurettes," 20- to 25-minute films that, at least by the standards of pornography, had characters and attempted to tell a story. The brothers did not do it because they wanted to advance the form or were trying to develop as artists. As Jim observed later, "Our movies reflect our daily effort to stay out of jail."

The Golden Gate Bridge is overwhelming in its beauty. When the fog is in, the towers are shrouded in ever-moving, ghostly mists. On a clear day, they soar to dizzying heights, monumental evidence that human aspirations are as vast as the big blue sky.

And, of course, commuters barely notice. Separated by only a row of orange plastic cones, cars roar across the bridge like it is a tunnel the drivers cannot wait to escape. But not on this afternoon in the summer of 1971. Something more riveting than beautiful scenery was happening on the bridge. Cars were slowing down, traffic was backing up, commuters were rubbernecking. *Somebody was making a movie.*

The traffic snarl soon attracted the attention of the police, who arrived with lights flashing. The two young women who were shooting the film inhaled sharply, tensed up, and exchanged uh-oh looks. They did not have the permit the city required before allowing film-makers to shoot on location. Their camera was a primitive Bolex that had to be reloaded every four or five minutes. Instead of "Action!" and "Cut!" the women's most frequent instruction to actors was "Freeze!" or "Hold it!" while they changed reels.

None of this mattered to the commuters or the cops. Necks kept craning and the cops did not inquire about what kind of film was being shot or ask to see an on-location permit. They jumped out of the squad car and began waving cars around the filmmakers.

Annie and Meredith puffed out their cheeks, exchanged sighs of relief and impish smiles, and turned back to their work.

A young woman with long brown hair walked toward the camera, numb as a mental patient on Thorazine. Her head was hanging down and her shoulders were slumped; her arms hung heavy and lifeless and her pretty face was empty, drained of all expression, even pain.

The woman stopped and turned to the rail. The stiff wind swirled her hair as she looked at the cold gray waves far below. She hesitated for a moment. Then she put a foot on the rail and pulled herself up. She was going to jump.

"Stop! Wait!" screamed a young man, who rushed up, hooked an arm around the woman's waist, and pulled her away from the rail. He told her she was young and beautiful and had her life ahead of her. He put his arm around her and the two turned and began walking slowly off the bridge.

"Cut!" Annie yelled, and she and Meredith gathered the equipment and collected the cast and scurried off the bridge as quickly as they could.

"I learned San Francisco shooting the socially redeeming parts of Mitchell Brothers movies," Meredith says with a laugh. "You've heard of jump cuts? Well, we had fuck cuts. Here's a shot of the Golden Gate Bridge. Here's the couple in bed, fucking."

"Actually, we always shot the sex scene first," Meredith continues. "That way, if an actor or an actress disappeared halfway through the shooting, as sometimes they did, we'd have the crucial part. The rest we could fake. One time we had to reshoot a talk scene and the girl who'd done the fucking didn't show up, so we used my brother Mark. He had long hair and we shot the back of his head."

The Bridge is a classic example of a Mitchell Brothers featurette. The plot was limited because the story line is limited when there are only two people in a film. Again, the plot was not there to tell a story or create tension or reveal character. It was there so that an attorney could tell a jury, "This film is not about sex. It is about *life,* life and death! The young lady you saw on the screen was going to commit suicide. The act of intercourse you saw her engage in with her rescuer is life-affirming. It is his way of welcoming her back to the land of the living. Sex is life-affirming, ladies and gentlemen! That is the message of this film. And it is that powerful message that gives this film redeeming social importance."

"We ended up making better movies because of the *Roth* decision," Meredith says in retrospect. "We probably would have gone on cranking out loops forever and never done any features because character development was not what the audience was there to see."

"Sooooo? What's it going to be? What'd you decide?" Jennifer, Meredith's sister, asked Artie.

The spectacular Northern California light was pouring through the kitchen windows of the apartment at Fillmore and Pacific. Still wearing the basketball shirt he had slept in, Artie was at the stove, waiting for a kettle to boil so he could fix himself a cup of coffee.

"Decide? Decide what?" Artie asked.

"Oh, come on, Artie!" Jennifer shot back. "One way or the other, make up your mind. I can't stay out here forever."

Jennifer had flown out from Massachusetts because Meredith had called to tell her family that she and Artie were going to be married. Meredith's parents, for obvious reasons, had decided not to attend the ceremony, so Jennifer and Meredith's younger brother Mark were representing the family.

Meredith and Artie had changed their minds about getting married before Jennifer got off the plane. To get married was to acquiesce to an authority a hip young couple like themselves did not believe the church or the state possessed. Who expected a member of the clergy to bless, or a justice of the peace to declare legal, a relationship that already existed between two people? Only the helplessly bourgeois.

A day or so after Jennifer arrived, Artie and Meredith changed their minds again. Why *not* get married? It would be a great party. But then they thought: Why not just have the party?

"You know what your problem is?" Artie asked, turning to face Jennifer. "You and your family think there's a right way and a wrong way. You think everything has to be done your way because your way is the right way. That's why you came out here. To make sure we did the right thing and got married."

"Artie, I don't care what you do. I just want you to make up your minds so I can get away from these cats," said Jennifer, who suffered from asthma and had been wheezing heavily.

"All right, all right, screw it! We'll do it! We'll do it today! You wanna do it today?" Artie asked Meredith, who had just walked into the kitchen.

"Why not?" Meredith said casually. "It's better than talking about it all the time."

"You find the minister and get a place. I'll call the theater," Artie said, handing Meredith a cup of coffee.

Meredith picked up the yellow pages and thumbed through until she found "Churches."

"Here's something," she said moments later. "This looks weird enough. 'The Church of Religious Science.' I'll call them."

Jennifer's wedding had been elaborate and perfectly choreographed, a major social event in the small town southwest of Boston. Now she gazed across the table at her counterculture sister and shook her head.

"I can't believe you're doing this," she said.

Meredith shrugged and dialed the number. Yes, the pastor did weddings. Yes, he would be pleased to do one today.

"Two o'clock this afternoon," Meredith said, hanging up the phone. Artie grabbed it and called the theater.

"Jim? Okay, tell anybody who's there: Meredith and I are getting married this afternoon." Artie gave his brother the time and location and added, "Tell them anybody who wants to can come."

Meredith selected a short, green leather dress with a beaded fringe. It was a copy of a dress Grace Slick, a former model whose clothes were as unique as her wit, had worn onstage with the Jefferson Airplane. Artie put on the gray felt top hat that had become his signature over the last year.

"And the ring? Where's the ring?" the Religious Science pastor asked when the couple was facing him at the altar.

Meredith looked at Artie, and Artie looked at Meredith. They did not have a ring.

Jim's prized possession was a ring with a dragon with emeralds for eyes that rested upon globs of gold. It was the first thing he had purchased when he had gotten out of the service. Now he slipped it off and handed it to Artie.

"That's a wedding present," he whispered.

The newlyweds adjourned to the Philosopher's Club, a corner bar on Market near Castro, an area that was rapidly changing from working-class to a gay enclave. Everyone ordered drinks and picked up a package of Twinkies from the box that somebody had bought as a substitute for a wedding cake. The whole thing was a goof, a great goof, and even Jennifer got caught up in the spirit. She began composing a parody of the wedding stories that run in the society pages.

"And in the emerald light glowing from the pool tables, the wedding party enjoyed Twinkies and beer to music played by an authentic American jukebox. A honeymoon is planned—

"Hey," Jennifer called, interrupting herself. "Are you guys going to take a honeymoon?"

"Due to professional and legal obligations, we are not," Artie replied.

"The groom, a major film director, and the bride, a leading cinematographer, are presently filming in everyone's favorite city, San Francisco. Due to a tight production schedule and the interest the local courts have taken in their work, the happy couple plans to honeymoon 'on location.' "

Everyone cheered, and Jennifer bowed in acknowledgment and raised her beer glass.

The new Mr. and Mrs. Mitchell kissed coquettishly.

5

A Stud
Is Born

"I DON'T WANT to see a skin flick. When I was in the Air Force a bunch of us drove all the way from Merced to see one and it was a total rip-off," said George McDonald.

"They're not a rip-off now," said George's friend Duane. "They've gone hard-core, my man. I see them all the time."

It was a Saturday night early in 1971 and George and Duane were cooped up in George's miserable little $3.00-a-day room in the Coronado Hotel on Ellis Street in the Tenderloin, trying to decide how to spend the night. Duane was one of George's few friends in San Francisco, a fat, sloppy-looking, lonely middle-aged guy who worked as a bookkeeper in a jewelry factory. Duane was also friendly, intelligent, and generous, quick to share his excellent marijuana and prescription diet pills. Most nights they were together, George swallowed a couple of Duane's pills and, jacked up on speed, they'd cruise the city until dawn while Duane delivered non-stop erudite lectures on architecture and minor San Francisco landmarks.

Twenty-two-year-old George was up for anything except a sex

film. He was working as a clerk in a dirty bookstore in the Tender-loin, selling soft-core titles like *The Truth About Bestiality* over the counter and hard-core titles under the counter. The store also sold 8mm films and a line of "marital aids" like dildos and artificial vaginas that could be filled with warm water. The men who bought the paraphernalia always purchased it for "a friend" as "a great gag." George earned $10 a shift plus 10 percent of everything he sold over $50. He worked a twelve-hour day on Saturday, and that was enough sex, even for George, who was fixated on sex. Besides, it was all George could do to pay the rent.

"Oh, you, I know you, it's money you're worried about," Duane said. "Come on, I'll buy. I want you to see this."

"In that case, you're on!" said George, who was in no position to turn down a free anything.

In addition to the mirror over the sink, the only thing on the wall in George's shabby room was a picture of the hot movie star Elliott Gould that George had cut out of a magazine. It was hanging there because people were always telling George that he was a handsome version of the star of the film *M*A*S*H*.

There were only a couple of things in life that George was really sure of: he was good-looking and he was a killer with the chicks.

The young man with the curly black hair and the even white teeth that flashed when he smiled had grown up an orphan in Fresno, California. For almost ten years, he had lived with a paint-ing contractor and his wife. The painter was distant and inarticulate and his wife was a dictator. The couple fought continually, separat-ing and getting back together, only to separate again. George had finally defied the painter one night, told him he was going to go out whether the painter liked it or not, and if he didn't, the painter could call the cops.

The painter called the cops. The ride in the back of the police car from George's "home" to a juvenile detention center had been the happiest trip of his life.

George was bounced around to eight different foster homes after that. The constant shifting made George wise to the ways of the world. If the father in a home made a homosexual advance, George fought him off but never said a word about it. He acted as if it had never happened, except when he and the father made eye contact, and then George let him know he hadn't forgotten.

It would not be long before the father was on the phone to the caseworker, saying what a shame it was they couldn't keep George. He was a wonderful boy and fit in perfectly, but the father had been laid off and they were going to have to move.

By the time he reached high school, there were two George Mc-Donalds. At home, George was a sullen, introverted boy who spent hours alone in his room, devouring book after book. He was scared, unable to trust, afraid that if he got close to someone he'd get hurt.

Outside his foster home, he metamorphosed into Super George, a Boy Scout with twenty-three merit badges and a paper route. He was an excellent student, a member of the track, football, wrestling, and debating teams, and the student behind the microphone at every assembly. His senior year at Herbert Hoover High, George was student body president, voted the class of 1967's "Most Likely to Succeed," and the recipient of the North Fresno Exchange Club's "Boy of the Year" award.

George's dream was to someday be elected governor of California. A true politician, he had an overwhelming need to be liked, to be the center of attention. George thought if he paid attention to what people were saying and did things that made them happy, if he worked harder than anyone else around, he could build a political career. It had certainly worked in high school.

But Super George, for all his achievements, was a rickety invention. Super George knew that a military career is fundamental to a political career, and he talked endlessly about going to West Point or Annapolis, but somehow, he never got around to taking the exams. He did take the U.S. Coast Guard Entrance Examination, but he choked up and failed it. So the day after he graduated, George joined the U.S. Air Force.

The Air Force was a drag, no challenge at all. George tested at the top of his class in every exam and soon found himself in a school, learning to program the bulky mainframe computers the military used in the late 1960s. The Air Force ended up sending him to Castle AFB near Merced, only forty miles from his hometown. George put the base's payroll system on a computer, and since no one else on the base understood how the system worked, his superiors left him alone.

George rented a small apartment in downtown Merced and it was there that he met the 1960s. Buddies from the base came by to hang out and have a few drinks, and before long they were arriving with hippie chicks from town. Every night there was a party, with jug wine and joints and, inevitably, sex—lots of sex. George never knew who was going to show up, who was going to end up on his lap, or with whom he was going to walk hand and hand into one of the bedrooms.

George picked up on the antiwar sentiment the townies brought to the parties and it wasn't long before Super George turned against the war and began wearing love beads under his uniform. He was interested in politics, but George wasn't nearly as aroused by the issues of the antiwar movement as he was by having sex with young hippies who opposed the war. Smoking dope and having sex seemed to be the primary ways of expressing your defiance of the corrupt social order.

George loved the hot physical intimacy, the spine-tingling excitement of entering a woman, especially for the first time. He reveled in the moments when he and a partner were going at it hot and heavy, in particular the moments when he was close to orgasm or actually coming. That was the only time when he was able to get outside himself and forget about Super George and the sad, isolated other George.

He also loved the conquest. George had learned how to con when he was living in foster homes. He knew how to focus on what a foster mother was saying, how to come up with the perfect answer to a question, when to flash his charming smile.

By the time he reached high school, George was turning the con on girls. He did things like take out ads in the newspaper to ask for a date; he listened intently to what a girl had to say and made her feel that he alone knew how special she was; he took her for walks by a waterfall so he could create ersatz romantic moments and tell her he knew the difference between meaningless sex and sex that mattered.

After George got laid, he'd settle into the pillow to wait for sleep or the next erection and go through his scorecard. Let's see now, he'd ask himself, was she number 27 or 28? Scoring did the same thing for George that winning a debate back in high school had done: both were empowering; both were ways to feed his insatiable desire to be somebody. Bedding a woman validated George to the one person who really mattered—himself.

George had assumed he was sitting out the war, serving on a base in the dusty San Joaquin Valley. But suddenly he found himself processing hundreds of requests for overtime pay from flight crews on B-52s and airmen who worked in munitions. Eventually, he found out that B-52s from Castle AFB were bombing targets in North Vietnam.

The missions were top secret. The planes were taking off from Castle loaded to the gills with bombs; they rendezvoused with KC-130s and refueled over the Pacific, and dropped their loads over North Vietnam. The immense bombers were then refueled and reloaded with munitions in Thailand. They bombed North Vietnam on the way back, were refueled again in midair over the Pacific, landed back at Castle, and then did it all over again.

Jane Fonda had just returned from her infamous trip to North Vietnam. When George saw the pictures she brought back of downtown Hanoi in rubble and nurses holding mutilated children, he scheduled a meeting with his commanding officer and announced that he could no longer support the U.S. war effort.

MPs placed George under arrest and locked him in the base jail. He was within an eyelash of being drummed out of the service with a dishonorable discharge when the judge advocate reviewing his case found an entry in George's record that described him as "the top NCO [noncommissioned officer] we've had here in the last 20 years." The judge advocate took the record to the base commander, who recommended that George be given an honorable discharge.

Now George was living in a roach-ridden hotel in the Tenderloin, working in a dirty-book store, and taking classes at the Bill Wade School of Radio and Television Announcing. George knew after the first few classes that the DJ school was a dead end. He knew that reading old news over and over wouldn't lead anywhere, and had all but given up going to classes. He was still dreaming about being elected governor of California one day, but he had yet to figure how to get out of the Tenderloin.

About the only thing George still had going for him was his charm. At Castle AFB, he'd had the key to the medal locker. He knew the paperwork was sloppy and that no one had any idea exactly what medals were in there, so just before he declared himself against the war, George had sneaked in, opened the locker, and scooped up a couple of bags of medals.

When he had a few bucks, George would go to a dating bar and strike up a conversation with a young woman. He'd buy her a drink or two and tell her he was on leave between tours of duty in Vietnam. He'd describe the war for her, let her see how heartsick and conflicted he was about it. And then, when it was getting late and the bar was about to close, he'd reach into his pocket and say, "You've been so great for listening, I feel like I've gotten to know you so well, I want you to have this. I've got no one else to give it to. Here, it's my air medal." Or "Here, it's my Antarctica medal."

"I was ruthless," George says. "But it worked."

Now George and Duane were walking through the Tenderloin and George was amazed, as he always was, at the human zoo he had landed in. Derelicts in greasy rags, their faces red from booze and busted blood vessels, were flopped against buildings, muttering gibberish at bottles of Night Train and Thunderbird. Hookers in outrageous miniskirts had every corner staked out.

The O'Farrell turned out to be a pleasant surprise after the heavy dose of urban squalor. George was impressed by how bright and clean and crowded the theater was. The lobby looked like an art gallery and the young woman behind the candy counter was really pretty.

George was even more impressed when the movie started. It was in color, it had sound, and the actress was stunning, absolutely beautiful. Her short blond hair was tied in an elegant scarf that hung over her right shoulder. George immediately wanted her.

"Boy, I couldn't wait to get away from that party," the man in the film said.

"I know," the woman replied. "I just wanted to be alone with you."

"Well, okay, let's do it," the man said.

Is that all they could come up with for a plot? George wondered. They got this really beautiful woman and that was all they could give her to say? Not that it mattered. He was anxious to see what the actress looked like with her clothes off.

She turned out to be even more beautiful than George had imagined, with large, firm breasts, a flat stomach, blond pubic hair that had been carefully trimmed, and long, gorgeous legs that George was accustomed to seeing only in ads in magazines.

Without even kissing him first, the woman immediately began giving the man a blow job. That must be the script, George thought. Women don't do that. When she stopped, the man was still soft. The audience groaned and began shifting in their seats. "The old spaghetti dick," someone a few rows away said, and men around George snickered.

The camera shifted to the man's face and George saw that he was terrified. George laughed out loud.

"You shouldn't laugh," Duane whispered.

"I know, but I can't stand it. There's so much tension on that guy's face," George replied.

"It's not that easy to do," Duane said.

"Are you kidding? With that fox? Hell, I could do that."

"No, you couldn't."

"I could," George said. "I could and I'm gonna."

The entire way back to his room, George had bragged about how much better he could have done than the guy in the film. It was one thing to screw with the lights off, Duane had insisted. It was quite another to get it up on demand under movie lights while surrounded by a crew and a director who was yelling, "Get your hands under her ass and move it around, she's just lying there."

No problem, George had said, smug as could be. Fucking was fucking.

George had spent all day Sunday thinking about what he had vowed to do the first thing Monday morning. He wished he hadn't been so damn sure of himself. If he chickened out, Duane would think he was a jerk.

George had always considered pornography filthy, foreign, something only sickos got involved in. One of the few things he liked about working in the dirty-book store was feeling superior to the furtive guys in business suits who ducked in, bought a couple of magazines and stuffed them in a briefcase, and ducked out again. At least he didn't have any problems in that area.

But that was exactly the point. George *didn't* have any problems with sex. That's why he thought he could star in a sex film. George was great in bed and proud of it. He didn't mind the world seeing him in action. In fact, it turned him on.

George thought the film he had seen at the O'Farrell was brutally honest. It had opened a door to show what people did when the doors were closed. There was nothing wrong with that. And George was very impressed by the fear on the face of the actor who could not get a hard-on. It was *so real.*

George was the kind of person who saw things in extremes. When Super George, the star NCO at Castle AFB, turned against the war, he had not thought twice about a possible court-martial and being sentenced to time in a military prison before he told his commanding officer he could no longer participate in what the United States was doing to Vietnam. When he joined the counterculture, George had decided that he was going to be as honest as possible about everything—unless, of course, he was trying to get laid.

There was no faking in a sex film. You did it or you couldn't do it. If the Mitchell Brothers had cast a guy who couldn't get it up in one of their films, they must be looking for a few good men. Well, George was a good man. He didn't fake anything. And he wouldn't fake it when the director yelled, "Action!"

The more he thought about it, the more George figured he had nothing to lose. He was lonely and broke, a nobody in the Tenderloin, lying on a sagging bed in a stinking little room listening to the radiator rattle and the drunks battle it out next door. If he made a film, he was at least taking a risk, trying to do something that might get him out of there. Anything was better than this.

They would pay George to be in those films. When they found out how good he was, they'd probably pay him lots of money. He did not have a girlfriend and he'd get to fuck beautiful women. He was good-looking and a born extrovert and had always suspected that he could act. What if he did really well in one of the films and somebody important saw it and cast him in a legitimate film? George read magazines; he knew that stranger things had happened to movie stars.

Most important of all, appearing in a sex film would give George an instant identity. He closed his eyes and imagined himself walking into the O'Farrell on a night when the film he was starring in was up on the screen. "Hey," the pretty girl behind the candy counter would say, "you're the guy in the movie!"

"That's right," George would say with a smile.

Monday morning found George pacing the pavement in front of the O'Farrell. He still had not fully resolved his inner conflict about making a film. A part of him was still Super George, Mr. "Most Likely to Succeed," the Big Man at Herbert Hoover High who was still dreaming about becoming governor. Several times he had walked up to the door only to turn around and walk away. Finally, George said to himself: Fuck it. Ronald Reagan made a lot of bad movies and he's governor!

With that, George walked inside.

The girl behind the candy counter, a blonde with large breasts, very white skin, and a lovely smile, was different from the girl who was working Friday night. George told her why he was there and she smiled and picked up a phone. She told George to have a cup of coffee while he waited, but he was far too nervous. He paced the lobby, his wet, clammy hands clasped behind his back to keep them from trembling. He was staring at a picture without really seeing it when someone shouted, "Hey, Elliott Gould!"

That's me! George thought. They've picked up on the resemblance already!

George turned and saw a tall, athletic-looking man with thick black hair and a mustache motioning to him. He found out later it was Jon Fontana, a friend of Jim's from high school. Fontana had been everything Jim was not in high school, a star athlete in three sports and the kind of student who didn't just answer a teacher's question, he expanded on it. Fontana had a degree in philosophy, loved abstract thought, and was the theater's resident theoretician. He and Earl Shagley were the Mitchell Brothers' cameramen.

"I was in the audience Saturday night and it looked like you guys could use some help," George said, referring to the leading man's inability to achieve an erection.

"Yeah, we sure could," Fontana said. "Do you know any women?"

"No," George said.

"Do you have a chick to work with?" Fontana asked.

"Well . . . uh . . . no," George stammered, while the fantasy about the Mitchell Brothers needing a few good men evaporated.

"Okay, look, we're shooting upstairs right now, so I've got to run," Fontana said. "But leave your name and number with Marianna at the candy counter and we'll call you if we get something. And call us right away if you find a chick to work with."

By 1971, the year George McDonald decided he wanted to star in a sex film, the hippie movement was as dead as Lyndon Baines Johnson's political career. But the effects of both were still being played out.

Hordes of kids were no longer arriving in San Francisco determined to make peace and love a reality. The seemingly endless stream of healthy, happy hippie chicks who didn't think twice about stepping in front of a camera and taking off their clothes for a few bucks had dried to a trickle. It was one thing to strip naked and fondle yourself on-camera; it was quite another to be filmed having sex with a man you had just met.

Some weeks, no women would answer the Mitchell Brothers' ads in the newspapers. Other weeks, four or five new faces would arrive at the O'Farrell. It was impossible for the crew to know who the women were or where they were coming from.

Some of the actresses had grown up in families near the bottom of the socioeconomic ladder in East Bay communities like San Leandro and Union City. Generally, they were not too bright and not too attractive. Ask one of them why she wanted to appear in a film and she was likely to say, "Well, I don't see anything wrong with it. And I need to earn some money because I dropped out of high school and now I want to go back and get a General Equivalency Diploma so I can enroll in a professional school and study to become a dental assistant."

Which, in fact, only a small percentage of the actresses ever did.

A few actresses, like the flutist in the Oakland Symphony Orchestra or the law student at Stanford, were there to collect the experience. Whether or not they had read Céline or Genet, they had an innate belief that if you descended into the lower depths, you would eventually come face to face with who you really were. A few were genuine intellectuals, rebels who had read Kerouac and John Osborne's plays and seen Marlon Brando's and James Dean's movies over and over again. They knew there were ways to be an Angry Young Man in America. They wanted to be Angry Young Women, a far more difficult task because there were no role models. Appearing in a sex film was certainly one way to try.

Still others had a score to settle with their parents. Appearing in a sex film is a powerful way to express both rebellion and rage. Bob Cecchini, Jim's Antioch High classmate who had joined the Mitchell Brothers' film crew, remembers actresses who dropped hints about why they were there.

"We'd take a break and a girl would say, 'My father is gonna love this. He's president of the school board back in my hometown in Nebraska,'" Cecchini says. "That was all they had to say."

Other actresses were sexual libertarians, swingers who swapped mates the way other couples did cards in a game of hearts. For them, sex was a way to play roles in a real live theater, to act out fantasies and bring drama to lives that otherwise had none. The majority of the swingers were married and living in suburbia, and were ordinary in every imaginable way except that on Saturday night, instead of going to see a film like *Bob & Carol & Ted & Alice,* they went to an orgy and lived the movie.

Finally, there were women appearing in the films because they were desperate for money and making a movie was easier and less frightening than turning a trick. You did not have to hustle a client, and you did not have to go into a motel room alone and close the door.

"There were times when the performers were having a good time and that was okay," Earl Shagley remembers. "Then we began to get people who needed money badly and wouldn't have done it under any other circumstances. I remember a woman who needed rent money because she had a new baby and the father had taken off. She didn't want to be there, so I didn't want to be there."

But as George McDonald found out when he visited the O'Farrell and offered to save the Mitchell Brothers from the scourge of the limp penis, there was a surplus of men who were eager to appear in sex films.

"Women were always tough to get," Cecchini says. "Guys—we'd have them lined up around the block. Everybody from bankers to doctors to street people wanted to be in the films. It was a kick to most guys, a fantasy they could make come true. We had a guy come in with two pet rattlesnakes. A guy going girl came in the middle of a sex-change operation. One time four guys dressed up as the Beatles on the *Sgt. Pepper* album arrived on motor scooters.

"We had everyone fill out a questionnaire," Cecchini continues. " 'What are your sexual preferences? What will you do? What will you not do?' Typically, the answer we got from guys was 'You name it, I'll do it.' "

Over the years, Mitchell Brothers' film crew members like Bob Cecchini evolved into sophisticated observers of sexual behavior. During a lull in the shooting or over a beer in the office, they'd occasionally argue about why so many more men than women were eager to appear in sex films.

A going theory was that men want sex and can't get enough of it —which was why the Mitchell Brothers were in business—and that women want romance—which is why Harlequin sells millions of books every year.

Another theory was that in the average relationship it is the woman who controls sex, deciding, or at least exercising veto power over, when and where to have it. On-screen, she has no power; she is *there* to have sex. Therefore, she has little or no interest in appearing in a sex film.

There were also discussions about the validity of the cliché that men are innately voyeurs—"There's no such thing as a Peeping *Jane*"—and that women are inherently exhibitionists—"Look at the way they dress, the way they showcase their tits and ass!" A majority of the crew felt that the cliché was contradicted by the fact that ten times more men than women were applying to be in the films, and that men who landed roles seemed to be at least as exhibitionistic as, if not more so than the women they worked with.

The crew also agreed that men were more predatory about sex than women, that it was common for a bunch of guys to discuss sexual conquests in exquisite detail and rare for women to do the same. They also realized that far more men than women seemed to invent themselves through sex. No one could think of a feminine equivalent for the word "stud," and it was hard to remember a woman, even the most shameless of the swingers, bragging about all the guys she'd had intercourse with.

The argument boiled down to the reason for the differences. Part of the crew felt that when it came to sex, men and women were biologically different. Men want to get their rocks off. Sex is more sacred to a woman, more closely associated with love and commitment, probably because she gives birth to children.

Other crew members, led by Artie, believed the differences were purely cultural.

"Give 'em permission to do it, Bob," Artie would say, whether or not Jim happened to be in the room. "Tell 'em it's all right to fuck and suck and do any guy any way they want. You'll have women standing in line to be in a film."

Many of the men who answered Mitchell Brothers' ads really were trying to fulfill some deep-seated stud fantasy. Oftentimes, when reality appeared in the form of a call from Bob Cecchini, the same applicant who had appeared wildly eager on the questionnaire would say, "Oh, I changed my mind." Or, what was far worse, the applicant would promise to be there and then fail to appear.

Some of the men no doubt chickened out because they developed acute cases of performance anxiety. More likely, time had elapsed and they had thought through the consequences of what they were considering—which, given the longevity of film, could last a life-time.

But not George McDonald. George pestered Fontana the same way an aspiring actor hounds an agent. He had convinced himself that appearing in a porn film was a quick way to get a starring role in life, and he was determined to get his shot.

Finally, Fontana called George. "We got something for you," Fontana said. "Be at the O'Farrell tomorrow morning at ten."

The soon-to-be celluloid stud did not sleep that night.

"I was totally terrified," George says. "It was 'put up or shut up' time. This was the ultimate blind date."

Waiting in the lobby of the O'Farrell the next morning, George kept sliding his hand in his pocket and touching his penis to make sure it had not shriveled or disappeared. Over and over he asked himself the same question he had asked himself as he twisted and turned on his thin mattress: "Can I get it up on demand?"

Fontana came down to the lobby to collect George, and George followed him up the stairs to the studio. Jim and Artie bounced out of their chairs and came over to shake hands. There was something familiar, something comfortable about the two ordinary-looking guys in jeans and polo shirts. When Jim happened to mention where he and Artie had grown up, George knew what it was.

"Hey, you guys grew up in Antioch? I'm from Fresno," George said. "We're valley guys!"

Jim gave George a quick tour of the studio and pointed out Earl Shagley, who was busy taking a brand-new $16,000 Arriflex camera, the most advanced movie camera there was, out of a packing crate.

"This is a big moment for us," Jim told George. "That's our first sound camera you're looking at. That means we won't have to dub sound anymore. We're gonna use it today, if we can figure out how it works."

George nodded, as if he visited a film studio every day of the week. Meanwhile, his heart was beating triple-time, his head felt light, his legs weak, the men moving around the studio were blurry shapes, and George badly wanted to sit down. Or maybe go back downstairs and think it over.

"Let's go across the hall and you can meet your co-star," Jim said.

They were crossing the hall when a young man came out of a room, walked quickly up to George, banged him with his shoulder, muttered, "You asshole!" and kept going. George thought: Jeez, what'd I do? and looked at Jim, but Jim didn't say anything, so George didn't ask. They walked through the door and Jim pulled a beaded curtain open.

"George, this is Lelania," Jim said.

George couldn't believe it: Lelania was the beautiful woman from the film he had seen with Duane, the woman he had been fantasizing about ever since. She had the same short blond hair and deep tan and was wearing a black see-through top and black pants that were skintight.

And then George realized that the guy who had just slammed into him in the hall was the guy who couldn't get it up in the film.

Jim explained that they would begin by shooting through the beaded curtain.

"That's for the socially redeeming part," Jim said. "We can go into court and claim it's an art film."

Fontana walked in and noticed what Jim was ignoring. George was as white as the paint on the walls, his upper lip was twitching, and he was shifting his weight from one foot to another like a kid in the principal's office. Screw in front of a camera? This guy didn't look like he could take his pants off.

"Why don't we give you two five minutes," Fontana said. "We'll turn off some of the lights and you can get to know each other. When you feel comfortable, let us know."

"Okay, sure," George said.

Fontana and Jim left, and George sat down on the edge of the bed and went into a full fetal tuck. Somehow, he had imagined that the camera would be hidden behind a one-way mirror. He never imagined there would be so many people around or that he would be so . . . out in the open.

"Well . . . hi," George managed to say, hating himself for being so inane. In bars, he always had his opening lines memorized.

"My name's really Judy and this is your first film, isn't it?" the woman said.

"Yeah," George replied. "Uh . . . I, uh, saw your film."

"You did? Really? Which one?" Judy asked, genuinely interested.

"It was about what happened after a party, I think," George said.

"Did you like it?" Judy asked.

"I thought it was really far-out," George said. "You were really beautiful. In fact, you're sort of why I'm here."

"You look a little nervous," Judy said.

"I am," George replied, looking at her for the first time.

"Well, here, let me help you," Judy said. She unbuttoned George's shirt and slid her hand onto his chest. Her hand was warm and soft and George was suddenly very excited.

"Jon!" George yelled without asking Judy. "We're ready!"

The long-haired members of the crew streamed in. Well, George thought, if I'm going to fuck in front of people, I'm glad they're freaks. Shagley and Fontana couldn't get the Arriflex running, so they set up the Bolex. Finally, they were ready to shoot.

"Okay, let's have both of you get naked right away," Jim said. "Lelania, you lie back on the bed, and George, you get on your knees over her chest. Then, Lelania, you go down on George. After you get him up, we'll go to a straight missionary position and move the camera over to the beaded curtain for the insert shots."

"Are you going to tell us when to move or when you want us to get into some other action?" George asked Jim.

"Just relax and let it flow naturally," Jim said.

Naturally? With all these lights and people around? How could anything be natural, George wondered.

As Jim was giving the crew final instructions, Lelania reached up and began to caress George's penis. George immediately got an erection.

I can do it! George told himself. I knew I could do it!

The lights came on and George felt like Alice tumbling down the rabbit hole. He had never seen himself under such intense light. He had never looked at a woman so closely before. He could see every hair on Lelania's arms, every pore in her skin. It was all super-real, and yet it seemed like a fantasy. It couldn't really be happening.

Lelania lifted her head and took George's penis in her mouth. George glanced to his left and Jim snapped, "Don't look at the camera!" He looked down and was astounded at what he saw.

George had had a lot of sex, but no woman had ever performed oral sex on him. And here was this beautiful woman with his penis in her mouth! George watched, fascinated, and began to rotate his hips to move his penis around. It felt very, very good.

Then he noticed that Lelania was grimacing. The position might look good on film, but it was putting a terrible strain on her neck. George thought that maybe they should stop.

Just then Jim scurried around to the head of the bed and signaled

George to perform cunnilingus. George had never done that before either. He hesitated for a moment. Jim and the crew were nonchalant, as if they had asked him to light a cigarette, so George figured there must be nothing to it. He slid down and got into position. He had always wondered what it was like to do this, and now, on-camera, he was going to find out.

Moments later, George sat bolt upright, gasping for breath. He had gotten so involved in what he was doing he had neglected to breathe.

It was now time for intercourse, missionary-style. George began taking long, fast strokes, pouring everything he had into them, determined to turn in an energetic performance. He was still going at it hot and heavy when Jim yelled, "Cut! Let's break here."

"Great, George, just great!" Jim said. "When we start again, do a couple of positions and then get back in the missionary. When you come, pull out and come on her stomach so we can see it. Got it?"

Got it, George thought, thinking how strange it was that this bald-headed guy was telling him when to fuck and when to stop and how to come.

George got out of bed and walked across the stage. A crew member came over and handed him a Dr Pepper.

"Hey, all right. A star," the crew member said.

George beamed.

"Yeah," said another crew member. "Way to get into it, man."

"Hey, thanks, guys," George said.

George was so excited he could barely contain himself. He bounced around the set naked with a goofy grin on his face, swigging on his Dr Pepper, checking out the equipment, nodding to the crew. Across the room, he noticed that Lelania was being interviewed by a reporter from KCBS radio. He got close enough to hear the reporter ask her a couple of questions about what it was like to be a porn star.

I knew it! George thought as he walked away with visions of the interviews he was going to give someday. I knew this was going to lead somewhere.

George and Lelania got back in bed. The lights went on and the camera started rolling. George immediately got an erection, but had trouble cranking up the passion he had going before Jim called for a break. He buried his head in Lelania's hair and smelled her perfume. That helped. He began stroking harder and harder and soon

Big brother holds little brother's cake on his third birthday. Jim always took care of Artie. Longtime friends of the Mitchell Brothers are convinced Jim was taking care of his little brother the night he killed him. (Photo courtesy of Meredith Bradford.)

A Wizard of Oz of their very own. J. R. Mitchell and his boys, circa 1951. In a world where other kids' dads punched a time clock in a mill, J.R. was a professional gambler who ambled into the cardroom at Blu's in Antioch to ask, "Who's ready for a game?" When they were young, the boys were ashamed of their father's occupation. Their love and admiration kept growing until they had turned J.R. into a mythical figure. As this picture shows, even at an early age, Jim was serious, Artie was the clown. (Photo courtesy of Meredith Bradford.)

J.R. at a cousin's wedding in 1969, a few years before his death. An intelligent man who lived by his wits, J.R. taught his boys to appreciate a good con. Jim and Artie built an empire on what they learned. (Photo courtesy of Meredith Bradford.)

Jim's (class of '61) and Artie's (class of '63) graduation pictures. Young men like these were destined to be "mill fodder" in Antioch, but Jim and Artie were determined to escape. Both photos are inscribed "To Pop." Jim wrote on the back of his, "To the best pop in the world. From the best son in the world." Artie wrote, "To that handsome man with a million friends, from his all-American son, with love." (Photos courtesy of Meredith Bradford.)

The all-American girl: Meredith Bradford's high school graduation photo (class of '64). Head cheerleader and a homecoming queen, Meredith was the daughter of a prominent Massachusetts physician and the eleventh great-granddaughter of William Bradford, the leader of the Pilgrims. Meredith was premed at Cornell and was on her way to medical school when she decided she wanted to live a different life than her parents had. She moved to Los Angeles, where she met and fell in love with an incipient pornographer named Artie Mitchell. (Photo courtesy of Meredith Bradford.)

Business as usual. Once you've seen it, you've seen it, and Dana Fuller, who worked with the Mitchell Brothers for many years, has seen it all. (Photo courtesy of Mike Bradford.)

The evolution of the O'Farrell, from the early 1970s, just before *Behind the Green Door* premiered, to today. The theater evolved from a movie house to a live sex emporium featuring attractions like the Green Door Room, where the curtain opens once every hour to reveal six women taking a shower together. (Photo by Costantini for the San Francisco *Examiner*.) Painted by artist Lou Silva, the murals on the back and west side of the O'Farrell are a San Francisco landmark. (Photo courtesy of Dave Patrick.)

"What do you think we should do, Bob?" "I don't know, what do you think, Bob?" The auteurs of porn: Artie, left, and Jim, clowning around during a shooting in 1971. (Photo courtesy of Meredith Bradford.)

The merry pranksters of porn: the Mitchell Brothers' staff in the early 1970s. Artie is at top left, playing the Mad Hatter. That's Jim, hiding behind his wife, Adrienne. Denise Larson, the head Nickelette, is standing next to her boyfriend, the hipster Vince Stanich. The man with the Amish beard in the front row is Bob Cecchini. Longtime cameraman Jon Fontana is next to Cecchini. Andy Finley is next to Fontana. (Photo courtesy of Meredith Bradford.)

On the town. Note the sartorial splendor of the boys from Antioch. Jim, Adrienne, Artie, and Meredith enjoy an evening with an unidentified singer in the lounge at the Fairmont Hotel in 1973. (Photo courtesy of Meredith Bradford.)

Marilyn Chambers, fresh and innocent as the high school girl next door, in a poster for her debut porn film, *Behind the Green Door*. (Photo by Phil Heffernan, courtesy of the San Francisco *Chronicle*.)

"BEHIND the GREEN DOOR"
starring
MARILYN CHAMBERS
a
mitchell brothers film group release

The student body president: George McDonald on his high school graduation day in 1967. A very big man on campus, George was an orphan who was raised in a number of foster homes (the sport coat came from a Goodwill store; that's why the sleeves are short). George was determined to become governor of California. He became San Francisco's first male porn star instead. (Photo courtesy of George McDonald.)

The Nickelettes onstage at the O'Farrell in 1973. Outrageous, antiporn, full of fun, the Nicks took on everyone, including their mothers ("M is for the million things she gave me . . . O is for the other things she gave me . . ."). The weekly Nickelodeon, a kind of crazy variety show, was a full flowering of San Francisco's bohemian underground. (Photo courtesy of Deborah Marinoff.)

In the 1960s, a loose coalition of sexual libertarians, leftists, gays, early feminists, and pornographers were united by a cause: freeing America from the shackles of its Puritan past. By the late 1970s, the coalition had dissolved and groups like Women Against Pornography (WAP) were demonstrating against S&M theme shows in the Ultra Room. (Photo by Palmer for the San Francisco *Examiner*.)

The Mitchell Brothers' response to the picketing was to fight fire with fire. Here that old sexual warrior, Artie Mitchell, is protesting censorship in Berkeley. The ideological battle between pro-censorship feminists like members of Women Against Pornography and "sex positive" feminists is still being waged today. (Photo courtesy of Dave Patrick.)

he and Lelania were both sweating and he could smell her sex. That helped too.

George looked down and saw that a pool of sweat had collected in the hollow under Lelania's breasts. Maybe she doesn't like me sweating on her, George thought, and instantly he was self-conscious and unsure of himself.

"It's really hot under these lights," George said. "You can't help but sweat."

"I know," Lelania said. "I like it. It really turns me on."

Lelania rubbed a hand across her chest and smeared the sweat over her body. George knew she was acting. Sweat didn't turn her on. She was doing it to make him feel good and forget about the crew and the lights and the camera. It was about the nicest thing anyone had ever done for George, and a wave of tenderness surged through him.

George kissed her, closed his eyes, and started a series of long, slow, heartfelt grinds. Suddenly he felt something cold on the back of his testicles. He whipped his head around and saw Jon Fontana holding a light meter an inch away from his scrotum.

"Sorry, man," Fontana said. "Just trying to make sure we got it right. We only get one come shot, you know."

George went back to the task at hand and was surprised to find that, although he was hard as a turkey neck, he could not come. He closed his eyes, buried his head deep in Lelania's hair, squeezed her legs together, and did some short strokes designed to agitate the head of his penis. When he finally reached orgasm, his penis felt so warm and tingly that he wanted to leave it in. But he was a pro now, he must do as the director told him, so he pulled out and, for the first time, watched his own orgasm.

A wonderful calm settled over George. He had done it. He had triumphed.

Jim showed George where to clean up and told him they would all meet in the lobby. They were going to Ocean Beach to shoot the socially redeeming part of the film.

Pornography is the opposite of life, George thought as he washed up. In life, you meet a girl, you go on a date, you maybe go to bed. In porn, you go to bed, then you have the date.

George went down to the lobby and sat down on a couch next to Lelania. She told him that the guy who had bumped into him was her husband, Johnny. Johnny was a former child star who had been in *Life with Father* and *The Fighting Sullivans*. He had walked over the Mexican border with some marijuana in his shoe and had earned the dubious distinction of being the first person arrested in Richard Nixon's Operation Intercept. He had jumped bail and they were on the run from the FBI.

Now it all focused for George. Jim and Artie had conned the couple into coming back, knowing that they were going to substitute George for Johnny. While he was pacing downstairs, they were upstairs talking the couple into it. No wonder the guy had been pissed off. The former child star had been bumped from a porn film, and a guy off the street was going to fuck his wife. They must really need the money, George thought to himself.

The shots on the beach were as much a fantasy to George as the sex scene had been. He and Lelania walked along holding hands, stopping to gaze into each other's eyes. Then, hand in hand, they walked up the stairs to the Cliff House, a San Francisco landmark that overlooks the ocean.

George let himself believe that Lelania had really fallen in love with him, that she really was his girl. And why not? He had done what her husband couldn't do. They were so good together, maybe they'd make another movie together. And another. Maybe they'd become famous together.

The shooting ended. George and Lelania hugged and said good-bye and she got into a car with a crew member who was going to give her a ride back to her apartment. George rode back to the O'Farrell in the Econoline.

"It was a silent and we usually pay twenty-five dollars for a silent, but you did so well I'm going to pay you fifty dollars," Jim told George back at the theater. "What are you doing tomorrow? Come back and we'll get you another girl."

George walked out of the theater coasting on a huge high. He had done it! He had conquered his fears. He had conquered Lelania, Lelania's husband, the camera, the crew, everything! Duane had been right. There *was* a difference between doing it in a dark bedroom and doing it for the camera. But George had done it! He had concentrated so hard that the camera and the crew and the lights had disappeared. He was a performer!

A new world had opened for him. George was going to make a living fucking beautiful women! He was going to be a movie star! He was going to be somebody!

After *Lelania,* George McDonald became a sought-after performer, a regular in San Francisco porn films. He was good-looking, he appeared gentle on camera, he did what directors told him to do, he never argued about money, and, most important, he always got it up.

Before long, George was as self-righteous about his work as a proselytizing minister. He felt superior to the film crews he worked with. He had to get naked and perform; they could hide behind the camera. He'd be in a bar and someone there would find out what he did, or he'd let someone know, and pretty soon he'd be surrounded by guys wanting to know what it was like to screw all those women. George would look in their eyes and see that he was living their fantasies. He was the guy who had the guts to do it, the guy who wasn't afraid to take off his clothes and let the world watch him fuck.

"I was the sexual outlaw," George says, describing the role he played off-screen. "I was literally the cock of the walk."

For George, it all came back to honesty. He had decided that the problem with America was that everybody was faking it. The bartender had a master's degree in English from Berkeley and said he was working on a novel, but he was faking it. The cabdriver who claimed to be a screenwriter was faking it. The artists and politicos and musicians who whiled away entire days over espressos at Enrico's, a cafe on Broadway in North Beach, were all faking it.

George may not have been in the most socially acceptable line of work around, but at least he wasn't faking it. They faked sex in Hollywood, and the result was a lot of ludicrous, dishonest films. The films George appeared in might be rank, but they were real.

George loved playing the sexual outlaw. The men who approached him were usually wary, filled with that curious mixture of fear and respect they reserve for outlaws ("This guy's got to be crazy to do what he's doing, I'd better watch myself.")

For some women, George was an archetype of sexual abandon. Every Saturday night, George went to an orgy hosted by a sensualist like Lowell Pickett or a swinger from the Sexual Freedom League. He was always the center of attention. All the women wanted to try on the porn star.

"It was like having constant honeymoon sex," George says in retrospect. "Sex is always the most exciting the first time. I'd have sex with a woman and then never see her again. It didn't bother me; there was always someone new."

The money wasn't very good, but that didn't bother George either. He was making a living and he had escaped the Tenderloin to a $200-a-month apartment in the heart of Sausalito. What he lacked in money he made up for in recognition. George was somebody.

The men who usually appeared in San Francisco porn films were transients who did one film and then disappeared. George did over forty films his first year in the business. He was intelligent, charming, and naturally loquacious, and he actively pursued interviews, calling up radio stations and saying, "Hey, porn is a happening thing in San Francisco. I'm in all the films, I'm San Francisco's first male porn star. You ought to interview me."

Michael Douglas and Karl Malden were shooting *The Streets of San Francisco* in those days, and if George happened to pass the crew while it was filming on location, he always looked around for Douglas. George considered himself Douglas's equal. Douglas was a star in one way, George was a star in another.

Paradoxically, the one place where George was *not* a star was on the set. The Mitchell Brothers and their crew had great contempt for anyone who was dumb enough, or crazy enough, to appear on the wrong side of the camera.

"I was never part of the club," George would say years later. "I didn't qualify. I was 'the meat.' I never had a say in shooting any of the films. If I said, 'Hey, I see this differently,' they'd cut me right off. 'Don't ever forget, you're just meat,' they'd say.

"It was tough because I really believed in what I was doing and they were really contemptuous of what they were doing."

The more films he appeared in for the Mitchell Brothers, the more ambivalent George became about the brothers. On the one hand, he loved Jim and Artie because they had given him a chance. They were a delight to be around. They paid promptly and ran a class operation, especially in comparison with some of the sleazeballs around town that George had worked for. But they seemed to have no respect for what they were doing, and they certainly had no respect for him. George hated them for that.

Jim was busy, telling a naked couple lying on a bed what acts to perform and the sequence he wanted them performed in. Artie sidled up to his old buddy Jerry Ward, whom the Mitchell Brothers had recruited away from Las Vegas, and whispered, "Can you believe it? My brother is trying to tell these people how to fuck."

Jerry had to put a finger in his mouth and bite down to keep from laughing out loud. Once again, Artie had nailed it. Fucking is fucking. How can you tell people how to do it? How could there ever be anything new about it? Adam and Eve had probably experimented in every position on their first night out of the Garden of Eden.

As an act, sex can retain the thrill of exploration, of conquest, of losing oneself in deep physical pleasure, of sharing a spiritual experience with another human being, for a lifetime. But unless you are fixated on it for some deep psychological reason, sex as a spectator sport becomes boring quite quickly. There are only a few orifices and only so many ways to fill them, and before long, flesh loses its enchantment.

Filming sex gets old even faster than watching it. Once you have shot all the positions and figured out how to use suction bottles designed to clear a baby's nostrils to produce realistic come shots—spelled "cum shots" in the trade—you have pretty much done it all.

"When you are immersed in sex, all the excitement is gone. It doesn't even approach excitement," says Mike Bradford, a member of the Mitchell Brothers' film crew in the early 1970s, "It becomes really boring because it is very labor-intensive. You spend a lot of downtime, waiting for a guy to get it up, thinking: Man, I'm hungry, or Isn't it time for a joint?

Shooting sex films had turned out to be not too much different from shooting the industrial films that Jim, Annie, and Earl had been so anxious to avoid. In porn, the actors changed, but the action never did. You shot a couple from the same angles walking up a beach or gazing at each other over a candlelit dinner. Then you shot them in action in bed. There are the obligatory shots of oral sex and the obligatory insertion shot, the obligatory shots of the woman in ecstasy and the man's face contorted with passion, and, of course, the all-important, obligatory "cum" or "wet" shot.

"We really did become oblivious to sex," Mike Bradford says. "A new girl would come in and we'd say, 'Take off your clothes, this guy's going to fuck you and then we're going to do some ass fucking.' She couldn't believe we were going about it with such aplomb, because it wouldn't be real for her until she walked into the studio.

" 'You're really serious. It's really going to happen, isn't it?' she'd ask. We'd say, 'Yeah, we're serious. Get undressed.' She'd take off her clothes and somebody would say, 'Aw, shit! She's got a pimple on her left cheek. We're gonna have to shoot her ass from the right side.'"

Mike Bradford had been a student at Ohio State University when his parents decided to leave Worthington, Ohio, and move to San Francisco. Mike came out to spend the summer with them, and the first thing his mother told him was that the lady in the downstairs apartment had the same last name they did. Her first name is Meredith, and you'll just love her husband, Artie. He's the most wonderful, charming fellow. Dad and I love them both. You'd never in a thousand years guess they were in the dirty-movie business.

A superb mechanic who loves machines, Mike immediately noticed that Artie had brush-painted by hand the Porsche he had bought in Germany.

"Artie had a flippant, 'Awwwww, fuck it!' attitude," Mike recalls. "It was his way of acknowledging that this stuff wasn't really important, even if you could afford it."

Mike found everything about Artie intriguing. Artie's favorite show was *The Prisoner,* and every week they'd tune in, get smoked up, and Artie would fire off a string of one-liners that were both funny and perceptive. He seemed instinctively to know that nothing is funnier than the truth. Artie divided the world into two kinds of people, those who got the funny part and those who didn't, and Mike was thrilled to be in on the joke. It made the nice college boy from Ohio feel hip and very special.

The annual KQED auction was the best. It stretched on for weeks, and every night Artie would get stoned, turn on the PBS station, and do a running commentary on the items that were offered. Somehow, he made the wine tours in Napa and the weekend getaways in Sonoma seem fatuous, something only dorks who voted Republican and had sex only on Saturday night would want to do. The chocolate extravaganzas the glib auctioneers described as "wild" and "naughty" doubled Artie up with laughter.

"Fuuuuuccckkkkk yooouuuu," Artie would yell at the auctioneer. "You want wild? You want naughty? How about a weekend upstairs at the O'Farrell? We'll even provide the chocolate."

Then, all of a sudden, an item would interest Artie and he'd turn deadly serious and grab the phone and start bidding. The Mitchells were now well beyond the days when they had to save every dollar just to buy a new camera. One night, Artie bought a Morgan, the classic little English sports car. Another night, he ended up the proud owner of a huge moose head.

Artie made the sanctimonious white liberals who ran the KQED auction seem incredibly tame. They were squares who did not have a clue how to have sex or raise hell or have a good time. None of them had ever taken any real risks, none of them had done anything with true abandon since their last big beer blast back in college, and even that had been more or less officially sanctioned. Well, Artie knew what it was like to be alive, and it sure as hell didn't have much to do with designer clothes, a weekend in the wine country, or a chocolate binge.

Sitting next to him, Mike realized that if he stayed in Ohio, there was a good chance he'd turn into a Fred MacMurray type, putting on yellow slacks and a madras jacket and cruising to the golf club for dinner every Saturday night. Mike began to see that as living death.

Mike spent a great deal of time at the O'Farrell that summer, astounded at what went on there. Beautiful women walked in the door, took off their clothes, did things Mike had never seen women do before, put their clothes back on, got paid, thanked everybody, and walked out the door like it was all in a day's work.

Who were these women? Who were the guys on the crew who went about their work with such cool indifference? What was it like to be part of the sexual underground? What was it like when you could have all the sex you wanted and did not have to go through the dating rituals Mike went through at Ohio State, taking girls to the Heidelberg on High Street and then going for a drive, all the time wondering: Will she? Should I try?

The political education Mike got at the O'Farrell was just as incredible. He had always assumed there were good guys and bad guys, and that someone like Daniel Ellsberg, who had released *The Pentagon Papers,* was definitely a good guy. But when Ellsberg visited the theater and spent some time upstairs, Jim and Artie had both been frosty. And when he left, Artie had muttered, "What an asshole!"

"Why? Why is he an asshole?" Mike had demanded. "He took on the whole establishment, the Pentagon, the White House, the FBI. What do you want from a guy?"

"He *is* the establishment, he's up to his eyeballs in it," Artie had replied. "We're supposed to make him a hero for spilling some secrets? Fuck! He was in on those secrets! I'll bet that as soon as the people he squealed on are out of power, he'll try to get back in. He's a classic halfway liberal, and I hate halfway guys!"

To insiders like Mike, the O'Farrell had become the coolest club in the world. Jim and Artie had created the best fraternity in America. The Betas or the Phi Delts at Ohio State certainly couldn't match the clubhouse upstairs at the O'Farrell, with its endless supply of available women, true eccentrics, marijuana, alcohol, and good guys, guys you could trust, guys who, when the spirit moved them, were ready to hop on a motorcycle, race the wind to Yosemite, and spend three days camping and fishing.

When men's movement guru Robert Bly was still a struggling poet, Jim and Artie had already established a ceremonial lodge where men could be men together. In the beginning, the sacrament was marijuana and the price of entry was friendship and talent. Later, the sacrament became cocaine and the price of admission was fame—Hunter S. Thompson, Warren Hinckle, Huey Newton.

But the unwritten rules never changed. Aging hipsters like Vince Stanich guided bright young men like Mike Bradford through the bowels of the metropolitan area. Men left their wives and girlfriends behind (women can be so complicating; they want to talk about feelings and commitments and plan the future) for the comfortable stench of marijuana and camaraderie.

"It was like a village in Sicily," says Mark Bradford. "It was a clan. When you were in, you were all the way in."

Mike returned to Ohio State that fall, but the Scioto River could not compare to the Golden Gate, and Woody Hayes's Buckeyes were no match for the scene upstairs at the O'Farrell. He missed his friend Artie, the sinister clown. He missed the warm, comfortable feel of being surrounded by a bunch of great guys upstairs at the O'Farrell. Everywhere he looked on campus, he saw future members of the Rotary Club.

Mike crafted a letter to Jim and Artie, exploring his feelings and ever so diplomatically asking for a job. A few days after he mailed it, Artie called and said, "Hell, you didn't have to write all that shit. All you had to do was ask. Come on out, you're now the eighth member of the film crew."

Cinema 7, the Mitchell Brothers' film operation, had moved from the studio upstairs at the O'Farrell to Stage A, a sound studio the size of an airplane hangar on Tennessee Street, near Potrero Hill. Mike built sets, scouted locations, unloaded and set up equipment when they shot on location, and filled in as a sound and lighting man.

Fun came before work. One of the first things the brothers did after leasing Stage A was to put up a basketball hoop. During breaks, the crew played game after game. The crew started every morning with a joint; throughout the day, they'd hit on joints to maintain the high. Often they could be found in Al's Anchor, a nearby tavern owned by an old sailor, downing beers and laughing about some outrageous thing that had happened on the set that day.

But for all the substance abuse, the basketball, and the general horsing around, the Mitchell Brothers' film crew managed to get a great deal of work done. Every week, an hour and a half of new film had to be on the screen at the O'Farrell. On a Monday, part of the crew would be doing the final edit on a film that was to premiere at the O'Farrell the next day. Meanwhile, Artie and Bill Boyer would be fleshing out the concept for the film the crew was going to shoot that week.

It is misleading to say that Artie and Bill Boyer were writing a screenplay. A screenplay implies a script with dialogue and a story line that has been plotted out scene by scene. The Mitchell Brothers did not have time for such niceties. The crew would brainstorm an idea—a concept, they call it in Hollywood—for a "Boy meets girl, boy fucks girl" film. They'd shoot it in two or three days, and then ask themselves: Okay, what do we do for next week?

"Oftentimes we didn't know what day of the week it was, but it really didn't matter," Mike recalls. "What mattered was, we were all buddies, we were all having fun."

When the money started rolling in, Jim and Artie seemed to stop caring about money. They weren't in it for the sex either. Some of the crew had "dick brain" and went "sport fucking," but most of them would much rather hang out with the guys than chase that week's porn starlet.

Pornography was a way to have fun, a way for a bunch of guys to hang out together. By hiring old friends from Antioch like Jon Fontana, Bill Boyer, and Alex Benton, Jim and Artie had essentially created a big-city version of the Studs. There was an Okie friendliness to the club upstairs at the O'Farrell. An old friend would show up and Jim would greet him with "Hey, how you doin'? Hope you don't have anything on for tonight. There's a barbecue out at Art's and you gotta come."

Women were not barred from the club, but few had gained admittance. Margo St. James, an ex-prostitute with a flair for drama who had founded COYOTE—Call Off Your Old Tired Ethics, the first prostitute's union—was a member, and so was Sharon McKnight, a razor-tongued cabaret performer who, besides being funny, could sing and act.

Meredith and Annie had, of course, been original members. But Annie was gone. She and Jim had broken up. Annie had finally decided that Jim and Artie were happy cranking out hard-core films and were much more interested in hanging out with their buddies than they were in making a real movie. Annie had learned all she could shooting pornos. She had quit and moved back to Los Angeles.

Meredith was not the diehard member of the club she had once been. She had a whole new set of responsibilities, for she had recently given birth to Liberty, a beautiful little girl. Meredith and Artie had purchased a Tudor mansion with a pool and tennis court on Frankie Lane in Lafayette. She spent most of her time out there, caring for the baby. Meredith still came around to the theater now and then, but the guys usually saw her only on weekends, when everybody drifted out to Lafayette to hang around the pool or the living room of the big house.

In the meantime, Jim had inducted—or tried to induct—another woman into the club. Jim had met Adrienne when she was working as a legal secretary for Dennis Roberts, one of the Mitchell Brothers' attorneys. They had moved in together and Adrienne had started working at the theater. She was in and out of the clubhouse a lot, but most of the guys resented her presence. Mike Bradford, for one, considered Adrienne "a classic bitch."

But Adrienne was only a minor irritant because most of the time she was home, keeping house or cooking elaborate dinners for Jim. Art and Jim had both begun living dual lives. At home, they were young men in stable relationships. The elaborate grounds at Artie and Meredith's were always freshly mowed and the water in the pool was always sparkling clean. Adrienne served dinner on English china and poured fine California wine into Swedish crystal glasses she had purchased at Gump's.

At the theater, Jim and Art were surrounded by sex and drugs and their buddies all day long. The boys in the club were, of course, perennial adolescents, smoking, drinking, playing poker, and bull-shitting with their buddies, just as they had done in high school.

"You could say the Mitchell Brothers never grew up," says Herb Gold, the novelist. "But look at the people who did grow up. They became partners in accounting firms. The Mitchells' attitude was: Who wants to be like them?"

Slowly, the Mitchell Brothers' circle had widened to include cosmopolitan literary figures like Gold. The cartoonist Dan O'Neill was living in the projection room, and the legendary R. Crumb, whose wonderful drawings come straight from the id, had become a regular upstairs. Huey Newton, a Michael Kennedy client, came by once in a while, and filmmakers from San Francisco State and aspiring young artists were flocking to the theater, hoping to become members of the in group that met upstairs.

By the early 1970s, the O'Farrell had turned into a bohemian outpost, a uniquely San Francisco version of a cafe on the Left Bank in Paris or a coffeehouse in Greenwich Village. Like all true bohemians, Jim, Artie, and their film crew were carrying on a mutiny against middle-class values. Waging that rebellion was the *real* fun.

From the days of William Bradford to the ridiculous films with titles like *Nice Girls Don't* that were shown to girls in high school physical education classes, sex in America has always been treated as sacrosanct and deadly serious. Jim and Artie and the crew at Cinema 7 were determined to subvert that, to be as wildly impudent and heretical about sex as they could be. Anything went; the bolder, the better.

It was inevitable that the sexual anarchists would take on the Catholic Church. Jim and Artie did so, not because they had high artistic aims, like exposing the Church as a male-dominated institution that is profoundly sex-phobic, but because the Church was such an obvious target.

For the film *Reckless Claudia*, Mike Bradford constructed a confessional out of cardboard. Claudia, played by a Stanford music major who was taking a walk on the wild side, feels guilty about the sexual sins she has committed and goes to a priest to confess. The priest is Artie. The questions he asks become more and more specific and the priest gets more and more turned on. Finally he can stand it no longer. He gets up, goes behind the confessional, and suddenly a raging penis pops through a hole in the confessional curtains. Claudia does five Hail Marys, crosses herself twice, and takes the penis in her mouth. Seconds later, the penis pulls out and splatters Claudia's face with semen.

The penis was not Artie's.

Part of the fun for the film crew—and a way to counter the boredom—was to pull off an endless number of in jokes. Sometimes the jokes were on each other, like the time they named the lead female in a film after Jon Fontana's high school girlfriend, without, of course, telling Fontana. Fontana's head popped up from the camera when he heard her name, but he kept shooting.

A standard gag was for members of the crew to appear in every film, but *only* in nonsexual roles. To cross the line was to become "meat," a performer, a jerk.

"We all had opportunities to stick our dicks in a girl's mouth and just get our dicks pictured, but we'd never do it," recalls Mike Bradford. "It wouldn't have been accepted, guys would give you too much shit for it.

"That's what happened when we were shooting *Reckless Claudia*," Mike continues. "It was a free blow job, but Artie wasn't going to do it and none of us would either. A guy named Jones was always hanging around the set, trying to get laid. He was tolerated but not appreciated, a pain in the ass we used when it was expedient. We asked him if he wanted to do it, and he said, 'Why not?' and climbed the stepladder. He came instantly, to the shock and horror of Claudia."

Everything was fair game in a Mitchell Brothers' sex film—death, religion, education (they made a point of filming *Wild Campus* at Diablo Valley College, Jim, Bill Boyer, and Artie's [almost] alma mater), and fantasies. Especially fantasies.

Immediately after the confessional scene in *Reckless Claudia*, Jon Fontana led the actress who was playing Claudia over to George McDonald, who was going to be in the next scene. She was wiping away semen, angry about what had happened and that no one had warned her, and she barely said "Hi" to George.

"Listen, Jon, can you tell me what I'm supposed to do? I always like to know so I can get into the character," George said to Fontana.

"It's a dream sequence," Fontana replied. "It'll be better if you find out as you go along."

Fontana walked away and George wondered why he was being so evasive. Then, out of the corner of his eye, he saw a giant gorilla head resting on a chair in a corner of the studio. Next to the chair on a raised platform was a bed covered with imitation-leopard sheets. A rope that had been tied to the rafters was dangling from the ceiling.

A sinking feeling came over George.

"Hey, Jon, wait!" George yelled. "Does that rope and stuff over there have anything to do with my scene?"

Fontana turned around.

"That *is* your scene, George," he said. "Hang loose and you'll find out."

Fontana and every crew member within earshot turned on their heels and walked away from George as quickly as they could. George stood there, feeling more naked than he did when he had his clothes off. How could Jim and Artie do this to him? He'd never done anything to them except give them his absolute best every time out. They were such wise asses. Everything was a goof to the Mitchell Brothers. Their idea of a joke was humiliating somebody, and George didn't like that, especially when the somebody was him.

It didn't help that when George looked around, he recognized a bunch of the people who hung out upstairs at the O'Farrell. It was just like Jim and Artie to invite their buddies to witness the spectacle. George thought about walking out, but he was dead broke and the rent was due. Ever since the other San Francisco filmmakers had followed the Mitchell Brothers' lead and begun making featurettes, George had been getting less and less work. In the good old days of the loops, there had been ten to fifteen ads for performers in every issue of *The Berkeley Barb*. By the early 1970s, filmmakers were taking a week or two to make a film, and only a few ads ran every week.

What the hell, George figured, I've done everything else. I might as well try this. He went off to a corner, pulled a fat joint out of his pocket, and smoked the whole number to help him get through what was coming.

George was told to get naked and put on the gorilla head. Holding a banana in one hand, he was supposed to swing on the rope, back and forth over the bed where Claudia was sleeping. Then he was to drop onto the bed and begin tearing away the jungle Jane ersatz leopard-skin outfit Claudia was wearing. Claudia would wake up terrified, and then—and this was the funny part—she was to attack the gorilla.

George swung on the rope, dropped onto the bed, and did a gorilla walk over to Claudia. He tore at her clothes. She woke up and lunged at George. He beat his chest a couple of times and lay back on the bed. Claudia went down and started performing oral sex.

At that moment, the sex scene George thought was going to be the hardest he had ever done turned into the easiest. The gorilla's head blocked out all the light. It was like he was still in the Air Force back in Merced, in a dark bedroom with a hippie chick. George relaxed and let Claudia do all the work.

The only difficult part of the scene came when he rolled over and they started to have conventional sex. George turned in a typically energetic performance and had so much trouble keeping the big gorilla head on that he had to hold it with both hands.

When the scene was over and George was finally able to take the gorilla head off, he looked up and Jim, Artie, the crew, and their entourage were all laughing at him. He put on his clothes, collected his money, and got out of Stage A as fast as he could.

In May 1972, for obvious reasons, sacrilege and "bestiality" among them, the San Francisco district attorney chose *Reckless Claudia* as the next Mitchell Brothers film to bring to trial. Surely sex in a confessional and George McDonald having sex in a gorilla costume would make a jury think twice about things like "contemporary community standards" and "redeeming social importance."

The trial was part of a two-pronged attack the Mitchell Brothers traced back to Dianne Feinstein, the antiporn crusader who was now president of the San Francisco Board of Supervisors. Under Feinstein's prodding, the board had abandoned its live-and-let-live attitude toward hard-core theaters and changed the rules of the game so that pornographers couldn't win.

For decades, theater permits in San Francisco had been issued by the fire department, whose inspectors looked for safety, not moral, violations. In 1971, the Board of Supervisors quietly approved an ordinance that required theater operators to apply to the Police Permit Bureau for an operating license before May 10.

Signs went up in the O'Farrell lobby asking customers who cared about "Freedom of Choice" to attend a hearing at the Hall of Jus-

tice on May 5. Instead of the usual crowd of citizens angry over the
smut blight in their neighborhood, the hearing was packed with
citizens who considered the O'Farrell a community asset. Robert
Charles, the owner of an upscale French restaurant a few doors
down the block, told the police commissioners that the Mitchell
Brothers were excellent neighbors, orderly businessmen who had
upgraded both their building and the neighborhood. A landscape
architect urged the commission to grant the permit because people
who liked hard-core films wanted a nice, clean place to see them in
and the "people who don't like these movies are free to go elsewhere."

The restaurateur and the architect might as well have stayed
home and watched *All in the Family*. The game was rigged. The
Permit Bureau had been created to deny applications to adult theaters, and that's what they did, to the Mitchell Brothers and every
other operator in town. The brothers appealed to the Board of Permit Appeals, and were turned down there too. Finally, Michael
Kennedy and his partner Joe Rhine went to federal court and won
an injunction that prohibited the city from instituting its new li-
censing procedures. The court later ruled that the new ordinance
was unconstitutional because it violated due process.

Kennedy and Rhine had proved their worth in the permit case
and now they were about to prove it again in the *Reckless Claudia*
trial. The stakes were high because Jim and Artie were coming off a
loss in the *Glowy Flesh* trial. A first conviction for showing an obscene film is a misdemeanor; a second is a felony that would carry a
five- to fifteen-year prison term. At least one member of the jury
had to get the funny parts in *Reckless Claudia* or the joke was going
to be on Jim and Artie.

After the loss in the *Glowy Flesh* trial, Jim and Artie had sat down
with Michael Kennedy and reframed their courtroom strategy. Joe
Rhine, a quiet, methodical attorney, joined his fiery partner in the
Reckless Claudia trial to give jurors alternative styles to choose
from. The idea was that jurors who didn't like Kennedy would like
Rhine, and vice versa.

Meredith did her part by sewing matching outfits for herself and
little Liberty. During every break, they stood in the hallway with
Artie, cute as an ad from *Family Circle,* visually telling the jury that
Artie wasn't an evil pornographer, he was the father of a lovely little
family.

The defense also introduced a brand-new tactic at this trial. In addition to arguing the obscenity law, Rhine and Kennedy had commissioned a poll that was conducted by the Field Research Corporation. The poll asked 1,050 men and women to name "the two or three most serious problems facing the country today."

"Adult Californians, our poll showed, were far more concerned with other issues of our times than they were with pornography," Peter N. Sherill, a Field Research vice president, testified on the stand.

During the two-week trial, Kennedy and Rhine kept coming back to Sherill's testimony. Of the people questioned, 61.1 percent said the war in Vietnam was the most serious issue facing America. Only 1.9 percent said pornography was a serious issue. Sixty-three percent of the respondents said that although there should be limits placed on advertising and promotion, there should be no restrictions on "the availability of sexual materials of any type to adults who wish to see them."

The poll worked better than the defense had dared expect. The most the Mitchell Brothers' side ever hoped for was a mistrial. This time, after deliberating six hours, the jury voted 12–0 for *acquittal*. It was the first time pornographers had won an acquittal in San Francisco.

A triumphant Michael Kennedy told the press the next day that jurors had told him after the trial that the case should not have been prosecuted, "especially in view of the fact that the theater advertises its wares as catering to adult patrons."

Jim and Artie were flying high. Clearly, it was becoming more and more difficult to convict a pornographer on obscenity charges in San Francisco. Especially pornographers who could pay for expensive polls and afford innovative attorneys.

"Jesus! What the hell are you doing!" Artie screamed.

"What the hell does it look like we're doing?" Earl Shagley shot back.

Earl and Maureen Shagley were outside on O'Farrell Street, picketing the theater, carrying signs that said, "Mitchell Brothers Unfair to Labor."

In the Mitchell Brothers' world, what Maureen and Earl were doing was akin to burning the flag. The O'Farrell Theatre was an extended family, a hippie commune. And here were two of the

O'Farrell's oldest employees walking a picket line like steelworkers outside a plant on the South Side of Chicago.

"Talk to Jim," Artie urged. "Just go upstairs and talk to Jim. Whatever it is, you two can work it out."

The Shagleys agreed and went inside the theater. Climbing the stairs, Earl was thinking about how much had changed in so short a time. Annie was long gone. The last Earl had heard, Annie was in Los Angeles, working in ceramics. Somebody had told him she was doing a bathroom for Bob Dylan.

Then there was the Adrienne problem. Six months after Artie married Meredith, Jim had married Adrienne, and now Adrienne was throwing her weight around the theater, telling old-time employees like Earl they had to do whatever she told them, even though Adrienne didn't have a clue about how to shoot a film. Meanwhile, Maureen, who was at least as smart as Adrienne and had been there much longer, was doing what she had done from day one, working on the sound.

Confronting Jim was not going to be easy. Shagley was sick of the porn business. He did not like the vast majority of people he had met, the distributors and the L.A. loop makers in their expensive leather coats. To Shagley, they were cheap hustlers with no moral character.

But that didn't apply to Jim. He still had great respect for Jim. Jim was one of the strongest people he had ever met.

Shagley remembered the night they were hanging out at the theater with a French filmmaker who was making a documentary on Jean-Luc Godard. They got to talking about the Bank of America billboards that were up all over town. The billboards featured a giant blank check, and they had decided it would be a great idea to spray-paint "Pay to the Bank of America: $100 billion for 100,000 lives" lost in Vietnam on one of the billboards. They got a can of spray paint, piled into an MG, and drove to a billboard that was located in the Fillmore.

They had just started climbing the steep ladder up to the billboard when a bunch of black guys poured out of a pool hall and wanted to know what they thought they were doing. Earl had started explaining about how radical they were, but somehow, surrounded by black men holding cues, they didn't seem so radical. If Jim hadn't stepped in and broken the tension by saying they were just a bunch of hippies who didn't know what they were doing, that messing with a B of A billboard had seemed like a good idea when they were smoking a joint but now that they were here, they realized they were on the wrong turf and it was time for them to be getting on their way, things might have gotten very nasty indeed.

But just because Earl liked and admired Jim didn't mean he was going to let Jim walk all over him. Perhaps only Annie and Meredith had worked harder on the early Mitchell Brothers films than Earl had. It was Earl who had learned how to use the Arriflex camera and Earl who had spent night after night in the editing room, working out a system that synched the sound to the action on the screen. Earl took the film to the printer and worried about whether the printer would tear it or overcook it in the developing "soup."

Now as he walked into the clubhouse-office, Earl was tired, overcome with a sense of futility. It had not been worth it.

"What's with this shit?" Jim asked, his eyes alive with anger.

"You gave the Antioch guys a raise. We didn't get one," Earl said.

"None of them are making as much as you are," Jim said.

"That's not the point," Earl replied. "We were here first. You're always giving them raises. Why do they come before talent? Why do they come first over everything?"

"We run a fair game, Earl," Jim said coldly. "You two walking around outside with those signs tells people we don't."

"Fair? You're talking fair to me?" Earl yelled. "How many times did you and I and Annie talk about solidarity and community and forming a company and dividing up the shares so everybody who did the work got a fair cut? How many times, Jim? That got washed away pretty fast when the money began flooding in."

"That's something we can talk about later," Jim said. "Right now let's keep it to your problem with the raises."

"Later! Later!" Earl shouted. "I've heard that from you before, Jim. After the first few times, you realize that later is never gonna come. That's when you decide you either take things the way they are or you move on."

"Which way are you leaning?" Jim asked.

"It's no fun anymore," Earl said quietly. "It started out as a cause. Now it's just a business."

The Shagleys and Jim managed to work out the salary dispute, but it didn't matter. A short time later, Maureen and Earl quit. Earl did several industrial films and then drifted out of the business.

Although he continued to live in San Francisco, he did not see Jim or Artie Mitchell again.

"In the beginning, we thought we were really going to change things by taking away the shock value and showing that sex wasn't shameful," Earl says. "But it goes both ways. You still have to have morals. You have to accept the responsibility of looking beyond the act to the consequences. Jim and Artie didn't want to do that.

"If you're going to have a real revolution, you have to spend a lot of time working at it. Jim and Artie realized how much work it was and decided just to get on the hog and go for the money.

"I think it backfired," Earl says, looking back on the sexual revolution. "I never thought there was anything socially redeeming in what we did. It was exploitation, and exploitation is inherently bad."

6

Behind *Behind* *the Green Door*

"JIM! COME 'ERE! Quick! Cybill Shepherd just walked in!!"

Jim hurried to Artie's side at the office window and looked down at the crowd that was milling around Stage A.

"The blonde, the blonde carrying the portfolio!" Artie cried. "See her? She's heading for the door!"

"Jesus, Art, you're right! It's her!"

Jim and Artie ran out of the office and stopped at the top of the long metal stairway.

"HEY! YOU!" Artie yelled.

People turned and looked up the stairs.

"YOU! By the door!" Artie yelled.

A slender, athletic-looking woman with short blond hair turned around.

"Who? Me?" she asked, pointing to her chest.

"Yeah! You! Come on up here," Artie cried.

"Oh no. No, thanks," she said, turning back to the door.

Jim and Artie raced down the stairs and ran after her.

"Where the hell are you going? What's the matter?" Jim asked.

"I didn't know it was going to be *that* kind of movie," the woman said. "All the ad in the *Chronicle* said was 'Now casting for a major motion picture.' "

"It *is* going to be a major motion picture. It's *our* major picture," Jim said.

"But it's a sex film!" the woman replied, opening the green questionnaire she was holding. "Question: 'Do you want a balling or nonballing part?' I read that and I'm thinking: Bowling? Is this a bowling movie? Then I read it again and realized what it said. That's when I headed for the door."

"At least come up and talk to us," Artie pleaded.

"Yeah, at least talk to us. You don't have to take off your clothes to talk to us," Jim said, giving her a sweet smile.

An image of an office flashed through the woman's mind. These two bald guys seemed nice enough, but they would lead her to a fat guy with a cigar who would have his feet up on the desk. They'd talk for a while and then the fat guy would remove his cigar and say, "Honey, you either get it on or you don't get the part."

"We're pretty good at talking," Artie said. "We get lots of practice."

The woman laughed. Could these guys really be making a dirty movie? They reminded her of boys back in high school who would spend weeks building up the courage to ask her out and then have trouble wrenching the words out of their mouths. They even looked like they could have grown up with her in Westport, Connecticut. One of them was wearing a sweater vest over a tie and button-down shirt. All that was missing to complete the preppie look was saddle shoes.

"Well, okay, it took me an hour to find this place," the woman said. "I guess we can talk."

"Great! I'm Jim and this is Artie. What's your name?"

"Marilyn Briggs," the woman said, sticking out a hand. "Pleased to meet you."

Marilyn followed the two look-alikes up the stairs, figuring they'd introduce her to the fat man. She'd hear him out, say no, and that would be that. She had done it before. Although she was only nineteen, Marilyn had been around.

Back in New York City, Marilyn had launched a modeling career and had done television spots for Pepsi and Clairol. In 1970, at seventeen, she had managed to land a small role in *The Owl and the*

Pussycat, a New York film that starred Barbra Streisand as a smart-mouth hooker and George Segal as a failing writer. Marilyn played the girlfriend of a minor character. Her one big scene was in bed, topless, with her boyfriend.

Streisand had refused to do the publicity tour, and Columbia, the studio that produced the film, had sent Marilyn out on the talk-show grind. Marilyn had wondered why. She had had such a small role, and had considered herself lucky to be getting the exposure. Then she landed in Los Angeles and discovered the real reason she had been chosen.

A Very Important Producer had visited her hotel room and told Marilyn he had been waiting for her to arrive ever since they met in New York. The producer then proceeded to pitch a package deal.

Marilyn was to be his mistress. In return, she would get an apartment, a car, acting lessons, walking-around money—and parts, that was the big thing. An unseen angel would be guiding her career. The producer had only one demand: She was his and his alone. Under no circumstances could she date another man.

The producer was in his mid-sixties, a bag of deeply wrinkled flesh with liver spots on his hands and a nasty potbelly. He reminded Marilyn of her grandfather, and the last thing Marilyn wanted to do was have sex with her grandfather.

Still, Marilyn might have gone for the deal. She knew enough about Hollywood to understand that this was a break. The producer was very commanding and could pull many strings. If all she had to do was be sweet and sleep with the horny old bastard once in a while, it might be worth it.

But the old man wanted to own her, that's what had bothered Marilyn. She imagined herself cooped up in an apartment somewhere, bored and lonely. Every two weeks or so, the producer would come over for dinner and sex. He'd grill her about where she'd been and who she'd been with. Sooner or later, she would start going out. How could she stay in? Sooner or later, he'd catch her and the whole thing would blow up.

Marilyn had thanked the producer and, as politely as she could, refused the offer. The producer was not a man who heard no very often and he did not take it gracefully. In Hollywood, a good bagel was harder to find than a beautiful young woman. For some reason, this spunky little blonde had caught his fancy and now the stupid little bitch had turned him down. Didn't she know this was the

Dating Game and she was the girl behind door number three? Didn't she know she was supposed to be thrilled he had picked her?

"I hope you're not thinking of working in this town," the producer had said over his shoulder as he walked out of the hotel room.

Marilyn had found an apartment and spent several months in Los Angeles trying to land a role, but she was not invited to audition for another film after *The Owl and the Pussycat*. She hated the ugly, sprawling, smoggy city and its twenty-four-hour-a-day traffic jams, and it had been easy for her to convince herself that she didn't want to work in Los Angeles anyway. If she wanted urban chaos, she could go back to her modeling career in New York.

But then she thought: Why not move up the coast to San Francisco? Marilyn had visited the city for the first time on the *Owl and the Pussycat* tour. San Francisco was clean and beautiful and seemed to be filled with young people just like herself. She could hook up with an agency and resume modeling, do some auditions and break into local theater, or perhaps land a role in a television production or even a film. San Francisco was a happening city; something would break.

In fact, San Francisco was not a happening city, at least not in film, television, or modeling. San Francisco was more of a charming backwater, a place for artists and actors who did not want to pay the dues necessary to break into the mainstream, or did not care about breaking in. Marilyn heard "Sorry, not interested" so often she began wishing she could replay that scene with the producer.

Marilyn had done some topless modeling in New York—everyone did topless in those days, it was no big deal—and had gotten desperate enough to take a brief stab at bottomless dancing after arriving in San Francisco. She had been a Junior Olympic diver in junior high, a high school cheerleader, and a high jumper and sprinter on the track team. Marilyn could really dance, but she had found bottomless depressing and soon quit.

She was working in a factory that produced musk and kama-sutra oils when she met Doug, a true hippie who sometimes played the bagpipes on the street for change. She and Doug had married and moved into an apartment near Potrero Hill, and Doug's friends— men who wore batik and women who had bells on their toes—had become her friends. She now had a gig as a hostess in a health food restaurant. When she and Doug were home, they usually had a joint working, and Marilyn liked to walk around the apartment carrying a can of beer.

When she spotted the ad in the *Chronicle,* Marilyn had run to the phone and called the number. A woman who answered told her they had already finished casting. "No! Wait! You have to wait for me!" Marilyn had cried. The woman on the other end had sighed and said she could come down if she absolutely had to, but she doubted it would do her any good.

Marilyn had grabbed her model's portfolio and run out the door. She finally found Tennessee Street and rushed into Stage A to find herself confronted by a crowd and a functionary who had handed her a green sheet of paper that had a strange question about bowling.

"Let's see your portfolio," Jim said after sitting down behind a desk. Marilyn handed it over, pleased that the nice bald guys, and not some gross fat man, seemed to be running the show.

The eight-by-ten glossies showed a woman who had sandy blond hair, dark blue eyes, a cute little nose, a wide, sensual mouth, and a very sweet smile. Marilyn projected the warmth and wholesomeness of a coed who has just pledged Kappa Kappa Gamma.

Jim and Artie knew this kid would be dynamite in a porn film. Any guy who had ever fantasized about fucking a cheerleader would want to fuck her. She was fresh, innocent, open, and unspoiled, the girl guys dreamed of taking to the prom. She reminded Jim and Artie of the good old days when San Francisco was full of sweet, idealistic hippie chicks who thought making a sex film was part of the trip. It was now the winter of 1971, only a few years after the summer of love, but already the hippie era seemed to have happened in another lifetime.

Jim turned another page and there was Marilyn in a bathing suit. She looked like a jock, a real athlete, and that was a bonus. The same guys who wanted to fuck her could fantasize about having her on their softball team at the company picnic.

Jim closed the portfolio and looked at Artie. They did not need to say anything. They knew what they had. There were a lot of applicants downstairs, but the truth was, they were rather a discouraging lot. The usual collection of low-class chicks had showed up, and so had the usual assortment of swingers, who seemed to be looking more and more hard-eyed these days.

Jim and Artie had gotten so tired of filming sex scenes with these kinds of people they had decided to spice things up by adding an element of the bizarre. The 325-pound woman downstairs who had showed up in a silver miniskirt had been given a role in the film, and so had her 125-pound husband.

It had been a disappointing casting call. The only fresh face that had surfaced was a Filipino airline stewardess, until Artie had caught sight of Marilyn. She was absolutely perfect for the film. Now, if they could just convince her to do it.

"You just happen to be who we're looking for," Jim said, closing the portfolio.

"Oh, really? Wow!" Marilyn said.

Marilyn was surprised Jim was so straightforward. The game was supposed to be played with hints and fakes. And she was surprised at her own reaction. She had blurted out "Wow!" like a naïve kid. It was probably because she had had nothing but rejections since arriving in San Francisco.

"You guys make the kind of movies where men take off everything but masks and black socks, right?" Marilyn said teasingly, trying to regain an edge.

"Only when they've got acne and their ankles are swollen," Artie shot back.

"I don't have anything against sex films," Marilyn said, lighting a cigarette. "I just don't want to be in one."

"Listen, you're classy and this is going to be one classy film," Jim said. "We're putting everything we have into it. Let us just explain the concept. Let us just tell you the story. The whole thing is a fantasy."

"Sure, go ahead," Marilyn said. "Fantasies are neat."

Jim slid his chair closer to Marilyn and Artie pulled up a chair, flipped it around, and sat down on it backward. The brothers told Marilyn the story together, taking turns, coming in so smoothly it was as if they had cues. As they got into the story, their professional calm gave way to a boyish excitement that Marilyn found charming.

"We've been pretty successful making hard-core films," Artie said. "This film here is our shot at breaking though to a mainstream audience. So it's not like we're asking you to star in a fuck film. This is going to be a real movie about real sex."

"Have you ever heard the story of *Behind the Green Door*?" Jim asked.

"Of course she hasn't," Artie said before Marilyn could reply. "She's not a guy."

Artie explained that *Green Door* was an anonymous story that men had been passing around at least since World War II. A woman named Gloria is kidnapped from a hotel and taken to a secret sex club where she is met by a group of women who strip her.

"It sounds terrible, doesn't it?" Jim said. "A woman being kidnapped and forced to do things against her will. We weren't even sure we wanted to do it at first."

"That sort of thing isn't our style," Artie added, leaning forward. "We've always been against violence. The turn-on in our films is that the women enjoy it as much as the men. Maybe even more."

Artie leaned back and gave Marilyn the leering grin that was becoming his trademark. Marilyn looked puzzled, as if she didn't know what to make of him.

"Anyway, Gloria doesn't get hurt," Jim said, regaining Marilyn's attention. "One of the women gives her a message, kind of helps her connect to her body. She tells her that years ago the same thing happened to her and it turned out to be the most amazing experience of her life. Let yourself go and just experience it, she tells Gloria. Be free."

"Gloria starts to relax," Artie interjected, getting swept up in the idea. "See, this is where the fantasy comes in! It turns out Gloria has fantasized about something like this happening to her. And now, because she's a captive under somebody's power, she's free to do things she would be afraid to try otherwise!"

"This is why it's such a neat part," Jim said. "While all this is happening, Gloria doesn't say a word. It's a throwback to the silent films. Gloria has to be scared and fascinated at the same time. Part of her wants it to happen and the other part wants to scream. And she has to convey that inner conflict with her face."

"It's a challenge for any actress," Artie announced.

"But you can do it. Just looking at you, I can tell you could bring it across," Jim added.

"How about it so far? Can you see yourself in the role? I don't know, maybe you've even had fantasies like Gloria's?" Artie asked.

"Let's leave my fantasies out of it," Marilyn said. "What happens next?"

"Okay. Listen, we gotta be up-front: here's where it gets a little heavy," Artie said.

"Heavy?" Marilyn asked suspiciously.

"A black guy. You fuck a black guy," Jim said, looking her in the eye.

"A black guy!"

"He's a stud," Artie said. "How many white girls dream of fucking a black guy? Lots of 'em, right? All we're doing is being honest. All we're doing is bringing the fantasy out of the closet."

"It's going to be done very nicely," Jim added. "The black guy we got, he's a real nice guy, you'll like him. He's been in a production of *Hair* and he's an ex-fighter, so he's got an incredible body. He's going to come out from behind the Green Door wearing white tights and white makeup around his eyes. It's going to be real powerful because, like my brother said, we think it's a really heavy-duty fantasy."

"Tell her the rest, Bob," Artie said.

"Well, without getting into it in too much detail because we haven't got the whole thing worked out, in the climactic scene you'll be surrounded by guys on trapezes."

"Trapezes! Oh, Jesus!" Marilyn yelled, and stubbed out her cigarette.

"It's wild, we're all excited about it, but not as wild as you might think," Artie said.

"Nothing really weird happens around the trapezes," Jim said. "It's all pretty standard sex. What's different is, it all happens at once."

Jim and Artie paused and looked at Marilyn. Marilyn was staring at the floor.

"So what do you think?" Artie asked.

"I don't know what I think," Marilyn said. "You sort of lost me back there with the black guy."

"It's just honest sex," Jim said.

"It's all about passion, the power of passion," Artie added eagerly.

Marilyn was surprised to find herself intrigued. She liked the idea that the film was a fantasy. It might be fun to live out a fantasy. But doing it in a bedroom was one thing; doing it on film was another. Marilyn had her long-term career to think about.

But that was the point. She had no career. And if she made a film like this one, she might never have one. She'd be damaged goods. What if she did break in and was on her way to stardom and *The*

National Inquirer found out she'd been in a sex film? She'd be ostracized forever.

Then again, maybe she wouldn't. Maybe this was the best thing that could happen to her career. The stigma against sex in the movies was breaking down. *Last Tango in Paris* and *Shampoo* were huge hits, people were talking about those movies for months. And the bald guys had said this was going to be a mainstream film.

Had they really meant that, or were they just blowing smoke? Stage A was huge; they seemed to be running a major operation. But were they big enough? Did they have the contacts to distribute a film nationally?

If they did, then maybe, just maybe, she was interested.

Any film going into national distribution would have to have good production values. You couldn't throw a piece of junk out there and expect to succeed. If the film did go national, Hollywood producers would see it. From what she had just heard, she would be the whole movie. If she did a great job; if she made the film really erotic, the studios would have to notice.

Marilyn Monroe had done her nude calendar. She had done it because she was broke, but it had ended up adding to her mystique instead of hurting her. Could this film be Marilyn Briggs's equivalent of Marilyn Monroe's famous calendar?

Marilyn thought about it for a few seconds and then decided no, there was no way it could be. Not if she had to fuck a black guy and do she didn't know what to guys on trapezes. Society hadn't come *that* far.

Artie saw that Marilyn was hesitating and decided to give her a little push. It had worked with women so many times before.

"Go for it," he said. "What have you got to lose?"

"Oh, nothing, nothing!" Marilyn said, waving a hand. "Just the rest of my life."

"Let us at least take a Polaroid," Jim suggested. "It'll give you a taste of what it's like and we'd like to see what you look like."

Marilyn was offended. Where do these guys get off, asking her to take her clothes off a half hour after meeting them? Then she thought: Wait a minute, this is their business. They're not playing games, they're serious. Of course they want me to take off my clothes.

But Marilyn didn't want to take off her clothes.

"I'm sorry, there's no way I can do this," Marilyn said, getting up to leave. "All of a sudden, it seems so stupid to be having this conversation."

"But why?" Jim asked.

"Well, one minute I'm sitting here listening to you talk about me fucking a black guy on-camera. The next minute you ask if you can take a Polaroid and I feel sick to my stomach. This isn't for me. Sorry, guys, I didn't mean to waste your time."

"No, wait, we don't need a picture. Sit down, we'll talk some more," Artie pleaded.

"Yeah, there's a big difference between taking a picture and making a film," Jim added. "Let us tell you what it's like to make a film."

Suddenly Marilyn was angry. These two baldies were going to tell *her* about making a film? She could tell *them* about how a film is made. They thought she was a naïve kid, a dumb chick they could dazzle by waving stars in front of her eyes. She'd show them.

"All right," Marilyn said, sitting back down. "First of all, how much are you paying?"

"For you? Maybe twenty-five hundred. That's five, maybe ten times more than we've ever paid a lady before," Artie said proudly.

"No way!" Marilyn said, and Jim and Artie both heard the scorn in her voice.

"All right, then. How much do you want?" Jim asked.

"At least twice that much, probably more," Marilyn said, suddenly realizing that she had entered a game of "Truth or Dare." What if they said, "Name your price"? What would she do then?

"You know something?" Artie asked, a bit angrily. "Girls, great-looking girls, have been happy to get fifty dollars to fuck in our movies."

"That was them, not me," Marilyn said. "Oh, and I'd have to have ten percent of the profits. Not the net either. The gross."

Jim laughed out loud. "Jesus, what'd you do, grow up in Hollywood?"

"No, but I know how it works," Marilyn said, and told them about *The Owl and the Pussycat.*

"Well, listen, it's been nice talking to a real live actress," Jim said with a smile that did not hide the ironic tone in his voice. "Tell you what. Give us your number and, as we say in the business, 'We'll call you.' "

After 30-minute featurettes like the notorious *Reckless Claudia,* the Mitchell Brothers had begun making 60- and 70-minute feature films. The brothers had pioneered both the featurette and the pornographic feature film in San Francisco, and now they had no choice but to keep making them. It wasn't just because films with a plot were easier to defend in court. The audience had come to expect films with a story line and characters, and felt cheated if they didn't get one.

Also, the pornographic features were drawing large audiences that, for the first time, included more than just single, lonely, frustrated men who were secretly scared of women. Middle-class businessmen and college kids had begun coming to the films regularly. And so, for the first time, had couples. They'd sit in the loge seats with their hands on each other's knees or thighs, or perhaps higher than the thighs, and they'd leave holding hands.

It made Jim and Artie and the inner circle feel good to see couples at the O'Farrell. They were no longer making films just for the horn dick daddies. Slowly but surely, their work was flowing into the mainstream.

The other adult theaters in San Francisco had followed the Mitchell Brothers' lead and begun showing pornographic features. Lowell Pickett and Arlene Elster at the Sutter were showing films that attempted to be both erotic and artistic. Alex de Renzy had run into problems with the IRS and had fallen into a rut trying to recapture the success of *Pornography in Denmark* by making pseudo-documentaries with couples romping around at staged orgies.

In plot, theme, and production values—especially sound, which they never did get right—the Mitchell Brothers' features were often as crude as their loops. But when compared with the absurd blue movies of the 1940s and 1950s, and to some of the truly vile films that were being made at the same time (a man rubs a broom handle with Vaseline and inserts it in a woman's vagina; three men gangrape a woman and finish the film with a golden shower, urinating on her hair and face), the Mitchell Brothers looked like the Elia Kazan of pornography.

Into their first features, the Mitchell Brothers wove a political message that was generally as sophomoric as the sex was coarse. In an early feature called *Inside the Flesh Factory,* George McDonald plays the co-owner of a bag factory that has just signed a contract to deliver $400,000 worth of grocery bags on a very tight schedule. (A bag factory may seem like an odd setting for a porn film, but the origin of the location is pure Mitchell Brothers. They were always in need of new locations; a friend who owned a bag factory said they could film there; they contrived a story about sex and industrial espionage.)

George and his partner tell the businessman who has placed the order that they need to hire extra help to fill it. "No problem," says the businessman. "I know a couple of girls who are looking for work. I'll send them over." Two angelic hippie chicks with long hair and colorful dresses arrive at the bag factory and George and his partner put them to work on the assembly line.

One of the women secretly sabotages a machine. She tells the distraught George that she has a brother-in-law who is an industrial mechanic and George begs her to give him a call. The brother-in-law arrives, checks out the machine, and says he can fix it, but it will take a while because he has to go to San Jose to get the part.

With nothing to do, the girls get to know George and his partner better—a lot better. The sex scenes involve all the positions and all the acts, including lesbian sex between the two hippies when George and his partner leave. The plot keeps staggering along, pausing to include more and longer sex scenes. The camera work is jumpy and distracting, the color is garish, the sound garbled, and the sex is repetitive.

The "wet" shots, the external "cum" shots that are as obligatory to pornography as infidelity is to soap operas, are a constant reminder that the film is about sex, that the sex is real, and that the true star of the film is an ejaculating penis.

"The origin of the wet shot was to show that a performer could come so he could get his next job," says Bob Cecchini. "I remember a director telling a well-known porn star, 'Okay, this time I want you to come inside her.' The guy looked up in disbelief. 'But they won't know I've come!' he said."

"They had to have wet shots," adds Debbie Marinoff, an art director at the O'Farrell, who later became Jim's girlfriend. "The old cum-a-roo shot was what paid off at the box office."

In every feature he appeared in, George McDonald played a sensitive young man who wanted to get to know, and to like, a woman before he had sex with her. That may seem less than earth-shattering, but in a world where a leading man's dialogue was confined to lines like "Suck harder, baby," it was something of a departure.

Before he had sex with one of the hippies in *Flesh Factory*, the character George plays sat down with her and told her he wanted to know everything about her. She told him about growing up in Wisconsin, the daughter of a pharmacist. George seemed genuinely interested and asked her a series of questions before they took off each other's clothes.

George's sensitivity paid off later when the woman, who had ended up liking him, confessed that she, her hippie friend, and her fake brother-in-law were industrial spies. There was nothing wrong with the machinery, she told George. She had removed a fuse. They were all working for the client who had placed the order for $400,000 worth of bags.

"He'll take over your business," the guilt-ridden young hippie told George. "He locks you into short-term delivery dates, and when you can't deliver, he comes with lawyers."

The woman replaced the fuse, George hit a switch, and the machine hummed with life. The women, George, and his partner work all night to fill the order and end up defeating the nefarious scheme.

Flesh Factory's underlying message is clear: Capitalism is rotten to the core. Business is corrupt, sex and women are tools to be used, anything goes.

The fundamental corruption of institutions is also the theme of *Wild Campus*, the film the Mitchell Brothers shot at Diablo Valley College, their alma mater.

The film opens with Dean Filbert, a fat, balding, middle-aged man, dictating a letter. "We pride ourselves in being the educational, social, and moral backbone of this community," the dean intones solemnly. "As you could see when you visited this campus, there was no indication of such immoral or uncivilized actions as violence or campus unrest. We are very proud of our students."

The secretary leaves and a young female student walks in. Dean Filbert discovers, as he reads her transcript, that she does not have much to be proud of, at least academically. She even got an F in pottery. The student leads the fuddy-duddy dean on and ends up on his desk, watching with a practiced eye as he performs cunnilingus.

"I could really get you in trouble for this unless you guarantee me a diploma," the less than innocent student says.

"You don't need to worry about that, baby," the dean replies. "I'll see that you get several diplomas if necessary."

Campus is as crudely produced as *Flesh Factory,* with the amateurish camera work, terrible sound, and stilted dialogue that was becoming the hallmark of Mitchell Brothers films.

For every foot of film that ends up on the screen in a Hollywood production, thousands of feet end up on the cutting-room floor. The Mitchell Brothers almost always shot one to one—every frame the camera recorded made it onto the screen. That led to such unforgettable moments in cinema as the scene in *Wild Campus* in which George is talking to a lovely young lady who shatters any illusion that she might be a bashful coed by casually announcing, "Excuse me, I have to take a piss."

George follows her into the ladies' room and they proceed to have sex.

"George, what a cock you've got," says the actress.

"Mark," says George, feeding her his character's name.

"Mark," she says, and the sex scene proceeds.

After hundreds of loops and dozens of features like *Flesh Factory* and *Wild Campus* (*Behind the Green Door* was scheduled to be their 337th film), Jim and Artie were finally ready to do what Annie and Earl Shagley had wanted to do from the beginning: make a serious film. They decided to film a fantasy, a wise decision because fantasy not only opened up the possibility of more imaginative sex, it enabled the filmmakers to take a step away from crudely realistic sex.

Although they were still having fun cranking out sex films, Jim and Artie were starting to get bored. They were making better films than anyone else in the industry and they were making money, but that wasn't enough anymore. They wanted to make a *real* film, a film that was about more than just copulating.

"Up to that time, nobody had done a great porn movie," recalls Mike Bradford. "Jim and Artie wanted to be the first to make one."

Part of the brothers' motivation came from Jim's desire to show Annie and Earl, his departed friends, that he did not need them to make the film they had spent so much time talking about making together.

But proving something to old friends, or wanting to make a film that had pretensions of being art, was definitely secondary. Jim and his brother were gamblers. They had an urge to play for higher stakes. They wanted to up the ante, to risk everything on a roll of the dice.

To make a better film, the Mitchell Brothers knew they had to come up with a better story than the hackneyed plots of *Flesh Factory* and *Wild Campus*. They couldn't just pull an idea out of the air and cobble a story together. For the first time, they would have to have a script. And the script would have to be good enough to justify the time and money the brothers were going to invest in the film.

The crew got together in the room behind Stage A to brainstorm ideas for the big film. They had almost as large a stake in the gamble as Jim and Artie. The cash flow at the O'Farrell was excellent, but it depended upon a new film going up on the marquee every two weeks. If the film didn't change, the audience dwindled and so did the cash flow.

Jim and Artie were planning to show reruns at the O'Farrell while they produced their blockbuster. That meant the cash flow was sure to decrease. To help make it through the lean time when they shot the film, the crew had agreed to work for lower wages in exchange for points in the film. If Jim and Artie were willing to gamble on producing a first-class film, they were too.

"We'd been using a lot of fantasies, and I remembered a story called *Behind the Green Door* that had been passed around in high school," Mike Bradford recalls. "It was a typewritten manuscript that somebody had xeroxed. I told them about it, and Jerry Ward, Artie's old buddy from the Army, piped up and said, 'Hey, wait a minute! I read that in New Jersey!'

"We knew we had something because here was an underground story that two guys hundreds of miles apart had both read," Mike continues. "We both remembered the trapeze. That was the unique thing."

Jim and Artie had never heard the story, but when they asked friends in the industry, they discovered that the *Green Door* story had been floating around at least since World War II, when the anonymous manuscript was a favorite with GIs. Jim and Artie were encouraged by the fact that since there was no author, they did not have to buy the rights to the story. They had Mike Bradford and Jerry Ward rough out the story and then Artie and Bill Boyer, among others, developed a script.

Things had gone along quite smoothly. The brothers had rented the stately Alta Mira Hotel in Sausalito to shoot the scenes in which the girl is kidnapped. Mike Bradford was going to play a parking-lot attendant, Jerry Ward was going to be a bartender, other crew members were going to be desk clerks, bellhops, and extras. Jim and Artie would play the kidnappers.

And now a nineteen-year-old blonde had come in and called their bluff. She was the absolute perfect leading lady, but Jim and Artie had let her walk out because she wanted too much money.

What should they do? How much were they willing to gamble? Were they really serious about making a great porn film, or were they going to screw around and produce a more expensive version of their usual half-assed effort?

In a thousand different ways, some subtle, some not so subtle, Jim and Artie had been told they were second-rate from the time that teacher had kicked Artie out of the meeting for kids who wanted to be crossing guards. They were Okies, white trash from a town nobody cared about. Their father was a gambler, a profession everybody looked down upon. They had gone to schools that anybody could get into.

They had made it in the big city, but in a segment of the entertainment business that was still, despite the sexual revolution, almost universally regarded as degrading. Jim and Artie knew that pornographers were probably condemned to ride in the back of the bus forever. But that did not mean the boys in the back could not make a first-class film.

Going first-class meant trying to sign the innocent-looking blonde with all the moxie. Why not get her? It was only money. All money did was up the ante and make things more interesting.

Marilyn Briggs had been back in her small apartment on Potrero Hill for two hours when the phone rang.

"Hi, Marilyn, it's me, Artie Mitchell," said a twangy voice.

"And Jim Mitchell. We're both on the line 'cause we both need to talk to you."

Marilyn had put the interview out of her mind almost as soon as she left Stage A. It was just one more out of one hundred that had led nowhere. If you dwelt on them or tried to analyze what happened, you'd go crazy.

"What's up, guys?" Marilyn asked.

"We've changed our minds," Artie said. "We really want you."

"We're gonna give you everything you want. Within reason," Jim added.

"You are?" Marilyn said. "But, but I'm still not sure."

"Hey, everything will work out," Artie said. "Give us your address and we'll be right over to talk it through."

Thirty minutes later, Jim and Artie knocked at the door.

"We've got to negotiate the points," Jim said after they had sat down. "We want to be generous but we can't be that generous."

"All right," Marilyn said. She kept telling herself she should say, "Look, guys, thanks, but I can't do this, I really can't." But it was "Truth or Dare" and she felt she couldn't back out.

"Don't worry about a thing on the set," Jim said. "Artie and I will be there the whole time. If there's something that really bothers you, something you really don't want to do, just tell us and we'll work it out."

Jim produced a contract and Artie handed Marilyn a pen.

"I guess this is what it feels like to sign your life away," Marilyn said, looking at her copy of the contract.

"This is going to be an adventure, a great adventure," Artie said with a sweet smile. "And, oh yeah, we've even come up with a name for you."

"Marilyn Chambers," Jim said. "How do you like it?"

"YOU DID WHAT?" Doug, Marilyn's husband of a few months, said when she told him the news over dinner that night.

"I signed up to do a porn film," Marilyn said airily, fingering her beer can. "It's not a grooty old stag film. It's a fantasy. It's going to be very classy. You'll like the guys who are doing it. They want me to bring you to the sound stage next time I go so they can meet you."

"When did you do this?" asked Doug.

"Today," Marilyn said.

"Today! You didn't even tell me you were going to answer a casting call!"

"I didn't see the ad in the paper until after you'd left."

"But why? Why make a fuck film? That's what it's gonna be, no matter how 'classy' they say it is."

"Well, the money's good," Marilyn said. "And I think I could do a good job."

Marilyn paused.

"And?" Doug asked.

"And so what!" Marilyn said.

"Look, it's your body, it's your decision, it's your life," said Doug, who, married or not, did not want to intrude upon his wife's "space." "All I'm saying is, think about it first, okay?"

Marilyn spent most of the next two nights awake, doing just that. She knew she could break the contract. What judge would uphold a pornography contract? She was trying to figure out whether she wanted to break it.

From the time she was in second grade, Marilyn, the third of three children, had spent her life trying, unsuccessfully, she felt, to compete with her older brother and sister for her parents' attention. In all the family pictures, Marilyn is the young actress, mugging for the camera. Marilyn was convinced her older brother and sister hated her for it.

Marilyn's father was tall and handsome, the former captain of the Brown University track team who had gone on to become a successful advertising executive in New York City. Every workday, he got on the train at 7 A.M. and arrived home in Westport, Connecticut, after 8 P.M. Marilyn adored him, wanted his love and attention more than anything, but felt she got little of either. At home, he seemed tired and aloof and wanted to be left alone.

Her mother was a nurse who had graduated from Pembroke, a fiercely independent woman who worked because she wanted to, not because the family needed the money. She had kept going back to school to earn advanced degrees and had ended up teaching licensed practical nursing.

When Marilyn came home from school, the house was almost always empty. She would wander through the rooms, feeling lonely and abandoned, and finally collapse in front of the television. She would get up and dash to the door when her mother or father arrived, but the way Marilyn remembers it, neither delivered the love and attention she craved.

"My father is English and my mother's side of the family is Scottish. They're both very cold, distant people. Growing up, there was never a lot of 'I love you's," Marilyn recalled years later.

In school, Marilyn was fiercely dedicated to doing whatever it took to win her parents' love and attention. Her father had been an athlete, so Marilyn became an athlete, taking up diving and joining the track team.

"I was a high jumper, just like my dad," Marilyn says. "It was 'Come on, Dad, *like me!* Please like me!'"

By the time she reached high school, Marilyn's need for attention

and approval had grown to include her peers. She gave up diving—
it was very hard work, no one came to the meets, and the payoff was
years down the line—for cheerleading. Cheerleaders were popular,
and more than anything else, Marilyn wanted to be popular.

If you are a pretty, popular teenage girl determined to impress
people, if you get most of your ideas from *Seventeen* magazine, it is
inevitable that, sooner or later, you will decide to be a model. Marilyn mulled over her momentous decision and decided the first person she wanted to tell was her father. He was in advertising. He'd
be so proud of her!

"Don't do it," her father responded. "You're not pretty enough.
You'll never make it."

Marilyn was devastated.

"I know that he did that to deter me from that cutthroat, horrible
business, but the way he did it was wrong," Marilyn recalls. "I didn't
think he loved me if he could say those things."

For weeks after that, Marilyn pouted in her room. Her father
didn't want her to work in his world and her mother expected her to
live the life she had lived. "Go to college, dear; choose a career like
nursing you can always fall back on, dear; marry a nice boy and
have children, dear."

Marilyn vowed that was not the way it was going to be. She was
going to do something that would blow her parents' minds, something that would make them snap to attention and say, "Wow, Marilyn! We never thought you could do that!" She'd *show them!*

Without her father's help, Marilyn had some pictures taken and
put a portfolio together. She hustled up and down Madison and
Lexington avenues and did pretty well for herself, appearing in TV
spots for Pepsi and Clairol and a half dozen photo spreads for other
national accounts. She had even appeared in *The Owl and the
Pussycat.*

But her successes had not impressed her parents. They had kept
warning her that while the work she was doing was very nice, it
would never lead anywhere. When she hit the wall in San Francisco, they'd said, "We told you so. Why don't you come back home
where you belong and start college?"

Marilyn had given up trying to impress her parents and win their
approval. She was convinced nothing she did would ever be good
enough for them. And since she couldn't please them, Marilyn was

determined to defy them. So instead of going back home, she had stayed in San Francisco and married a hippie.

Now Marilyn had a chance both to defy and to impress her family in a way they would never, ever forget. This was her chance, really and truly, once and for all, to be her own person. Her parents had ignored everything else she'd ever tried to do. Let them try to ignore this.

Marilyn decided to go through with the movie. She convinced herself that it was a great challenge. She had heard somewhere that actresses in porn films chewed gum and sneaked looks at their watches while they were doing it. She was determined to bring the same intensity to her role in *Green Door* that Streisand had brought to her role as a hooker in *The Owl and the Pussycat*.

"I don't really think I knew what I was getting into," Marilyn says in retrospect. "It was a step into the world beyond. I knew it was going to be naughty, but I didn't consider it dirty or obscene. I thought I could make it erotic, sexy, and beautiful."

Jim and Artie gave her a script to read, but after thinking about it, Marilyn decided not to read it. She wanted her performance to be real. The best way to do that was for her to experience things for the first time, just as Gloria was.

"That's why I think the film hit," Marilyn says. "I lost my inhibitions on-screen at the same time Americans everywhere were losing theirs."

Mike Bradford walked into a drugstore at Twentieth and Texas streets and stood at the end of a line of elderly ladies who were waiting for the pharmacist.

"Hi," Mike said when it was his turn. "I'm making a porn film. We just got a new high-speed camera we're going to use to shoot some slow-motion ejaculation shots. Any idea what we could use for sperm?"

The pharmacist stared at Mike.

"Are you putting me on or could this, by any chance, be for real?" he asked.

"Oh, it's for real, all right," Mike said. "I'm part of the Mitchell Brothers' crew. You know, the O'Farrell Theatre?"

The pharmacist did know. A conversation that started simple and became increasingly technical ensued, and Mike ended up leaving with a large quantity of high-grade hand lotion.

From the pharmacy, Mike drove to Center Hardware at Fourth and Townsend, one of the last true hardware stores in San Francisco. Center carried everything from bath mats to commercial plumbing supplies and was staffed by old men who knew the location of every dusty washer. They loved Mike. He was always coming in for the supplies he needed to build sets, and he always told amazing stories and handed out passes to the O'Farrell.

"What can we help you with today, Mike?" an elderly salesman named Monte asked.

"Trapezes, Monte. I have to build trapezes and I don't think I can do it without your help."

"Mike! No! Trapezes! Oh God, I know what it's for, but, Mike, you go ahead and tell me."

"Here's what I've got so far," Mike said, carefully removing a drawing from a folder.

"Let's go in the other room and talk about your contract," Jim told George McDonald as he led him away from the commotion in Studio A and into the room where the crew brainstormed scripts.

George knew he was going to be playing a lead in *Green Door* and had been eagerly anticipating this meeting. George had appeared in 48 films, 18 for the Mitchell Brothers, and this was the first time he had ever been offered a contract. The brothers were really going legit.

There hadn't been much work lately. George looked down at the battered old Hush Puppies he had picked up at a Salvation Army store and let himself fantasize about how much Jim was going to offer to pay him. The most George had ever made on a Mitchell Brothers film was $350. He was hoping for $1,000 this time. With a grand, he could pay his rent and buy some decent shoes.

"I'm going to have you sign two contracts," Jim said, leaning against a window and looking down at George, who was sitting in a chair. "We're paying everyone a day rate, but you and Marilyn Chambers we're going to pay a flat rate. She's your co-star, by the way. You haven't met her yet but you will. How's two thousand dollars sound? Five hundred up front and the rest deferred for six months.

"Well, I . . ."

"Deferring the money is the only way we can do this," Jim interrupted. "This is really costing us."

"But, Jim, how can a contract be legal when the act we're performing is illegal? Couldn't it be used against us in court?"

"Fuck court. Let the lawyers worry about court," Jim said. "Now, because we're deferring most of your money, we're going to give you a piece of the film. How's two percent sound?"

George's head was spinning. He had asked the legal question to stall for time until it slowed down.

George half hated Jim Mitchell. He'd give anything if he and Jim could change places, if Jim could experience what it felt like to put on a gorilla head and fuck a girl and then have the crew and a bunch of Mitchell Brothers cronies laugh up their sleeves at you. But now, here was Jim offering George twice the money he was hoping for and talking about throwing in points too. Had George died and gone to Hollywood?

"You'll like the role," Jim said, trying to move beyond the numbers.

George's leg started vibrating.

"Jim, man, two grand, two points. Hey, man, that sounds great!" George said, and jumped out of his chair to shake hands with Jim.

"Okay, here's the thing. You're going to play a junior adman, so you'll have to cut your hair."

George loved his long black hair.

"Maybe I could just tie it up under my neck, Jim," George said.

"You're gonna get it cut," Jim said. "We've hired a stylist. And a makeup girl."

"Wow! We've never done that before," George said.

"And we're going to be shooting on location. At the Alta Mira Hotel," Jim said proudly.

"That beautiful old hotel?" George cried. "That's on the hill above my apartment in Sausalito!"

"We got it rented," Jim said with a big smile.

"Rented! Man! Going on location has always been more like a bank robbery than a film shoot. Leave the engine running, jump out, shoot the exterior, and make the getaway before someone comes out and asks what we're doing. We're finally going first-class, Jim!"

"We're going to shoot Marilyn checking into the hotel and then we'll shoot you coming into the lobby and watching her walk up the stairs," Jim said. "It's a really crucial scene because later you're in the audience at the highly secret sex club where members are forbidden to interfere with what happens onstage, no matter what goes down. You recognize her as the girl from the hotel. You know she's been kidnapped. You wait for the right moment, you rush the stage, pick her up and carry her out of there, and then you and Marilyn get it on."

"Sounds good, Jim," George said. "By the way, who's directing? You?"

"No. Artie's the director. I'm producing this one," Jim replied. "He'll get you a script in a day or two so you can work on your dialogue."

"Dialogue!" George said.

"Dialogue!" Jim smiled.

George walked out of the meeting feeling what he had wanted so badly to feel since the day of his first conversation with Jon Fontana more than a year earlier. He wasn't just a porn star who fucked for a living. He was an actor. A real actor.

The crew was set up and ready to go. The hairstylist and the makeup girl had worked on everybody. Extras playing bartenders and waiters were walking around with napkins tucked in the necks of their rented tuxedos so they wouldn't get makeup on them. Jim and his wife, Adrienne, had taken George McDonald shopping, and George, looking very convincing in a double-breasted blue blazer, gray slacks, blue shirt, and rep tie, was strolling through the lobby of the Alta Mira Hotel, waiting to play his scene.

On any other Mitchell Brothers film, the time it took for a scene to develop and the time it took to shoot it would be the same. But because this was their big roll of the dice, Artie was calling for take after take. The camera angle on Marilyn was right and then it wasn't right. When George played his scene, his expression was too serious or not serious enough. Finally, late in the afternoon, Artie said he had what he needed.

The next morning, George was reknotting his tie for the third time when the phone rang. An assistant production manager was calling to say the second day of shooting at the Alta Mira had been called off because Jim and Artie wanted to see the rushes before they continued. George decided he wanted to see the rushes too, so he put on the Levi's and cowboy boots he had bought with his up-front money and rode a bus across the Golden Gate Bridge.

When he walked into Stage A, George thought someone had

been hurt. Technicians were leaning against walls, staring at the floor. Other crew members were wandering around aimlessly, occasionally shaking their heads.

"What's going on, man?" George asked a crew member.

"Yesterday was a disaster," the crew member said. "The lighting was all wrong. Everything we shot turned out black. We can't use a goddamn thing. Don't go near the office, man. Jim and Artie are up there right now, fighting it out."

"You stupid fuck! Why are you such a stupid fuck? Why are you so fucking incompetent?" Jim yelled.

"You wouldn't have done any better, don't tell me you would have," Artie yelled back. "You've fucked up plenty of times but nobody makes a big deal out of it because they're afraid you'll fire 'em!"

"Name one thing, just one thing, you've done on your own for this company. Come on, Art, just one fucking thing," Jim said angrily.

"I brought Jerry Ward in. And Gish," Artie said defiantly. Jim Gish was an Army buddy who had served with Artie in Germany. He was calm and intelligent, one of the O'Farrell's most valued employees.

"All right, I'll give you that," Jim said grudgingly.

"And I'd do a lot more if you'd fucking let me," Artie screamed. "If you didn't insist on being the one in charge of every fucking thing!"

"If I don't, who will?" Jim asked. "You can't handle it, you sure as hell have proved that!"

"You know something?" Artie asked, inching toward his brother. "You can't handle it either. You can't shoot film, man. You don't know what the fuck you're doing. The crew freaks out every time you pick up a camera. They think your ideas are for shit. Every time you go out there, they're prayin' you'll leave before you fuck something up."

"That's bullshit and you know it, Art," Jim said, waving a hand at his brother with the same motion he used to flip away a fly.

"Bullshit? It's not bullshit!" Artie screamed. "They'd tell you themselves if they had any balls. And you fucking know it. You hired guys like Fontana so you'd never have to hear that you don't know shit about shooting a film."

"You're talking about balls? I can't believe you're standing here talking to me about balls," Jim yelled. "You fucked up, Art. If you had any balls, you'd admit it."

"You set me up, motherfucker," Artie screamed back. "You wanted me to fuck up so you could take over. Being in control, that's all you give a fuck about. That's all you've ever given a fuck about."

"Fuck you, Bob!" Jim screamed.

"Fuck you too, Bob!" Artie yelled back.

"When Jim and Artie got into a fight, I turned into a wimp like everyone else," Bill Boyer recalls. "It was better to let them play it out than to figure out how to go in with a suggestion. If you tried, you'd end up like the policeman who wades in to break up a fight and has both parties turn on him."

The Mitchell Brothers had grown to be adults and had gotten married, but they were eternal little boys, forever locked in a power struggle that grew out of the big-brother and little-brother roles that had been firmly established by the time Jim took Artie's hand and led him off to first grade.

Jim and Artie had become almost as close as Siamese twins. Together, they formed a more complete person than either one was alone. Artie was flamboyant, a blithe spirit whose bonhomie lubricated group interactions on the set and in the clubhouse. Jim was the quiet, serious businessman who had a hard time relaxing and having fun when his little brother wasn't around.

When you are as close as Jim and Artie, it is difficult—maybe even impossible—for one brother to see the other as a business partner, even though that's what they were. It is difficult to see your brother as a married man with a life independent of your own, even though he has a wife. He is forever your brother. You don't like him; you love him. You don't dislike him; you hate him. And because he is your brother, you never stop competing with him.

"They tormented each other daily," says Mark Bradford. "Jim absolutely loved Artie, and Artie absolutely loved Jim, but there was no in between, no understanding for what one or the other might be going through. It was a hundred percent one way or the other. When they were fighting, they were firing cannonballs. Usually the fight wouldn't last too long. One or the other would storm out and they wouldn't talk for a week or two and then it would be 'Hi, Bob' and 'Hi, Bob' and everything would be all right again."

In the end, Jim always won the battles. He was the older brother, and older brothers always win.

"The final decision was always Jim's," Mark Bradford says. "Jim would humor Artie, but if Artie ever really challenged him, it would turn into a fight and Jim would win and that would be that. Jim put Artie down because he didn't want Artie to be better than him. There was never any doubt that Jim was the dominant one."

"Art had the toughest job in the whole theater," adds Jack Harvey, nicknamed Fast because of his rapid-fire speech. A great handyman, Harvey has designed sets and has been adding rooms to the O'Farrell for more than twenty years.

"Art's job was being Jim's younger brother, playing second fiddle," Harvey continues. "That was the whole problem."

Jim and Artie had assembled a staff that was far more diverse and talented than any other group of people who had ever drawn a paycheck—or been paid cash—in pornography. Phil Heffernan, Mark Bradford's best friend from Exeter, had come out to be the theater's art director. Heffernan loved the job because he got to experiment and do almost anything he wanted, as long as he delivered on deadline. Jerry Ward, whom the brothers had recruited away from the Flamingo with the promise of a $500-a-week salary and $1,000 a week's worth of experiences, was the O'Farrell's general manager.

But all was not well. Despite the camaraderie of the crew and the good times in the clubhouse, the Mitchell Brothers' employees were not the big, pot-smoking extended family that Jim and Artie thought they had created. And that was largely due to the fact that Jim and Artie did not have the placid, equable relationship they had sold to the press.

Jim and Artie had become competitors, so it was inevitable that their employees would fall into two camps: Artie's people and Jim's people. If you had a choice, the camp you wanted to be in was Jim's.

"Art was my in, but when I wanted to bring Phil Heffernan in, I knew damn well he'd be a lot better off coming in on Jim's side than Artie's," recalls Mike Bradford. "So I introduced him to Jim, and Jim interviewed him and hired him. That meant Phil was Jim's guy, and they got along great.

"The reverse was true with me," Mike concludes. "Jim never liked me that much because I'd come in through Meredith and Artie."

One of the reasons Earl Shagley had quit was that he resented the arrival of Jim and Artie's old buddies from Antioch, and the tensions between the people who came from Antioch and employees who had been hired in San Francisco continued.

"When Jim and Artie got people who were smarter than they were, it made them nervous," says Debbie Marinoff, a young artist who took a job at the O'Farrell because she considered it the center of the San Francisco underground. "Jim would hire some of the best people from the Art Institute, people who were much smarter than he was. He'd keep them around because he stole their ideas. He got all his best ideas from other people. And when they intimidated him, he got rid of them."

There were other reasons why Jim and Artie had surrounded themselves with good ole boys from Antioch. When you are on foreign turf and under attack, as the Mitchell Brothers constantly were, it is instinctive to build a fort and fill it with people you can trust. The guys in the fort fulfilled the same function that kin had for J.R.: they were an extended family you could rely on in an often hostile world.

The guys in the fort were like the "Lost Boys" who joined Peter Pan in Never-Never-Land. In the fort, Jim and Artie could be bickering brothers forever and none of their buddies would ever tell them to grow up and knock it off. In return, the guys got to smoke dope, drink beer, listen to music, pick up girls, hang out, and occasionally raise hell. In short, they got to be eternal adolescents.

"George! I need to talk to you!" Jim yelled after he had stormed out of the meeting with Artie and double-timed it down the iron stairs.

"I'm taking over for Art. I'm going to direct," Jim told George.

"Okay." George nodded.

"We're changing the script," Jim said. "You're not a junior adman anymore. You're a truck driver. The next time we shoot, show up in your Levi's."

"That's cool," George said. "I'll feel more comfortable."

"And think of some truck driver dialogue," Jim said as he walked away.

Several days later, George arrived at Stage A at 7 A.M. to find it transformed into an exotic nightclub. Huge drapes and Persian carpets were hanging from the walls; large, overstuffed Victorian couches faced a stage. Trapezes hung over the stage and looming behind them was the ominous Green Door.

Two hours later, remarkably quick for a Mitchell Brothers production, the cast of about thirty had been made up, rhinestone masks were in place, black ties and gowns had been carefully adjusted, and Jim had yelled, "Action!"

Six women dressed in black robes like the witches in *Macbeth* led Marilyn Chambers onto the stage. The six weird sisters held her down, took off her white gown, and began making oral love to her.

Marilyn was terrified, and she wasn't just acting. She looked at the women hovering over her and couldn't believe that she was actually going through with this. On the other hand, what was happening was definitely titillating. It wasn't the things that the women were doing. It was the fact that she was the star of the show, the center of attention. There was an air of expectancy in the studio. Everyone was waiting to see what would happen next, and Marilyn found that especially exciting, because it was going to happen to her.

The camera panned to George, who suddenly recognized Marilyn as the girl from the hotel. (Jim had reshot the scene outside on the veranda of the Alta Mira; it was harder to screw up shooting in the bright California sun, and it was cheaper than paying to rent the lobby again.) The women led Marilyn to a huge black pillow in the center of the stage. They continued to suck on her breasts and perform cunnilingus, and then the spotlight shifted to the Green Door. The door opened and Johnny Keyes, an ex-fighter with a tight upper body, did a slow walk through the door.

Johnny was as black as Marilyn was white. White lines crossed his forehead and met between his eyes, which were also heavily made up. A bear-claw necklace hung from his neck and his muscular legs were sheathed in white tights that were cut away at the crotch.

Johnny was doing his slow matador's step to the center of the stage when Jim yelled, "Cut!"

"Would one of you chicks give him a hand?" Jim asked motioning to the six women who were holding Marilyn on the pillow. "We've got to get him up before he walks out of that door."

A girl named Candy jumped up and escorted Johnny back behind the Green Door.

A fluff girl! George thought to himself. In all the films he had worked on, this was the first time they had ever had a get-him-up girl.

A few minutes later, Candy ran back to her position.

"Action!" Jim yelled.

Johnny Keyes came through the door again, as erect as Dionysus on a Greek vase.

Johnny reached Marilyn and performed what seemed like endless cunnilingus. Marilyn tried to close her eyes and pretend he wasn't there and this wasn't really happening. Then she told herself: It's no big deal, it's like going to the gynecologist. But it wasn't like visiting the gynecologist and Marilyn knew it. She reminded herself that this was an adventure, that she was Gloria and that while Gloria had no say over what was happening, she didn't have to like what was happening either. A look of anguish crossed Marilyn's face and she looked around with eyes that were pleading for it to be over soon.

Johnny moved up onto Marilyn's chest and inserted his penis between her legs. He began taking long, hard strokes and Marilyn closed her eyes, winced, and looked away. Johnny moved further up on her chest and waited for her to open her eyes. When she did, he looked down at her, silently saying: I'm fucking you, I'm fucking you, look at me. It feels good, it feels good, it feels good.

Gloria/Marilyn looked away, and Johnny followed her eyes, silently insisting that she recognize him. Marilyn thrashed about and then the part of her that was resisting decided to surrender. She threw an arm over Johnny's shoulders. With that one movement, the passive Gloria/Marilyn was transformed into an active sex partner. Johnny lifted his head to kiss her and Gloria/Marilyn returned the kiss.

"Cut! Great scene!" Jim yelled after Johnny had his orgasm.

It was time for the big scene. Mike Bradford took a deep breath and lowered his trapezes to the stage. He didn't take another breath for what seemed like an hour.

Five men in white tights with the crotches cut out walked onto the stage. Three of them climbed onto the three trapezes and one man lay down in the middle, on the floor. Once again, the weird sisters appeared with Marilyn.

"Action!" Jim cried.

The sisters guided Marilyn down to the man who was lying on his back on the floor and he inserted his penis into her vagina. Marilyn had smoked a joint before the shooting started, it was no big deal, but now she felt like she was on an acid trip. It was happening, but strangely, nothing felt real. It all seemed to be happening in a dream. Because it was a fantasy, Marilyn was able, somehow, to distance herself from what was happening at the same time she was doing it.

She took the penis of the man on the trapeze in front of her in her mouth and, for a moment, was once again utterly amazed at what she was doing. I wonder how this is going to look on film? Marilyn asked herself. That caused her to shudder, and she quickly went back to being Gloria again.

Gloria/Marilyn began masturbating the men on the trapezes on either side of her. A fifth man scurried around, trying to find a position to suck her breasts. The weird sisters crowded around, trying to fondle her. Marilyn began stroking the men harder, anxious to see what was going to happen or to get the whole thing over with, she wasn't sure which.

"All right, everybody in the audience, start masturbating!" Jim commanded as he walked among the onlookers.

George was happy to fuck on cue, but no one could pay him enough to jack off in front of people. He pulled his shirt out of his pants, covered his lap, and faked it.

"Okay, go!" Jim shouted a few minutes later. "Girls, attack the guys!"

According to the script, the action onstage became so hot the audience broke into a spontaneous orgy that was started by superheated females who attacked the men. Two women rushed George. A tall, dark-skinned woman with long legs pulled him onto the floor and sat on his face. Another woman unzipped his pants and began performing oral sex.

"All right, George! The next time I yell, 'Action,' I want you to push your chick off, pull up your pants, and rush the stage. Gather up Marilyn and take her through the Green Door," Jim said. He paused for a moment, then yelled, "All right, everyone, ready! Action!"

George hopped into his pants one leg at a time, ran up, and

picked Marilyn off the floor. He raced for the Green Door and banged Marilyn's head on the doorjamb.

"Cut!" Jim yelled. "Let's try it again. And this time, take it a little easier on the star, okay, George?"

"I'm really sorry," George said after Marilyn had assured him that she was all right. "You didn't know you were going to be rescued by Don Knotts, did you?"

7

The Boys
Hit It Big

"SEARCHLIGHTS and ushers in tuxedos greet the sleazerati as they arrive at the O'Farrell Theatre here in San Francisco on opening night of *Behind the Green Door,* the Mitchell Brothers' latest and biggest film," a TV reporter holding a microphone and looking into a camera was saying as he stood under the O'Farrell marquee. "Marilyn Chambers, the star of the film, arrived just moments ago in a stretch limo, and it's no stretch of the imagination to say she left the crowd wanting to see more, which they undoubtedly will.

"Now, let me hastily add that when I say 'sleazerati,' I am by no means including the man standing next to me," the reporter continued, faking an anxiety attack as the camera did a slow pan up a very large man. "That trademark handlebar mustache of course belongs to none other than Ben Davidson, the former all-pro defensive end for the Oakland Raiders. Ben, they tell me you have a role in *Green Door.*"

"That's right," Davidson growled.

"Ah, Ben, is it an, uh, action role?"

"What do you mean, 'action'?" Davidson barked.

"Ah, you know, Ben. Action as in action."

"Maybe you better come inside and find out," Davidson growled, pretending to pick the reporter up by the collar and carry him into the theater.

In his playing days, especially in one memorable game in 1968 when he used his helmet to spear Kansas City Chiefs quarterback Len Dawson in the back, Ben Davidson epitomized the Oakland Raiders. Back then, the Raiders were the outlaws of professional football and Davidson was the bad-assed leader of the defense, a give-no-quarter player whose attitude was: If you can't take it, get the hell off the field.

Davidson was now the proprietor of the ironically named Gentle Ben's, an upscale bar in Danville, a wealthy community in Contra Costa County. Davidson thought it would be a kick to appear in a porn film—in a nonsex role—and agreed to play the bouncer who guards the Green Door and intimidates visitors by squeezing a football until it explodes. Jim and Artie were elated. With Davidson they had two hooks for their film—a fresh young starlet who looked as if she could play Wimbledon and a gnarled NFL veteran who looked as if he could have been in the ring with John L. Sullivan.

Inside, the O'Farrell lobby had taken on the look of a huge living room. An antique barber chair sat in one corner and a large saltwater aquarium took up most of one wall. Artie and Jim were wearing tuxedos, and the younger brother was everywhere, hugging someone over here, bursting into laughter over there.

Because of where they were and the kind of film they were going to see, the 200 people crowded into the lobby that night had a license to get loaded and overindulge. Waiters circulated with silver trays full of champagne and people were snatching the glasses so fast the waiters didn't have time to lower the trays.

The shift from the communal 1960s to the hedonistic 1970s was evident in the drugs that were being consumed. In the lobby, somebody would fire up a green "house joint"—compliments of the Mitchell Brothers—take a couple of hits, and hand it to the person standing next to him. Then he'd turn around and get handed another green joint. Meanwhile, the true insiders, the ultra-hip who could afford to, were disappearing into washrooms and reappearing with flecks of white powder under their noses.

George McDonald arrived with his girlfriend, Gunilla, a nursing student from Sweden. He had met the classic Scandinavian beauty on the street in Sausalito and charmed her with small talk. Smokey, George's roommate, had also come along. Smokey was from Florida, a former biker who had been so messed up on drugs when the police raided the biker clubhouse that he had collapsed face down in a mud puddle. The cops had charged the bikers with resisting arrest and Smokey had used TV footage of himself passing out to beat the charge. Now he was working as a sound man on pornographic films.

Fat Larry, George's attorney friend, completed the McDonald party. Six feet two and 300 pounds, Fat Larry was a brilliant attorney who had edited the *Law Review* as a student at Hastings, the University of California law school. Unfortunately, his drug lust was even larger than his appetite for food, and his practice was going downhill faster than a semi truck with burned-out brakes.

To get prepped for George's big night, George, Smokey, and Fat Larry had snorted some crank, or methamphetamine. When the crank kicked in and they were feeling hot-wired, they had eaten a rather alarming quantity of clear-light LSD. Then they had all hopped into Fat Larry's big black Lincoln and cruised to the O'Farrell. Within moments of entering the lobby, Smokey and Fat Larry were on their hands and knees, searching the carpet for a joint they had finished in the Lincoln.

The premiere was supposed to start at exactly 9 P.M. It was already after ten, but no one had noticed. Guests who were still able to remember why they were there were in no hurry to stop the fun to see a movie.

But Bob Cecchini, loyal employee that he was, began to get edgy. This was a big night for the Mitchell Brothers, and Cecchini was worried that somebody might get so messed up on all the drugs floating around that he'd screw something up. Cecchini left the lobby and strolled into the theater to make sure things weren't getting out of hand. A few couples were sitting together talking, and in a side aisle a couple was screwing.

Maybe I should tell them to stop, Cecchini thought to himself. What if there's a cop here with one of those infrared cameras? They'd sure make a great picture. Then he calmed himself. There aren't any cops here, Cecchini told himself. Reporters from every newspaper and television station in town were out in the lobby with a slew of important attorneys and big-time nightclub owners. Taking down the O'Farrell tonight would be like shutting down a club on Bourbon Street in the middle of Mardi Gras. The cops were dumb, but not that dumb.

Cecchini walked up to the projection room, where crew members were hanging out with the ever-affable Vince Stanich. An aging hipster with a pompadour and a thin mustache, Vince was usually an isle of calm. Tonight, he was worried and distracted, picking up the phone every few minutes to call the film lab.

"They're going crazy at the lab, trying to add things at the last minute to the sound track," Vince told Cecchini. "Every time I call they say, 'Don't worry, the film is on the way.' But the film ain't here, and it ain't gettin' any earlier."

Finally, a courier arrived with three canisters of film. Vince grabbed the canister marked "Reel No. 1" and threaded it into the projector. Somebody downstairs in the lobby flicked the lights off and on, and the drug-sated opening-nighters filed into the theater.

George McDonald had made a point of never seeing any of his films. He was afraid that if he had an image of himself up on the screen that was larger than life, the next time he closed his eyes on the set that image would flash into his mind and cripple his performance. Tonight especially, George did not want to see himself in action. He was very nervous and he was tripping on acid. What if he went in and the George on the screen turned into the gorilla from *Reckless Claudia*?

This was the biggest night of George's career. If any film was going to catapult him to stardom, it would be *Green Door*. If it bombed, it wouldn't be long before he was back in those Salvation Army Hush Puppies.

George picked up a full glass of champagne, lit a cigarette, sat down on a couch, and waited for the film to end.

Green Door was half over when a woman wearing an elegant black dress came out of the theater. She was tall, thin, and handsome, in her late thirties or early forties, with long salt-and-pepper hair and, George noticed, nicely defined calves. He immediately pegged her as a Pacific Heights socialite, the type he saw in Sausalito every day, having lunch.

"You! It's you! I just saw you in there," the lady said when she spotted George.

"How's the film?" George asked.

"I found it very disturbing," the lady replied.

"Oh, hey, I'm real sorry," George said. "A lot of people have that reaction. This kind of thing isn't for everyone."

"I left my son in there," the lady said. "I am really very disturbed."

"Well, jeez, I am sorry," George said. "Nobody means to offend."

The woman stood over George and hiked her black dress up to her hips. George saw she was wearing panty hose over black bikini underpants.

"I'm not disturbed *that way*," the lady said, lowering herself onto George's lap. "I'm disturbed *this way*."

The lady began to rock back and forth on George's Levi's. George looked down and saw that he had an erection.

"I want you to fuck me, Mr. Stud. I want you to fuck me right here," the lady said, her voice full of determination.

"Here? No, really. I mean, not here," George said, gently but firmly lifting the lady's hips. "We'll upstage the film."

"I want you to fuck me!" the lady insisted.

George lifted her off and hopped off the couch.

"Another time," he said, flashing his winning grin. "Give me your phone number and I'll come by."

"Oh, all right, then, since you insist on playing the temperamental movie star," the lady said. She picked her small black purse off the couch, dug out a pen and a small pad of paper, jotted down a number, and handed it to George.

"I'll be hearing from you, then?" she asked.

George nodded and put the number in his wallet. The lady went off to the rest room and George walked outside to get some air.

Seventy-two minutes after *Behind the Green Door* began with Marilyn Chambers driving a red Porsche convertible up a winding road, the film ended and the ushers threw open the doors. George stubbed out his cigarette and returned to the lobby. Mellow jazz was playing on the sound track and his heart began beating very fast. Trying hard to appear cool, he leaned against a wall where people could see him and he could study their reactions.

"You were great!" said a man as he walked by.

"Fabulous!" agreed the lady on his arm.

"It didn't make a bit of sense, but I loved every second!" said a man, giving George the old thumbs-up.

"Long as it's hot, who cares if it makes sense, right, George?" echoed a tall man whom George had never seen before.

Didn't make any sense? What's this, didn't make any sense?

George wondered. He waited for the crowd to thin and then walked over to one of the ushers and asked how things had gone.

"Binky fucked up," the usher said, calling Vince Stanich by his nickname. "He was in such a rush to get the film up on the screen, he got the reels crossed. The sequence he showed was one-three-two."

George's head dropped. Tonight was breakthrough night. Representatives of every major media outlet in the city were here. And the Mitchell Brothers had blown it.

"Hey, don't look so down, man!" the usher said. "Take a look around! Everybody dug it!"

The usher was right. People were laughing and chatting, obviously on a high from the film, feeling very select, very hip, very glad to be there.

The happy crowd depressed George. Ultimately, nothing mattered. The Mitchell Brothers had screwed up the most important night of their careers. Of his career. And it didn't matter.

Only in pornography could you show a film out of sequence and have it not matter.

Even shown in sequence, *Behind the Green Door* doesn't make much sense. A crucial fifteen minutes had burned up in the developing soup at the lab. The 16mm film was grainy and sometimes blurred, and the sound, as was usual in a Mitchell Brothers film, was inept.

But none of that mattered. The *Green Door* reviews were sensational. *Playboy* called it "Catnip for young couples," and Arthur Knight in the *Saturday Review* wrote, "In terms of lighting, photography, technical experimentation and erotic content, it stands pretty much alone. It's sex as ritual, sex as fantasy, sex as it can only be in the movies."

In the first year it was out, *Green Door* played primarily in three theaters—the O'Farrell, another theater Jim and Artie owned in Berkeley, and a third porn house the Mitchell Brothers owned in Richmond, an oil-refining town north of Berkeley on San Pablo Bay —plus a few selected theaters across the country. Instead of changing the films every two weeks in the theaters they owned, the brothers had shown *Green Door* continuously.

It had cost the Mitchell Brothers around $18,000 to put *Green Door* on the screen—with deferred payments for the crew and actors, the total cost rose to around $60,000. Yet in the ten or eleven months it had been playing, the film had grossed almost $2 million.

But as the film approached its first anniversary, the box office numbers were beginning to slide. It was time to make another film, a film that would also star Marilyn Chambers.

On her way to the O'Farrell to discuss the new film, Marilyn was wondering if her parents would ever see one of her movies. They hadn't seen *Green Door,* of course. But they had certainly *heard* about it.

"Oh my God, Marilyn! You've ruined our image!" Marilyn's mother had told her not long after *Green Door* had premiered.

"What image? What do you mean? It's me who did it, not you," Marilyn had replied.

"Our friends are totally appalled, that's what I mean!" her mother had shot back. "We keep hearing 'Oh, you poor things, you're going to have to live with this!' "

Despite her parents' revulsion—or perhaps because of it—Marilyn had agreed to do another film. Doug had liked *Green Door* and they were both pleased with her performance in the film. She felt that she was the major reason for the film's success and that she had, in fact, accomplished what she'd set out to do. She had brought something new, something erotic, to the sex film.

Marilyn could act, and acting mattered, even in pornography. She knew that she was a sex fantasy up there on the screen. She knew she had to live that fantasy, to feel it, be it, get lost in it, so the audience could live it through her.

Sooner or later, somebody in Hollywood would notice that it took genuine talent to turn people on.

Marilyn walked into the clubhouse, and Jim and Artie jumped up from the poker table they used as a desk to give her a Mitchell Brothers hug. Artie got in front, Jim got behind her, and they squeezed her into a sandwich. Artie rolled a joint and Jim went over to the refrigerator and got Marilyn a Heineken. After the small talk was over, the discussion turned to *The Resurrection of Eve,* Marilyn's next project.

There were to be two Eves. The first, to be played by Mimi Morgan, a rather nondescript brunette, would be living with Frank Paradise, the hottest of the cool late-night FM disc jockeys. Frank becomes insanely jealous of Eve's friendship with championship fighter Johnny Keyes. Eve becomes so upset by Frank's accusations she rushes out and smashes up her car.

The Eve who emerges from major plastic surgery is Marilyn Chambers. Filled with remorse that is mixed with awe over Eve's new beauty, Frank marries her, and Eve settles down to become a happy housewife. But Frank is bored and strong-arms Eve into attending an orgy. The inevitable happens: Eve is disgusted by the first orgy, but Frank drags her to others and Eve gradually discovers she likes impersonal sex.

At an orgy that is Roman in scale, Eve breaks free of all restraint and has wild sex with Johnny Keyes. In the final scene, she tells the insanely jealous Frank their marriage is over.

"The story line in *Green Door* was a joke, really," Artie told Marilyn. "What made it work was you being so beautiful and experiencing things as you went along. This story is much, much stronger. There are real characters and you're really going to get a chance to act."

"We're real high on Matthew Armon, the guy we got to play Frank Paradise," Jim added. "He's done some Shakespeare down in Santa Cruz and he's got a great voice. He really sounds like a late-night DJ."

Marilyn was nodding her head and sipping on her beer.

"We'll be shooting in thirty-five millimeter," Jim continued. "We did *Green Door* in sixteen millimeter 'cause we wanted that grainy, realistic feel. *Eve* is really going to feel like a feature."

"Oh, you know what, guys?" Marilyn said. "I don't mean to interrupt, but I keep forgetting to tell you. Like two years ago, I modeled for the Ivory Snow box. I'd forgotten all about it till the other day. The agency called and said the box was going to be on the shelves any day now."

For once, Artie was silent. He stared at Marilyn, and then he looked at Jim. Jim looked at Marilyn, his face as blank as an empty wall.

"Tell us . . . again . . . what you just said," Jim said.

Marilyn repeated the story and described the photograph. She was holding a baby, gazing down lovingly into his adorable little WASP face.

This was the defining moment in Jim's and Artie's careers. They were always looking to put one over, always thinking about the next big score. And life had just handed them a piece of action that was beyond anything their father could conceive, beyond anything they could ever have dreamt up.

"Ninety-nine and forty-four one-hundredths percent pure," Jim said to Artie, his voice calm.

"The good little mommy is a very bad girl," Artie said with an evil grin.

Jim methodically gathered the papers on the poker table together. Then he uncharacteristically threw them in the air and screamed, "I DON'T BELIEVE IT!!!!"

Artie jumped up and hugged Marilyn and started running around the room, pumping both fists in the air like a victorious fighter.

"This is the killer! This is the all-time killer!" he kept shouting.

The Mitchell Brothers spent the rest of that day, and many days after that, on the phone. They talked to dozens of journalists and hired the most high-powered PR firms they could find in New York and Chicago. When the soap box with Marilyn's picture came out, they bought Ivory Snow by the crate. They had thousands of T-shirts and buttons manufactured with Marilyn's picture on the soap box.

"They really knew how to capitalize on something like that," Marilyn recalls. "When it came right down to it, what they did best was deal with the press."

Marilyn soon found herself in the biggest suite money could buy in the Plaza Hotel, doing nonstop television, radio, and print interviews. Articles began appearing with headlines like "Is She the Next Marilyn Monroe?" *Green Door* was playing at the World Theater in New York, where *Deep Throat* had had a spectacular run, and in hundreds of theaters around the country. Johnny Carson, America's ultimate arbiter of pop culture, was doing Ivory Snow jokes on *The Tonight Show*.

Procter & Gamble finally pulled the box with Marilyn's picture off the shelves and replaced it with a box that featured an idealized *drawing* of a young woman. (Twenty years later, Marilyn's box is a collector's item and the drawing is still on the box.) But it was too late. Marilyn Chambers was forever after "the girl on the Ivory Snow box," the perfect symbol of the mainstreaming of pornography. Marilyn was the girl next door who liked sex.

It always takes a few years for popular culture to catch up with the avant-garde, and, as the lines waiting to get into the World

Theater in New York to see *Green Door* demonstrated, mainstream Americans wanted to see pornography. What had happened in San Francisco during the 1960s was now happening across the country. Suppliers were responding to the demands of consumers; massage parlors, bars that featured topless and bottomless dancing, and XXX theaters were popping up in every city and town that was big enough to have a McDonald's.

The mainstreaming of pornography was one of the true social phenomena of the 1970s. Only a few years earlier, a young man from a state in the heartland or the Bible belt who wanted to see a pornographic film in a movie theater would have had to go to San Francisco, Times Square, or Sunset Boulevard. Now, even in a traditionally conservative town like Tucson, Arizona, where Baptist ministers were denouncing the spread of filth, the young man—and his date—could see a sexually explicit film in a theater downtown.

Acts that had always been considered deeply taboo in middle-class America—exotic positions (i.e., positions other than man on top, woman on the bottom); oral sex; group sex; lesbian sex; anal sex; sex between white women and black men and, far less frequently, black women and white men—were up on the screen where anyone eighteen or older could see them.

There can be no doubt that some members of pornography's new audience went home and tried to replicate events that had happened on the screen, and, in the process, they no doubt discovered that the spectrum of "normal sexual behavior" is far broader than they had been led to believe by their parents or high school health teachers.

One of the first to feel the effects of porn going mainstream was George McDonald. George was finally the star he had longed to be. At the height of *Green Door*'s popularity, he was getting stopped on the street or approached in a restaurant two or three times a day.

Like many a celebrity before him, George discovered that fame was not liberating; it was a burden. Every film star or famous athlete has bizarre stories to tell about incredibly intrusive people who barge into their lives. George's experiences were especially strange because, as George was finding out, in-vogue films like *Green Door* were bringing to the surface fantasies and sexual insecurities that had been deeply buried.

"Women would always go, 'OOOHHH, you did that?'" George recalls. "They tended to be less inquisitive, less verbal, and more physical than men. Sometimes they'd want me to take them to see the film. The idea was, we'd see the movie, then go some place and fuck.

"With men, well, when you talk about sex, you're always confessing," George continues. "Most guys wanted the notion that it was hard to get it up on demand verified. A certain type of guy wanted to kick my ass. He'd watched the film with his wife or girlfriend and she'd gotten turned on, and now he wanted to kick my ass.

"Strangers would sit down at my table in a restaurant and start describing a scene from the film and it was always the same. They could always have done it better. It was too bad I was such a bad fuck. If only they could have done the scene."

For a psychiatrist like Dr. Martin Blinder, porn becoming part of popular culture was a healthy cultural event. When fantasies and fears surface, people can examine them and better understand their own sexuality. But to an antiporn crusader like Charles Keating, the filth washing across the country was not only debasing what it meant to be human, it was unlocking demons that lurked deep in the human heart. Once released, those demons had the power to drive men to rape, molest, and even kill.

"Sometimes, I'd get accosted by the most venomous right-wingers you can imagine," George recalls. "They'd say, 'You're a dirty-movie star! You exploit women!' I learned that nothing I could say could change their minds, so I always just sat there and let them tell me I was responsible for the decline of American civilization. Sometimes I'd run across a real weirdo. He'd rag on me for a while and then he'd end up saying he hadn't meant to do that to his dog, it had just happened."

A cultural phenomenon of this magnitude did not go unnoticed, and heavyweight essayists waded in to explain, condone, or condemn the fact that explicit sex had become readily available in the capitalist marketplace. Pornography was no longer simply dirty. It was *important*.

In "The Pornographic Imagination," Susan Sontag saw the spread of pornography as further evidence of the collapse of the Christian vision that had once united the Western world, a disintegration that Matthew Arnold had mourned so powerfully in "Dover Beach."

"Perhaps the deepest spiritual resonance of the career of pornography in its 'modern' Western phase . . . is the vast frustration of human passion and seriousness since the old religious imagination, and its secure monopoly on the total imagination, began in the late eighteenth century to crumble," wrote Sontag. The "ludicrousness and lack of skill of most pornography . . . points to something more general than even sexual damage. I mean the traumatic failure of modern capitalist society to provide authentic outlets for the perennial human flair for high-temperature visionary obsessions, to satisfy the appetite for exalted self-transcending modes of concentration and seriousness."

Kenneth Tynan, the always exciting critic who crossed the critic/author line to write *Oh! Calcutta!*, a nude review that ran forever on Broadway, believed that if literature could give rise to feelings of sorrow and pity, anger, peace, love, and spirituality, literature could certainly arouse lust. Tynan did not consider hard-core pornography crude or dehumanizing. In his essay "Dirty Books Can Stay," Tynan called hard-core porn a peculiar art form "which is orgasmic in intent and untouched by the ulterior motives of traditional art." Hard-core porn should be judged on its own standard, which is to cause "physical enjoyment." Since masturbation is the "physical enjoyment" pornography most often generates, Tynan reasoned that it was the fear and hatred of "self-abuse" that drove pornography's critics.

"A century ago, when it was generally believed that self-stropping led to loss of hair, blindness and mental paralysis, I could have understood this attitude," Tynan wrote in his typically ironic tone. "Nowadays, I find it as baffling and repugnant as when I first encountered it, at the age of fourteen. The debating society at my school was discussing the motion: 'That the present generation has lost the ability to entertain itself.' Rising to make my maiden speech, I said with shaky aplomb: 'Mr. Chairman—as long as masturbation exists, no one can seriously maintain that we have lost the ability to entertain ourselves.' The teacher in charge immediately closed the meeting."

The prominent essayist George Steiner attacked pornography on the grounds that it was a totalitarian assault on the individual. There are no great characters in pornography, Steiner wrote in "Night Words," because pornographers have no love or respect for "the sanctity of autonomous life . . . the tenacious integrity of existence." Pornographers treat their characters like slaves who are commanded to "strip, fornicate, perform this or that act of sexual perversion. So did the S.S. guards at rows of living men and women."

Steiner believed pornography is most dangerously fascist in its assault on the last vestige of human privacy.

"Sexual relations should be one of the citadels of privacy, the night place where we must be allowed to gather the splintered, harried elements of our consciousness to some kind of inviolate order and repose," Steiner wrote. "The new pornographers subvert this last, vital privacy; they do our imagining for us . . . The images of our love-making, the stammerings we resort to in intimacy, come prepackaged . . . Sexual life, particularly in America, is passing more and more into the public domain. This is a profoundly ugly and demeaning thing . . ."

Marilyn Chambers's performance in *Green Door* became a lightning rod in the debate over pornography. Defenders of pornography saw in Marilyn's character a "nice girl" who discovers herself through sex. The more sex she experiences, the more she wants to experience until she emerges as completely liberated.

Opponents of pornography took exactly the opposite view. Marilyn's character is enslaved from the moment she is kidnapped. The acts she is forced to endure are designed to humiliate her and break her will, to inflict such deep wounds in her psyche that she will emerge from the sex club as a robot that has been programmed to say yes.

Jim and Artie loved the fight. Nobody knew better than the Mitchell Brothers that nothing sells tickets to a porn film like a good, hot controversy. They had struck a vein of gold that ran deeper than any that the thousands of 49ers during the gold rush had hit. Now they had to make sure the gold flowed into their pockets, and not into somebody else's.

"We're going to be partners," said the man who had introduced himself as Robert DeSalvo. "We're going to be partners, fifty-fifty, whether you want to or not."

Jim and Artie were sitting behind the poker table upstairs at the O'Farrell. They were dressed in tank tops, Levi's, and running shoes, staring at the two men wearing business suits who sat across from them.

"You see, you got no choice," DeSalvo continued. "We have your film. We have already made copies. We intend to distribute it. If we can get together on this, we'll both do nicely. If not, well, as I just said, we have your film."

"Gentlemen, we are not interested," Jim said.

"Not interested at all," Artie echoed.

"May I suggest you are making a mistake?" DeSalvo said.

"We've made 'em before, we'll make 'em again," Artie replied.

"Well, I think you should think this through very, very carefully," DeSalvo said. "We'll be checking back in to see if you've changed your minds."

"The mob!" Jim said after the two men had left.

"The fucking mob!" Artie said in disbelief. "It finally happened. We finally crossed paths with the mob."

"What do we do, Bob?" Jim asked.

"I don't know, Bob," Artie replied.

"Let's find out who they are."

"Good idea, Bob."

"Jim and Artie talked to people in the porn business and found out the people who had approached them weren't really Mafia; they were Mafia wannabes," Meredith Bradford says. "But that doesn't mean their decision to stand up to them didn't take a lot of guts."

It did take guts, and it was thrilling too. It was good guys against the bad, a chance to play war with real guns. And what made it especially exciting was that for the first time Jim and Artie were the good guys.

"Jim and Artie always reminded me of little kids playing fort in a playground," says Jack Harvey, the talented handyman who has worked at the O'Farrell for over twenty years. Jack is a dedicated family man who has remained fascinated by the goings-on at the O'Farrell without ever showing more than a casual interest in the product the theater sells.

"Jim and Artie would talk and talk and build castles out of air," Harvey says. "Air castles, I called them. No substance, just air."

Mostly, Jim and Artie's "air castles" were overreactions to actual events. During the energy crisis of 1972–73, Jim bought a four-wheel-drive Eagle van and had a diesel engine and extra fuel tanks installed. "It probably cost fifty thousand in the end, and as far as anything Jim would want it for, it was totally useless," Mike Bradford says.

Convinced the social order he had never really believed in was about to crumble, Jim became a survivalist, stocking the basement of the O'Farrell full of fifty-gallon drums of water, gasoline, and case after case of Honey Bee brand dried foods. Artie lacked his brother's paranoid streak and considered the hoarding ridiculous, but went along with it anyway.

"The survival thing was definitely a Jim kick," Meredith says. "Art would go, 'My fuckin' brother. He's paranoid. But let him do it. It keeps him occupied.' "

From Jim's response to OPEC flexing its muscle, it was easy to predict how he would react to the visit of the two men in suits. This was his chance to play fort for real.

"There was all this talk about gangsters trying to take over," Jack Harvey recalls. "I don't know whether it was true or whether it was the drugs. Drugs can make people very paranoid.

"But ultimately it didn't matter, because we fortified the place," Jack continues. "We put concrete in the windows so they couldn't throw Molotov cocktails in. We tried to seal the place up so they wouldn't have an easy lob in. And then they got guns, lots of guns."

Until 1973, the mob was involved in pornography only in an ad hoc, local way. Mobsters like Lou and Tony Peraino, who had made *Deep Throat,* were just two more guys in New York City who were financing pornographic films. Typically, the mob is drawn to enterprises where there is a huge cash flow—legal and illegal gambling, racetracks, union pension funds. They considered pornography small potatoes because the films were shown in only a few theaters, so the "handle" was small. Besides, pornography was a lot of work. You had to deal with unreliable people like junkies, and you had to keep cranking out films to meet the porn audience's constant demand for new faces.

But in 1973, at the same time the mob was starting to take a serious look at pornography because of all the XXX theaters popping up around the country, the U.S. Supreme Court came down with a decision that had precisely the reverse effect that Chief Justice Warren Burger had intended. *Miller v. California* did drive serious pornographers like Arlene Elster out of the business. But it also gave mobsters an opportunity to get into the business.

The crucial part of the Burger Court's decision in *Miller v. California* revolves around the phrase "community standards." The conservative Chief Justice and his allies on the court were upset that adult theaters, dirty-book stores, and massage parlors had spread from San Francisco and Times Square to Main Street, U.S.A. *Miller* was the Court's attempt to beat back the blight.

Before *Miller,* a local court could find a film obscene based on "community standards," but lawyers could appeal the case to a higher court where a national standard, however vaguely defined it might be, was used to determine what was obscene and what was not. In *Miller,* the Supreme Court declared, within its own borders every community had the right to determine what was obscene and what was not obscene. When it came to obscenity cases, every community was a duchy, free to write its own laws.

The ruling caused consternation to more than just pornographers like Jim and Artie Mitchell. Several days after *Miller* came down, the police in Salt Lake City closed a theater that was showing *Last Tango in Paris.* Jack Valenti, president of the Motion Picture Association of America, said that it was now impossible to determine in advance whether a film violated obscenity law because the Burger Court's ruling in *Miller* created "50 or more fragmented opinions as to what constitutes obscenity."

The Burger Court, said the New York *Times* in an editorial about the *Miller* decision, gives "license to local censors. In the long run it will make every local community and every state the arbiter of acceptability, thereby adjusting all sex-related literary, artistic and entertainment production to the lowest common denominator of toleration. Police-court morality will have a heyday."

After *Miller,* pornographers who did not have a hot film like *Green Door* on their hands, who lacked the money to pay attorneys, did not have the stomach to wage an endless war in court, and did not want to end up in jail, got out of the business.

"*Miller* made it all but impossible to distribute a film across state lines," says Arlene Elster, who is now running a commercial plant nursery in California's Sonoma County. "I knew the films would never get better if you couldn't distribute them, so I gave up and got out."

Jim and Artie had originally confined *Green Door* to the three Bay Area theaters they owned and a few carefully selected theaters across the country because they did not want to take on the feds. Getting busted for obscenity in a city like New York, which happened to the Mitchells when *Green Door* premiered at the World, was a hassle for a pornographer. But he could always hire attorneys and fight the case on the grounds of artistic or redeeming social value. And if he lost, it was a misdemeanor that carried a small fine, which he could always appeal.

What pornographers really worried about was *the feds.* If a California pornographer got convicted of showing an obscene film in a city like Memphis or Wichita—which, after *Miller,* was much more likely to happen than it had been in the past—and if the feds could prove the pornographer had shipped the film over state lines, the pornographer was in big, big trouble.

Getting busted for shipping an obscene film across a state line was a federal offense. It is much more time-consuming, and therefore much more expensive, to try a case in a federal court than in a local court. And if a pornographer got convicted in a federal court, he faced penalties that were more severe.

With people standing in line to see *Deep Throat* and *Green Door,* a mob guy didn't have to be Meyer Lansky to recognize an opportunity. The mob could distribute the films under the table, thereby taking the heat off the producers, as Robert DeSalvo had suggested to Jim and Artie. Or the mob could copy the film and distribute it themselves, which was also happening.

"*Green Door* was popping up all over the place. We'd find it being shown in storefront theaters in places like Phoenix," says Bob Cecchini. "We tried to stay ahead of it. I used to get on red-eyes and hand-deliver prints all over the country."

Eventually, the Mitchell Brothers got help from an unlikely source: the FBI. Agents visited the O'Farrell and told Jim they had evidence that Robert DeSalvo was distributing bootlegged copies of *Green Door.* If Jim and Artie were willing to testify, the government was ready to bring charges against DeSalvo.

"The FBI didn't get in because they wanted to protect anyone," says Bob Cecchini. "They might do that for Universal Studios, but they weren't going to do it for pornographers. It was just a way to get to organized crime."

Jim and Artie had a tough decision to make. Should they testify for the government, the same government that had been trying to put them in jail for years? Did they dare cross the mob? Even the wannabe mob?

The brothers finally decided they had to testify. *No one,* not the cops, not the mob, was going to drive them out of the pornography business.

"Their attitude was 'This is a low-level mob guy,' " Meredith recalls. " 'If we don't take a stand now, the big guys will roll over us.' "

The trial took place in a federal court in Houston, and both Jim and Artie were called to the stand—for the first time as part of the prosecution's case. The defense argued that no crime had been committed because copyright laws do not extend to pornography.

In a landmark decision, the court ruled otherwise. Pornography was protected under the copyright law. For the first time, pornography, the toad in the erotic garden, had the same protection as the precise and somehow coldly clinical descriptions of sex in John Updike's *Rabbit Redux*.

Despite the copyright victory, the problem of interstate distribution remained. Jim and Artie eventually decided that although huge profits could be reaped by distributing a film nationally, the money wasn't worth a term in the federal pen in Leavenworth, Kansas. Wisely, the Mitchell Brothers decided to create their own chain of theaters *inside* the state of California. At their peak, they would own eleven theaters, from the Bay Area to Orange County.

Most of the theaters were big, beautiful old buildings with baroque or rococo façades in downtown areas. Jim and Artie were able to snap them up at bargain prices because the grand old theaters were being abandoned as the industry feverishly built multiscreen complexes in the suburbs. Each theater was run by a manager the Mitchell Brothers trusted, and each manager called the O'Farrell every night between 12 and 1 A.M. to deliver an exact accounting of that day's box office.

But Jim and Artie weren't through with the mob after the trial in Houston. A few years later, Michael "Mickey" Zaffarano, a truly substantial mob figure, bought the distribution rights to *Autobiography of a Flea* before the Mitchell Brothers had started shooting the film. Zaffarano was an old-line mobster who was a captain in the Carmine Galante organization in New York City. He owned the D.C. Playhouse, an upscale adult theater two blocks from the White House, the Pussycat Theater in New York, and had an interest in several theaters in Southern California.

Zaffarano was under intense FBI scrutiny and the Mitchell Brothers eventually got out of the deal. "Mickey brought too much heat," Artie would say later. But it had been exciting to rub elbows with a real-life mobster. Jim and Artie went out to dinner with

Zaffarano regularly and listened with wide-eyed interest to the old man's stories.

One time when Zaffarano flew into San Francisco, the brothers arranged to have him picked up in a limo with a hooker waiting on the leather seat. Jim and Artie had paid the hooker to give the mobster a blow job on the ride into town, but Zaffarano declined. The back of a limo, even with smoked windows, was not a proper place for sex.

Then there was the time Jim got a call from a heavy in Chicago who had been stealing Mitchell Brothers films for years.

"I think his name was Murray," Jack Harvey recalls. "He came out to San Francisco to shoot a porn film. He had an Asian story and an Asian porn star lined up and then she left, wouldn't do it. So he calls Jim and says, 'I need an Asian porn star.' And Jim says, 'Wait a minute. Why should we help you out? You thievin' bastard, you're stealing films from us!'

"The guy says 'Look, I'm in a bind right now. You send me a porn queen and I'll never steal from you again.'

"That sounded fair. They sent [a porn star named] Jana over and made the movie. And I understand he never stole from us again. They made hundreds of thousands of dollars in profits off the sales of films to this guy."

"We have a very important announcement to make," Jim said, pausing for effect.

"I'm pregnant," Adrienne announced.

"Oh my gosh! Adrienne! That's wonderful!" Meredith said, jumping off the couch to embrace her.

"Hey, Bob, congratulations!" Artie said to a beaming Jim.

"When did you find out?" Meredith asked.

"Yesterday," Adrienne said. "You're the first ones we've told."

"This is so exciting!" Meredith said. "I've got all my maternity clothes packed away. I'll get them out tomorrow and you can come over and pick out what you want."

"That'd be great!" Adrienne said.

"You'll love being a dad, Bob," Artie said. "Having a kid, it's, it's, well, nothing else compares to it."

"So you've told me," Jim said. "Many times."

"If it's a boy, you've already decided to name him Artie, right?" Artie asked.

The two couples had just finished another one of Adrienne's fantastic dinners. They talked pregnancy and obstetricians and how after getting up three times a night to comfort a crying baby night after night, you begin to feel crazy. And then it was time for Meredith and Artie to leave. There were more hugs and kisses and congratulations at the door.

Meredith and Artie climbed into their car and Artie started the engine. He pulled the transmission lever down to D but kept his foot on the brake and looked over at Meredith.

"She's lyin'," Artie said.

"I know," Meredith replied. "She's already told me she had her tubes tied."

When Jim first met her, Adrienne was a legal secretary with a BA from Cal/Berkeley who was working for Dennis Roberts, one of the Mitchell Brothers' attorneys. The guys in the Mitchell Brothers' inner circle did not consider Adrienne sexy or even particularly attractive. She was flat-chested and rather plain-looking.

In short, Adrienne was the opposite of the women who appeared on the screen at the O'Farrell, and that was part of the reason why Jim was attracted to her. Adrienne was older than Jim, a serious, strong-willed woman who had a past.

"Adrienne had three children by her first husband," Meredith says. "She told me it was better for her because it was too traumatic fighting with her ex-husband, so she gave custody of the kids to him."

Jim wasn't looking for sex or excitement when he married Adrienne. Those things he had in abundance. He wanted stability, a quiet domestic life that was as removed from the O'Farrell as possible. Adrienne had provided that for him. An elegant dresser who loved to shop, she had filled their home with crystal and fine china, beautiful rugs and Scandinavian furniture.

Adrienne and Eleanore Kennedy, Michael's wife, another intelligent, socially conscious woman with impeccable taste, had become close friends. The Kennedys were frequent guests at Adrienne's wonderful dinner parties, and Adrienne and Jim and Meredith and Artie went to Eleanore's soirees in Pacific Heights, where they rubbed shoulders with radical-chic elite like Huey Newton, Jane Fonda and Tom Hayden.

Meredith and Adrienne spent almost as much time together as

Jim and Artie did. Adrienne loved to garden and was wonderful with Liberty and little Storm, Meredith and Artie's second child. She and Meredith went shopping and hung out at the O'Farrell together. On weekends, the two couples went to the Tivoli restaurant on Grant Avenue in North Beach and sat watching the passing parade, or they drove over to Sausalito and sat in the sun on the deck of the Trident.

There were problems, of course. Although they were "new" pornographers whose films were based on women enjoying sex as much as men, it is difficult, if not impossible, to be in a business where women are a commodity to be exploited *and* be a loving husband who has an I-Thou relationship with his wife.

Meredith and Artie got around it by being buddies. Jim's instinctive way of dealing with it was to find a woman who was as far removed from the sex-sated world of the O'Farrell as possible, a strong woman who could control him, keep him from being swept away on the currents of sex and drugs that ran through his life. But Jim was used to being in control, and he wanted to control Adrienne as much as he wanted her to control him.

When Adrienne moved in with Jim, he was sharing an apartment at Taylor and Broadway with Jerry Ward. Jerry was one of the few members of the inner circle who got along well with Adrienne. Most evenings, Jerry got home earlier than Jim did, and he and Adrienne liked to sit down on the couch and get stoned.

"We'd be in there having a good time and Jim would come in and get pissed off, so pissed off he passed a rule: Adrienne wasn't allowed to smoke dope until Jim came home," Jerry recalls.

The more Jim tried to control Adrienne at home, the more she tried to exert her influence in his world. Her attempts to call the shots in the male-dominated world at the O'Farrell earned her the enmity of the boys in the club.

"Adrienne became the classic wife of the president of the company," says Phil Heffernan, the Mitchell Brothers' art director at the time. "She walked around with this manipulative smile on her face that said, 'You do what I tell you or I'll tell Jimmy you're a fuck.' I really don't know what her role was, except to collect her salary and meddle where she wanted to."

"She had a level of authority at the theater that was completely out of scope with her ability," adds Mike Bradford. "She was your basic bitch, a whiner Jim could never do enough for. I think the world of Jim and I could never understand why he couldn't do better than Adrienne. It was particularly strange because he had a mother who has so much character. You'd think his taste in women would come from her.

"I think what happened was, Jim confused bitchiness with strength," Mike concludes. "Or he got a bigger dose of bitchiness with the strength than anyone could endure. Jim was right—Adrienne was strong. She was just of no use."

Jim could overlook his problems with Adrienne because his primary relationship in life wasn't with his wife, it was with his brother. But there were problems with that relationship too.

The brothers' closeness, sadly but inevitably, had caused them to hate each other almost as much as they loved each other. The Mitchell Brothers gave each other the strength to take on society's conventions, the cops, and the mob. Artie could always make Jim laugh. "Having a brother you're close to, whenever the going gets tough, we've got each other to talk to and laugh about it," Jim once said. "It's a lot easier having someone to goose around with and keep your spirits up."

But Jim and Art also made each other miserable. They were so close they had no perspective on each other, no way to detach from each other, no hope of understanding the forces that were shaping their lives.

Artie instinctively disliked anyone who came between him and Jim. He had been jealous of Annie, constantly needling her, calling her Mouse, which she hated, and taking shots at her work. Now Artie hated Adrienne.

Adrienne had a cackle for a laugh that drove Artie up the wall. She would laugh one too many times or say something that angered Artie, and he would start teasing her in his kidding-serious way until an annoyed Adrienne would plead, "Jim! Make him stop!"

Jim would keep staring off into space, as if nothing was happening.

At the same time, Jim was locked in a deep, unconscious rivalry with his younger brother, a rivalry that Adrienne had been quick to join. Meredith rented a piano because she liked to play. Adrienne bought a grand piano and began to take lessons. Artie and Meredith moved to a new, more expensive apartment. Jim and Adrienne moved to a new, more expensive apartment. Artie and Meredith bought the Tudor mansion in Lafayette. Jim and Adrienne scurried around and ultimately purchased an equally spectacular house with a wonderful glass atrium in San Francisco.

There was a push-pull, attraction-repulsion character to the Mitchell Brothers' relationship. They would get into a fight and go their separate ways and sulk, often for a week or more. If their estrangement lasted long enough, inevitably someone would say something disparaging about one brother to the other. Just as inevitably Jim or Artie would explode with righteous indignation and defend his brother.

"He's a hard man but he's a fair man and I love him!" Artie would say.

"He's got more guts than anybody I've ever met and I don't want to hear people talking shit behind his back," Jim would warn.

It wasn't so much his brother's character that Jim and Artie leaped so quickly to defend. From the time they were little boys, the brothers had been taught that no relationship in life was as crucial as theirs. Any kind of criticism made it seem that that relationship was failing. That triggered remorse over the endless head-to-head competition, or the fact that they had had a nasty fight. Remorse quickly changed to fear. Where would I be without my brother? Who would I have without my brother? How could I handle things without my brother?

Jim and Artie tried to mitigate the tensions in their relationship as best they could. They ignored each other's irritating habits, and made a show of keeping things equal. If Jim bought a new shirt, he bought one for Artie too. If Artie bought a new CB radio, he bought one for Jim too. They leased identical cars and owned the same boats. They kept themselves surrounded with friends and, more often than not, invited three or four couples over for dinner so that Jim and Artie or Adrienne and Artie would not start swiping at each other.

The precautions helped, but did nothing to curb the one-upmanship that was as basic to their relationship as love. Jim was always quick to give Artie equal credit for their success. But Jim never stopped competing with his little brother, never stopped striving to obtain something better than Artie had. Including a better wife.

"Jim was thrilled to find Adrienne," Meredith recalls. "She was like me, she wasn't from the theater and she had a degree, which to him was a very big deal. I never bothered to cook and she was a great cook and that was a big deal too, because *she could outshine me.*"

Where Adrienne could not outperform Meredith was as a mother. But that was being taken care of too, because now Adrienne was pregnant. Or was she? Adrienne started wearing Meredith's maternity clothes, but weeks passed and her stomach stayed flat.

"Things got more and more strained," Meredith says. "I didn't dare say, 'Adrienne, I don't believe you're pregnant.' But I couldn't help myself. I'd go, 'Have you been to the doctor?' She'd say, 'Oh yeah, I've been,' and I knew she hadn't. I knew everything she did, because we spent so much time together."

Artie, characteristically, was much more indelicate.

"Your old lady isn't pregnant," he said to Jim one day at the theater.

"You're just used to Meredith and Meredith's a pig," Jim replied. "She put on way too much weight when she was pregnant. Adrienne's taking care of herself."

Artie was the only one who had license to question Jim directly about Adrienne's pregnancy. The rest of the gang watched with morbid fascination and whispered about "Adrienne's baby."

"It was a little tough on the underlings," Mark Bradford says. "Half the camp is saying, 'Adrienne is pregnant,' and the other half is saying, 'Bullshit, bullshit, bullshit.' The months go by and the months go by and eight and a half months later, it's now clear that this woman is not pregnant. But the fantasy is being maintained."

"It went on and on," Meredith adds. "It got to be ten months. Then eleven months. I kept saying, 'What's the doctor saying?' She kept saying, 'He says it's just late,' and I'd say, 'But you're so small!' "

"Hi, Meredith. It's me, Adrienne."

Jim and Artie had taken a motorcycle trip to Los Angeles. Meredith thought she knew what was coming next, and waited for it to play out.

"I have some bad news," Adrienne said. "I went into labor last night and lost the baby."

"Oh no!" Meredith said. "What happened?"

"I took a cab to the hospital," Adrienne said. "I didn't want to bother anybody."

"Where did you go? What kind of hospital was it?" Meredith asked.

"A Kaiser hospital," Adrienne said.

"Who took care of you? What was the doctor's name?"

Adrienne gave Meredith the doctor's name, and Meredith jotted it down.

"Will you call Mae and tell her the baby's dead?" Adrienne asked.

"Ah, okay, yeah," Meredith said.

Meredith knew, but she had to be 100 percent certain. She got the number of the Kaiser hospital, and talked to someone in Admitting. An Adrienne Mitchell had not checked in last night. The doctor whom Adrienne mentioned had left the hospital staff eight months earlier.

That evening, Meredith answered the phone.

"Hi, Meredith, it's Adrienne. Did you call Mae?"

"I did call her," Meredith said.

"What did you tell her?"

"The truth."

"The truth? What do you mean, 'the truth'?"

"I told her there never was a baby, Adrienne," Meredith replied. "I said, 'Mae, Adrienne wanted me to call and tell you the baby died. But no baby died. I know how excited you are about Jim having his first baby, but there never was a baby and I'm not going to let you believe you had a grandchild who died.'"

"You bitch! I thought you were asking some pretty rude questions!" Adrienne shouted before hanging up.

That call marked the end of the friendship between Meredith and Adrienne. The Mitchell Brothers' inner circle talked about "Adrienne's baby" among themselves—"I remember Art saying to Fontana, 'You sucker, you gave them a cradle!'" Meredith recalls— but no one ever spoke to Jim or Adrienne about it.

"Adrienne and I did not speak after that," Meredith recalls. "We were civil when we went to Cannes, but it was very touchy. I was pregnant with Mariah and I was throwing up the whole time we were there. But Art and I didn't tell anybody until I was so huge it was impossible not to notice. We were afraid of mocking Jim and Adrienne by actually being pregnant."

"This is it! Tonight is *the* night!" Artie said, reaching into a wicker basket for another croissant.

"I'm having so much fun I almost don't want the film to go on," Marilyn Chambers said.

"Isn't that the truth!" Meredith Bradford agreed. "I miss the kids, but I wish this could go on forever."

Meredith looked around and still couldn't believe that she, Doug, Marilyn's husband, Jim, Artie, and Adrienne were sitting at a table outside a château overlooking Cannes and the blue Mediterranean. The château rental had been arranged by friends of Michael and Eleanore Kennedy who owned a château nearby. Bougainvillea and other exotic flowers were blooming everywhere, and the wonderful lady who cooked and cleaned house had just brought out a spectacular herb omelet.

After years of fighting obscenity cases in America, what a wonderful feeling of freedom it had been for Meredith to go down to the stony beach, take off her top and lie in the sun, with no one paying any particular attention. This, Meredith had decided, was what it meant to be civilized.

Meredith's Yankee parents had been horrified when she had first married a *pornographer*. In her imagination, Meredith had concocted all sorts of terrible scenarios about what would happen the first time she brought Artie home. And, of course, it had taken Artie all of five minutes to win them over.

Her mother loved Artie; he had such energy and he was so funny. In his new son-in-law, her father had found one of the few people who loved to fish more than he did. Meredith and Artie went back to Cape Cod every summer, and Artie and her father could never wait to get in the boat and out on the water where the bluefish were running.

This trip had been the best. Meredith had been nervous about leaving Storm, her baby, and Liberty, her two-year-old, with her parents. But other than the daily call to Massachusetts, which sometimes took an hour or two to complete, and the ongoing tensions with Adrienne, Cannes had been a wonderful holiday.

It had been a typically audacious move on Jim and Artie's part to enter *Green Door* in the world's most prestigious film festival. They had expected the entry panel to turn the film down, and when the panel accepted it, Jim had argued that they had to go abroad. Showing a film at Cannes was the fulfillment of a dream for the former San Francisco State filmmaker. He could forever thumb his nose at anyone who accused him of never making a "real" film. What could be more "real" than showing a film at Cannes?

Besides, Jim kept saying, there was no downside. If the French didn't like it, so what? They had still shown a film at Cannes. Who would have believed a couple of Okies from Antioch could do that?

But as each day brought them closer to the *Green Door* screening, Meredith grew more worried. She didn't want the film to bomb and spoil the trip of a lifetime.

"Wow! You guys look great! If the critics would review you instead of the film, we'd be sure of gettin' four stars!" Artie said when the three couples had gathered on the terrace to sip chilled white wine before climbing into the limo that was going to take them to the Cannes premiere of *Green Door*. With their tans and elegant summer dresses, Marilyn, Meredith, and Adrienne were models of the "health is beauty" idea that California represented to the world. Jim, Artie, and Doug were dignified in their new summer suits.

The theater was packed when the Mitchell Brothers' party arrived. They filed into their reserved seats in the rear of the theater; the lights went down and there was Marilyn, driving the red Porsche.

The film ended and the lights came up. The audience stood as one and turned to face the Mitchell Brothers' party. People stared and stared. The silence was terrible.

"Jesus," Artie whispered to Meredith, "they hated it! They're gonna grab us! They're gonna carry us out of here and string us to the streetlights!"

The silence continued.

"Do something, you fucking frogs!" Artie said under his breath. "Get it over with!"

Someone started clapping. Jim and Artie jerked their heads to see who it was. More people clapped, and then the entire audience was applauding.

"Bravo! Bravo!! Bravo!!!" echoed off the theater walls.

The standing ovation went on and on. Jim and Artie and Marilyn finally stood, and Marilyn, after raising her hand for quiet, delivered a lovely little thank-you speech in high school French. That brought even louder cheers.

"It was incredible in Cannes after that," Meredith remembers.

"The film was reviewed in all the local papers and there was a mob scene outside the theater every night. We were instant celebrities. We couldn't go into a restaurant without causing a fuss."

In 1878, Henry James, the master of the novel, published *Daisy Miller*. The heroine, Daisy, is a pure product of America, fresh, innocent, full of life and insouciance. She falls for an Italian nobleman and, against all advice, meets him in the Colosseum at night. The nobleman is a symbol of European decadence. He is so corrupt, and Daisy so pure, that their tryst is fatal. Daisy dies of cholera that had bred in the fetid pools at the bottom of the Colosseum.

Less than a hundred years later, things had turned 180 degrees. As *Green Door*'s triumph at Cannes showed, it was now Americans who were teaching Europeans—and the French at that!—about decadence.

Estimates are that *Green Door* grossed $50 to $60 million before it ended up on videocassette. Those figures could be wildly high, or they could be twice as large. There really is no way to tell. In pirated versions, *Green Door* played in theaters across America and around the world. People who bootleg films do not report their grosses to the IRS or *Variety*.

The Mitchell Brothers did not even know how much *they* had earned on *Green Door*. They had discovered their accountant was an embezzler.

Jerry Ward had become suspicious of the accountant and had done some research and discovered that a "substantial" amount of money—to this day, no one is sure of the exact figure—was missing. As was usual with Jim and Artie, the brothers had intuitively trusted the accountant because he was "a friend," a good guy who was on their side in a world where it was us against them.

Like entrepreneurs in any business, Jim and Artie were great at pioneering new markets because they loved to take risks. Also like many entrepreneurs, they were less skilled at running a business day to day because that was so much less interesting than rolling the dice on a film like *Green Door*. Standard business procedures had never been a priority in the Mitchell Brothers' world.

"Their accountant landed his twin-engine plane down in Mexico," says Mike Bradford. "Public accountants generally didn't have twin-engine aircraft, but Jim and Artie weren't businessmen enough to know that. The Mitchell Brothers always thought good management was spontaneous. With their accountant, they were just doing what they thought was right, which was to trust him."

However much he got away with, the accountant's betrayal hurt the Mitchell Brothers emotionally more than it did financially. They had trusted him and he had betrayed their trust. He was a member of the club and he had screwed his friends. A guy had to be a real jerk to choose money over friends.

Friends and having a good time had always been the Mitchell Brothers' highest priorities, and now that they had made it big, the brothers decided they were going to have fun in a big way. That was not as easy as it sounded. The snap had always come from doing things that most people did not dare to do. But now high school kids were having sex and stockbrokers were smoking dope on weekends. The Mitchell Brothers had to figure out bigger and better ways to go for it.

Joseph Campbell thought the secret to living a truly happy life was to "follow your bliss." Jim and Artie decided to follow their whims.

The brothers got interested in bicycles because Mike Bradford was a hot racer. The brothers had Mike order them the finest tandem bike on the market, but by the time it arrived, their interest had passed. They never even took it for a ride.

Guns were another toy. Bradford is an expert marksman who saved his money until he could afford a Feinwerkbau air pistol, which he describes as "probably the most accurate launching device in the world."

"It's really a beautiful piece of equipment, and when I told Artie and Jim about it, one of them went, 'Gee, we'd like one,' and the other said, 'No, we need two.' I arranged to get them two guns and I went up there and showed them how they worked. They were all excited and they set up a target in the office, but they got tired of it pretty soon and I don't know what ever happened to the guns. It was just a flash in the pan."

Cars were, of course, yet another toy. Jim and Artie had grown up in Antioch, ogling the cruisers as they rolled by. Now that they could afford anything they wanted, it was only natural for them to go out and buy the hottest, most exotic machines available on four wheels.

Jim bought big, powerful pickup trucks and spent a fortune adding customized engines and transmissions. He and Artie owned an

array of cars over the years, everything from matching 560 Mercedes sedans to a truly wild early 1930s Ford truck powered by a big
Corvette V-8, a Morgan, a drag-strip Corvette that did wheelies
when you popped the clutch, and a genuine Checker cab. When
they got tired of one vehicle, they sold it and got another.

Motorcycles were another interest that was triggered by Mike
Bradford. Jim and Artie sponsored Mike's racing career, and Jim
often went to see him race at Laguna Seca or Sears Point. Inspired
by what he saw, Jim bought a beautiful 750 Honda. He parked it
outside the O'Farrell and the bike was stolen. The police managed
to recover it, and Jim promptly brush-painted the entire bike a really
ugly Army green. He parked it outside the O'Farrell every day after
that, and the bike was never touched.

"Artie didn't want to be left behind, so in his own inimitable way,
he went out and got this shitty little 160 Honda he couldn't hope to
go fast on because he didn't want to go fast, he just wanted to play
around," Mike Bradford recalls. "He bought a can of white paint
and he brush-painted that fucker from the handlebars to the engine
and then he went out and rode it.

"We'd go for a ride every Sunday morning with motorcyclists from
all over the Bay Area and we'd stop at a cafe somewhere and all
these beautiful bikes would be lined up outside, but the one that
really stood out was Artie's little Honda.

"They both enjoyed those Sunday rides, but they never really got
serious about bikes," Mike continues. "It was never the activity or
the satisfaction of participation that they enjoyed. It was the people,
being involved with a group of guys who were into something that
they enjoyed."

Fishing was the one Mitchell Brothers passion that developed
into a serious pursuit. Jim and Artie had loved to fish since J.R.
taught them to tie on a heavy sinker and let the bait lie on the
bottom of the river until a catfish came by.

As soon as the Mitchell Brothers realized they had salt water in
their veins, they began accumulating boats the way they had cars.
Jim bought a sailboat called the *Manteca Peek* and eventually ran it
aground in the Sausalito harbor. He also bought a beautiful, hand-
made teak boat out of Hong Kong called the *Choy Lee*.

In time, the brothers decided they could have a second career as
commercial fishermen. They bought a 42-foot fishing boat and,
with the self-disparaging humor that distinguished them, named it

the *Bottom Feeder*. Trade magazines that covered commercial fishing began appearing in the office upstairs, and Jim and Artie began spending more time talking about nets and trawlers than they did discussing slow-motion cum shots.

"They were expected to be great San Francisco filmmakers and heavy political activists," says Marilyn Chambers. "What they really were was pool-playing, beer-drinking fishermen. That's what they wanted to be—fishermen."

Perhaps the only thing Jim and Artie liked better than fishing was throwing a party, and it did not take them long to discover their two favorite sports went together beautifully. After partying a night away at the O'Farrell, everyone would pile into the cabs and ride down to Fisherman's Wharf, where Jim and Artie would herd them onto the *Bottom Feeder*. The Mitchell Brothers and their friends would watch the sun rise over the Berkeley Hills as they were passing under the Golden Gate Bridge.

Sometimes when they were out fishing, Jim and Artie would start talking about the old days in Antioch. They had no idea why life had been so good to them and they knew better than to ask. A gambler never questions his luck.

Only one really bad thing had happened to them. J.R. had died in 1972.

J.R. and Mae were in high spirits because Storm, their second grandchild, had just been born. They were thrilled to be grandparents and had doted on both children. Meredith and J.R. had become exceptionally close because J.R. had spent so much time helping her take care of Liberty.

J.R. and Mae had gone out for a drive. J.R. had complained about not feeling well and pulled over. He suffered a massive heart attack and died there, parked beside the road.

It was always an event when J.R. visited the O'Farrell. The brothers literally would roll out the carpet that was reserved for distinguished journalists and give him the grand tour, going into every little detail of their operation. J.R. had always ended up holding court in the clubhouse, playing cards and telling stories. And now he was gone.

Friends who knew Jim and Artie casually saw only the happy-go-lucky princes of pornography. The people who really knew them knew that, deep inside, the Mitchell Brothers were little boys who could not get over their father's death.

Jim and Art could not pick up a deck of cards without thinking of their father. They could not go fishing without wishing he was on board. They spent more time putting together the annual J. R. Mitchell Lo-Ball Tournament at the O'Farrell than they had on most of their films.

Little boys are prone to breaking into tears, and years after J.R. was gone, Jim and Artie were still crying for him.

Georgia Mae remembers Adrienne telling her that "Jim started crying on an airplane once, he just missed his dad so." A girlfriend of Art's remembers a night during a vacation in Mexico when she came into their hotel room and found him looking out over the ocean, sobbing. She rushed to his side, put a hand on his shoulder, and asked him what was wrong. Artie shook his head and kept crying. Over and over again, he said, "I miss my dad. I miss him so much."

8

Real-Life
Theater

"NICKELETTES!"

"Nickelettes!"

"Nickelettes!"

It was midnight on a Tuesday and the O'Farrell was SRO, but not, as usual, with horn dick daddies. After fifteen hours of continuous suck-and-fuck films, the businessmen had picked up their briefcases and gone home and the old men had stumbled back to their sad rooms. On the way out, they had been surprised to see a line of freaks snaking down Polk Street and into the alley behind the theater, a line of happy, eager longhairs who had fallen by the theater earlier that day to purchase the coveted nickel ticket.

The freaks were a show in themselves. Women were wearing small tiaras and clinging velvet gowns they'd dug up at thrift shops. Men wore huge old double-breasted jackets with big lapels over shirts that had been hand-woven by campesinos in the Yucatán. And now they were all in the theater, passing joints and chugging jug wine, stomping their feet and yelling, "NICKELETTES! NICKELETTES!"

Al Rand, a lonely fifty-seven-year-old man who lived in a hotel near the O'Farrell and had played a dirty old man in several Mitchell Brothers' films, had found new life as the Nickelettes' mascot. Tall and bald, Rand roller-skated onto the stage wearing a straw boater and carrying a cane.

"Good evening, art fans! Thank you for your good breeding and patience!" Rand said, bowing deeply. "I shall now reward your courtesy by bringing out those dancing dolls, the one and only NICK-ELETTES!"

Rand pointed his cane stage right and roller-skated off as eleven young women, short and tall, skinny and fat, dressed in prom dresses and wearing outrageously heavy makeup, danced onto the stage singing, "Ain't we sweet, can we take a peek at your meat? / Now we ask you very confidentially, can we take a peek at your meat?"

"NICKS! NICKS!" roared the audience, and here and there in the crowd men stood up and mimed unzipping their pants.

The Nicks moved into "There's no job like a blow job," sung to the tune of "There's No Business Like Show Business," and then, to a loud roar, launched into their theme song.

"Put another nickel in, in the nickel bag of sin / All we want is hash and grass and ga-ga gin-nnnnnn."

The lights dimmed, the mood turned serious. Head Nick Denise Larson stepped into the spotlight. To the tune of "Leader of the Pack," she sang, "I used to live in a little town / People tried to put me down."

"Down! Down!" chanted the Nicks.

"So I went to where people were just like me / I went to Kook CITT-TEEE."

The audience leapt to its feet and delivered a long standing ovation. The bond was complete. They had all come to Kook Citt-teee to be freaks together.

The Nicks snaked off and Al Rand roller-skated back on. He was about to introduce the next act when an earsplitting roar came from backstage.

"Oh no!" Rand said, suddenly in fear of his life. "It's . . . it's . . . Awful Knawful!"

Rand roller-skated to safety, and Mike Bradford, dressed as Evel Knievel, roared onto the stage on a Honda 350. Mike raced toward a ramp that had an incline of about two degrees. At the last moment, he chickened out and hit the brakes. The audience booed.

"What do you want for a nickel?" asked the Nicks, who had suddenly appeared on stage. The audience booed again and the Nicks began throwing nickels at them.

Mike rode back into position and made another run at the terrifying ramp. This time he cleared it, achieving a height that might have cleared one of the wine jugs that were being passed around in the audience. Mike promptly gunned it, popped a wheelie across the stage, and did a stunt crash into a wall. The audience roared.

Next, Al Rand brought on Freaky Ralph Eno, a street performer and guitar wizard. Freaky Ralph put his guitar behind his back and turned around to show the audience the Colonel Sanders mask he was wearing on the back of his head. Freaky Ralph played a satirical song he'd written about the Colonel up there in chicken heaven. Next came the Bourbon Street Irregulars to do their trademark tune, an incredibly fast, demonic version of the "William Tell Overture."

A wry young comedian named Don Novello came out dressed as the character he would make famous a few years later on *Saturday Night Live*: Father Guido Sarducci. The band that became the Tubes, one of the most interesting bands to come out of San Francisco in the 1970s, did a couple of numbers. Al Rand judged a yo-yo contest. And then it was time for the films.

First came the twelfth chapter of John Wayne's 1930s adventure serial, *Hurricane Express*. Very campy, very high-tack. That was followed by several experimental films made by students at San Francisco State. And then "Let's Sing a Western Song" flashed up on the screen. The San Francisco freaks followed the bouncing ball and sang their hearts out.

"The stars at night are deep and bright / Deep in the heart of Texas."

The Nickelodeon was the creation of Vince Stanich, the O'Farrell projectionist, underground denizen, and genuinely sweet man. Vince knew most of the experimental and student filmmakers in San Francisco. The O'Farrell had the biggest X-rated screen in town and the 16mm equipment most of the filmmakers were using. Why not let them show their films one night a week?

Jim and Artie did not want to abandon pornography, but they did want to be more than just pornographers. In whatever ways they could, they had begun reaching out to the larger community beyond pornography. People might think their movies were dirty; you couldn't change their minds about that. But you could show them that the brothers who made the movies weren't meanspirited low-lifes; they were genuinely good guys.

Jim and Artie had begun hosting fund raisers for progressive politicians, and among fund raisers for social causes the brothers were becoming known as "the easiest touch in town." Along with other causes, the brothers contributed to environmental action groups and convicts' rights organizations. Jim and Artie had a definite affinity for men and women serving time behind bars. When you have been busted dozens of times for doing something you do not believe is wrong, you begin to believe that nobody can do anything wrong.

To show the community that the O'Farrell was anything but a sin palace, the brothers had commissioned artist Lou Silva to do an astonishing mural of a figure that was part monarch butterfly and part woman rising from a bed of flowers on the Polk Street side of the building. (That mural was eventually replaced by an exquisite mural of undersea life that Silva did in painstaking detail. Later, Silva painted another mural depicting life in a rain forest.)

And now Vince Stanich had come up with another way of going beyond pornography, while remaining true to the spirit of the O'Farrell. As soon as he told the brothers about it, Jim and Art had said, "Great! Let's do it!"

"We put together packages of experimental films, underground classics like *Reefer Madness*, rarely seen animated films, trailers of commercials, and generally the craziest stuff we could find," Vince says, explaining how underground theater started at the O'Farrell. "We charged a quarter at first and nobody came. We dropped the price to a nickel, called it the Nickelodeon, and packed the place."

The Nickelettes were the creation of two very live wires who worked at the O'Farrell. Debbie Marinoff, whose family owned one of the largest title companies in Los Angeles, had grown up rich in Beverly Hills. She had come to San Francisco to study art and had ended up working as the Mitchell Brothers' art director.

"I was a snob," Debbie says. "I hated pornography. I thought the Mitchell Brothers were total fuck-ups and I always wondered how long the kind of dumb luck they'd had with *Green Door* would continue. On the other hand, they were true revolutionaries who made things happen. They were the only people in the San Francisco underground who had the money and power to get something done."

Debbie's co-conspirator was Denise Larson, the cashier-receptionist at the O'Farrell. Denise had majored in theater at San Francisco State and was very serious about serious drama. Working at the O'Farrell paid her rent while she and her friends did experimental plays. One play was based on *The Diary of Anaïs Nin* and another, *The Erotic Neurotic*, was about Dracula.

"I was the receptionist-deceptionist," Denise says. "My job was to control the buzzer that locked and unlocked the door to the upstairs, and to lie to people Jim and Artie didn't want to see. My favorite was this guy who was always trying to set up a business meeting with Jim and Artie. One day he called and I said, 'They're not here. They're in Cannes, France.' And he said, 'They're always in conference!' "

Denise and Vince Stanich were living together, and one day Vince casually suggested, "Why don't you come down and do a cheerleader act at the Nickelodeon?" Denise liked the idea, but her co-writers in the theater did not.

"The two women I was working with said no," Denise recalls. "They were into high art. So I got together a group of women and we did it and it was really fun and we kept doing it. We never rehearsed and we let anyone join who wanted to.

"The Nicks became a scene, everybody wanted to see them," Denise continues. "I was still working on the Anaïs Nin play and one day somebody said, 'Why don't you forget that and do the Nicks all the time?' I thought: My God, how can they say that? I want to be a *serious artist*. Then it dawned on me: The Nicks were serious. They were a vehicle, a way of making a statement."

The Nicks' primary statement was a repudiation of pornography. They were innocents, virgins in residence at the O'Farrell.

"The Nicks were *for* women; the Mitchell Brothers *used* women," says Debbie Marinoff. "The bottom line was, we could not be bought and sold, which was the antithesis of what the Mitchell Brothers were about."

The Nicks loved to spoof pornography. If Marilyn Chambers could become a star by sucking and fucking, they could be stars too. It didn't matter if Denise was the only one with talent, if the rest of the Nicks couldn't really sing and couldn't dance, or if they were fat

—one of the Nicks, Priscilla, weighed 250 pounds. The amateurishness was the point!

The Nicks were serious about only one thing, being outrageous, and in that they succeeded. They satirized sex, marching onstage swinging rubber dildos and singing a song about "an itch I can't scratch and a libido to match." They poked fun at high-minded feminists who were too serious to get the funny part—the Messiah comes back as a fertility goddess and ends up being crucified on White Flower Day, a sales event at Macy's.

The Nicks even took on their mothers. They all invited their mothers to a special performance on Mother's Day, and came out holding huge letters they flashed up one at a time as they sang:

> **M** is for the million things she gave me
> **O** is for the rest of what she gave me
> **T** is for the thousands of things she gave me
> **H** is for the hundreds of things she gave me
> **E** is for everything she gave me
> **R** is for the rest of what she gave me

"Our mothers hated it," Debbie says, grinning at the memory. "They were mortified."

Years before performance art became a happening thing, the Nicks took performance art to the streets. One night, they put on Brownie uniforms and, over the little brown suits, strapped on the huge plastic tits Debbie Marinoff had ordered from a supply house in Hollywood.

"Growing up in Beverly Hills, I developed a serious tit fetish," Debbie says. "My best friend was Jayne Mansfield's daughter. It was tits tits tits everywhere. I never got them myself, so I suppose the Brownie/tit raid was my revenge."

The Nicks jumped into a van and drove to North Beach to make a guerrilla raid on the Condor, the tit capital of America, where Carol Doda performed night after night for tourists. The Nicks were determined to make a statement about the exaggerated importance of mammary glands.

"We made our point," Debbie says. "We did a number on the stage at the Condor after Carol went off, and then we went outside and walked up Broadway. Guys kept charging up to grab our plastic tits."

One night, the Nicks had a slumber party and were sitting around with their hair in curlers and their feet cozy in bunny slippers when they decided they just had to do their act.

Bolstered by the acid they had dropped earlier, the Nicks threw coats over their pajamas, crowded into a couple of cabs, and rode up Nob Hill to the Mark Hopkins, one of San Francisco's oldest and most snobbish hotels. They piled into the glass elevator for the ride to the nightclub at the top of the hotel and everyone went "OOOHHH" and "AAAHHH" as the elevator rose above the lights of the city.

"Ladies, please!" the elevator operator said sternly. "You are at the Mark!"

There was only a scattering of people at the tables and the band was going through the motions, waiting for quitting time, when the Nicks stormed into the room. The bandleader immediately agreed to play "Put Another Nickel In" and the Nicks did their act. They were scurrying back to the elevator when a purple-haired lady stopped Denise and said, "That was very nice, dear. Which sorority are you pledging?"

But the best raid by far was the one the Nicks staged at the opera. San Francisco prides itself on being a world-class city, the cultural equal of any capital on the Continent. An opera famous for lavish productions is crucial to that claim, and opening night at the opera has long been the highlight of the San Francisco social season. Each season, dowagers wrapped in minks and dripping jewels step out of limos and gracefully accept the tuxedoed arm of a retail magnate or a newspaper publisher.

The Nicks figured the opera was definitely ripe for attack. Debbie Marinoff, who uses women's clothes in her art, rounded up prom outfits and Mexican wedding dresses and added large amounts of glitter. While the Nicks were putting the finishing touches on their gowns, Debbie and Denise were plotting the raid with Vince Stanich.

On opening night, the Nicks jumped into a van Vince owned that had a big rainbow painted on both sides. Vince drove slowly down Van Ness and joined the limos waiting to pull into the carriage entrance at the opera. When the van stopped at the carpeted entrance, the Nicks jumped out and someone shouted, "There they are!"

Young men in coats and ties and 1940s fedoras with "Press" cards stuck in their hatbands came charging out of the press section.

They were the Nicks' boyfriends, and they were all carrying flash cameras. Flashbulbs popped and the "photographers" furiously reloaded to shoot the preening, vamping Nicks. Television cameramen caught the Nicks' act, and that night they appeared on all the local newscasts. The Nicks had done it. They were famous.

The publicity and the never-ending outrageousness kept bringing more freaks to the O'Farrell at midnight every Tuesday. People waited in line for hours to get in, and some who hadn't gone by the theater during the day to pick up a ticket showed up with counterfeited tickets. The Nickelodeon had been one big party from its inception, especially in the huge projection room, where the true insiders gathered to smoke dope and sample that night's chemical smorgasbord. There was always hashish around and often mescaline or peyote, which insiders like Mike Bradford used sparingly as a "toner."

But now drug use was escalating. The Mitchell Brothers were doing coke, as were many of the insiders and members of the audience. Lately, during intermission, freaks from the audience had been going into the rest rooms to shoot heroin.

Artie had attended a few of the first Nickelodeons and then had stopped coming. The Nicks made Artie uncomfortable. He knew that Denise and Debbie considered him a yahoo, because they did not try too hard to conceal it. After working on almost 350 porn films, Artie had grown used to having women do whatever he told them to do. And now, all of a sudden, here were the Nicks proclaiming that they were "free" and that nobody could "use" them, and flaunting the fact that they considered pornography, and the people who made it, stupid. The Nicks were putting him down, and Artie didn't like that.

In his own way, Artie was as controlling as his older brother. He had become a star in the underground, a free spirit and court jester, the living symbol of the O'Farrell Theatre. Except on Tuesday nights, when the Nicks took over. If Artie couldn't be a star and the center of attention, he wasn't going to make the scene. Tuesday nights became one of the few nights that Artie stayed home in Lafayette with Meredith and his kids.

Jim had helped the Nickelodeon get started, ordering equipment and arranging work schedules. But he, like Artie, had faded into the background. Denise, Debbie, and Vince didn't need Jim. The Nickelodeon was their show.

The more popular the underground variety show became, the more Jim resented its presence in the O'Farrell. It was his theater. He called the shots. And look what was happening. The freaks were running amok!

Jim and Artie talked about it and decided that from now on the O'Farrell was going to be theirs seven nights a week, not six.

"We're going to pull the plug on the Nickelodeon," Jim told Vince one afternoon. "We've got no choice. The drug use is out of control; we're begging the narcs to raid the theater. The crowds are too large; we're violating the fire code. We're trying to shoot *The Resurrection of Eve* and the Nickelodeon is interfering with the schedule."

Vince Stanich, characteristically, said okay and kept his mouth shut. But few employees in the inner circle bought Jim's reasons. They believed Jim had pulled a power play that was designed to reinforce the fact that they were part of an extended family. Jim was the daddy, and the daddy called the shots.

"What it all came down to was, the O'Farrell was Jim and Art's game," Mike Bradford concludes. "They were going to play it their way. If you worked there long enough, there came a time when you had to decide whether the benefits of being part of the family were more enduring than certain fairly shallow methods of managing."

The Nicks went on to play other theaters, and Denise Larson produced several full-length shows—*Anarchy in High Heels* and a version of *Peter Pan* in which Peter is a rock star, Tinkerbell is played by the 250-pound Priscilla, and the pirates are lesbians. In October 1982, they played on a bill at the Danceateria in New York City that included "the world premiere of Sire recording artist Madonna." But it was never the same after Jim closed the show at the O'Farrell. The anarchy, the sense that "we're stars, we can do anything," was gone.

Debbie Marinoff and Jim had become good friends, and she was dating Dan O'Neill, the brilliant underground cartoonist, whose drawings covered the walls in the clubhouse and who had lived, off and on, in the projection room at the theater. Debbie loved being a denizen of the underground, meeting artists and writers and filmmakers and watching theatrical people live their theatrical, screwed-up lives.

"We're so cool, we're not underground, we're underwater. We're not just culture. We're ultra-culture," Debbie was fond of telling Jim.

Debbie didn't realize just how "ultra," or how far underground—or underwater—the O'Farrell was until late one night when Dan O'Neill said, "Let's go over to the O'Farrell. There's a scene coming down you won't believe."

The theater was dark when Dan and Debbie arrived, but Dan tapped on the door and Jerry Ward suddenly materialized and let them in. An employee was setting half gallons of whiskey, vodka, and gin on the candy counter and another was busy with ice, plastic cups, and swizzle sticks.

Jim Mitchell had taught Debbie an important lesson. "When you don't know what is going on," Jim had told her, "shut up and watch. People won't think you're dumb; they'll think you're cool."

Debbie leaned against a wall and watched while an employee stacked pornographic magazines on a table. The Mitchell Brothers bought them for a $1.00 or $2.00 each and sold them to Japanese tourists for $10 to $15 each. Debbie began to wonder if tonight's activity had something to do with the Japanese.

For years, Japanese tour buses had been pulling to the curb in front of the O'Farrell. The tour guide would clap his hands twice, and the Japanese, who as often as not were accompanied by their wives, would file off the bus. They were orderly as always, until they spotted the magazines. Then they went into a feeding frenzy. Although slasher movies were legal in Japan, hard-core pornography was not, and the tourists eagerly stocked up, buying as many as ten magazines apiece.

When Japanese customs cracked down and began confiscating the magazines, the Mitchell Brothers had started stocking small pornographic magazines called "pocket pals." The Japanese were able to avoid the prying eyes of customs officers by stuffing the little magazines in their pockets when they walked through customs. The pocket pals cost as much as the full-sized magazines, and on every magazine they sold, the Mitchell Brothers kicked back $1.00 to the tour guide.

The Japanese always stayed to see a feature and, as far as Debbie knew, went from the O'Farrell to the next San Francisco attraction. But now it was after 1 A.M. Japanese tourists wouldn't be out this late, would they?

Sure enough, a few minutes later, two shiny new Mercedes tour buses with huge windows pulled to the curb and Japanese men in suits and ties climbed off. They were silent and serious and they scurried off the street and into the theater as quickly as possible. When the last tourist had gotten off, the buses pulled away from the curb and vanished down O'Farrell Street.

A makeshift box office had been set up at one end of the lobby and the Japanese obediently lined up in front of it. Debbie strolled by and saw that whatever was going to happen, it was expensive. The Japanese were paying $15 a head.

After they had paid their admission, the men stocked up on magazines and some of them purchased a drink before going into the theater. O'Neill motioned for Debbie to follow him up the stairs, and they went into the projection room.

Debbie was surprised to see that the projector was empty. A couple of employees were fiddling with the lights. Vince Stanich was adjusting a spotlight. Somebody handed Debbie a joint and Dan O'Neill brought her a drink, and they walked up to the glass and watched the all-Japanese audience settle in.

The house lights went down, and rock 'n' roll came blasting over the loudspeaker system. A young woman in a miniskirt came bopping onto the stage, ripping off her clothes as she danced to the music. And then Debbie's head snapped back. A friend of hers named Mark had suddenly appeared onstage. Mark was carrying a camera and he began taking pictures of the woman. The more pictures he took, the more aroused he became. Finally, he ripped off his clothes, embraced the woman, and they fell to the stage.

It was a pretty standard sex show. The couple performed oral sex on each other and then went through a repertoire of positions before Mark had his orgasm and the woman faked hers. The Japanese clapped politely when it was over and filed out of the theater. The tour buses appeared magically at the curb, and within minutes they had vanished.

Debbie and O'Neill went back to the projection room and shared another joint with Vince. Jim and Artie were nowhere to be seen, but Debbie knew they had set this whole thing up. It wouldn't have happened otherwise.

Debbie had always affected a "You can't fool me, I'm hip" attitude. But now, sitting in a chair in the projection room, she was stunned. Not because of the live sex show; that had barely fazed her. She had had an epiphany. Debbie understood the Mitchell Brothers.

Jim and Artie had shut down the Nickelodeon, killing the most exciting theater in San Francisco, because it was "out of control." And yet here they were, running far greater risks to put on an illegal live sex show for the Japanese. If the cops stumbled in, they would padlock the front door and throw away the key.

Why had they done it? Jim and Artie didn't need the money, not after *Green Door*. They didn't need to win business with the Japanese. Japanese tourists had been pouring into the O'Farrell to see movies and gobble up magazines for years.

Debbie's epiphany was that Jim and Artie did it to do it. They hated authority. The live sex show was a weapon, a way of getting even. The more they got away with, the better they felt about themselves.

Debbie had thought that Jim and Artie had closed down the Nickelodeon because they weren't in control and it wasn't their scene. Now she realized that was only part of the reason. The Nicks, for all their high spirits and wild satire, were too tame for Jim and Artie. When it came to taking on the establishment, the brothers weren't interested in spoofs or fun and games. They wanted to get down and dirty.

"That was the first of many live shows they had like that, and they pulled them off with a complete nonchalance," Debbie says. "I never got over being pissed at the brothers for closing down the Nicks, but at the same time I loved their insanity, their ballsiness, their outrageousness."

The Resurrection of Eve was not the worldwide hit *Green Door* had been. Pornography was now part of the entertainment marketplace, and since it was no longer daring to go to a porn film, pornography was no longer chic. A large part of the huge audience that *Green Door* had attracted had apparently decided that if you have seen one pornographic film, you have seen them all.

But measured by any standard other than *Green Door, Eve* was a hit and Marilyn Chambers was established as the one star in pornography who had wide appeal. Linda Lovelace was considered a one-trick pony. Nobody was going to want to see her give deep throat again. Besides, Lovelace was mousy, vapid. Georgina

Spelvin, the star of *The Devil in Miss Jones,* was hard and cold, not really fantasy material.

But Marilyn was a kid. She could play the all-American, blond-haired, blue-eyed girl on a sex trip for at least another ten years. To keep scoring at the box office, all the Mitchell Brothers had to do was keep putting her in the right films.

"Hi, guys," Marilyn said one afternoon as she bounced merrily into the office. Jim and Artie, as always, jumped up and hugged her.

"I got some news, guys," Marilyn said after everyone had sat down. "I'm leaving."

"You are?" Artie asked. "You're taking a trip? Where you going?"

"No, I'm leaving. As in leaving," Marilyn said.

"Leaving town?" Jim asked. "You're moving?"

"Leaving, period," Marilyn said.

She paused before adding, "I'm going with Chuck Traynor."

"You're what???" Artie shouted.

"You're what???" echoed Jim.

The brothers could not have been more shocked if Marilyn had come traipsing in to tell them, "Guess what, guys, I'm really an undercover FBI agent and you are both under arrest."

"You can't do that, Marilyn," Jim said.

"It's already done," Marilyn said. "I've already signed the contract. Chuck is my exclusive agent."

"He's a scumbag!" Artie screamed. "A fucking Rasputin! You know how he got Linda Lovelace to give deep throat head? He hypnotized her to shut off her gag response. He'll ruin you, Marilyn!"

"No, he won't. Our interests are the same. He wants to handle a star and I want to be a star. He's got all kinds of ideas for ways I can cross over into Hollywood films."

"I can't believe you'd do this to us, Marilyn," Artie said, anger building in his voice. "We discovered you. We took care of you."

"Hey, it's not like I was some fucking charity case," Marilyn said. "You guys did pretty well selling Marilyn Chambers."

"You owe us, Marilyn," Jim said.

"You make 'owe' sound like 'own,' as in 'We own you, Marilyn.'"

"You've betrayed us, Marilyn," Jim said. "You could have at least talked to us before you did this."

"It's just something I felt I had to do, Jim," Marilyn said. "It's my career, not yours and Artie's. And hey, we can still work together."

"You owe us, Marilyn," Artie said.

"You'll have to talk to Chuck about that," Marilyn said, and stood up to leave.

Chuck Traynor did indeed hypnotize his wife and business product, Linda Lovelace, so she could perform deep throat oral sex.

"It's a trick I learned in Bangkok," Chuck says. "I saw it done over there and taught it to Lovelace. It's something like the sword swallowers use. I've got a degree from the American Institute of Hypnosis and I used a form of self-hypnosis to let her experience a pleasurable rather than a choking feeling."

Chuck is a self-described country boy from Homestead, Florida. He has always dressed like a cowboy, with boots, jeans, a belt with a big rodeo buckle, and Western-style shirts. He is lean and wiry and his face is windburned and deeply lined. The baseball cap he almost always wears covers his thinning hair. He will reveal almost anything about himself except his age.

"I'm over twenty-one but that don't mean nothin'," Chuck snaps. "Inside, I'm twenty-one. *All men are twenty-one.*"

Chuck speaks with a drawl he uses to hide a shrewd and calculating mind. After twenty-five years of crisscrossing America in the sex business, Chuck can go into a community and learn everything he wants to know by spending thirty minutes with the local paper. Not the news sections. "They're filtered through reporters," Chuck says. "You can't trust that." Chuck reads the classifieds. "The classifieds never lie," he says.

If the price of cars is down, that tells Chuck the local economy is down. Is the price of guns cheap? Are there a lot of openings for security guards? That tells Chuck the town has a crime problem. Are there ads for "artist's models"? If there are, the town is loose, because "artist's models are always a scam, they're ads for hookers." A personals column full of ads from single women is another indication the town is open (hookers again). A lot of personal ads from divorced women with children who are looking for a husband tells Chuck the community is fairly conservative.

Back when he was in the Marine Corps, Chuck won a three-division marksmanship contest. His prize was a date with Natalie Wood. After the Marine Corps, Chuck worked as a crop duster before getting into the sex business in South Florida the same way Jim Mitchell did in San Francisco: shooting stills of nude women.

In the late 1960s, Chuck opened a bar called the Las Vegas Inn in North Palm Beach, Florida, and hired topless dancers. He eventually married Linda Lovelace, a lonely, unhappy young girl.

In her pathetic but painful autobiographies, *Ordeal* and *Out of Bondage,* Linda says that Chuck turned her out as a prostitute and describes all kinds of physical abuse and degradation. In an age of victims, Linda portrays herself as the ultimate victim, a lost creature who has fallen under the spell of a modern-day Svengali and has fewer options than a Muslim woman married to a brutal husband in Khomeini's Iran.

Chuck doesn't really dispute the events Linda describes. He simply insists that Linda was a willing participant. Chuck had always demanded nothing less than absolute obedience from Linda, and after *Deep Throat* hit and she became a star, she was less inclined to submit and do exactly what he told her. When Linda became disobedient, Chuck began to think about getting rid of her.

"All Linda had to do was stay in harness and become famous, but she didn't do that," Chuck says with disgust. "Soon as we got to Hollywood, everybody started telling her what a big star she was and how I was handling her all wrong, and she listened to 'em.

"Women have serious cramps once a month because they deserve them," Chuck says before expanding on the metaphor he introduced when he used the word "harness." "I raise quarter horses, and these days they've got this little thing they put on a horse's neck to prevent PMS. I don't know why they can't do that for women, why we can't get these little things you can stick on their necks to make 'em work right."

You need not have passed Psych 101 to realize that Chuck Traynor is a misogynist.

"I don't believe that anyone ever signed a piece of paper saying that you can sell apples but you can't sell pussy," Chuck says. "I just don't believe that. As long as you do it fairly, there's nothing wrong with either one."

When you are selling the latter, sentiments like sexual love and fidelity are irrelevant. That is Chuck's major criticism of the Mitchell Brothers. They kept getting emotionally involved with "the product."

"Jim and Artie had reached a point where they didn't know where to go with Marilyn," Chuck says. "Maybe they were both in love with her but hadn't figured out how to make the move without pissing off the other. That probably fucked them up because the biggest thing you have to learn in this business is that possession and jealousy can't exist."

Chuck suggests that because Jim and Artie were human enough to be afflicted with passions like jealousy, they were less suited to the porn business than he was. "I always felt that you could screw my old lady and I won't care," Chuck says. "But if I catch you holding her hand under the table, I'll shoot your ass, 'cause if you hold her hand under the table, what you're trying to do is take away my management position, and I get real upset about that. You can drive my race car, but don't come around at night and try to steal it."

Chuck had approached Marilyn Chambers while he and Linda were still married. A theater in Florida had offered Linda a huge amount of money to dance nude, but Linda couldn't dance. Chuck had called Marilyn and tried to interest her in the gig, but Marilyn had turned him down.

After he and Linda split up, Chuck began pursuing Marilyn in earnest. Marilyn finally agreed to meet Chuck while on a trip to New York, and Chuck had a limo waiting for her at the airport.

Basically, Chuck convinced Marilyn Chambers that he, better than anyone else in the business, knew how to appeal to the eternal twenty-one-year-old lurking within all men. He told her that the Mitchell Brothers had started her on the road to stardom, but they would never take her any further. They were amateurs who did not see the big picture. To make it as big as Marilyn could make it—and Marilyn could make it very big—she needed Chuck.

Marilyn didn't just go for the business deal Chuck pitched. Within a year, she had divorced Doug, her husband, and married her manager. The wedding was held in Las Vegas, and the best man was Chuck and Marilyn's new best friend, Sammy Davis, Jr. Mr. Bojangles was a kinky little guy with an enormous thirst for sex, a thirst Chuck and Marilyn helped to quench, however temporarily.

Hard as it is to accept that any woman who has not been badly beaten as a child or had a lobotomy would marry Chuck Traynor, there are reasons why Marilyn Chambers turned herself over to him. Marilyn wanted to be a star, and young men and women who yearn to be stars are famous for overlooking a lot of abuse. That is what makes Hollywood Hollywood.

"Chuck was there because of my career," Marilyn says. "I felt I was using him to further my career, and he was using me to make money. That's show biz."

Marilyn did not think Jim and Artie were smart enough business-men to guide her to the fame she wanted, the fame that would show her family: "I did it!"

"They were always talking about some half-assed idea I knew wouldn't come off," Marilyn says. " 'Flakes' is a terrible word, but they were, in a cute sort of way."

But it went deeper than Marilyn wanting someone to run her career. She wanted someone to run her life.

Marilyn had become a queen in the most male-dominated indus-try in America (except, perhaps, for the Catholic Church). Whom did she have to help her make decisions? Not any of the women she had met in the business—they were jealous and competitive. Not her father—he refused even to discuss the business she was in. Not her ex-husband—Doug was a hippie who wanted to play his bag-pipes. Not Jim and Artie—they were flakes whose main job seemed to be smoking dope, going fishing, hanging out with the guys, and taking the occasional bust.

So when Chuck Traynor came along and said all you have to do is exactly what I tell you to do and I'll make you a star, Marilyn quickly said yes.

"I had a dominant-submissive relationship with Chuck," Marilyn says. "He was definitely the stronger one. I relied on him for every-thing."

Marilyn had left two hurt little boys behind in San Francisco. Jim and Artie did what hurt little boys always do: They hit back.

The Mitchell Brothers had their crew comb through the outtakes of Marilyn's movies. Then they spliced them together, added some interviews, and called the pastiche *Inside Marilyn Chambers*. Mari-lyn had no idea what Jim and Artie had done until the film was about to be released.

"I hated the film and I still do. It's supposed to be the story of my life, and it's not true. Jim and Art ripped me off. They felt I'd be-trayed them. 'How dare I not be loyal? How dare I go behind their backs!' I felt they'd betrayed me, and for many years, we didn't speak. Only when money was to be made did we start talking again."

———

It was 102 degrees in the golden brown hills outside of Livermore, California, and George McDonald, his penis lubricated with olive oil, was up in a glorious live oak tree, out on a limb with a new porn starlet named Gina Fornelli. George and Gina had just met, and one of the first things she had said to him was "I'm going to be a bigger star than Marilyn Chambers will ever be."

George and Gina were engaging in anal intercourse, for they were in the land of Sodom, where the god Anu, to prevent famine caused by overpopulation, had declared, "No man may violate a woman's cunt or they will face the penalty of death."

"You're hurting me," Gina cried.

"Want me to stop?" asked the ever-sensitive George.

"No, use more olive oil," Gina said.

While this was taking place, Lot and his daughters, who had just arrived in the vicinity of Sodom, were searching for fertile land to till. Lot paused under the live oak tree. Hearing a rustle, he looked up just in time to have a wad of semen splatter into his eye.

Sodom and Gomorrah went downhill from there.

In 1973, the justices of the New York Supreme Court had ruled that four films, including *Green Door,* contained so many "acts of sexual perversion, [they] would have been considered obscene by the community standards of Sodom and Gomorrah." With their typical "Fuck you, we'll show you" attitude, the brothers had decided to make a film called *Sodom and Gomorrah: The Last Seven Days.*

Jim and Artie were riding high after *Green Door* and *Eve.* They figured there was nothing they could not do in pornography, because they had already done so much. Why not *really* go for it? Why not become the Cecil B. De Milles of pornography?

This time out, the Mitchell Brothers were battling their own success. They had to make a film that was bigger, better, and more successful than *Green Door* or *Eve.* And they had to do it without Marilyn Chambers.

Jim and Artie decided they could blow everybody away by making an epic that went beyond the scale of any previous porn film. They were going to film a larger-than-life spectacle that would be shot on location with real sets, authentic costumes, crowd scenes, and innovative cinematography. They would break new ground by making a biblical epic that had *real* sex. When Jim and Artie were finished, Cecil B. De Mille would look like an old fuddy-duddy.

The Mitchell Brothers ended up spending between $450,000 and $700,000 on what may be the dreariest, dumbest, most unerotic film in the annals of pornography. *Sodom and Gomorrah* was supposed to solidify Jim's and Artie's reputations as filmmakers and forever lift them out of the porn ghetto. Instead, the film brought to the surface the considerable weaknesses of the Mitchell Brothers Film Group.

Too much money, too much power, egos the size of hot-air balloons, and too much cocaine, the same factors that have destroyed many a Hollywood film, are what turned *Sodom and Gomorrah* into the pornographic equivalent of *Cleopatra* or *Heaven's Gate.*

Jim was convinced he was a big-time filmmaker. He had had a hit at Cannes, and he was determined to behave like a heavyweight, no matter what it cost. He rented part of a ranch outside of Livermore and paid the rancher to tear down a barbed-wire fence because it would ruin the biblical verisimilitude. When the shooting went over schedule and the rancher couldn't get his cattle out onto the range, Jim had to buy extra feed because the people of Sodom were shepherds, not cowboys. He rented a crane for $500 a day because he wanted to take boom shots. He flew to Hollywood and went on a spending spree, buying props and costumes that had been used in biblical epics.

After years of shooting one to one, Jim, now the *auteur,* shot reel after reel of film. And the more he shot, the more the story got away from him.

"Twenty-seven hours of film were shot on a movie that doesn't go from A to B," Jack Harvey says, shaking his head. "A year of production and twenty-seven hours of film in the can, thousands and thousands of dollars spent on just unbelievable crap!"

When you are shooting a low-budget porn film, even a small-budget film like *Green Door,* you can take a slapdash, "what the hell, just do it" approach to filmmaking. You cannot be that cavalier on a big-budget film that calls for complicated scenes and a large cast. Jim and Art did not have a solid script when they started shooting, and they did not establish a template for shooting the film. No one in the cast or the crew was ever sure exactly what story they were telling, or what scene they were going to shoot next.

That led to constant indecision and turmoil, and the turmoil led to internecine warfare, particularly between the Mitchell Brothers.

Once again, Jim and Artie were behaving more like little boys locked in an eternal power struggle than like two business partners. They did not sit down and try to come up with solutions to problems. Jacked up on cocaine, nerves jangling and the veins in their temples popping, Jim and Artie blamed each other for the chaos on the set and ended up fighting like two bantam roosters. It was "Fuck you, Bob, you don't know what the fuck you are doing" and "Fuck you, Bob, you don't either."

Jim and Artie were too close to have ever taken the two steps away from each other that are necessary to gain perspective in a relationship. They had never developed the language needed to discuss their problems with each other. They would get into an argument, scream at each other, and, as often as not, get physical. Sometimes, they'd end up on the floor, wrestling; other times, they'd exchange punches.

When Jim and Artie were kids in high school, no one except their parents had particularly cared if they had a fight and didn't speak for a week or two. But now they were in charge of a major production. It was costing hundreds of dollars a day to shoot on location, and Jim and Artie were still behaving the way they had back in high school. They'd get into a fight and instead of patching things up and going back to work, the brothers would spend days ignoring each other or Art would jump in a car and take off.

Meanwhile, work on the film would come grinding to a halt. Then, for no apparent reason, Art would reappear and the brothers would act as if nothing had happened. Work on the film would resume where it had left off.

If Jim and Artie could ignore their problems, so could the cast and crew. *Sodom and Gomorrah* eventually evolved into little more than an excuse to throw the longest party in Mitchell Brothers history, and they had thrown some epics.

The *Sodom and Gomorrah* set was a small tent city built around a marketplace that had a large open fire. It was a long way back to San Francisco, and there was no reason to commute—the cast and crew could live in the tents. There were plenty of drugs, a smorgasbord of sex, and an abundance of good food because Jim felt that everything had to be first-class. Every day one of San Francisco's best caterers brought food out to the set. The bill was staggering.

Why make a movie when you can *live* a movie? Why do all that hard work when you can get loaded and get laid, and then get loaded and get laid again? Night after night, the cast and the crew and the hangers-on binged on booze, drugs, catered food, and non-stop sex.

When the brothers finally did get down to filming, the scenes were not nearly as vital and erotic as the sex that was happening off-camera. The sex in *Sodom and Gomorrah* was downright weird.

The Mitchell Brothers' reputation was based largely on the fact that women in their films liked sex as much as the men. But by the time they reached *Sodom and Gomorrah,* Jim and Art were burnt out on straight sex, no matter how many couples were doing it. So, as the sex-sated have done in other cultures and in other times, the Mitchell Brothers turned kinky.

But kinky in a crude, Antioch kind of way. In *Sodom and Gomorrah,* an anteater is thrust into a woman's groin. There are sex scenes featuring a banana and a giant zucchini. As punishment for violating Anu's laws, a man's penis is coated with honey and placed over an anthill.

"Flutie," a six-foot-ten-inch member of an urban commune who had shown up at the O'Farrell and been given a routine questionnaire, had answered "I can give myself head" to the question "Do you have any specialties?" Jim and Artie had immediately written him into *Sodom and Gomorrah.*

"This is where we went in the wrong direction," Bill Boyer says in retrospect. "There was a lot of pressure on Jim and Art to top themselves, and they tried to do it with gimmicks rather than attempting to make a serious film with nice, erotic, sensual sex. If a guy walked in and said, 'I can go down on myself,' Jim and Art said, 'Great! Let's put it in the movie!' even if the movie was half finished. If a woman said, 'I can take a zucchini,' it was 'Great! Write her in, she's now Lot's wife!' "

The nonstop party and endless filming came to an abrupt halt when the cast and crew awoke one morning to discover that Adrienne Mitchell, *Sodom and Gomorrah's* wardrobe director, had disappeared. Before long, someone noticed that Bram, one of the actors, was also missing. One and one made two: Adrienne and Bram had run off together.

Jim was deeply wounded and wanted to shelve the whole project. Losing Adrienne did not hurt as much as the blow to his ego. He was the porn king and his wife had deserted him for an actor. Actors were "meat."

Joy Horner-Greenberg, a former employee at the O'Farrell and, like Meredith, a close friend of Adrienne's until they had a falling-out, ran into Adrienne after she had left Jim.

"Adrienne told me she and Jim hadn't gotten along in a long time," Joy recalls. "She said they were always in some kind of power struggle. She wanted to be in control and he wanted to be in control and they never compromised."

In addition to power, there was another reason why Jim and Adrienne's marriage had ended up in the hands of divorce attorneys. After years of using women in films, Jim and Artie were using them in real life. It was much more complicated than simply finding a young woman attractive and sneaking off with her to have sex. Sex had become an exercise of power. It had become a tool to gain ascendancy over friends.

It had started with Jim before he married Adrienne, and it continued after he remarried and started a family. Artie's promiscuous sexual behavior began when he was married to Meredith and escalated over the years until, by almost any definition, Artie developed a full-blown sexual psychosis.

To many of the employees at the O'Farrell, Vince Stanich was the heart and soul of the theater. Vince was always steady and had a knack for saying things that made people laugh at themselves.

But when it came to hitting on his girlfriend, it did not matter to Jim or Artie that Vince was one of the oldest and most valued employees at the O'Farrell. It did not matter that he was one of their closest friends. It did not matter that Vince and Denise Larson were living together and were serious about each other. Jim and Artie both wanted to have sex with Denise, that was what mattered.

"They were both very much into the classic madonna-whore thing," Denise says, looking back on Jim and Artie. "They'd get married, have kids, and then they'd stick them out in Oakland or the suburbs. While the families were out in the suburbs, they'd stay late at the theater and have girls on the side. The women at the theater were their little play toys.

"If they couldn't have you, that made them want you more," Denise continues, referring to herself. "Artie kept coming on to me when I was with Vince. He was relentless. Jim came on to me too. We'd all gone to Hawaii together and he started calling right after we got back. Jim would call me right in front of his wife. He'd go, 'I know Vince is down at the theater. Can I come over?' I'd go, 'No!'

"Maybe he was trying to one-up Vince," Denise concludes. "After

Vince found out he was doing it, we didn't spend any time with Jim anymore. But the way things turned out, Vince's ultimate loyalty was to Jim."

Vince and Denise eventually split up. Denise left the O'Farrell; Vince stayed.

Jim and Adrienne eventually got a divorce. After he got over being dumped, Jim took up with Debbie Marinoff. Jim vowed to Debbie that he was going to "break" Adrienne and make her pay for running out on him. In the course of a deposition that Adrienne gave, it became apparent that he had fulfilled his vow. His lawyers fought her on every point, no matter how minute.

"He wins," Adrienne said, breaking into tears during her deposition. "He warned me. He said, 'Adrienne, if you don't take my offer, I'm going to make it so miserable for you.' He wins. He's stronger. He always wanted to be stronger. He wins. I want my life back."

After taking time off for Jim to recover from Adrienne's departure, Jim and Artie returned to work on *Sodom and Gomorrah*. Looking at the rushes, Jim decided the "serious" biblical story he had intended to turn into a porn epic would never work. The only way to salvage the film was to turn it into a spoof.

Inspired by Erich Von Daniken's insipid best-seller, *Chariots of the Gods?,* the Mitchell Brothers' brain trust developed a subplot about Tarzania, a spaceship sent by Yahweh to cure the Sodomites of gonorrhea. Yahweh is a chimp who talks like John Wayne.

Jack Harvey built an elaborate spaceship in the studio of a building on Turk Street that the Mitchell Brothers had recently purchased. Jim and Artie got the crew back together and shooting began again. But the chimp and the spaceship were not funny and only added confusion to a film that was already a mess. The Mitchell Brothers knew that *Sodom and Gomorrah* was a huge turkey, but released it anyway.

"We had no choice but to release it," Bill Boyer says. "We had to try to get some of the money back. We'd always had great openings and the slogan for this one was 'It was some party!' That slogan was Jim and Artie's way of trying to sweep the film under a rug."

There was no way a slogan could hide a gobbler of this magnitude. The *Chronicle,* thanks largely to critic John Wasserman, was the first daily newspaper to review pornographic films on a regular basis. The *Chronicle* had always been kind to the Mitchell Brothers, but not this time. The review in the *Chronicle* trashed *Sodom and Gomorrah,* said watching the film was "as dull as watching a pile driver on a construction site . . . [It is] an abysmally shoddy spectacle of sex and violence that is . . . without humor, imagination or production values, a skimpy, painfully witless, dunderheaded retelling of the story of Lot and his daughters in Sodom."

Sodom and Gomorrah was the Mitchell Brothers' watershed as filmmakers. After the film bombed, Jim moved onto a houseboat in Sausalito to lick his wounds, and eventually came up with the idea for a series he called *Ultrakore.*

"We were broke after *Sodom and Gomorrah* and had to go lean and get a lot of product out, so we went back to story lines that were basically 'Hi. Let's fuck,'" recalls Bill Boyer. *"Ultrakore* was the obvious next step—nudie, beaver, split beaver, soft core, hard core, ultrakore."

Ultrakore was a return to the loops that dominated pornography when the Mitchell Brothers broke in. Porn was no longer chic, fewer couples were arriving at the O'Farrell to see a film, and the hard-core audience of horn dick daddies was growing bored with features built around plots that were increasingly stupid. Most important of all, the San Francisco DA had given up trying to prosecute films on obscenity grounds. That meant that things like story lines and "redeeming social importance" were no longer crucial in pornography.

The idea behind *Ultrakore* was to reinvent the loop by shooting in 35mm and laying down scorching sound tracks. *Ultrakore* was also a parody of the genre it was reinventing. *Hot Nazis,* for example, burlesques sadomasochism, with female Nazis who had fake German accents chanting, "We are hot Nazis, we are hot Nazis." Jim wanted *Ultrakore* to be hot and fun to produce, but basically it was the same old stuff repackaged in a glossy format. And, as Bill Boyer says, "it wasn't fun anymore."

By the late 1970s, the Mitchell Brothers were exhausted as filmmakers. When the *Ultrakore* series burned itself out, the brothers went back to making feature films, but the films were haphazard and lifeless.

"Once we learned how to do it [make films], we didn't want to do it anymore," Jim said in 1978. "That's our problem."

CB Mamas capitalized on the CB radio craze. The husbands go to work; the wives get on the radio and put out a call to all the horny good buddies out there. The women are hard, cold, and unattractive; the men are out of shape and stupid; the sex is unimaginative.

Artie described *The Grafenberg Spot* as "a six-day wonder made to raise money for legal expenses." Its sequel, *The Grafenberg Girls Go Fishing,* is a truly ugly film, particularly the first half, where dildos protrude from vaginas and anuses like terrible spikes and the sound track has more lowing than a dairy farm at feeding time.

The film from this period that stands out is *Autobiography of a Flea. Flea* is an old story about a remarkably verbal insect who witnesses some very human events in a seventeenth-century monastery. The film is elegant in parts, with style and wit and a real character in the flea. But it was not really a Mitchell Brothers film. *Flea* was directed by Sharon McKnight, the actress, singer, and cabaret performer Jim and Artie had known for years.

"*Flea* is our finest film, but Sharon is a show biz person, she's not into porn, and there's no sex in the film," Jack Harvey says. "After it was all shot and done, they had to go back and shoot some real close-up stuff and cut it in to add some sex to the film."

The Mitchell Brothers' failure to develop as filmmakers cost them some key employees. Mike Bradford had said something about a "fucking cocksucker" in front of the grandmother he loved, and suddenly realized how coarse he had become. Mike quit and crossed the Bay Bridge to study accounting at Cal/Berkeley. Bill Boyer left because he didn't want to spend his life cranking out sex films. George McDonald retired because he didn't want to spend his life acting in them.

Jerry Ward left because of a financial dispute. Like Earl Shagley, Ward learned that no matter how close you were to Jim or Artie, you were still an outsider. Ultimately, the Mitchell Brothers' inner circle consisted of only Jim and Artie.

Ward owned 19 percent of the dummy corporation the Mitchell Brothers had formed to produce *Green Door* and 18 percent of the corporation they had formed to produce *Eve.* Jerry kept asking when they were going to pay the residuals and Jim and Artie kept putting him off. Artie, quoting a line from *The Godfather,* kept saying, "It's nothing personal. It's business."

"But after a while," Jerry says, "it becomes personal."

Jim and Artie finally sent Jerry to their accountant, who showed him "a sheet of paper, *a single sheet of paper.* It looked like a restaurant menu. That really pissed me off. If they'd opened the books, even the phony books, if they'd just have showed me something, it would have been different. I knew they were having the biggest laugh about this, I knew they were going, 'We really gave him the old snow job.' It was just such an affront. I quit and ended up filing a lawsuit." (Jerry settled out of court for $50,000.)

"It was really too bad," he says. "After the lawsuit, I couldn't go to the theater anymore. Artie was the closest friend I've ever had. And I never saw him again, even though we lived in the same town. When it came down to it, Artie chose Jim over me. Artie chose Jim over everyone."

Jerry Ward joined Mark Bradford and Phil Heffernan, who had left because they wanted to do what the Mitchell Brothers had failed to do: make a truly erotic film. The film was called *Sip the Wine,* and, like the film it was modeled on, François Truffaut's *Day for Night, Sip* was a movie about making a movie. Instead of the old vacuum cleaner salesman meets horny housewife plot, *Sip* was about a porn director who falls in love with one of his actresses.

"We felt we'd establish a conflict between making art and making porn, and that when the director and the porn star go to bed, the sex would really be erotic because they'd have been through a lot and really fallen in love," Phil Heffernan says.

Sip got very good reviews when it opened in San Francisco, but like a country-rock act that is too rock for country and too country for rock, *Sip* was too XXX for mainstream theaters and not XXX enough for porn houses.

"We set up a meeting with an L.A. distributor and he came over to our house," Jerry Ward recalls. "We went on and on about what a sensitive sex film we've got. He listened and then he asked his first question: 'How many wet shots you got?' "

"That was our lesson. You can't just make films, you've got to sell them," Phil Heffernan adds. "It was a wonderful experience, though. Opening night was one of the great nights of my life. I just wish our investors had gotten their money back."

There are a number of theories on why the Mitchell Brothers never made a serious, mainstream film. Or a truly erotic film. Or at least a really good film. It wasn't for lack of money; they had money to burn after *Green Door.*

"We've pissed a lot of money away and had a real good time doing it," Jim said in 1978. "[Something] like twenty-five million dollars . . . We've paid the people who work for us well, and the lawyers have gotten a ton of it. There's fines, taxi bills, tequila, a lot of good stuff to smoke to keep us going. We're happy being the Mitchell Brothers."

It was easier to keep being the Mitchell Brothers than it was to keep taking risks. The odds were 100–1 against any legitimate film the Mitchells made, no matter how good it was, becoming a phenomenon like *Green Door*. Why should they risk trying to make a *real* film and fall on their faces?

Loyalty—and arrogance—were also reasons not to try. It was more important to Jim and Artie to keep the Antioch crew together than it was to go to Los Angeles and come back with a hotshot screenwriter and director and a cinematographer. And even if they had hired real pros, it is doubtful Jim and Artie would have taken their advice. It was more important to them to make their movies their way than it was to grow as filmmakers.

"The Mitchell Brothers had a chance to do something and they never did because they had no intellectual capacity," says Lowell Pickett, their old competitor. "Their films were sophomoric because they were living out fantasies they'd formed in eighth grade. They had no aspirations to make better films because they had everything eighth-graders want—buddies to go fishing and be macho with."

It's true that Artie and Jim were risk takers, but only in a limited way. They were white trash from Antioch who had transformed themselves into good-guy outlaws, the Peck's Bad Boys of San Francisco. To make a legitimate film was to risk giving up that outlaw status. They would be judged not by the standards that outlaw pornographers are judged by. They would be judged by the same standards that Francis Ford Coppola and George Lucas were judged by. And they were afraid they could not measure up to those standards.

"I tried to get them to make a real movie," says Richard Lackey, Jim's old friend from the Studs. "Jimmy will probably get mad at me for saying this, but I don't think they ever could have done it. I'm sure Jim wouldn't have been able to stand up to the criticism. It's hard to criticize a pornographer who keeps breaking ground, because there are no comparisons. But if you do a straight film, you've got all kinds of comparisons."

The Mitchell Brothers demonstrated the same impeccable sense of timing getting out of pornographic films as they had when they got in. By 1978, Americans were buying VCRs the way they had once bought electric toasters. The VCR was the ideal medium for the pornographic film. Couples and horn dick daddies no longer had to go to the O'Farrell to see a sex film. They could slide a tape into their VCR and slip under the covers in their bedrooms. They no longer had to slink into a store that sold dildos and inflatable dolls to purchase a sex film. The mainstreaming of pornography that Jim and Artie Mitchell had done so much to bring about was now complete.

After the VCR revolution, the pornographic film industry moved to Los Angeles, where producers and directors—that is, anyone who can hold a minicam steady—began flooding the marketplace with pornographic videotapes. Today the market is so crowded with product, the rule of thumb in the business is that if you invest more than $30,000 in a porn videotape, you will never get your money back.

"We gotta talk," Artie said, hovering over Meredith.

"All right, Art. Sit down, have a beer," Meredith said.

"No!" Artie said.

"Did you have a game tonight?" Meredith asked. Artie was the sure-handed third baseman for—what else?—the Beavers, the Mitchell Brothers' softball team.

"No bullshit, Meredith, we gotta talk," Artie said desperately.

"All right, Art, talk," Meredith said.

Meredith and Artie's three children were four, two, and one. On her one night out a week, Meredith played softball on a woman's team. They had just finished a game and Meredith had gone back to the bar that sponsored the team to have a beer. Now Art was standing over her, very agitated.

The two women Meredith had been sitting with excused themselves and left.

"Listen, Meredith, I know why you're so hot to play softball," Artie said. "It's so you can hang out here. You're hot for the band, for somebody in the band."

Meredith laughed.

"Art! You're jealous! You've never been jealous before! It makes you look kind of cute."

Artie scowled.

"No bullshit," he warned.

"Come on, Art, lighten up," Meredith said. "You know me better than that. I'm not interested in anyone. I don't even know anyone in the band. I've never even stayed long enough to hear them do more than a song or two."

Artie sat down and sighed, his anger suddenly gone.

"Meredith, look. Listen, please, okay? I don't want to get a divorce," Artie pleaded, and tears welled up in his eyes.

Meredith looked at him for a moment without speaking.

"Art, I'm sorry. I'm really, really sorry," she said finally. "I feel so bad for making you feel bad, but we've been over this and over this."

Meredith hadn't stopped loving or enjoying Art. She had decided to divorce him because she was tired of coming in a distant second to his brother.

Art was never home. Night after night, after the kids were in bed and the mansion on Frankie Lane was quiet, Meredith wandered around thinking: This is shit. I want a life. Night after night, Art was down at the theater, playing the genial host, shooting pool, smoking dope, and bullshitting with the guys.

Meredith felt isolated from Art; his real life was at the theater. She was not her husband's soul mate; his brother was. Since she left the inner circle to have children, Meredith and her children's relationship with Artie had deteriorated to the point where they were little more than window dressing, a pleasant backdrop that had publicity value ("Porn King Is Actually a Devoted Dad").

There was no way Meredith could work through any of this with Art. If she tried, Art erupted, stormed out, and headed straight to the theater.

"It'll be different, Meredith," Artie pleaded. "I'll stay home more. I'll see the kids more. I don't want to lose them. I don't want to lose you."

"Art, I've thought about it and thought about it and I'm sorry, but I don't think things will ever change. Jim's your first wife, I'm your second. The theater is your first home, ours is your second. I'd rather be alone than be second, Art."

"But that's what I'm saying, Meredith! You're not second. You've never been second. And I'm gonna show you you're not."

"You won't, Art. You can't. It's not really your fault, it's just the way it is. I'll never be as close to you as you are to Jim. You two are Siamese twins. I don't want to be married to Siamese twins anymore."

"What the fuck do you mean, Siamese twins?" Art asked, suddenly angry.

"It's like, like I can't reach you," Meredith said, struggling to find words to express what she was feeling. "In a relationship, you expect to grow, right? We never have. Every time I try to deal with some problem we've got or something I'm feeling, like why I stopped feeling comfortable with you, you refuse to deal with it. You don't have to deal with it because you've got Jim. You can go be with him. I feel like there's this emotional tug-of-war that's been going on for years. I'm tired of it, tired of tugging against Jim."

Artie stood up.

"Meredith, I've never begged for anything from you. From any woman. But I'm begging now. Don't get a divorce."

"I'm sorry, Art, I'm really, really sorry, but I'm not going to change my mind."

"All right, then fuck you!" Artie yelled.

Art drew his fist back and smashed Meredith in the mouth, dislocating her jaw.

It would not be the last time that Artie Mitchell hit a woman.

Lisa Loring in her prom dress. The daughter of a professional dancer, Lisa developed routines for her stage show and found performing at the O'Farrell artistically fulfilling. She felt she and the other dancers were "going to change the world through our clever way of presenting sex." (Photo by Barry Shapiro, courtesy of Lisa Loring.)

"Feel the Magic." Marilyn left the Mitchell Brothers for Chuck Traynor, who had managed and been married to Linda Lovelace. She returned to the O'Farrell as a live act in the mid-1980s and ended up getting arrested for lewd and lascivious conduct, among other charges. (Photo courtesy of Dave Patrick.)

When Dianne Feinstein became mayor of San Francisco, the police began raiding the O'Farrell with a vengeance they had not shown in years. The Mitchell Brothers retaliated by putting the mayor's phone number on the marquee. She would change it; the brothers would find out and immediately put up the new number. (Hardy for the San Francisco *Examiner*.)

The Siamese twins. Two halves of a whole, Jim and Artie were so close they looked more like each other with each passing year. (Photo courtesy of Dave Patrick.)

Missy when she was still Elisa Florez. The daughter of a prominent Republican, a former aide to Senator Orrin Hatch who had worked for the Republican National Committee, Elisa came to California and transformed herself into "Missy, the Republican porn star." (Photo courtesy of Dave Patrick.)

Elisa after her transformation. She and Artie were living together in San Francisco's Marina District in 1986 when Missy starred in *Behind the Green Door: The Sequel*. This photo was taken that year at the Adult Film Association of America awards ceremony in Los Angeles. (Photo courtesy of Dave Patrick.)

Joanne Scott and Artie Mitchell in Cabo San Lucas with a prize marlin. A dancer at the O'Farrell who was deeply devoted to Artie, Joanne had an on-again, off-again relationship with him that lasted almost eight years. Joanne found Artie's sudden departures, his relationships with other women, his crank calls in the middle of the night intriguing. "It was part of an elaborate game we were playing," she explains. (Photo courtesy of Joanne Scott.)

Jim and Artie pose above Ocean Beach in San Francisco, where the brothers and several of their sons came close to drowning in the vicious surf. Artie came out of the freezing water with hypothermia and a thyroid condition, which lessened his resistance to the large quantities of drugs and alcohol he was consuming. (O'Hara for the San Francisco *Chronicle*.)

The house where it happened. Artie had lived in a number of elaborate homes around the Bay Area. He moved into this nondescript house in Corte Madera, a commuter community across the Golden Gate Bridge in Marin County, to be near his three youngest children. The only concessions to his former lifestyle were a huge hot tub (which had required a crane to install in the backyard) and a wall-sized television set. (Photo courtesy of Eric Voss.)

Jim and his defense team confer at his trial. Michael Kennedy, who had handled most of the Mitchell Brothers' obscenity cases, left his Park Avenue office in New York to defend Jim against Marin County Assistant District Attorney John Posey, who wanted to send Jim to prison for thirty years. Kennedy, on the far left, was assisted by Nanci Clarence, who seemed to enjoy playing hardball with Posey. (Photo by Dave Patrick.)

Liberty Bradford on the stand at her uncle's murder trial. Smart and articulate, Liberty was an effective witness for the defense, but she has since filed a wrongful death suit against Jim. So have her younger brother and sister. (Photo by Katy Kaddatz for the San Francisco *Examiner*.)

Vince Stanich in his office in the summer of 1991, booking performers for the O'Farrell. Those are copies of *War News* on the wall. (Photo courtesy of Andy Finley.)

Please join us for a
Bereavement Ceremony
in Memory of
Artie Mitchell
on Sunday, June 23, 1991
1 – 4pm
at the O'Farrell Theatre
895 O'Farrell Street,
San Francisco.

Please rsvp Nancy at (415) 776-1016

The invitation to what must rank as the most bizarre wake in American history: not only did it feature nude dancing, it was hosted by the murderer of the deceased.

Chuck Traynor in his office in The Survival Store, an indoor shooting range and gun store he owns and operates in Las Vegas. Married to and the manager of Linda Lovelace and then Marilyn Chambers, Chuck makes little if any distinction between women and the quarter horses he owns. (Photo courtesy of Andy Finley.)

Marilyn Chambers reprises her old Ivory Snow box cover with her daughter, Mckenna, who was two weeks old at the time. (Photo courtesy of Andy Finley.)

Georgia Mae Mitchell and Meredith Bradford in Georgia Mae's home in a suburb of Sacramento, California, during the summer of 1991. (Photo courtesy of Andy Finley.)

9

The Theater
of Sex

JIM AND ARTIE had pulled another coup in the sex industry when they opened the Ultra Room at the O'Farrell on January 4, 1977. There was nothing new about aboveground live sex acts; couples had been simulating sex acts in North Beach clip joints back in 1967 until the cops put a stop to it. And for several years, Alex de Renzy had had two women doing an act on a raised platform in the Screening Room.

But Jim and Artie had never been interested in doing anything similar. Except for the surreptitious live acts they staged for the Japanese (where the sex *was real*), the brothers were disdainful of live acts. Live sex shows were as phony as studio wrestling.

And the laws in San Francisco that governed live sex acts were even screwier than the laws that determined what was obscene in films. Two women could get on a stage and perform cunnilingus until they were blue in the face, and because they were of the same sex, the cops would not raise a finger. But if a woman *and* a man appeared on the stage and cops were in the audience, they would bust the show as soon as a finger or lips invaded an erogenous zone.

The brothers' view of live shows had changed during a trip to New York City in 1976. Out of professional curiosity as much as anything else, Jim and Artie had gone to the Melody, a sex club located near the old Winter Garden Theatre. By the mid-1970s, the brothers had grown a bit smug about being in the vanguard of commercial sex and the millions they had made by shocking the straights. But this time it was the brothers who were stunned.

Four naked women walked onto a stage, lay down on four mattresses, and spread their legs. Men got out of their seats and lined up at one end of the stage. One at a time, the customers walked onto the stage and took a baby wipe out of a plastic box. A customer wiped the vagina of the first woman and then kissed it and/or inserted his tongue. Then he proceeded to the next woman and did the same thing. Wipe, kiss. Wipe, kiss. Wipe, kiss.

This wasn't fake, this *was real*. Jim and Artie had always prided themselves on being more outrageous than anybody in the sex industry, but this was further out than anything they had ever done. They absolutely had to come up with something that was wilder and more imaginative than what they had seen at the Melody.

The brothers left New York fired up. They were going to do for live sex what they had already done for the pornographic film. This was a challenge, and Jim and Artie needed a challenge.

The brothers had grown bored living off the reputation that *Green Door* had brought them. They didn't care about making movies anymore, and the O'Farrell pretty much ran itself. But now Jim and Artie felt like film directors who get a chance to do a play on Broadway. They were going into live theater, and they were going to do something *really outrageous,* something no one else would dare to do.

Jack Harvey's status at the O'Farrell was instantly elevated from set builder and handyman extraordinaire to consulting architect. He and Jim pored over plans and eventually decided they would re-create the old-time arcades with their rows of tiny individual booths. Jim gave Jack an unlimited expense account and the freedom to turn a sketch into reality. Jack was happier than a kid with a new Erector Set.

The red-carpeted room was twenty feet long and ten feet wide. A trapeze hung from the ceiling over the Leatherette platform, and a black Leatherette runway elevated three feet above the carpet ran all the way around the room. Dildos, chains, whips, and paddles were scattered on the runway. The walls were sectioned into many small partitions made of one-way mirrors. Above the glass, hand-holds were embedded in the black wall.

Behind the one-way mirrors were tiny compartments, half the size of a telephone booth. A light came on when a man slipped into a booth and closed the door behind him. The performers could see the light and a vaguely defined figure standing in the shadows.

Jim and Artie had decided the new venue should be called the Ultra Room—the name had a nice ring; like *Ultrakore,* it suggested you could go no further. And they wanted the shows to have an S&M/bondage theme. After years of being immersed in sex, Jim and Artie had grown kinky. They thought that because *they* wanted to see S&M, everyone would.

"After they opened one of the rooms at the O'Farrell, Jim de-manded that the girls who were performing there come out with strap-on dicks [dildos]," recalls Joanne Scott, the studious-looking daughter of a career Army officer who performed at the O'Farrell for eight years. "Jim really wanted to see that, and he thought the audience would too. Not only did he talk the girls into it, he made them each buy [a dildo] for thirty-five dollars. The audience didn't like it. The girls did one show and refused to do it anymore, and that was the end of that."

There are almost as many theories about S&M as there are schools of psychology. Some theorists contend that since sex is closely related to aggression, there is nothing "abnormal" about boots and whips between friends. Some radical feminists believe it is an expression of what all sex really is: violence against women. Others consider S&M a highly stylized theater where people who have accumulated a busload of fears and guilt about sex can pay homage to their demons *and* have sex. Some men—or women—are so afraid of the opposite sex they can only approach a partner sexu-ally when she is wearing a leather mask and has her hands hand-cuffed behind her back. Other men—or women—are so hamstrung by the puritanical idea that lust must be punished they can only get turned on by being a "slave" to a dominatrix.

Jim and Artie had in mind something like S&M lite. The shows in the Ultra Room would sketch S&M themes—the heavily choreo-graphed interplay of dominance and submission; the idea that pain administered in a sexual context is pleasurable (in that sense, S&M appears to be a throwback to fifth grade, when a girl socking a boy on the arm can mean that she likes him). The brothers knew the customers had no stomach for hard-core S&M, with whippings that drew blood, men tied by their scrotums and lifted into the air, or nipple piercings. Their goal was to give the uninitiated a peek into a world they would not otherwise enter.

Two weeks after it opened, the Ultra Room was already on its way to being a major financial success when the *Chronicle* sent ace columnist John Wasserman to the O'Farrell to evaluate the Mitchell Brothers' foray into live sex. A sexual epicure, Wasserman mentioned in his column that "in the line of duty [he had] seen exhibitions in Amsterdam and Copenhagen that made the activities of the Ultra Room seem almost coy." But that did not stop the columnist from bringing on the band to cheer the new room. The Ultra Room was something new under the pornographic sun!

"In an arena that has been combed, sifted, raked and circumscribed for centuries, the brothers have come up with what may well be an authentically new and unique gimmick," Wasserman gushed. "The secret of the Ultra Room is that it exploits the most forbidden, hence exciting, of all forms of voyeurism—that of the Peeping Tom. Not only is the show watched in total privacy . . . but further, it is watched through one-way mirrors, so one is also spared surveillance from within . . . It's genius, I tell you, pure genius."

Jim and Artie had installed the one-way mirrors in the Ultra Room, and had established a firm "no tipping" policy, in the belief that if there was no contact between the audience and the performers, if the performers did not accept pay for "sexual services," there was no way the cops could bust them for running a house of prostitution. But the precautions were for naught.

On June 13, 1977, six months after it opened, San Francisco police raided the Ultra Room and issued citations to five employees, charging them with "indecent exposure to elicit vicious or lewd thoughts or acts."

In addition to the O'Farrell, the cops raided the Arena, a live sex club on Sutter Street that had opened only a month earlier in a blatant attempt to copy the Mitchell Brothers' success. Police sources told a *Chronicle* reporter that officers had hit the two theaters because "live sex shows have been so successful, other porn theaters might follow their lead if action wasn't taken."

Jim and Artie were more angry that the raid had taken place than they were worried about the legal consequences. It just proved that the DA hated sex. There was no such thing as a certain amount of sex the authorities would tolerate. You had to fight for everything in the sex business.

Jim and Artie were ready to fight. And they were going to fight in their own unique way.

"You don't have a thing to worry about," Jim and Artie assured the three "Ultralettes" and two ushers who had been arrested. The cops had only issued citations, and, usually, citations are no big deal. "We could pay the fines, but we're not going to. We're going to take this to court and battle the DA until he's bloody. It's going to cost him thousands of dollars to collect a few hundred bucks."

After all the legal battles the Mitchell Brothers had fought, Jim had emerged as an expert on the First Amendment. "There are constitutional issues of freedom of speech and freedom of expression at stake in the case," he told the five employees who had been arrested. "We've got great lawyers on our side. They'll fight this all the way to the U.S. Supreme Court, and none of you will be liable for a cent."

To Jim and Artie, the Ultra Room bust was reminiscent of the first time the cops had hit the O'Farrell, in July 1969. Back then, the brothers had deliberately started "soft" to avoid being arrested, and had ended up busted. When they opened the Ultra Room, Jim and Artie had done the same thing. And sure enough, the cops had hit the Ultra Room anyway.

In the late 1960s and early 1970s, Jim and Artie had ignored the busts and defied the legal system and kept making films that were more and more hard-core. Things had worked out just fine. Now the brothers were determined to do the same thing all over again. The DA was *not* going to dictate what they could and could not do in the Ultra Room.

So instead of backing off after the raid and cooling down the shows, the brothers pushed things one step further and removed the one-way mirrors in the Ultra Room. For $5.00 or $10, depending on who was performing, a patron could lean out of his booth and bury his face, however temporarily, in a performer's vaginal area. He could also, on special occasions, pay to witness a live sex show featuring *a man* and a woman. Some of the special shows starred John Holmes, the well-known porn star who had appeared in over a thousand porn films.

There were lines down the block waiting to buy tickets to the Ultra Room.

The cops temporarily halted their raids while San Francisco city officials busied themselves developing legal ways to eliminate live sex theaters. Spurred on by Supervisor Dianne Feinstein, who had a large city map in her office with pins marking the sites of rapes (most of the rapes did indeed occur in or around the Tenderloin, where most of the city's sex theaters were, but that area was also home to most of the city's felons, prostitutes, drug addicts, and drifters), the city enacted a set of stringent new controls.

The new regulations were not unlike those that govern behavior at a junior high dance held in the gym of a Catholic school. There was to be no sitting on laps; no touching in sexual areas; and girls must be properly clothed at all times.

Attorneys for the Mitchell Brothers, and the operators of other live sex venues, went to court and were able to get judges to issue a series of temporary restraining orders (more time was needed to prepare for trial, constitutional issues were involved, etc.) that kept the police from enforcing the new rules.

Meanwhile, Supervisor Feinstein was trying to get the Board of Supervisors to pass legislation that would confine establishments that offered adult entertainment to an area between south of Market Street and Potrero Hill (the O'Farrell would automatically lose its license because it was not located in that area), but Feinstein was unable to get liberal Mayor George Moscone to support the measure. In October 1977, Moscone signed a compromise measure that placed a four-month moratorium on the opening of new adult theaters or bookstores.

While their lawyers kept the authorities at bay, Jim and Artie were on a roll reminiscent of the good old *Green Door* days. Reporters were calling to request interviews, and cognoscenti like Herb Gold were dropping by the theater to check out the new action.

An excited Artie gave friends a private tour of the Ultra Room and asked them if they had ever been to Neiman-Marcus down on Union Square. "You've seen how all those fancy designers each have their own boutique, right?" Artie would ask. "Well, that's what we're going to do at the O'Farrell. We're going to turn this place into the first boutique of sex!"

It was Artie who came up with the idea for the next room. He called it the Kopenhagen Intimate Lounge, and it was going to be softer and cozier than the Ultra Room. Jack Harvey and his crew worked around the clock, creating a room off the O'Farrell lobby that, compared with what would follow, was exceedingly simple.

Jack built a platform two and a half feet high and three feet wide that ran all the way around the room. He carpeted the floor and the platform with thick shag and hung mirrors on every wall. To add to the mystery and sense of enticement, the glass doors that opened into the room were covered with thick velvet curtains. Big, soft, inviting pillows were scattered on the platform. A flashlight with a long red phallic extension, the kind that are used in airports to guide planes to their gates, was placed next to each pillow. And the Kopenhagen was ready.

Once every hour, two dozen men were let into the Kopenhagen. As the minutes ticked by and nothing happened, apprehension and curiosity increased as the men toyed with their flashlights and traded self-conscious jokes.

Suddenly, rock music began blasting off the mirrored walls and the lights dimmed. Two and sometimes three women in long, flowing lingerie entered the room and glided past the men, letting them get a whiff of their perfume. The women met under a spotlight in the center of the room and exchanged deep tongue kisses while their hands crept under the lingerie and explored each other's bodies. Soon the lingerie was removed and the women were on their hands and knees, performing cunnilingus while emitting deep moans. Men who tried to hide their astonishment behind blank expressions kept their flashlights trained on orifices.

A song ending was the performers' cue to hop off the floor and jump onto the platform between two startled patrons. Using both hands to balance themselves against the mirror, the performers would wait a few seconds for the next tune to begin—the Rolling Stones' "Beast of Burden" was a favorite at the time—and then, slowly, rhythmically, the performers lowered their vaginas to a customer's face. Grinding their hips in slow circles, the performers would bring pubic hair within inches of a mouth before moving on to the next man.

Back on the floor, the women slowly, teasingly, opened cosmetic bags and produced their "toys," body oils and dildos of different sizes and substances—plastic, silicon, and steel. The performers made a great show of fondling and oiling the dildos before inserting them. Then, in the grand finale, they jumped back on the platform.

Hovering over a patron, a woman raised one foot to the mirrored wall and kept inching her foot up the mirror until her legs were spread almost 180 degrees. Her partner ducked in under her and inserted a dildo. Then she removed it, and the women repeated the performance on the other side of the room.

The Mitchell Brothers were once again leading the pack. Nobody in the country had a show this explicit, not even the Melody in New York City.

Jim had replaced Jerry Ward and other key members of the Mitchell Brothers' original extended family with two more old friends from Antioch: Jeff Armstrong and Richard Mezzavilla. Armstrong became the general manager of the theater and Mezzavilla the comptroller. Both were excellent pool players with razor-sharp wits. Both were honest and fiercely loyal to Jim.

And neither man would dare tell Jim how to spend his money.

Jim liked nothing better than purchasing extravagant, one-of-a-kind pieces of machinery. He loved buying boats, and the exotic and extremely expensive transmissions and engines he had dropped into a string of trucks had made him a legend in custom shops from San Francisco to Los Angeles. He had spent thousands to purchase a showroom-sized window made of spun sugar from a prop shop in Hollywood, so he could fulfill a Steve McQueen fantasy by crashing his motorcycle through the window in one of the *Ultrakore* loops.

Now that the O'Farrell was being transformed into a live sex arena, Jim was behaving like a manic, type A executive who is obsessed with every detail of the house he is building as a monument to himself. He was driving Jack Harvey crazy with ideas for adding more theme rooms to the O'Farrell.

"Air castles, it was all air castles," Jack recalls. "They'd sit up there all day, smoke that weed, and come up with air castles. Jim, he's got a Winchester complex, it's build, build, build," Jack says, referring to Sarah Winchester, the widow of the famous repeating-rifle manufacturer, who believed that if she kept adding rooms to her home in San Jose, California, she would never die. (The mansion eventually reached 106 rooms.) "It was great for me. I got a machine shop with rolling machines, lathes, and all kinds of power tools. I learned all kinds of trades and professions, all at Jim's expense. My job was to spend Jim Mitchell's money."

Some of the ideas Jim came up with were relatively simple and revealed his conception of women, like the shoeshine stand where a customer could have his shoes shined by a naked woman. Others were incredibly elaborate fantasies.

Jack spent months building a room called the Streets of Paris. There was a cobblestone street, wrought-iron balustrades, swirling lights, and small iron Kewpie dolls. The street was lined with doorways; in each a girl was supposed to be leaning out of a half-door, inviting a customer in for a round of mutual masturbation. But the cubicles turned out to be too small to hold two people, there were access and egress problems, and after months of work, Jim scrapped the Streets of Paris.

The Shower Room was another idea that Jack spent months working on. The idea was to have women step into a shower and get all soaped up. Men watching behind a glass partition would then stuff quarters into a slot, pick up a squirt gun, and use it to wash soap off the women. Jim loved the idea at first but cooled on it after Jack had installed the plumbing, and the room never opened.

The most grandiose "air castle" was the Pyramid Room. Jack Harvey argued against the room the entire time he was working on it. But Jim kept telling him, "Hey, it's your job to build it, it's my job to sell it," and Jack agreed and kept right on working.

The pyramid Jack constructed was an elaborate structure with huge hydraulic doors that opened onto a platform. The doors closed and the platform descended to a small cockpit where a harem was waiting to put on a private sex show that was designed to arouse the most jaded sultan.

"I kept telling Jim, 'You can't put people down there. It's claustrophobic, somebody will go berserk, people will die,'" Jack Harvey recalls. "Finally, Jim said, 'Yeah, you're right, we can't do it.' But by then, we had already spent a hundred thousand dollars. Over and over we did that."

Not all of Jim's ideas turned out to be so farfetched. He had Jack scale down the original auditorium, put in a new screen, construct a new stage made of highly polished hardwood, and put in new seats. The Cine Stage, the Mitchell Brothers called it, a dark, comfortable theater where X-rated films played continuously.

To keep the action going while customers circulated from the Kopenhagen to the Ultra Room to the Cine Stage, the Mitchell Brothers decided they needed an updated version of an old burlesque house. Jack Harvey built New York Live, a small theater with only a few rows of seats built around a T-shaped stage. Jim spent a fortune on the most exotic sound and light systems available, and had closed-circuit television installed so that dancers could be seen on large monitors mounted on the side walls.

As skilled as Jack's work was in New York Live and the other rooms, his crowning achievement was the Green Door Room. Built to resemble a small nightclub, the Green Door Room had a semicircular stage that faced an open area filled with small round tables. A row of elevated semicircular booths were built into the back wall. Above the stage, Jack installed a series of shower heads that delivered a very fine mist from the ceiling.

Once an hour, while a DJ was building expectations—"You are about to witness a show like no other, a spectacle that could only be presented at the O'Farrell Theatre"—the showers came on and the curtain opened to reveal six very attractive naked women standing back to back with their arms on each other's hips. There was much oohing and aahing while the women looked up and opened their mouths and stuck out their tongues to catch the spray and celebrate the sensuality of it all.

While loud, crystal-clear rock music bounced off the walls, the women broke into couples and began rubbing, fondling, and exploring the body's deepest orifices. When the song changed, four wet women ran into the audience, threw big white towels over the small tables, slid onto the tables, and writhed about on their backs and stomachs while one couple continued to do a girl-girl under the showers.

Whether they were tourists from Peoria who had screwed up their courage to visit the O'Farrell or connoisseurs of explicit sex who had been to dozens of sex clubs, customers left the theater shaking their heads, more stunned than aroused. They had never seen anything like this before, because there wasn't a sex club as innovative as the O'Farrell anywhere in the world.

"I been to Bangkok, I been to Amsterdam, I been in most of them, and the O'Farrell is the best in the world," says Chuck Traynor, who may be the ultimate expert on such matters.

There is a despondency, a depressing gloom that characterizes sex clubs, whether they are in San Francisco, Tijuana, or Amsterdam. The women appear defeated or high on drugs, and seem to be there because there is no place else they can be.

The male patrons tend to be silent and sullen. If a man has no sensitivity at all, if all he sees in front of him is meat wrapped in different packages, he is a brute, and louts are always oppressive. If he is loud and macho, chances are he is covering his fear of women with contempt. If a patron is sensitive, no matter how many drinks he has, he is usually unable to silence a small voice that keeps telling him he is taking advantage of women who have not had many options in life, and that makes him conflicted and withdrawn.

The O'Farrell had never been gloomy or meanspirited; that was what differentiated it from sex theaters the world over. That the theater retained its energy and sense of jauntiness after it metamorphosed into a live sex venue was due largely to the fact that Jim and Artie were able to attract performers like Lisa Loring. To Lisa, the theater was a cause as much as it was a job.

Lisa's father was a professional musician; her mother was a flamenco dancer who eventually started a successful dance troupe modeled after the June Taylor Dancers. As a child, Lisa had been part of the act. A miniature version of the adult dancers, Lisa dashed onto the stage, radiating charm that melted an audience. When she got older, she attended Holy Names, a Catholic girls' high school in Oakland, and assumed she would join her mother's troupe when she graduated.

"All I'd ever wanted to do was dance, but it didn't work out," Lisa recalls sadly. "Maybe I made my mother feel too old. Maybe I didn't look right because I was too short. It upset me very much."

In the mid-1970s, Lisa enrolled at San Francisco State and landed a role in a student production of *Tommy*. The play got good reviews, attracted an audience that went beyond the campus, and enjoyed a long run. Lisa loved being part of the cast, and auditioned for a role in a professional production of the X-rated live musical *Let My People Come*. She was a finalist, but did not make the last cut.

Discouraged, she began looking around for a job to support herself while going to school. She did not want to type or answer the phone in an office; that was too boring. Lisa had grown up in a show-business family and wanted a job where she could express her talent. Eventually, she spotted a "Nude Performers Wanted" ad in the *Chronicle* classifieds. She called the O'Farrell Theatre and somebody told her to come down and look at the shows. If she thought she could handle it, they'd talk about hiring her.

Lisa saw the show in the Ultra Room—"It was amazing; three women were really being *wild*"—and went upstairs to talk to Artie. Artie charmed her. He was so straightforward, so nonjudgmental.

"The pay is twenty-five dollars a performance in the Ultra Room. You can do five or six performances a shift, and I really want to emphasize the word 'performance,'" Artie explained to Lisa. "The Ultra Room is theater. It's the theater of sex. Sex is dramatic. Sex is exciting. Some people think what happens in the Ultra Room is lurid and obscene. Fine, let 'em. But all we're doing is taking sex out of the closet. That's all we've ever done."

"I'd just found a wonderful house I wanted to rent in Berkeley and I needed a job that paid good money," Lisa says. "I wanted to have fun and I wanted to dance, because that was really all I knew. Maybe I was still angry with my mother, maybe it went back to high school and the way the nuns suppressed us."

Lisa got used to being nude much more quickly than she had thought she would and was soon completely comfortable in the Ultra Room. The whips, paddles, chains, and handcuffs were simply props, part of the choreography.

What made Lisa eager to get to work was the discovery that she had the power to cast a spell over the men in the booths. After the one-way mirrors came down, Lisa saw awe and concentration in the customers' faces that bordered on reverence—"It sounds strange to say this, but they looked like they were in church," she says—and realized she could do with them as she wished. Lisa would look at a man and wink and the man would flinch. She'd smile at the guy and watch while the guy struggled to produce a shy smile. She owned him.

"Oh, hi, daddy," Lisa would say when she hopped up on the runway to give a customer a close-up view. "You want to look? You're so hot, I just know you do!"

The guy would be beaming when Lisa left, and not just because Lisa had displayed herself. She had affirmed his sexuality, made him feel special.

The Ultra Room was Lisa's stage, and like most of the other performers, she took great pride in where she worked. It was the performers' duty to clean up the booths between shows—the Mitchell Brothers provided the women with a *four-page* booklet of instructions—and Lisa didn't mind the job. Many of the men knew they were going to have an orgasm and had prepared by ducking into the men's room and slipping on a condom before entering the booths. But others took no such precautions.

"Lots of times you'd have to clean up cum," Lisa recalls. "I'd tell somebody about it and they'd go, 'That's gross!' To me, it was comical. Somebody just got a little too excited."

When the Kopenhagen Intimate Lounge opened, Lisa had a chance to double the money she made by working in both rooms, but she decided not to. You couldn't fake it in the Kopenhagen, you really had to perform cunnilingus, and Lisa wasn't a lesbian.

No one pressured Lisa to work the Kopenhagen room. The Great American Music Hall, one of the top venues in San Francisco, was a few doors down the street. O'Farrell employees got free passes to shows at the Music Hall and Music Hall employees got free passes to the O'Farrell. Artie knew Lisa loved music, and sometimes when a Kopenhagen show was about to begin and Lisa had an hour or two to kill, Artie would walk into the dressing room and say, "Come on, Lisa, let's go catch Van Morrison's second show."

But the Kopenhagen intrigued Lisa, and before long she was standing behind the curtain with the technicians, watching the shows. The men had the same awe, the same looks of respectful fascination that she saw every day in the Ultra Room. The Kopenhagen was theater, just like the Ultra Room.

Lisa decided to try the Kopenhagen and discovered she liked the intimacy; she also decided she liked the fact that the women were not faking it. She was a sex performer, and the sex was real.

Lisa also relished the fact that the Kopenhagen had become a *women's* show. A group of performers had approached Jim and Artie and told them they had some ideas for lights and music in the Kopenhagen. Sure, go ahead, try them out, the brothers had said, and performers had begun doubling as sound and light technicians.

"I felt like I was part of the women's revolution," Lisa says in retrospect. "We were in charge and we were teaching men about sex, helping them feel that sex isn't dirty, it's artistic. We were very open, very proud of what we were doing.

"With Japanese tourists and people from all over coming to the theater, I felt like I was part of something the whole world was looking at," Lisa continues. "I was one of the girls who had a mission to prove that nice girls could have a healthy attitude toward explicit sex without being degenerate. That was definitely a turn-on."

Lisa was able to express her artistic longings when Jim and Artie opened New York Live, the mini-strip club. Yes, the whole idea of the room was to get naked and let 'em look at it. But the beauty of the O'Farrell was, Jim and Artie didn't care *how* you got naked. In fact, the more imaginative a performer, the more the brothers respected her.

Lisa did a cowgirl act with a trick lasso, but her favorite routine was prom night. While Danny and the Juniors' "At the Hop" played on the sound system, Lisa pranced onstage dressed as a prom queen. Eddie Cochran's "Summertime Blues" came next, and by the time the Big Bopper opened "Chantilly Lace" with his immortal "HELLLL-OOOOO, BAAA-BBEEE," the gown was discarded, the bra and panties were gone, and Lisa was prowling the stage with a large ice-cream soda, licking the whipped cream off the top and smearing it on her body.

"We called you together because we've got an announcement to make," Artie said. "We're making a policy change that affects all of you, so listen up."

The dancers were sitting in seats in the Cine Stage. Jim and Artie were on the stage, looking uncomfortable. Each waited for the other to speak.

"I'm gonna tell you right up front, you're going to hate this for a lot of reasons," Jim said finally. "But stay with us and give it a try because you are going to make a lot of money."

"It's a matter of economics," Artie said. "You'll make more money and we'll make more money."

The brothers announced that performers would no longer be paid for doing shows. From now on, they would earn the minimum wage. In return, the brothers would allow them to accept tips. The catch was, the performers would have to work for the tips.

"We want you to go out into the audience," Jim told the women. "We want you to be nude when you go. We want you to sit on laps. Lots of laps."

The performers exchanged surprised glances. "I don't know about this," someone murmured. "I don't either," someone else replied.

"We've talked to the lawyers and they tell us as long as you don't solicit, we'll be all right, even if we get busted," Jim continued. "We're not asking you to do anything that's riskier than what you've been doin' in the rooms or onstage in New York Live."

"It's just a way of bringing the customer closer to the action," Artie added.

For Lisa Loring, things were never the same after that. She more than doubled her salary, regularly earning $300 to $400 a night in tips. Men threw ones, fives, tens, and sometimes twenties at her when she was performing in the Ultra Room, and they stuffed bills into her hands in the Kopenhagen. They laid money on the stage when she was dancing in New York Live, and when she had finished her set, she looked into the audience and saw men waving bills, inviting her to sit on their laps.

But no matter how much she made, Lisa hated working for tips. It cheapened what she was doing. And the men could be so casually cruel. Lisa was short and brunette and had stocky legs. She'd approach a customer and ask if he wanted some company. "No, beat it, you got big old legs. I'm waiting for that one over there," the guy would say, pointing to a leggy blonde across the room.

Sometimes, sitting on a lap was worse than being told to go away. Some of the young guys weren't so bad. They'd try to grab or pinch her and Lisa would say, "Hey, that's no way to behave," and the guys would wilt and apologize.

"It's kind of nice to have the power to do that," Lisa says.

She didn't mind sitting on the laps of the older men who told her about wives who had died. She felt sad for the plain, painfully shy men who appeared in the theater every night. After a few moments of small talk, it was clear they had no idea how to relate to a woman, much less develop a relationship. At times, Lisa took it upon herself to be an unlicensed therapist, telling some poor dork, "Look, there's nothing to be afraid of. I know there's a girl somewhere you've got your eye on. Just be friendly and outgoing, and when you think the time is right, ask her to have dinner."

It made Lisa feel good to keep men company for a while and leave them feeling better. What she hated was the endless, mindless small talk.

Hi. Are you from San Francisco?

Hi. Is this your first time here?

Hi. How do you like the show so far?

And she hated answering questions about herself. She had heard them so many times she could mouth the words as the customer was speaking them.

Do your parents know you're doing this?

You seem like a nice girl. Why are you working in a place like this?
What do you get out of this? Besides money, I mean?
Do you have a boyfriend? Does he know you're doing this?
Listen, could we meet after you get off?

"I wanted to be a performer onstage, wrapped in a mysterious façade," Lisa says. "I didn't want to go into the audience and be me and talk about my life. When you cross the invisible line that separates the performer from the audience, you shatter the illusions you've worked so hard to create onstage."

Even worse, the tipping and audience contact policy helped destroy the camaraderie and sense of professionalism that had made Lisa so proud of her work.

"Word got out that you could make a lot of money, and it attracted a lot of hustler girls who didn't care about working together and didn't have that loyalty, that passion for trying to change the world through our clever way of presenting sex."

The "hustler girls" were there to get money, not to be performers. Instead of elaborate costumes and choreographed fantasies, like Lisa's prom-night routine, the hustlers would take the stage in a leotard, stumble around to some music, wiggle out of the leotard, get down on the floor and display themselves, and then hurry back into the audience, where the money was.

Sitting on customers' laps had evolved into a form of simulated sex the performers called "lap dancing." A woman would sit on a man's lap and move around until she felt his erection. Then she would squeeze her buttocks together and release and squeeze them together again while rocking back and forth on his lap. While the charge was negotiable, the tacitly agreed amount was a dollar a minute.

But after the "hustler girls" arrived, Lisa would go into the dressing room to hear one of them boasting that she had just gotten a guy to pay her $5.00 a minute for a lap dance.

Overcharging for lap dancing was the least of what some of the hustlers did. To make big money—and Lisa heard girls bragging about making $800 to $1,000 a night—some of the hustlers were being explored digitally by forty or fifty men a shift. Others were performing oral sex in the Kopenhagen Intimate Lounge. It was common practice for a dancer to take a man into the back row of New York Live and masturbate him. Others let men penetrate them as they sat on their laps in dark back rows.

Ushers patrolled with flashlights, and if they caught a dancer with a patron who had his zipper down, they reported her to Jim and Artie, and the dancer, Lisa says, "was fiercely fired." Lisa and her allies did their best to police the theater too.

"The girls who worked there and loved it protected the place," Lisa says. "If we caught somebody in a back row doing something they shouldn't, we'd say, 'Don't do that! You'll get us all in trouble!'

"If we caught a girl a second time, we usually reported her to management, although sometimes we dealt with it ourselves," Lisa continues. "That's what we were doing that day in the Ultra Room with Suzie. We decided it was better to scare her, to really, really scare her, than it was to report her to Jim and Artie. And we surely couldn't report her to the police. The police wanted to take the theater away from us!"

That is exactly what the police wanted to do.

Lillian Wright, whose stage name was Dede, was a beautiful twenty-one-year-old black woman from Pittsburgh who loved working at the O'Farrell as much as Lisa Loring did. Lillian had grown up as the only child in a Roman Catholic family in which sex wasn't so much taboo as it was nonexistent. Now Lillian was getting paid to explore her sexuality and her power as a woman. She loved performing in New York Live. The rapt attention, the men who were all but drooling, "makes you feel like king shit," she says.

To Lillian, working the audience was an exciting game. Other dancers asked, "Would you like some company?" Lillian prided herself on never using that line, because, to her, company meant work. She always said, "Hi. Would you like to play?" If a guy answered by asking, "How much is this going to cost me?" Lillian replied, "I'll tell you what. I'm going to sit here and visit, and if you want to tip me out of courtesy or donate to the cause, that's up to you." If the man didn't respond, Lillian would softly kiss his cheek.

"I'm going to leave now, but you're going to miss my black ass when I'm gone," Lillian recalls saying. "The next time I came around, he'd want to talk to me."

Late in the afternoon of July 9, 1980, Lillian had finished performing in New York Live and had just walked into the audience. She spotted a handsome young man with short, carefully combed hair, a nicely trimmed mustache, and a tailored jacket with a color-coordinated pocket puff handkerchief in the breast pocket.

"Hi. I'm Dede. Want to play?" Lillian asked, using her stage name. Without waiting for an answer, she sat down in his lap.

The man froze and shifted uncomfortably in his seat. He put his hands down to his sides, and Lillian, seeing an opening, slipped her hand inside his unbuttoned sport shirt and began stroking the thick hair on his chest.

"I don't want to play. I want to watch the show," the man said.

"That's okay, you don't have to tip, I'm going to sit here anyway," Lillian said. "You're cute. You look like Burt Reynolds."

The customer tried to gently push Lillian off his lap.

Lillian saw that his face was drained of color and his hands were trembling, and that encouraged her to continue. She liked making men uncomfortable. It made her feel powerful.

Lillian put both legs over the arms of the chair and, straddling the chair, brought her breasts very close to the customer's face. The customer's head jerked back as he tried to avoid contact with her nipples.

"Are you always this uptight?" Lillian asked, gently touching his face and leaning close to smell his aftershave. The customer tried to ignore her and looked around her at the dancer who was performing onstage.

Lillian glanced around and saw that the dancer was nude and directly above her. Slowly, the dancer turned around and touched her toes.

"Do you like her ass?" Lillian asked.

"It's all right," the customer said.

"Do you like mine?" Lillian asked.

"I can't see it," the customer replied.

Lillian jumped off the chair, turned around and dropped the panties she always wore into the audience. She wore them because it was fun to tease men with her panties.

"Now do you like it?" Lillian asked.

Before the customer could answer, someone blew a sharp, piercing whistle. A deep male voice from somewhere in the theater commanded, "ALL RIGHT, EVERYBODY! STAY WHERE YOU ARE! THIS IS A RAID AND YOU ARE ALL UNDER ARREST!"

"Burt! Quick! You better get out of here!" Lillian cried.

Burt jumped out of his seat and opened a button on his jacket. Beneath the jacket, he was wearing a star and carrying a revolver, a police radio, and two sets of handcuffs. Instantly, Lillian understood why he was so tense and why he had kept his hands over his hips.

"Burt!" she cried in disbelief. "You're with the cops!"

Fifteen vice cops were fanning out across the theater, taking pictures of nude women sitting on laps and placing them under arrest; others were racing up the stairs to the office to confiscate employee tax records.

Jack Harvey was busy working on an addition to the Green Door Room when he heard the whistle and the screams coming from New York Live. Seconds later, a young man wearing a badge on a sweater came racing up to him.

"Hold it right there. This is a big bust," the cop said.

"Oh yeah?" Jack replied calmly.

"Who are you?"

"I'm an outside contractor, hired to do some work here."

"Well, you better stop hammering now," the cop said before hurrying away.

Moments later, Jon Fontana, the Mitchell Brothers' cameraman, walked in and picked up a tool belt and began hammering nails in the wall. Other crew members appeared and picked up hammers and began pounding nails into the wall. When Alex Benton, the sound man, appeared, there were no more hammers left, so Benton picked up a board and began walking around the room.

"Who are these guys?" the cop in the sweater asked when he returned ten minutes later. Alex Benton was still walking around the room carrying the board.

"My crew," Jack replied.

"All right," the cop said, and left the room.

The cops hauled away twenty-nine people—seven performers, seven members of the Mitchell Brothers' staff, and fifteen members of the audience. Lillian Wright was not arrested because "Burt" looked after her.

In the upstairs office, police found a .45 caliber submachine gun and three ammunition clips welded together into a large banana clip, plus two rifles and a sawed-off shotgun. Officers also discovered a leather sap, or blackjack, a pair of sap gloves filled with lead, brass knuckles, a police baton, a bag of marijuana, and a white powdery substance believed to be cocaine.

No charges were filed on the drugs or weapons because they were not included in the search warrant.

On November 28, 1978, a former San Francisco supervisor named Dan White had scheduled an appointment with Mayor George Moscone to discuss reversing his decision to resign from the Board of Supervisors. A former police officer and firefighter, White had grown frustrated with city politics and had also discovered that he could not support his family on a supervisor's salary. He and his wife had opened a hot-potato stand at Pier 39, a tourist attraction near Fisherman's Wharf, and White had resigned from the Board of Supervisors to help her run it.

White had then reconsidered and decided he wanted his seat back. Mayor Moscone had first agreed to reappoint him, but then the mayor changed his mind. This further evidence of city hall perfidy had sent White into a blind rage.

On the day of his meeting with the mayor, White slipped through a side door of city hall that did not have a metal detector. A short time after entering the mayor's office, White pulled a police revolver and shot the mayor dead. Then he went down the hall and killed Supervisor Harvey Milk, the leader of San Francisco's gay community.

The Board of Supervisors elected Dianne Feinstein to succeed George Moscone.

Like all citizens of San Francisco, Jim and Artie had been stunned and saddened by the killings. It was bad enough to lose George Moscone, whom the brothers had considered a good guy. Now their very own version of the Wicked Witch of the West was calling the shots under the huge city hall dome, just a few blocks south of the O'Farrell.

With Feinstein as mayor, Jim and Artie had not been surprised when, after a two-year hiatus, the cops had started raiding the O'Farrell again (the brothers were now calling it the O'Farrell Eros Center). On March 1, 1979, police hit the theater and arrested eleven people. On August 1, the cops raided again and arrested eleven more dancers and office personnel. That was followed by the big raid on July 9, 1980, when twenty-nine people were arrested.

Jim and Artie publicly accused Mayor Feinstein of being behind the new harassment each time the cops made a raid. They began putting "For show times call Mayor Feinstein" and the mayor's office number up on the marquee. Every time the mayor changed it, the brothers put up the new number.

To attract even more attention, Jim and Artie closed the O'Farrell's doors on July 17, 1980—at the press conference called to announce the closure, the two showmen referred to the theater as "part of the cultural heritage of San Francisco"—temporarily putting fifty female performers out of work.

"We've been arrested a hundred and fifty times and we've never been brutalized like this," Jim said at the press conference, and went on to denounce the "thug cops" who had used "Gestapo tactics" during the July 9 raid.

"One girl was punched in the stomach and kneed by a policewoman," Jim told the reporters. "I'm not going to sit here and sell a ticket and have some guy have a heart attack or get beat up by a vice cop. It's not worth it."

A few days later, an informal agreement was reached: the theater would reopen and the cops would not come back, pending the outcome of a trial that was to be held in December 1980.

The lead attorney representing the Mitchell Brothers was Paul Halvonik, the former head of the Northern California affiliate of the American Civil Liberties Union. (Michael Kennedy had grown increasingly expensive and the brothers had begun using him sparingly.) Halvonik had a brilliant legal mind that had attracted the attention of Governor Jerry Brown, who had appointed him to the state Court of Appeal. But Halvonik and his wife had gotten into trouble for growing marijuana, and he had resigned from the Court of Appeal as part of a plea bargain.

His opponent was assistant district attorney Bernard Walter. Walter was a member of an old San Francisco family who had spent eight years as a Buddhist monk in Sri Lanka. He found the business the Mitchell Brothers were in deeply offensive because he felt it dehumanized women in the same way that enemies are dehumanized—Gooks, Chinks, Krauts, Commies—in wartime.

"Pornography is insidious because we associate sexual intimacy with love and trust," the soft-spoken, dark-haired Walter says. "A shortsighted social observer trained to think in terms of instant gratification may not consider porn a clear and present danger. It is indeed exceptionally rare for someone to look at *Hustler* and then pounce on the next sexual object and commit a deviant act. But education is incremental. Advertising demonstrates that. You don't buy a Toyota because you see one ad. You buy a Toyota because you see lots of ads.

"That's what pornography does," Walter concludes. "Through repetition, it wears away the idea that sex is based on love and trust. In the process, it dehumanizes women."

Walter had tried to convince his boss, DA Joseph Freitas (and later DA Arlo Smith), not to prosecute patrons who had been arrested at the O'Farrell. The theater was open for business; how could a patron who was visiting from Kansas, or even from Marin County, know beforehand that what was taking place inside was illegal? Walter also was not interested in prosecuting the female performers. They were only doing their jobs. It was the two brothers whom Walter was after.

(Despite Walter's entreaties, three O'Farrell performers were brought to trial by another assistant DA. In two of the cases, the jury was unable to reach a decision. A third dancer was found guilty of accepting money for a lewd act and was given a thirty-day suspended sentence and ordered to perform thirty-two hours of community service.)

To Bernard Walter, allowing the Mitchell Brothers to operate the O'Farrell a few blocks from city hall was as unfair as it was unseemly. If the cops arrested a black pimp who was running two or three women in the Tenderloin, the newspapers did not write about it. If the pimp hired an attorney, the attorney did not make the pimp out to be a hero who was defending the sanctity of the First Amendment. Walter considered Jim and Artie no different than that pimp. They just operated on a broader scale.

"The difference between a street pimp and the Mitchell Brothers is just business sophistication," Walter says. "If the theater, which was run as a whorehouse for years, was run by two dark, swarthy Sicilians, do you think the city would tolerate it? If it was run by two black brothers from Harlem? No way! Minorities who pimp women are sent to prison.

"Jim and Art got away with it because they were two clever, blue-eyed guys from Antioch who seduced the press, who seduced politicians, who seduced members of society," Walter continues. "More than one reporter has told me the Mitchell Brothers were generous with their cocaine. The women [performers at the O'Farrell] themselves have told me they were used as favors for members of the press and for celebrities like Sammy Davis, Jr., and [*Screw* magazine publisher] Al Goldstein."

Walter had no intention of trying to stop what went on *onstage* in New York Live. He believed that was covered under First Amendment guarantees of freedom of expression. What he wanted to stop was the contact between the performers and the audience. He researched red-light abatement statutes in an attempt to discover precisely what was, and what was not, prostitution. He was pleased and surprised to discover that the statutes defined prostitution as "the touching of women's breasts and genitals for the purpose of sexual arousal or gratification in exchange for money or other considerations."

The statutes did not say anything about *intercourse*. Touching in exchange for money was prostitution, and Walter had a slew of pictures taken by undercover officers with infrared cameras that showed customers doing everything from oral copulation to fondling the women's breasts.

"Buttocks, genitals, and breasts were being touched, groped, kissed, and sucked every day by hundreds of people," Walter says. "In terms of the statutes, that was prostitution."

The trial, which began on December 12, 1980, proved to be uneventful. Paul Halvonik, the constitutional law expert, argued that there was no clear evidence that prostitution had occurred at the theater and that, in any case, the theater was protected under the Constitution's provisions for free speech. Walter argued that acts of prostitution had indeed occurred and produced police reports and photographs taken by undercover officers to prove it.

Superior Court judge Ira Brown spent several weeks considering the arguments and issued an order on December 30. The ruling prohibited the owners and operators of the O'Farrell from "allowing the occurrence, continuance or recurrence of acts of lewdness or prostitution upon the premises."

"It's a major victory," Jim told the *Chronicle*. "The judge simply ordered us not to break the law and we're not. We don't consider what goes on here either lewd or prostitution."

Bernard Walter also claimed victory.

"We couldn't have asked for more," Walter told the *Chronicle* reporter, and added that the vice squad would be checking to see that the Mitchell Brothers abided by the judge's decision.

In truth, the Mitchell Brothers had won. Walter had asked Judge

Brown to require the theater to post a sign that would say: "This theater is licensed by the City and County of San Francisco. Employees are not permitted to (1) engage at any time in sexual conduct; (2) remove all of their clothing; (3) expose their genital areas; (4) allow patrons to touch their breasts or genital areas; and (5) touch the patrons." Judge Brown's order hadn't gone that far.

A day after Judge Brown's ruling was made public, the *Examiner* sent a reporter to the O'Farrell to see what effect the order prohibiting "acts of lewdness or prostitution upon the premises" was having on the theater. The reporter found that onstage in New York Live, a "dancer removed all of her clothing and bent over backwards, fondling her genitals with her fingers and, at one point, a long feather." Meanwhile, in the audience, a customer "held up a tip. A woman sat on his lap and the customer fondled her bare breasts."

Bernard Walter may have lost the first round, but he was not finished with the Mitchell Brothers. Undercover vice squad officers kept visiting the O'Farrell, collecting evidence of, as Walter says, erogenous zones "being touched, groped, kissed, and sucked every day by hundreds of people." It took eighteen months, but when Walter was finally convinced he had enough evidence, he went back into court and charged Jim and Artie Mitchell with contempt of court for repeatedly and knowingly violating Judge Brown's order.

This was serious. If they were convicted, the theater would be closed and the brothers would face six months in jail and heavy fines. Undercover officers had taken dozens and dozens of pictures of performers and customers doing things that, by almost any standard, were lewd. Simply put, the DA had them.

This time, Dennis Roberts, a tough, articulate attorney from Oakland, was handling the case. The more Roberts and the brothers studied the case, the more convinced they were that their best defense was to try to take the DA's case away from him.

A month before the trial, the brothers announced that they had entered into an agreement with the DA's office. Plexiglas would be installed in the Ultra Room. "No tipping" signs would be prominently displayed throughout the theater. Female performers who roamed the audience would wear bras and "pants or shorts the legs of which shall extend no less than five inches below the crotch area."

Dennis Roberts called it "a good-faith showing on our part," a way of demonstrating the Mitchell Brothers were lawful businessmen. Bernard Walter said, "In a very quiet way, the city has gained a major victory."

But the agreement did not get the brothers out of the legal woods. They still had to stand trial for contempt of court. That trial, which began in San Francisco Superior Court on July 14, 1982, did not have the usual drama that is produced by a prosecutor and a defense attorney battling over two versions of one event. The case the defense presented was so bizarre that the trial took on the surreal feel of the theater of the absurd.

Ignoring the evidence of oral copulation and digital intercourse that was presented by undercover officers, Dennis Roberts told Judge Frank Shaw that the O'Farrell was not a house of prostitution where men went to be sexually aroused. Roberts described the theater as a place men visited out of "curiosity and interest." The O'Farrell was not a house of prostitution because men did not go there to get up, over, and out. Indeed, they weren't even *getting aroused*.

"Arousal and gratification means more to me than a quick sniff," testified Margo St. James, an expert witness for the defense. St. James was the former prostitute who had founded COYOTE, Call Off Your Old Tired Ethics, the country's first prostitutes' union.

"Arousal doesn't happen in a group setting with other men," testified Rev. Ted McIlvenna, another expert witness for the defense. A Methodist minister and professional sexologist, McIlvenna was and still is the director of the Institute for the Advanced Study of Human Sexuality on Franklin Street in San Francisco, the first graduate school of sexology in the United States.

"A few men might get an erection," McIlvenna testified, "but most men would not in a group of other men."

Judge Frank Shaw could not believe what he was hearing.

"You're going to tell me that oral copulation is curiosity and enlightenment?" he asked Rev. McIlvenna.

"It's ludicrous to suggest that the type of conduct [that goes on at the O'Farrell] would not lead to sexual arousal in a male," the judge told Dennis Roberts later in the trial.

"Perhaps in a romantic setting," Roberts quickly replied.

"It doesn't have to be romantic," Judge Shaw snapped.

When the trial ended, the judge gave lawyers on both sides ten weeks to present written briefs in the case. It appears that nothing in the brief the defense presented altered the impressions Judge

Shaw had formed in court. On December 2, 1982, he sentenced Jim and Artie to six months in jail and fined them $62,000 for contempt of court.

Lawyers for the Mitchell Brothers appealed the conviction to the state Appeal Court. The prosecution prevailed there, but a majority of the justices on the California Supreme Court ruled that the Mitchell Brothers were entitled to a jury trial, and the conviction was overturned.

When things quieted down, Jim and Artie rescinded the "no tipping" policy and dancers clad in see-through bras and skimpy panties went back into the audience. But these changes were cosmetic compared with less obvious, but far more potent changes that were taking place in the political and cultural milieu.

The sexual revolution of the 1960s, which was based on the idea that the freedom to explore sex is fundamental to the idea of freedom, the "do your own thing," "get your laws off my body" movement that had united sexual libertarians with early feminists, gays, lesbians, and pornographers like the Mitchell Brothers, had been shattered. And nobody exemplified the split better than Jim and Artie.

In the late 1960s and early 1970s, the Mitchell Brothers had considered gays allies. Gays were persecuted for their sexual preference; the brothers were getting busted for bringing sex out of the closet; they were all in it together. But after the Ultra Room raids of the late 1970s and early 1980s, the Mitchell Brothers had not been content to lob verbal cannonballs at Mayor Feinstein, the cops, or the DA's office. The brothers had begun attacking the gay community.

"This city is getting weird," Jim told the *Chronicle* after the July 9, 1980, raid. "They give homosexuals the right to fornicate in public places, but they don't give a second thought to depriving heterosexuals of their rights. . . . Gays don't get bothered because they are a political force. Heterosexuals' rights are being trampled because we're in a minority group."

Further evidence of the split in the old 1960s sexual coalition were the women who on occasion began picketing the O'Farrell. Members of a group called Women Against Pornography, or WAP, marched in front of the theater carrying signs that condemned pornography for promoting violence against women.

The WAP marchers were shock troops in a bitter battle over pornography that is still being waged in San Francisco and in cities across the country. On one side are the "pro-censorship feminists"; on the other side are the "sex-positive feminists."

The two sides do not like each other.

"Gloria Steinem sold out and made an unholy alliance with the right wing, and I'd like to shake [radical feminist] Andrea Dworkin until her teeth rattle," says Maggie Rubenstein, a sex therapist and instructor at the Institute for the Advanced Study of Human Sexuality. "The women's movement took this retarded position that anything about sex that isn't flowery or sweet is taboo. They think porn causes all the ills in the world, as if there were no rapes or brutality toward women before the printing press was invented.

"The problem with sex today is fourteen-year-old pregnant girls," Rubenstein concludes. "Pornography doesn't cause that. Porn is a reflection of a sex-phobic society, and so, I'm sad to say, is the women's movement."

The feminist movement of the early 1970s was in large part an exploration of women's sexuality, of *Our Bodies, Ourselves.* At a typical National Organization for Women conference in 1972 or 1973, there were seminars on abortion, methods of contraception, the anatomy of reproduction, and the nature of women's sensual pleasure. Nora Ephron was writing essays with tag lines like "Happiness is knowing what your uterus looks like."

But as the women's movement explored sexuality, it inevitably ran head-on into the dark side of human sexuality. That led to provocative investigations of rape and sexual abuse like Susan Brownmiller's *Against Our Will.*

Studies like Brownmiller's are among the women's movement's lasting and most important contributions. Incest, child abuse and molestation, wife abuse, and date rape have emerged as major social issues that are no longer ignored. Newspaper feature sections and television talk shows have become forums for discussions about sex as an expression of power between an employee and her (or sometimes his) boss; between a priest or a minister and a parishioner; between a therapist or a doctor and a client.

Inevitably, the feminists' exploration into the relationship between sex and abuse or sex and violence focused on pornography. In a landmark essay in the August 1977 *Ms.,* Gloria Steinem portrayed pornography as an ugly manifestation of a master-slave relationship between men and women. The women in pornography are "power-less and without alternatives." The pleasure men obtained from pornography is not sexual; it is the pleasure the conqueror gets grinding his boot in the face of the conquered.

"Pornography," Steinem wrote, "is the pleasure of the powerful in the humiliation and dehumanization of the powerless."

In her introduction to *Out of Bondage,* Linda Lovelace's second autobiography, Steinem presented Lovelace as a symbol for the captive women who work in the sex trade, a victim who only did what she did because she was held prisoner by the evil Chuck Traynor. Lovelace was one of "thousands of teenage runaways, terrified women and even children who are victims of forced prostitution and pornography each year, victims who are forced to coexist and depend for their lives on their victimizers for far longer than the duration of a rapist's attack." Lovelace was a heroine for mustering the courage to tell her story because it "would help not only herself but others forced into pornography and prostitution."

Steinem's views on pornography seem tame when compared with the militant views of Andrea Dworkin and her ally, the legal scholar Catharine A. MacKinnon. To Dworkin, pornography is "Dachau brought into the bedroom and celebrated." Not only is pornography produced by Nazis who are emblematic of the age-old domination of women by men; it is a window into the deepest caverns of men's minds. Men are beasts; the penis is the weapon they use to dominate and inflict pain. According to Dworkin, "intercourse remains a means or the means of physiologically making a woman inferior; communicating to her cell by cell her own inferior status, impressing it on her, burning it into her by shoving it into her, over and over, pushing and thrusting until she gives up and gives in—which is called *surrender* in the male lexicon."

Dworkin and MacKinnon are not cerebral feminists who are content to denounce porn from behind a lectern or a word processor. They are activists who have been instrumental in attempts to pass civil rights ordinances in Indianapolis and Minneapolis that would make pornography a form of sexual discrimination and enable citizens to file suit in civil court to ban hard-core porn—and to collect damages for whatever harm the plaintiffs could prove had been done them by pornographers.

Because of its prominence in San Francisco and the large number of performers the O'Farrell employed (at any given time, 60 to

100 female performers work there), the O'Farrell became a focus for the debate between the pro-censorship and the sex-positive forces. To the WAP activists who picketed the theater, the dancers were victims, like Linda Lovelace. Their work at the O'Farrell was both a continuation and a public expression of the terrible abuse they had suffered in private.

The sex-positive forces took exactly the opposite view.

"Gloria Steinem is full of shit. Are we going to say that all the women in erotic art—and we have the world's largest collection—are abused? That Salome took John the Baptist's head because she was abused? Come on!" says Rev. McIlvenna, whose ire rises at the mention of the pro-censorship feminists.

"It's a feminist lie that women in the sex industry are abused. Feminists lie all the time!" McIlvenna continues. "We've done sexual histories on forty or fifty dancers at the O'Farrell and not once did we encounter a pattern of abuse."

Ted McIlvenna founded his Institute for the Advanced Study of Human Sexuality back in the 1960s because he felt that "the mission of the church is to set people free. Sex is the one area where less information is supposed to be better than more information. That's stupid." The institute, McIlvenna believes, has become an alternative to the "stuffy, conservative" Kinsey Institute in Bloomington, Indiana.

"The women who work at the O'Farrell are there because they *want* to be there," McIlvenna says, denouncing the belief that pornography and violence are inextricably linked. "The O'Farrell is a symbol of freedom in this community. It's the one place you can go for remedial sex education and feel good about it. The Mitchell Brothers and the women who work there have done more for the sexual health of this community than all the sex therapists combined."

The truth is, there have been and still are dancers at the O'Farrell who fit neatly into *both* the pro-censorship and the sex-positive feminists' image of women who work in the sex industry. Lisa Loring and Lillian Wright and a former medical student who is now a practicing physician in Northern California are examples of women who worked there because they were being paid to explore an area that had always been hidden and mysterious.

A surprisingly large number of dancers at the O'Farrell—at any time, the percentage hovers around 40 percent—are gay. When they describe their work, the gay dancers are likely to talk about what a kick it is to "gender-bend," and the feeling of power that comes with knowing you are gay at the same time you are turning on a roomful of men.

"The O'Farrell was a lark, an adventure," says Debi Sundahl, a former O'Farrell dancer who is a co-founder of *On Our Backs,* a magazine of lesbian erotica. "It was a chance to infiltrate a man's world, and that was perversely fascinating.

"When I started working at the O'Farrell, I found working with someone of the same sex incredibly exciting," Sundahl continues. "Sex is incredibly fluid, there's so much to learn. I discovered my body was capable of sexual feelings I didn't know it had, and of course I wanted to explore that completely. I felt I was exploring feminism firsthand, and getting paid to do it."

For a long period during the 1980s, a large number of O'Farrell dancers were followers of the Bhagwan Shree Rajneesh, the Hindu guru who established a commune near Antelope, Oregon, that attracted large numbers of followers. In the end, the Bhagwan may have loved the string of Rolls-Royces his devotees showered on him more than he did anything else.

Corrupt though he may have been, the Bhagwan was part of an ancient tantric tradition that believes sex can be a form of yoga. The Bhagwan preached that guilt is learned and there is no such thing as sin, particularly sexual sin. Sex is a natural desire and desires are created to be satisfied. The root of all evil is the failure to satisfy these desires. Sexual frustration produces sadistic hypocrites who condemn and ultimately try to destroy those who have experienced the joy they have themselves been denied.

The Bhagwan's followers who performed at the O'Farrell were doing his work. They lived very cheaply in San Francisco, often crowding into small, sparsely furnished apartments. When they had earned a large amount of money, they left for Rajneeshpuram, the divine city the Bhagwan was building in Oregon. It was a rare customer at the theater who knew the tip he was handing a dancer was going to help pay for another Rolls-Royce for the Bhagwan.

But many of the O'Farrell dancers did not believe sex was a cause. Rev. Ted McIlvenna and the sex-positive feminists to the contrary, many sex performers confirm the belief of Steinem, Dworkin, and the pro-censorship feminists that women who work in pornography have inevitably been battered and sexually abused.

"Find a woman who grew up with nurturing parents who made her feel loved, who raised her to the age of eighteen so she's happy and well adjusted, and there's no way you could get that woman to take off her clothes for money," says Dave Patrick. "Something weird had to happen to make her want to work in the sex industry."

Dave Patrick is as far from a feminist ideologue as you can get. An intelligent, forthright man who is tall and good-looking, has blond hair, a thick mustache, and a passion for bowling and beaches, Dave is the renegade editor and ace photographer for *The Spectator*, a weekly newspaper that covers the sex industry in the Bay Area. *The Spectator* is the epitome of a pro-sex, pro-pornography, anti-censorship paper, and Dave has been a staffer since the paper spun off from *The Berkeley Barb* in 1978. He has interviewed and photographed hundreds of sex performers. During a six-year period, he dated dozens of women in the industry.

"The reality is, every woman in the sex business that I've ever spent any time with was abused," Dave says. "One hundred percent. No exceptions. So what do they do? They end up making a living being fondled by strangers for money. It's perpetuating the thing that made them nuts in the first place.

"It's almost like they feel comfortable in that role; it's something they are real familiar with," Dave continues. "Some women feel sex is their only power. I've met women who are real smart who don't know they're smart, they've been beaten down their whole lives, been told they're worthless and no good. The only thing they have at their disposal is their body. They know they can manipulate people by using their sexuality. They go with that because they don't know what else to do with their lives."

Dave was attracted to women in the sex industry because he identifies with them. In a two-part series he wrote in *The Spectator* about his experiences dating sex performers, he said, "I was sexually abused as a child. The memories are so terrible I've almost completely blocked them out, but the scars that will probably never heal continue to affect my life today. That's why, no doubt, I was attracted to the kind of 'impossible' women who populate the sex industry in such large numbers. I'll admit, at times, I can be a pretty 'impossible guy.'"

Dave had a white-knight complex. He'd get to know a performer, find out she had a horrible past, and decide, "Gee, all she needs is for a good guy to come along and show her that not all men are horrible. I can save her, and once I do she'll appreciate me and love me because I pulled her out of the pits."

It never worked.

"A nice guy comes along and they don't know how to handle it," Dave says. "I'd get close to somebody and she'd be scared of being that close to a man, so she'd do things that were unforgivable so I would have to leave. I'd try to be real patient and talk to her and say, 'Look, I'm not a wimp, you did this horrible thing, don't do it again,' but it didn't work, she always did it again. It was like, if I wasn't beating on her, if I wasn't really pissed off, then I must not care about her."

Over his fifteen years in the business, Dave Patrick has seen a pattern repeated over and over again. "The prettiest, nicest dancers are the ones going out with the scuzziest, most abusive guys," Dave says. "Every night, these women have guys telling them how beautiful they are. Every night, they get paid a lot of money for doing nothing. I think in their heart of hearts they feel there has to be some payback. If they get a guy who dumps on them, then somehow it's even.

"I also think that these women have hated men for so long they don't want to forgive them," Dave continues. "They pick bad guys over and over again so that they can say, 'Yeah, all men are scum. I have a right to hate them.'"

Dave Patrick has done stories about dancers at the O'Farrell like Tanya, a beautiful black woman who drank herself into an early grave, and Megan Leigh, a young O'Farrell performer who committed suicide in 1990. He has seen women drink themselves into oblivion, but he is convinced that the sex industry is the most dangerous drug of all.

"I think maybe the most destructive thing about the sex industry is, it allows these women to live out their delusions," Dave says. "It takes years of hard work to make it as a legitimate performer. A sex worker doesn't understand that. The appeal to her is, it's all today. She picks her songs and her costumes and she walks out onto the stage and it's all there—the lights, the music, the rapt audience. While she's onstage, she's Madonna, she's a star!

"There's no dues to be paid. It's all instant gratification. That's why so many performers get hooked on cocaine. Performers get to the point where they want whatever they can get right now. They get used to the attention and the easy money and they don't learn to do anything else. They talk about going back to school or learning a trade but it just never happens.

"By the time a performer hits thirty she's done a lot of drugs and alcohol and she's usually finished, trashed out," Dave concludes. "She doesn't have any skills. She doesn't have a résumé. What's she going to do then?"

10

Family Affairs

"MEREDITH, what's the possibility of me spending some time at the Cape this summer?" asked Jim.

Meredith and Jim were in the Mitchell Brothers' business offices in a suite in the Jack Tar Hotel on Van Ness and O'Farrell, a block from the theater. The brothers had rented the suite because, with the ever-present possibility of a raid and the continuing parade of good buddies, weirdos, and semi-naked women through the clubhouse upstairs at the O'Farrell, the hotel was a much more suitable place to deal with legal and business matters.

Meredith had been in her second year of night classes at John Fitzgerald Kennedy Law School, and was working part-time for a law firm that did debt-collection work, when her ex-husband had approached her. "Jim and I have talked this over and we think it would be a good idea if you'd go to work for us," Artie told her. "We're getting hit with astronomical legal bills, fifteen hundred to two thousand dollars a day during a trial. You could do the legal research and file the briefs. That way, we'd only have to pay Kennedy and Joe Rhine for the actual hours they worked on a case."

Meredith had agreed and started as a certified law clerk. After she passed the bar, the Mitchell Brothers had hired her as their full-time, in-house attorney. Jim and Artie were happy with her work, and Meredith—who still loved being around Artie—was delighted to be part of Cinema 7 again. She was seeing ten times more of Artie than she had when they were married, and she and Jim had developed a comfortable business relationship.

There had always been something about Jim that scared Meredith. The things she loved about Art—his lightness, his sense of fun —were absent in Jim. Jim was authoritarian, almost dictatorial. Adrienne was a good example of that. Jim had buried his marriage to Adrienne so thoroughly that she had become a nonperson. If her name happened to come up, Jim's face stayed blank, as if he'd never heard of her.

Now that Meredith was no longer married to Artie, her relationship with Jim had improved. He no longer considered her a rival. He listened to what she had to say and they worked together to reach a decision. She had scrupulously kept her private life separate from her business life.

But now Jim wanted to go to the Cape.

Momentarily stunned by his request, Meredith looked down at the floor. This, she thought, is a classic piece of one-upmanship by Jim. He knew that Meredith and Art had spent parts of five summers on Cape Cod, and that Artie had loved every minute. One of the first things Art had said after Meredith asked for a divorce was "Does this mean I can't go to the Cape anymore?" And now here was big brother Jim trying to invade what had been his little brother's favorite turf.

"Well, sure, you can come to the Cape. Why not?" Meredith replied, unable to think of a way of saying no.

"Hey, that's great!" Jim said. "I've always wanted to get back there."

With five other families, the Bradford family had purchased a section of the Cape Cod shoreline back in the late 1950s, when the price, by today's standards, was reasonable. Meredith was spending so many summers there she had begun to feel she was imposing on her family, and after she and Artie had divorced, she had asked her father for permission to build a house on the family property, where she had a small beach house built.

"I'm not going to be able to get back there until sometime in early

July," Meredith told Jim. "Why don't you take my house during June?"

"Done!" Jim said. "The sooner the better. I really need to get the hell out of San Francisco."

After his split with Adrienne, Jim had rebounded to Debbie Marinoff, the talented, strikingly pretty former art director at the theater. Adrienne was tough and strong-willed; Debbie was soft, creative, and flexible. Although she had never forgiven him for closing down the Nickelodeon, Debbie liked Jim immensely. Debbie was a rich Jewish girl from Beverly Hills and Jim was her idea of a pure American, an Okie from the plains who had fulfilled the American Dream by coming out of nowhere and creating himself anew. Away from the theater and his role as the tough porn entrepreneur, Debbie had found Jim to be gentle and caring. Sexually, he was very straight.

But there were things about Jim that Debbie did not like. No matter how sweet he acted when they were alone in her apartment, Jim spoke about women in a crudely sexist way that drove Debbie up a wall.

"He'd always refer to women as either brood mares or whores. They were always one or the other," Debbie recalls. "I was different, I was an *ingenue,* a member of the club. He liked me and he liked my art, but he liked my tight pussy best. Jim could be really sweet, but the bottom line was, he wanted women to shut up and spread their legs."

What bothered Debbie most was that Jim wanted to dominate her. She had started a small design and advertising business and Jim wanted her to fold it and marry him. He insisted on making every decision, and when Debbie didn't acquiesce, "Jim pulled the silent treatment." He would turn cold and aloof and speak to her only on business matters until Debbie would say, "Oh, come on, Jim, stop being silly." She would sit down on his lap and pat his bald dome, and pretty soon Jim would smile.

In time, Debbie saw that she was surrendering more and more of herself to Jim. She was a strong woman who was determined to make it as an artist—that is why she had come to the O'Farrell in the first place. Feeling strangled, Debbie moved back to Los Angeles. Jim visited her every weekend, and eventually they moved into an Art Deco mansion at the top of Laurel Canyon next to Hal Ashby, the film director. Debbie was in her element; she had grown up in the house that Orson Welles and Rita Hayworth had lived in when they were married, and had gone steady with David Cassidy before he became a teen heartthrob. But Jim never adjusted to life at the top of Laurel Canyon.

"Jim couldn't cut it in L.A.; he was a redneck with a big old truck and all his dogs," Debbie says. "He kept saying, 'You're going to leave me because I'm an Okie,' and he was right. I was a nice Jewish girl; he was a pornographer. There was no way I was going to marry him. My parents wouldn't even consent to meet him."

Jim and Debbie finally split up. Debbie tried to get a job in advertising, but her pornography portfolio did not impress the agencies. After a few months of trying, she gave up and took a job selling Mercedes-Benzes for L.A. Motors in downtown Los Angeles.

Debbie was walking the showroom floor, making a statement about herself and her product by wearing a stylish three-piece suit, when the door opened and Jim Mitchell strode in. Debbie stopped in her tracks; Jim spotted her and stomped past the gleaming sedans.

"I want you back," Jim said.

Debbie stared at Jim but did not say anything. There was something different about him, something strange. His eyes were cold and he seemed tense, as tightly wired as the ignition system in the big Mercedes SL Debbie was standing beside. Then it hit her. Jim was coked up.

"You're not so cute anymore," Jim snarled, eyeing her suit.

"What's this cute shit?" Debbie yelled, her voice echoing across the sedate showroom. Here and there, a head turned.

"Huh? What's this cute shit?" Debbie repeated in a quieter voice. "What am I? The eternal chick?"

Debbie calmed down, and that night she and Jim went out. They did lines of cocaine and went through their relationship once again. Debbie wanted a career; Jim didn't want her to have a career. Jim wanted children; Debbie didn't want children.

Jim returned to San Francisco and months passed. And then Debbie changed her mind and decided she really did want Jim. But by then it was too late.

"He was already with Mary Jane, and she was pregnant," Debbie recalls. "I said, 'Come on, marry her,' and he did."

Mary Jane Whitty was in her mid-twenties and worked as a cashier and dancer at the O'Farrell. Ordinarily, to Jim, that meant she was someone of little or no consequence beyond the economics of the sex industry. But according to Debbie Marinoff, Jim had a white-knight complex, just like *The Spectator*'s Dave Patrick.

"Mary Jane was a damsel in distress," Debbie says. "Jim rescued her, he took over her life. He loved playing that role."

Like Lisa Loring, Mary Jane was a graduate of Holy Names, a Catholic high school for girls in Oakland. Mary Jane was an aspiring artist, a tall, not particularly attractive woman with short brown hair she occasionally tinted red. She dressed, Artie was fond of pointing out, "like an Antioch schoolteacher," favoring conservative, flower-print dresses. Like Lisa Loring, Mary Jane had taken a job at the theater to explore a world that was forbidden and secret.

After Meta, Jim and Mary Jane's first child was born, Artie and Meredith's first child, Liberty, became their babysitter. Liberty loved Mary Jane. Mary Jane was her adult friend, someone she could talk to. Mary Jane was also wonderful with Storm and Mariah, Liberty's younger brother and sister.

"Mary Jane was always really, really sweet to me," Liberty says. "I got the impression that I liked her better than the adults did."

Liberty's impression was valid. The boys upstairs at the O'Farrell did not intensely dislike Mary Jane, as they had Adrienne, but they were not about to invite her to join the club either.

"I think Jim's thinking was: 'This woman is a good bet for stability. She'll make a good mother for my kids.' Jim was very unsophisticated about women," says Mike Bradford.

"I think Jim was doing what J.R. had done," adds Richard Lackey, Jim's high school buddy. "He picked a young woman, someone he could train."

After Meredith offered to loan Jim her summer house at the Cape, she had called her parents and told them that Jim, Mary Jane, and little Meta would be spending June there. "Don't make a big deal out of it," Meredith said. "Say hello, be pleasant, but don't worry about having them over."

The Bradfords invited Jim and his family to dinner shortly after they arrived on the Cape, and invited them again and again. Dr. Bradford and Jim hit it off exactly as he and Artie had years earlier. Soon they were fishing for tuna and bluefish, and spending hours together puttering around the property.

For Jim, Dr. Bradford was a substitute father, someone who filled the gaping hole that had opened when J.R. died. For Dr. Bradford,

Jim was a wonderful new friend, someone who was as interested in his hobbies as he was.

Jim had such a great month that the next year, 1981, he decided that he and Mary Jane were going to be bicoastal; their growing family (they now had two children and would eventually have four) would spend six months of the year on the Cape and six months in San Francisco.

At heart, Jim was a gambler and an outlaw, but after countless arrests, endless legal battles, and the incessant, unbridled hedonism of the porn business, he had grown weary of it all. Assistant DA Bernard Walter once described Jim as the kind of guy who would go out and feed his parking meter every two hours; Artie, Walter said, would ignore the meter and give the meter maid the finger if he saw her slipping a ticket under his windshield wiper.

At age thirty-eight, it was time for Jim to indulge the quiet, stable side of his character.

The temporary retreat from porn was not the result of a philosophical decision Jim had reached. Jim was not a philosophical guy. He had developed a "Jones," a nasty cocaine habit. He was not about to check into a hospital that had a chemical dependency program, or join a twelve-step program like Alcoholics Anonymous or Narcotics Anonymous. He was a Mitchell Brother and the Mitchell Brothers were antiestablishment; they did not trust institutions. Jim was going to deal with his habit his own way. He was going to move 3,000 miles away from his suppliers and kick it on his own.

Jim bought a large Colonial house inland from the Bradford property and, in his typical grandiose way, had an immense garage added to store the cars and boats he intended to collect. One of his prized possessions was a cherried-out '56 Ford pickup. Every time he spotted the truck, a delighted Dr. Bradford would call out, "Here comes Jim in his little red truck!"

Unfortunately, the truck, Jim, his wife and kids, and Mary Jane's women friends from the O'Farrell visited the Bradford property too often, and a cultural clash developed.

Yankees have a respect for property that borders on the divine. There are parts of New England that have remained unspoiled because the flinty descendants of old families that inherited them would rather live "land poor" than sell to developers and watch the fields and wood yards be subdivided. And Yankee propriety says that you enter someone's house only after being invited in.

Jim was the product of Okie hospitality, of a world where the door is always open and whatever you want is in the refrigerator. Somehow, he and Mary Jane had gotten the idea that the Bradfords' house and the private beach they shared with the five other families were theirs to use as they wanted. Jim, Mary Jane, their children, and their guests descended on the Bradfords. They used the house as a beach house, leaving things on tables and diapers in the toilet, traipsing in and out to use the bathroom or the phone. And the women were sunbathing topless.

The Bradfords' sense of privacy and decorum were both violated. It was their house, their retreat; they had a right to decide who came and went. But they were in agony. Nobody wanted to alienate Jim.

Finally, as Yankees often do, the Bradfords decided to deal with things directly.

"Jim, I don't want to drive you away for good, but this is our house," Mrs. Bradford said one afternoon, after she and her husband had asked Jim to sit down in the kitchen. "You don't own it and Mary Jane doesn't own it. You can't come in here and take what you want and use what you want. We need our space, Jim."

"It just can't go on like this, Jim," Dr. Bradford added. "You and I don't see it because we're usually out fishing, but the feeling around here is, we've been invaded. Things are getting touchy and before there is any unpleasantness, we thought we'd let you know how we're feeling."

"We love having you here, Jim," Mrs. Bradford said. "We just can't allow you and your friends to take over the property."

Jim was inhaling deeply on a cigarette and looking at the floor. He had the deadpan look of a tired gambler on his face, the look he habitually wore when he was listening to someone pitch a business proposition. When the Bradfords were finished, he remained silent and kept staring at the floor.

"I understand what you're saying," Jim said finally. "I didn't realize things had gotten so out of hand."

Jim got up slowly and crushed his cigarette in an ashtray. "I'll talk to Mary Jane about it," he said, and then he walked out the door.

The Bradfords were greatly relieved. Jim had taken it well; things were going to work out. Dr. Bradford was not going to lose his friend.

An hour or so later, the phone rang. It was Mary Jane. Ordinarily quiet and pleasant, Mary Jane was furious.

"How could you treat us like this! Like we're dirt!" Mary Jane screamed at Mrs. Bradford. "We're all family!"

Mary Jane hung up and then called Meredith and screamed at her. That afternoon, when Meredith drove up to her house, Jim was waiting. She got out of her car and Jim walked up and pointed a finger at her.

"You're fired!" he said, and turned his back and stomped away.

Meredith called her office the next day and learned that Jim had also fired Dianne Ferguson, her legal secretary.

"It was a really *drastic thing* to do," Meredith recalls. "We were doing all kinds of briefs to the Court of Appeal and the Supreme Court. Dianne was the only other connection to the cases and she was just excellent, really competent. Firing her was a big mistake. She was the only one who could have explained what we were doing to whoever Jim hired to replace us. But Jim didn't care. He wanted us out."

What the Bradfords thought was carefully worded criticism had turned out to be gasoline that hit the inferiority feelings smoldering just below the surface in Jim. The Bradfords were WASPs, insiders who had gotten there first; people like them always had the final say on what was right and wrong. Jim had been fighting people like them all his life.

Jim had thought he had finally crossed the line and been accepted for who he was. He had adopted a new father who could teach him to behave like people who had impeccable manners, people who did the right thing instinctively. And his adopted father had betrayed him, had made him feel like a trespasser, an Okie rube who didn't know any better.

That whole summer, Jim did not come back to the Bradfords'. If he happened to cross paths with Dr. Bradford in a store, Jim looked right through him.

"My dad was brokenhearted," Mark Bradford says. "He missed the hell out of Jim."

Meredith kept thinking that Jim's firing her over something that had happened on the Cape wasn't fair. She had done a really good job for the Mitchell Brothers. Before coming to the Cape, she had spent thirty days in trial in Santa Ana, California, battling the forces of Charles Keating and the CDL in the Mitchell Brothers' longest, most bitter, and most expensive case.

Santa Ana is the heart of Orange County, the place where John Wayne and Ronald Reagan are folk heroes. The battle began in 1975 when the Mitchell Brothers bought the former United Artists Theatre in upscale Honer Plaza, renamed it the Santa Ana Theatre, and replaced *The Apple Dumpling Gang* with *Sodom and Gomorrah*. There would not have been much of an outcry if the theater had opened in a run-down area of downtown Santa Ana. But because the porn theater was in a nice mall, the citizens' reaction was "Oh my God! It's coming to *our* neighborhood."

The outrage was so great that the Santa Ana city council hired James J. Clancy, perhaps America's most fervid antiporn crusader, to drive the Mitchells out of town. Clancy was the point man for Citizens for Decency Through Law, and had spent years on the road, organizing chapters for the CDL.

"The council basically told Clancy, 'Go get 'em!' " Santa Ana councilman Gordon Bricken told the Los Angeles *Times*. "We expected to go out there and scare them away. . . . The theory was that the big guy on the block could just knock 'em out. In reality, the council discovered the Mitchell Brothers are a savvy group of guys."

The council passed an ordinance stating that the Santa Ana Theatre specialized in "lewd" films and was therefore a "public nuisance." Because it was a public nuisance, like an unsafe building or a toxic dump, the city had the right to close it down. Meredith and other attorneys for the Mitchell Brothers argued that although the courts had the legal right to declare a film obscene, the courts did not have the right to close a theater for showing obscene films. They won time after time.

"The judge in Santa Ana hated my guts," Meredith recalls. "He hated porn and here was this *female* representing the pornographers, and that made it double disgusting. But he had to rule in my favor on all the legal issues. He didn't want to look stupid; he didn't want to be overturned. You could almost hear him crying as he ruled for our side."

(The Santa Ana Theatre was taking in over $1 million a year at the box office, making it one of the top five XXX theaters in the country. But the longer it stayed open, the more determined the good citizens of Santa Ana were to close it down. The city ended up filing over forty lawsuits and spending $500,000 to try to rid Santa Ana of the Mitchell Brothers.

(Eleven years after they started the fight, the Santa Ana city council threw in the towel. In 1987, the city agreed to cease filing lawsuits and to pay the Mitchell Brothers $200,000 to cover attorneys' fees and settle claims of legal harassment. In return, the brothers agreed to stop placing the names of the films on the marquee. A few years later, the brothers sold the theater, and the new owners turned it into a mainstream movie house.)

All that summer, Meredith kept thinking that Jim would calm down, remember how she had helped beat the CDL in Santa Ana, and rehire her. She was especially hopeful because she had Art on her side. Art wouldn't let Jim run over her like this. Art had his children to think of.

Meredith had felt so bad about divorcing him that she had not aggressively pursued child support and was receiving just $150 per child per month. It was Meredith who was supporting the children. Surely, Art would protect her livelihood. Surely, he would turn Jim around.

"What are we gonna do?" Art asked every time Meredith called that summer. Meredith didn't know, but she felt better, knowing Art was on her side. Meredith returned to Lafayette after Labor Day so the kids could start school, but was not asked to return as the Mitchell Brothers' attorney.

When the Mitchell Brothers had first hired Meredith, she was chugging around the Bay Area in a beat-up 1972 VW. The brothers were driving big Mercedes 500SLs. Artie had decided Meredith and his children deserved better and had arranged for Cinema 7 to lease a $16,000 Volvo for Meredith.

Meredith knew it was over when she received a letter from the leasing company informing her that Cinema 7 had ceased paying the monthly fee. If she wanted to keep the car, she was going to have to pick up the payments.

Meredith did not have the money to make the payments. The economy went into a bad slump in late 1981 and 1982, and jobs, even for attorneys, were tough to locate. Meredith had trouble finding a position, and for a while she and the children were on food stamps.

Jim returned to the Cape the summer after he had fired Meredith, but he did not go near the Bradfords. The next summer, he put his house up for sale and never returned. He and Meredith met at family gatherings over the years, but they never spoke again.

Meredith could live with that. She had always known how rigid Jim could be. What tormented her was what Art had done. He had promised to help and had not done a thing.

Meredith wondered if Art, once again, had sided with his brother, even at the expense of his three children, whom he had always claimed to love deeply. Perhaps he was still badly wounded by the divorce; perhaps leading her on and then not doing anything was his way of getting revenge. Perhaps it was Karen, Art's second wife. Karen was jealous of Meredith and the three kids.

Probably, Meredith thought, it was a combination of all three.

It was Christmas 1982, and the Mitchell Brothers were throwing a holiday party at the Great American Music Hall for the O'Farrell's 75 female performers. There was a band, male strippers, an open bar, and a buffet the most jaded rock star would find adequate. Married employees brought their families, and children were chasing each other through the crowd. Everyone was loose and happy and Lisa Loring was sitting on Jim's lap, snuggling and, every now and then, kissing him lightly.

Lisa felt Jim's body grow tense and glanced at his face. She followed his gaze to the door. Standing there, glaring at her, were Karen and Mary Jane, the wives of Artie and Jim. Mortified, Lisa hopped off Jim's lap and walked away.

Lisa knew that Mary Jane was extremely protective of Jim. If Mary Jane walked into a room and found Jim talking to a dancer, the dancer got the evil eye. If she thought that Jim and a dancer were becoming friendly, she demanded the dancer be fired.

Karen was just as possessive, maybe more so. Karen had met Artie when she was working for the company that did the catering during the shooting of *Autobiography of a Flea*. She and Artie had begun a relationship, and Karen—who found Artie and the world he inhabited fascinating—had ended up performing in the Ultra Room. When Lisa arrived, Karen was running the Ultra Room, hiring and firing the Ultralettes and supervising the show. Lisa thought Karen was remarkably beautiful, with her long red hair, large breasts, and long, slender body.

"I was one of the few women who could get along with Karen,"

Lisa says. "I always liked her, but I didn't always trust her. I felt if my back were turned, the claws would come out."

Now the claws were sure to come out. The wives were sure to demand that she be fired, even though her relationship with Jim and Artie was strictly platonic.

The day after the Christmas party, Lisa tiptoed into the clubhouse upstairs at the O'Farrell. The room was generally off-limits to dancers unless they were invited. Sometimes a dancer would wander in without asking permission and Jim or Artie or one of the managers would order her out. But Lisa was an old-timer—she would eventually spend seven years at the O'Farrell, which is close to a record—and she *had* to talk to Jim.

"Knock-knock," Lisa chirped in her birdlike voice.

Jim looked up from the poker table that doubled as a desk.

"Hey, Lisa, come on in," Jim said, flashing a smile.

"Jim," Lisa said tentatively, "do I still have a job?"

Jim smiled and lit a cigarette.

"Well, Mary Jane and Karen don't want you to work here anymore," Jim said, smiling through the smoke. "But I told them, 'Hey, Lisa and I are buddies. We were just having fun.' I told them if they wanted to get those nice gold watches for Christmas, they had to be cool."

Lisa kept her job, but other performers who got too close to Jim or Artie did not. It is impossible to blame either of the wives for being jealous and possessive. Jim and Artie *were* having sex with some of the dancers. Around the theater, Artie had become to sex what Jack Harvey was to everything else: the Mr. Fixit Man.

"The only time in all my years at the theater when I was frightened by one of the girls was the morning Pixie wanted to see me," Jack recalls.

It was early one morning, and Jack, who was forever repairing a shoe or fixing a clasp on a costume for one of the dancers, figured Pixie wanted him to mend something. But when he arrived in the dressing room and asked what he could do, Pixie said, "I need to be laid," and pulled her panties down.

"Holy shit! She wasn't kiddin'!" Jack recalls. "I said, 'Hold that thought!' and ran down the hall to the office. Artie had just gotten in and was readin' the *Chronicle* sports section. 'Art,' I said, 'Pixie's in the back all alone. She's got her drawers down and wants to be laid.'

" 'She does!' Art said, slamming down the paper and getting up. He went back there and fucked her."

Artie Mitchell and Karen Hassall were married under the redwoods in a park off Skyline Drive south of San Francisco in June 1979. Aaron, their first child, was one year old at the time, and Artie said later it was his son he was marrying, not Karen. Eventually the couple moved into a large farmhouse in Canyon, a lovely little community hidden deep in the Oakland Hills. Karen and Artie raised ducks, chickens, pheasants, marijuana, and, in the fullness of time, three children.

When Karen and Artie were first together, Meredith's three children had enjoyed visiting their father and his new girlfriend. Karen was pretty, energetic, and athletic. She took the kids on shopping trips and she and Artie took them camping and skiing in the Sierra. Karen, or Kay as everyone called her, was always fussing over Artie, telling the kids how much she loved him, how skinny he was when they met and how healthy he had become, now that she was cooking for him.

Artie basked in the attention. When he casually asked his older children, "What do you think? Should I marry Kay?" the answer was "Yeah! Sure! Why not?"

"As soon as that wedding ring was on, Kay changed," Liberty remembers. "She's so volatile. She'd be so nice one minute and so mean the next."

As the oldest child in a divorced family, Liberty had been forced to grow up fast. She became a second parent, baking cakes and making lunches for her younger brother and sister, refereeing fights, and getting them dressed and off to school. More than anything, Liberty wanted the two families to peacefully coexist. But the time came when, no matter how hard she tried, Liberty could not make things work.

Liberty, Storm, and Mariah began seeing less and less of their father and stepmother. They were supposed to spend every Saturday in the wonderful farmhouse in Canyon because their mother was going to law school and had Saturday classes. But Friday night, Artie had begun calling Meredith to plead, "I know the kids are supposed to come, but please don't push it, Kay is in a bad mood," or "Please don't make me take them; Kay is on the rag."

"The whole law school ended up knowing my kids because they'd spend Saturdays in the lunchroom while I was in class," Meredith recalls.

The Saturdays the children did spend in Canyon became increasingly miserable. Kay talked glowingly about trips the older three children had not been invited to take. If they went shopping, she bought things for her children, but not the others.

"My mother or my father never hit me, but Kay did," Liberty says. "I was using a wooden spoon to scoop frozen orange juice out of a can and she said, 'You shouldn't use a wooden spoon, you'll break it.' I went, 'Soorrr-eeee,' real sarcastic, and whap! She nailed me. I just stood there, I didn't even move.

"I remember when I told Dad, he went, 'Well, that's what you get.' He didn't even try to defend me."

More frightening to Liberty than being hit were the blows that Karen and her father exchanged when they got into fights, fights that started in one room and raged through the house.

"It was horrifying for a child. They'd do it right in front of us," Liberty recalls. "Kay started it a lot. She was every bit as violent, if not more violent than he was. They'd be scratching and kicking and falling down staircases. She'd scream—those screams will echo in my head forever—and run at him with her fingernails out. They'd pick up vases and throw them at each other. I'd be hiding with a baby underneath a table."

Finally, the visits all but stopped. Meredith's kids didn't want to visit their father and stepmother. When she was five, Mariah flatly refused to go anymore, telling her mother that she was afraid of Kay.

"I told her she didn't have to go and for about a year she didn't," Meredith recalls. "Art didn't really notice. Then the other kids stopped going too. I'd call Art and say, 'Are you going to come over and see them? It's been four months.' He'd go, 'Has it been that long?'

"He really was devoted to his second family. He figured he'd messed up the first time and was determined to do it right the second," Meredith concludes. "So he spent all his time with his second three kids. With my kids, he became an absentee father."

Things had gotten tough for Meredith and her three children. Artie was earning over $139,000 a year and driving a Mercedes, Kay was shopping at Neiman-Marcus, and they were whisking off to vacations in Hawaii and Mexico. Meanwhile, Meredith was driving a battered old Rambler, shopping for clothes at Kmart, and struggling to establish her own law practice.

Meredith finally took Jim and Artie to court, charging them with defaulting on an agreement they had reached when they hired her. Tom Steel, the attorney who had replaced Meredith, represented the brothers; Meredith represented herself. She won a default judgment for $50,527.80, but, playing hardball, the Mitchell Brothers had Steel challenge the decision. A San Francisco Superior Court judge set aside the award and ordered the case reopened.

The years passed, with Artie showing up on birthdays and holidays to give each of the children $100. Liberty, Storm, and Mariah's feelings of abandonment, of coming in a distant second to Karen and Artie's children, continued to grow until, finally, they became outwardly hostile to their father. In fourth grade, Storm began signing his name "Storm Bradford" instead of "Storm Mitchell," and his two sisters decided they wanted to change their names to Bradford too.

Growing up, Liberty felt she was composed of two irreconcilable halves. On one side, she was a Bradford, a member of an aristocratic New England family, the "nicest, cleanest people. They're *so safe,*" she says. On the other side were "these wild Okie outlaws and, like it or not, I was a porn princess. Both sides wanted to own me and I was trapped somewhere in the middle. When I was with the Bradfords, I felt like a Bradford. When I was with the Mitchells, I felt like a Mitchell."

Liberty especially liked her grandmother Georgia Mae. Mae was "a pistol," full of life. After J.R. died in 1972, Mae had become very serious about psychic phenomena and had spent years studying under a veteran psychic. Jim and Artie had put her on the payroll and Mae was collecting a healthy salary as "VP of Psychic Research." Her job was to do charts on the judges and prosecutors who were handling the Mitchell Brothers' cases.

But when she grew older, Liberty learned from her mother that Mae had not always been the live wire that Liberty loved so much. When J.R. was alive, Mae had done whatever he told her to do. She had cooked, cleaned, played the perfect hostess, and listened eagerly as he told stories she had heard over and over. After years of teaching and taking care of J.R. and her boys, Mae was worn down and looked dowdy. At family gatherings, she would get a cup of coffee, sit in a chair in the corner, and nod off.

After J.R.'s death, Mae had been reborn. She had begun her career as a psychic, enrolled in square-dancing lessons, and started wearing hot pants. She went on cruises, and men were calling, wanting to date her.

It was great to have a grandmother who was fun to do things with, but that didn't make it easier for Liberty to come to terms with the fact that her father was a pornographer. There was a terrible incident that grew out of the birthday party Artie threw for her when she turned nine. The parents of one of her little friends had gone to the police and accused Artie of showing dirty movies to the children. They reported that Artie had removed his clothes and gotten into his hot tub nude with the little girls. During a game called "Light as a Feather," where everyone at the party lifted one girl in the air, Liberty's nine-year-old friend told the police that Artie had "pushed aside her panties and inserted his finger in her vagina."

"I'd rather be charged with murder than child molesting," Artie said outside an Oakland courthouse after entering a not-guilty plea.

At the trial, it turned out that the dirty movie was *Hoppity Goes to Town*, a cartoon Artie had taped from a television show. Four of the seven girls at the party had decided to take off their swimming suits and go skinny-dipping in the hot tub, but Artie had not taken off his suit. And the judge did not believe the nine-year-old's testimony about the alleged molestation, saying he had "problems with her credibility."

Meredith told Liberty she believed that the girl's parents had filed the suit to get money. Things like that happened to people who were in the pornography business, Meredith had explained, and the incident had finally passed. But when Liberty reached junior high school in the early 1980s, the Ultra Room was being raided on a regular basis, the Mitchell Brothers were in the news, and kids kept approaching Liberty to ask if her father was one of the infamous Mitchell Brothers. Liberty told them no, her father was a commercial fisherman.

"It wasn't a lie, but it wasn't the truth either," Liberty says. "When my dad found out I was having trouble telling people what he did, he yelled at me for being ashamed of him."

It was during one of her birthday parties that Liberty's father first came into focus for her. As his relationship with Karen continued to deteriorate, Artie had begun bringing his girlfriend of the moment to family events. They were all dancers at the O'Farrell, and Liberty regarded them as pieces of fluff. Inevitably, the girlfriend would corner Liberty and tell her, "Your dad is incredible! He's the greatest guy I've ever met in my whole life!"

"He must have briefed every one of them that he and I were having problems, because they were all his little agents," Liberty says. "They'd always say, 'You know, your dad really, really loves you.' I'd go, 'Uh-huh.' "

Watching while his latest flame sat on her father's lap and played with his beard and giggled at everything he said, Liberty realized that this was a porn magnate's version of J.R. and Georgia Mae's marriage. Her father really did want a girl just like the girl that married dear old dad. Someone who would wait on him hand and foot and hang on his every word. Someone who would never, ever challenge him.

Her father couldn't deal with women who stood up to him, Liberty decided. That's why she was having trouble with him. That was probably why he and Karen were always fighting. He and Karen had been fine when she was all goo-goo over him and making such a fuss over taking care of him. As soon as she started to assert herself, the problems began.

That was Artie's dilemma. He wanted totally compliant women, but he was attracted to strong women like Meredith and Karen. (Liberty hated Karen, but she would never accuse her of being weak.) And he couldn't handle their strength.

"My dad had the most problems with my mom, me, and my little sister," Liberty says. "My mom was the only one who ever left him; everyone else *he* left. He never forgave her for that. He punished all of us for her doing that.

"The three of us were the only women he couldn't get over on," Liberty continues. "All his other women bought the porn king, the Party Artie role he played. We didn't, and he felt really intimidated by that."

Tanya, a beautiful black performer at the O'Farrell, had just come out of the Kopenhagen and was so shaken her entire body was trembling. Spotting Jack Harvey, the theater's resident father figure, she rushed up and threw her arms around him.

"Tanya honey. What's the matter?" Jack asked.

Tanya stepped away from Jack and grabbed her forearm near the elbow.

"I put my fist this far up Marilyn's ass," Tanya said, throwing herself back into Jack's arms and starting to cry.

It was January 1985, and Marilyn Chambers's career had come full circle. She was back at the O'Farrell, this time as a live act.

A woman becomes a star in pornography by doing things that few, if any, other performers will do. Marilyn was doing things at the O'Farrell that even her old mentors, the Mitchell Brothers, could not believe.

Marilyn had lived for most of a decade on a ranch outside of Las Vegas with Chuck Traynor, her husband and manager. They weren't home very much. Most of the time, they were crisscrossing the country as Marilyn headlined one porn theater after another. Marilyn had also appeared in several plays in Las Vegas and other cities, including London—*Mind with a Dirty Man,* co-starring Phil Ford and Jane Kean (who had played Trixie on *The Honeymooners*), *Last of the Red Hot Lovers,* and *The Sex Surrogate,* during which Marilyn was nude most of the time, having sex with imaginary clients. She had also been the lead singer in a country and western band called Haywire.

Wherever they went, Chuck had insisted that Marilyn be Marilyn Chambers twenty-four hours a day. Being Marilyn Chambers meant answering the door nude when a busboy delivered a room service dinner and telling him, "Forget the tip. Come into the other room and I'll give you a blow job."

"To create the perfect porn star, you have to create an image of a totally uninhibited sexual creature who would be happy being anything you wanted her to be," says Chuck Traynor. "You have to make it so there are no barriers between this chick and the audience, so men will think she'd enjoy doing anything they wanted her to do.

"When Marilyn said to the room service guy, 'Let me suck your dick,' it was all part of that image," Chuck continues. "The bellboy fucks Marilyn Chambers or she blows him and he's an instant Marilyn Chambers fan. He goes downstairs and tells all the bellboys and pretty soon all the bellboys are out there pimping for Marilyn Chambers."

After living her image all day every day, Marilyn had forgotten who she was and had become Chuck Traynor's creation. Chuck had even refused to let her take a few courses at the University of Nevada, Las Vegas, because if word leaked out she was going to school, it would harm the fantasy. Marilyn had no friends in the sex business. The other female performers were jealous and competitive and there had never been time to work through that because Chuck kept them away from her. There was always another plane to catch or a limo waiting to take her to another gig. Marilyn loved to drink beer, she drank it the way most people drank water, and she liked smoking grass and doing cocaine. But Chuck let her use drugs only when he said she could, which was sporadically, usually after an engagement or when they were home on the ranch in Vegas.

Still, it wasn't a bad life in other senses. She had become a star, if only in the netherworld of pornography.

"For me to be put on a pedestal and adored by millions of men, I loved that," Marilyn says. "I never felt exploited by Chuck or anybody else. *I* exploited me."

Marilyn had also developed an affection for Chuck. He was smart and funny and, in his own way, very honest. When they were off the road and alone, they both forgot that Marilyn was a product and had good times going hunting or skydiving or riding horses in the desert.

And Marilyn appreciated what Chuck had done for her career. The fact that she hadn't made it in Hollywood wasn't Chuck's fault; it was Hollywood's.

Marilyn thought the breakthrough was going to come when she auditioned for the role of the daughter who runs away to become a porn star in *Hardcore*. But the casting director took one look at her and said, "You don't look like a porn queen. You look too clean and wholesome."

"But that's the point! That's why I'm probably the biggest thing there is in porn!" Marilyn replied.

"Hollywood's concept of sex is so corrupt," Marilyn says in retrospect. "The *Hardcore* people wanted a woman with orange hair who chews gum, swings a big purse, and wears stiletto heels. That's such a cliché. When I was making *Green Door* with Jim and Artie, I'd say, 'I can't do this scene,' and they'd come up with a beer in one hand and a joint in another and their baseball caps on backward and say, 'Sure you can! Think about being really turned on. Think of the millions of people you're going to turn on.' They made me feel really attractive and like a real actress.

"In Hollywood, they still think sex is dirty. They're afraid of it. They were afraid to show people that a porn star was smart and had talent and could act. That works against what society thinks."

Where Marilyn did meet Hollywood stars was at the parties Sammy Davis, Jr., threw after his shows in Vegas. "Sammy was kinky," Marilyn says. "Sexually, he was into everything. He came down from a show by cooking and having sex. He'd call and say, 'Come up to the suite after the show, I'm cooking chili.' I'd say, 'And then we'll have an orgy afterward, right, Sammy?'"

Marilyn had introduced Sammy to Jim and Artie and, because of his sexual proclivities, Sammy had adopted the brothers.

"'They're my kind of people!' Sammy used to say about the brothers," Marilyn recalls. "Jim and Artie set him up with women, they did use women for that, but I don't think they thought it was pandering. I think they thought they were giving somebody a good time."

(Just how voracious was Davis's sexual appetite? The last time Chuck Traynor saw him was two days before he died. "He was still Sammy but he could hardly talk—the cancer had moved into his throat," Chuck recalls. "One of the last things he said was 'Chuck, I'm going to start fucking those sixteen-year-olds. I don't have to worry about AIDS now.'")

After being dominated by Chuck, after being sex queen Marilyn Chambers twenty-four hours a day for almost a decade, Marilyn had finally rebelled. She was tired of having to please Chuck and every man she met; she was tired of playing gig after gig, because "no matter how hard I worked, there never seemed to be enough money."

In 1982, Marilyn went back East to do a gig in New York City and visit her parents. It was the first time Chuck had ever let her go on the road alone. At the club she met a bodyguard named Bobby D'Apice, and ended up going to bed with him.

"You've been drinking!" Chuck said when he met Marilyn at the Las Vegas airport. Chuck did not allow her to drink unless he okayed it first.

"That's right," Marilyn replied, getting into Chuck's truck. "Listen, stop at the first convenience store we pass, will you?"

Chuck did and Marilyn went in and bought a pack of cigarettes.

"Things are going to be different around here," Marilyn said, lighting a cigarette. Chuck had forbidden her to smoke too.

"I'll be goddamned if they are!" Chuck yelled.

"I'm leaving," Marilyn said. "I'm leaving as soon as we get home!"

"The hell you are!" Chuck replied.

Marilyn moved out that night, but the fight continued for months. Chuck wasn't all that concerned about losing Marilyn as a wife; he was upset about losing "income property." Eventually, Marilyn and D'Apice moved in together and she reached a truce with Chuck by signing a contract allowing Chuck to take 50 percent of everything she earned over the next five years. So when she returned to the O'Farrell early in 1985, Chuck was still her manager and was still calling all the shots, even though they had separated.

Except for the fact that dancers were wearing bras and panties when they went into the audience, the O'Farrell was as wide open as it had ever been. Jim and Artie had no real interest in complying with the agreement they had made to get the DA out of their hair. As a former employee told the DA's office during a deposition, "Charlie Benton [a manager at the O'Farrell] came up to us and said, 'Unless a wad hits you in the eye, don't worry about what goes on. We don't want you to go into New York Live and look [to see] if a girl is doing this or that. We don't care what she's doing. Stay outside and check tickets.

"Charlie said that came from upstairs. I took that to mean Jim and Artie and Vince [Stanich]," the former employee continued, going on to describe numerous acts of fellatio, cunnilingus, and the hundreds of condoms performers were using. For $5.00, performers were placing a condom on a man's penis and masturbating him.

"It was a direct, flagrant violation of the contempt order," the employee said. "We felt that this was like telling the judge, 'Hey, fuck you.'"

After she broke free of Chuck, at least partially, Marilyn had begun running wild, indulging with reckless abandon in all the things he had controlled. She smoked and drank and did cocaine nonstop. Looking back on it, Marilyn describes herself as a walking mass of addictions. She was hooked on coke, on the rush that begins with scoring the stuff and chopping it into lines. She got high watching the Mitchell Brothers count the gate. "It was 'Ohhh! Look at all the money I brought in!'" But the biggest high was watching an audience watch her in utter astonishment.

"I felt I had to fulfill my reputation when I came back to the O'Farrell," Marilyn says. "I wanted to be the best. Chuck always told me, 'You've got to give the audience what they don't expect.' He said, 'Tina Turner starts wild and ends wilder. That's what you've got to do.' That was some of the best advice I ever got. I always wanted people to go out of a show saying, 'My God! Did you see what she did? I can't believe it!!!' "

Being "the best" at the O'Farrell meant doing S&M with heavy-duty whipping and bondage in the Ultra Room. "It was all real," Marilyn says. "I don't believe in faking." In the Kopenhagen Lounge, it meant locking the door and letting men fulfill their fantasies—oral sex, intercourse, whatever they wanted to do, Marilyn did. It also mean being "fist-fucked" vaginally and anally.

"It was a question of showing them how much I could take," Marilyn says. "I showed them that I could take a fist up my butt and have hot candle wax dripped all over me. People would go, 'Oh my God! That's amazing! How could you do that?' I loved people telling me I was amazing. I loved it that the Mitchell Brothers couldn't believe what I was doing and that there were lines around the block. It was great!"

Onstage, being "the best" meant putting on a show that had been choreographed by Chuck Traynor. Two black dancers—one of whom was Tanya, who died an early death from cirrhosis of the liver—in long, flowing negligees ran up and down the stage while strobe lights flashed and loud rock music played. Then the music stopped, the theater went dark, and a spotlight hit Marilyn in the center of the stage. The music came back even louder, and Marilyn, wearing a long gown covered with rhinestones, boogied off the stage and into the audience. By now, the audience was cheering and clapping with the music.

The dancers eventually undressed Marilyn and, while she was lying on her back on the stage, shoved steel balls in her anus. Slowly, one at a time, Marilyn pulled the balls out. The dancers surrounded Marilyn and began making oral love to her. Suddenly, the house lights went out again. Marilyn screamed, as if she was having an orgasm, and the dancers used turkey basters to squirt the audience with warm water.

The show was called "Feel the Magic," Marilyn was "a touchable fantasy," and when the lights came up, she bounced off the stage and went into the audience for the "feel" part of the show.

"Jeez, Lieutenant, my partner and I did a routine walk-through of the O'Farrell today and you wouldn't believe what's going on there!" a uniformed officer told Lieutenant Dennis Martel, the head of the San Francisco vice squad, on the evening of February 1, 1985. "Marilyn Chambers is onstage and guys are grabbing her, there's digital intercourse, it's incredible!"

Martel, a straightforward, honest cop with short blond hair, a mustache, and a weight lifter's upper body, had been head of vice for only a few weeks. He was leery of going into the O'Farrell. Every time the department went near the theater, the press jumped on them and citizens called to complain that the cops were harassing innocent customers instead of busting muggers. Still, Martel had a job to do, and he decided to check out the tip.

Later that night, the lieutenant and five other officers walked up to the O'Farrell box office, showed their badges, and announced they were there to conduct an inspection. If Marilyn had been in any part of her act but the "feel" of "Feel the Magic," perhaps nothing would have happened. But the cops' timing was impeccable. As the officers walked into the theater, Marilyn was just entering the audience.

In the report he filed, Lieutenant Martel stated, "I observed approximately twenty patrons have sexual contact with Ms. Chambers. At least five patrons touched or put their mouths on her breasts and nipples as she offered her breasts to some patrons. Chambers raised her vagina and anus to other patrons and positioned her body enabling patrons to touch these areas. I observed at least twelve patrons inserting their fingers into Chambers's vagina while she made undulating motions. I observed at least four patrons touch the anus area of Chambers as she bent her buttocks directly in front of the patrons' faces. I observed at least two patrons appear to make penetration of the anus with their fingers. I observed a white male orally copulate Chambers's vagina for approximately fifteen seconds. I observed Chambers have contact with at least five additional patrons, and then start to dance down the aisle toward the rear stage."

Martel had seen enough. He ordered his officers to arrest Marilyn, and two officers went through the black curtains that blocked off the backstage area and grabbed the naked, sweating dancer. Bobby D'Apice, Marilyn's boyfriend-bodyguard, ran up and tried to stop the cops. The cops arrested D'Apice for interfering with an arrest and discovered he was carrying a .45 that was cocked and had a round in the chamber. D'Apice did not have a license to carry the weapon.

Meanwhile, out in the theater, the cops had arrested the customer who had orally copulated Marilyn's vagina and were attempting to round up other patrons who had felt the magic. Customers were yelling and banging into each other as they dashed for the front doors. Martel called for backup and another five uniformed officers arrived at the O'Farrell.

"Can I get dressed before we go?" Marilyn asked the cops.

It was the first time she had ever been arrested and she was trying to be cool. She wasn't worried about what the cops might do. She was worried about the briefcase in the dressing room that contained cash, cocaine, and another pistol.

The cops said sure, go ahead, and when Marilyn went into the dressing room, she looked around for the briefcase, but it was gone. Someone had already hidden it.

Marilyn put on a pair of jeans and her blue fox coat and was taken to the city jail on Bryant Street. The cops put her in the drunk tank, and then, one at a time, officers began coming into the tank with a Polaroid camera, respectfully asking if Marilyn would pose for a picture.

Marilyn was charged with soliciting prostitution and engaging in lewd conduct in a public place, and was released on $2,000 bail at 3:44 A.M.

Ordinarily, the arrest would have led to another battle between the DA and attorneys for the Mitchell Brothers over what constituted prostitution. Bernard Walter was ready to charge that the $20 patrons had paid to see the show and engage in the fondling the cops had witnessed constituted prostitution. The brothers' attorneys would have argued that Marilyn was a performer whose freedom of expression was protected under the First Amendment. And since she had accepted no tips from the audience, even though men were waving as much as hundred-dollar bills at her, how could it be prostitution?

But this was no ordinary case. This was Marilyn Chambers, the city's favorite bad girl. And Warren Hinckle was on the story.

A natty dresser who wears an eye patch, a heavy drinker who hangs out in Irish bars, Hinckle is a San Francisco version of Jimmy Breslin. A legend when he was editing *Ramparts* in the 1960s,

Hinckle can be an excellent journalist when he is digging into the story. But as a rule he is more interested in being a character than in being a journalist; he would rather be righteous than right; and, even for a columnist, he is more of a politician than a journalist, using his column to attack enemies and praise friends.

Like Jim and Artie, Hinckle loves drama. He loves to insert himself in the middle of an event, and the cops were dumb enough to make him a star in the Marilyn Chambers affair.

Hinckle wrote a column saying that during the raid dozens of cops had come running to the O'Farrell, and that ten cops had escorted Marilyn to her dressing room. "These porn dancers can be dangerous; one has to watch closely to make sure they don't pull a concealed weapon from some orifice," Hinckle wrote. After arresting Marilyn, Hinckle said that it had taken "25 to 30 lawmen to drag Ms. Chambers off to jail as naked as Venus stripped for her tub."

Two weeks after the Chambers bust, the cops arrested Hinckle for walking his basset hound without a leash. The hound is as much a Hinckle trademark as the eye patch. It seemed an obvious retaliation for the columns Hinckle had written about Marilyn. Hinckle's arrest gave the Chambers story new life, and Hinckle was in his glory at the center of the biggest flap in town.

The SFPD had been buried under a flood of bad publicity in the months before the cops had hit the O'Farrell. At a party at the Rathskeller restaurant held to celebrate rookie cops' induction into the force, vice cops had tied up a rookie and watched while a prostitute performed oral sex. The gay community was charging the cops had used excessive force during a raid on a club called Lord Jim's. There were also stories in the papers about hackers in the police department secretly gaining access to and reading public defenders' court files.

And now the cops were picking on a 110-pound sex performer and a one-eyed columnist.

"Our credibility is at stake in regards to our arrests," police commissioner Jo Daly told the *Examiner*. Daly said she had received fifty-one calls from citizens protesting the raid at the O'Farrell, including one from a seventy-nine-year-old woman who told the commissioner, "By golly, [Marilyn's] act was not the worst of crimes."

The pressure on the cops kept mounting, and police chief Cornelius Murphy kept his head in the sand, refusing to answer the department's critics. Finally, the DA dropped the charges against Marilyn, Bobby D'Apice, and Warren Hinckle.

But for Jim and Artie the best was yet to come. In the wake of the Chambers's arrest, the Board of Supervisors voted to strip the police of their power to license the city's adult theaters.

The red-light abatement laws that had cost the Mitchell Brothers hundreds of thousands of dollars to fight, the laws which were the most serious threat to their license to run the O'Farrell, were gone. Six months after the Chambers raid, the police commissioners voted to pay the Mitchell Brothers $14,000 for damages they had suffered as a result of the raid.

The brothers had beat the cops, the DA, the red-light abatement laws and Mayor Feinstein. It was their greatest victory.

It was also one of their last.

11

Artie Ups
the Ante

"MISSY, this is going to be really great! We're both going to fuck this girl!" Artie was saying as he drove his long white Mercedes 500SL south on the James Lick Freeway.

"Whatever's next," said Missy Manners, who was sitting beside Artie in one of the big leather seats.

Artie and Missy had been doing cocaine, drinking, and smoking dope all night long. A Grateful Dead tape was playing—Artie and Missy always played the Dead—and Missy was feeling numbed and curiously detached. At the same time, Missy felt the deep throb of sexual excitement—coke always did that to her.

Lately it occurs to meeeeeee, what a looonnnggg . . . strange trip it's been, Missy sang along with the band, feeling in every bone in her body that the Dead had nailed down the ultimate truth about life. Life was indeed a long strange trip, and if you didn't take it, you didn't live. Missy knew that from firsthand experience. Here she was, stoned out of her gourd and yet not feeling half as sedated as she did during all the years she had spent as Elisa Florez.

Elisa had grown up in Salt Lake City, the daughter of John

Florez, a confidant of Senator Orrin Hatch. Florez was a VP at the University of Utah who had gone on to be chief of staff of the Senate Labor and Human Resources Committee, and was later appointed to the U.S. Civil Rights Commission by President Reagan. Elisa's mother was an alcoholic and she and her stepmother did not get along. But Elisa had always tried to be her father's daughter, a model young Republican. She had worked as a page for Senator Hatch, graduated from Georgetown University, and had worked for the Republican National Committee. Elisa had impressed power brokers like Senator Hatch with the long hours she labored to elect conservative candidates.

But Elisa had been an unhappy, dowdy young woman with short, ugly hair and pasty flesh who dressed in frumpy, unimaginative clothes. Pleasant enough on the surface, Elisa boiled with anger on the inside, anger at her father because he insisted on making every decision ("He came to visit me and the first thing he did was rearrange all my furniture"), angry that her sisters were considered prettier, and, at the bottom of it, angry at herself for not having led her own life.

Elisa's frustration grew until she turned her back on the insular world inside the Washington Beltway and moved to the Bay Area to take graduate courses at the University of California/Berkeley. She went on a diet and took the most demanding aerobics classes she could find; she let her hair grow and dyed it blond. Over time, ugly duckling Elisa metamorphosed into a lean, limber, large-breasted young lady with pearly-white teeth, large almond-shaped brown eyes, and a dazzling smile.

Elisa was thrilled. She was pretty! And she had done it all herself!

Elisa had begun sunbathing on nude beaches, and one day a friend suggested that she enter the Miss Nude America contest at the Civic Auditorium. As a lark, she did, and she loved every minute of it. It was exciting to have an auditorium full of men watching her and to hear them yell as she flaunted her body.

"I grew up being told what to do, and I always just wanted to be my own person," Missy says. "I found out I liked shocking people. I liked exploring that part of my life that had always been buried. Sex was never anything that was discussed in my family."

"You had so much fun at the Miss Nude America contest, you ought to give the O'Farrell a try," another friend told Elisa. "What's the O'Farrell?" Elisa asked. The friend explained it was the most

famous sex club in San Francisco, and that every Monday was amateur night. The winner got $100 and often was offered a job at the
theater. Elisa decided to give it a try.

She got a costume, carefully picked out her music, and threw
everything she had into a dance that combined aerobics with strip-
ping. She won the $100 prize and Artie Mitchell himself came
down and invited Elisa and her friends to join a little party he had
going upstairs.

Elisa was apprehensive: she had never been in a sex club before.
What if this bald guy with the big smile wanted her to join an orgy
or something? But she was on a roll, she had just won the amateur
contest, and her friends were with her. What was the danger?

She was following Artie up the stairs when a small envelope
dropped out of his back pocket. One of Elisa's friends picked up
the envelope and opened it. Inside were two grams of cocaine. The
friend showed it to Elisa and they laughed and decided to do the
cocaine themselves. Artie was so messed up, he never noticed
the envelope was missing.

Elisa found herself attracted to Artie, despite the fact that he was
wasted. He was the opposite of the politicians she had known in
Washington, men who calculated the effect of everything they said
before opening their mouths. A couple of times when he thought
someone was trying to bullshit or put too fine a point on things,
Artie warned, "Hey. No excuses." He seemed to be totally there,
completely engrossed in what he was doing, whether it was lining
up a pool shot, sucking on a joint, or listening to something Elisa
said. She was used to talking to Washington types whose eyes kept
traveling across the room as they figured out whom they were going
to approach next.

Artie was attentive to Elisa that night, sidling up to suggest she
work at the O'Farrell, wandering off and then coming back to say,
"You really should work here, you know." Elisa was intrigued by
Artie and by the O'Farrell. Artie was an outlaw, and Elisa was interested in becoming one.

"Artie was definitely his own person and I definitely wanted to be
my own person," Missy recalls. "The sex industry seemed a way to
do it. It was naughty, something my parents wouldn't like. It was a
way to say 'Fuck you!' to my parents and the whole Republican
establishment."

Elisa dropped by the theater a few days later—she just "happened" to be in the neighborhood—to ask Artie if he would like to have a drink. They went to the Blue Light Cafe on Union Street, a place owned by soft rocker Boz Skaggs, and Elisa was having a wonderful time until Artie suddenly announced that he had another date and had to go.

Elisa was miffed and figured she would never see Artie again, but he called a few days later to ask her out. They became instant best friends, talking freely and easily about deeply personal things. Artie told Elisa to call him A.J. because that's what people had called him when he was a child. He also told her that she made him feel young again. They ended up at Artie's house in Walnut Creek, a suburban community in Contra Costa County, making love on the living-room floor.

Elisa thought she had found a soul mate, but it was not that simple. Artie had not initiated her yet.

Soon after their first date, Artie called and told Elisa to meet him at the theater and they would go out to dinner. Elisa arrived to find Artie surrounded by beautiful young O'Farrell dancers, several of whom turned out to be Rajneesh devotees. Elisa knew that Artie had a lot of girlfriends, and these, obviously, were a few of them. Especially one girl, who glared at Elisa when she walked in. She appeared mesmerized by Artie.

Artie was drunk and very high, and when they piled into Artie's Mercedes, his friend Dave got behind the wheel.

"Okay, everybody name a restaurant they want to go to," Artie commanded.

When it was Elisa's turn, she named a restaurant and Artie snarled, "I figured you'd want to go to some yucky place like that."

Elisa was stunned by the ferocity of Artie's hostility. What had she done? She was insecure to begin with; the other women were sex performers, insiders who had known Artie for a long time. She was the new kid on the block.

"Artie. What did I do? What did I say?" Elisa asked. Her heart was beating so fast, she felt light-headed.

"You slut, I just knew you'd say something like that," Artie said, biting off the words. "All you swine think alike."

Elisa started to cry. Artie reached over and yanked her hair. And then he slapped her. The other women watched and were silent. The only sound in the big quiet Mercedes was Elisa sobbing.

They drove to Maxwell's Plum, a restaurant in Ghirardelli Square near Fisherman's Wharf.

"I'm going to take a cab and I'm going home!" Elisa announced as she got out of the car.

"Oh, fuck you!" Artie cried. "I knew you didn't have any guts. I knew you couldn't stand up. You can sail the ship or you can be an anchor. If you're going to be an anchor, get the fuck off!"

Elisa wanted to break free, to enter a strange, forbidden world. She thought she was escaping her past; instead, she was repeating it. This suddenly nasty Okie porn king was making a bid to dominate her. Artie's methods were different, but he was doing the same thing that Elisa was enraged at her father for having done.

Elisa decided to show Artie she could take it and followed him into the restaurant.

"I'm sorry, we don't have any tables," the maître d' informed them.

"We can't have a table? Are you certain?" Elisa said through her tears.

"Oh, my dear girl!" said the maître d', who assumed Elisa was in tears because he couldn't seat her party. "By all means, come right this way!" he said, and led them to a private room with a glorious view.

Months would go by before she and Jim and Artie came up with her new name—Missy (as in missing) Manners—but that night, Elisa became Missy. (Judith Martin, who writes the "Miss Manners" etiquette column for the Washington *Post*, later sued Elisa and the Mitchell Brothers over the name "Missy Manners." The defendants settled out of court and agreed to stop using that moniker. After the settlement, Elisa became just "Missy.") Something let go inside her. She knew the more outrageous she was, the more attention she would get; the more exciting she was, the more Artie would like her. Missy had a need to be outrageous, to be the center of attention. She had been on her way to being a star inside the Washington Beltway; now she was determined to be a star in the outlaw world of Artie Mitchell.

The incident in the Mercedes faded and was forgotten as Missy and everyone else at the table tried to match Artie drink for drink. They began competing to see who could come up with the best sexual innuendo, and everyone was laughing and giddy when Missy slid off her chair, crawled under the table, and proceeded to have oral sex with everyone there, men and women alike.

"I'd been so uptight in one way, I decided I might as well go all the way in the other direction," Missy recalls. "Everybody at the table thought it was really hysterical. The waiter would walk in with a salad or something and I'd be missing and they'd all have these funny looks on their faces. We were all having a really good time."

After the dinner, Artie dropped the dancers off at their apartments.

"Please, please, come in with me," pleaded the dancer who was madly in love with Artie when they stopped at her apartment.

"No, I'm with Elisa," Artie said.

"No, please! Please come with me. We'll both fuck you," the dancer begged.

"I can't, I'm going to be with Elisa now."

Missy soon learned that the incident in the Mercedes wasn't an aberration or an isolated test. It was a reflection of Artie's character. Missy had heard from people who knew the Mitchell Brothers that Jim was the controlling brother and that Artie was the free spirit. But that had turned not to be true. Artie was just as controlling as his older brother. His methods were different, that was all.

Artie's method of asserting power was to set up situations he could dominate. He did that best at parties, which is why he had earned the nickname "Party Artie," or "Party Hearty Artie."

Upstairs at the O'Farrell, Artie called the shots. The party started when he said it started. If Artie wanted to play pool, they played pool. Artie played the renegade hero, telling stories about his numerous arrests or outrageous sex acts he had witnessed or participated in, or asking a dancer, "Hey, how about a blow job?" Artie turned his audience on to lines of coke, hits of acid and Ecstasy, tightly rolled joints made from the most potent sinsemilla marijuana grown in Humboldt County, and a never-ending supply of whiskey, tequila, and Heinekens. Missy intuitively understood that while Artie may have had shortcomings as a director, his instincts were deeply theatrical. Artie liked nothing better than to create a scene and watch it play out.

As for Missy, she was hungry to bring drama into her life and eager to play a subordinate role in Artie Mitchell's real-life productions.

Rather than tell Artie she understood him, Missy decided to show him. Showing is so much more dramatic than telling. One night, she slipped a pair of regulation police handcuffs under Artie's pillow.

"I never said, 'I'll be your sex slave forever' or anything like that," Missy recalls. "I just put the handcuffs under his pillow. He took them, and it was really clear that he understood I was willing to be submissive for him."

Missy starred in an endless series of real-life dramas that Artie directed. If a half dozen people were having sex on the pool table upstairs at the O'Farrell, Missy was one of them. If she and Artie hit it off with some women in a bar and one of the women said, "God, you guys are great!" Artie would immediately ask, "Oh yeah? Wanna come home with us?" If the women said yes—which they did a surprising number of times—Missy and Artie had group sex.

"One time I walked out of the O'Farrell and down Polk Street totally naked," Missy recalls. "I got in the Mercedes and stood up and poked my head through the sun roof and we took off. Somebody started finger-fucking me and I sat down and we all started having oral sex and fucking all the way over the Bay Bridge to a friend's house, where we continued to have sex for the rest of the night. It was just wild like that."

Artie and Missy were upstairs at the O'Farrell one night when a tour bus full of Japanese pulled up to the curb.

"Look at this," Artie said, peering through the blinds. "The Japanese are going to bring me so much fucking money. Come on, Missy, you're going to go down there to greet them."

Missy climbed on the bus and pulled off her top.

"Hi, I'm Missy Manners and I want to welcome you to the O'Farrell!" Missy said, walking down the aisle.

Japanese men began opening briefcases or pulling out wallets.

"I wanna fuck at you!" a man in a suit and tie yelled, waving a fistful of money.

"I wanna fuck at you!" another yelled, leaning into the aisle and waving money at Missy.

In seconds, every man in the bus was shouting, "I wanna fuck at you!" and the tour guide was screaming at them in Japanese. Missy put her top on and hopped off the bus. Artie loved it.

Another time, Missy and Artie received invitations to the grand opening of the Fog City Diner. Fog City is the epitome of a trendy San Francisco restaurant where food is fun before it is anything else. The invitation was highly prized and all the regulars in Herb Caen's column arrived to witness the transformation of a 1950s diner into a chic 1980s restaurant. Artie and Missy got very drunk, and around one in the morning Artie started chopping up lines of cocaine on the marble-top counter.

"My girl's beaver, you gotta see it," Artie started telling the people who were sharing his coke. "Come on, Missy, show it to 'em."

Missy, who was sitting on the stool next to Artie's, swung away from the counter, hiked up her skirt, pulled off her panties, and placed them on the counter. Then she sat back down on the stool with her legs spread and her dress up.

Five people dropped their drinks. The busboy took his own sweet time sweeping up the glass. People kept strolling by to have a look, and the bartender handed Missy a pen and asked her to autograph her panties.

"Artie was always increasing the ante," Missy says. "It was 'Okay, so you're going to be my sex slave. Let's see how bizarre you can take things.' "

On the night that Missy and Artie were traveling south on the James Lick Freeway, Artie was upping the ante higher than it had ever been. Nothing he and Missy had done was as bizarre as what they were about to do.

Artie got off the freeway and weaved the big Mercedes through side streets behind San Francisco General Hospital. The car would drift to the left; Artie would catch it and overcorrect, jerking the car too far to the right. Then he would overcorrect again.

Missy hardly noticed. Driving while intoxicated was just one of the ways they pushed things to the limit. One time when Missy and Artie were high on Ecstasy, Missy was driving and started hallucinating. Artie crawled over her and took the wheel while they were going fifty miles an hour over the Bay Bridge.

"This is gonna be amazing," Artie said as he pulled into a parking space at a ninety-degree angle to the curb on a street that headed up a steep hill.

Missy followed Artie up a set of wooden stairs that ran up the outside of a drab little house that had been sliced into two apartments. Artie knocked on the door and it was opened . . . by a gorilla.

The gorilla removed its head, revealing itself to be Joanne Scott, a veteran O'Farrell performer who had been Artie's off-and-on girl-friend for years.

"Art! How could you?" shouted a furious Joanne.

"Get the hell in there! Both of you!" Artie yelled, shoving Missy into a tiny three-room apartment.

The apartment was a shrine to Artie Mitchell. Everywhere there were pictures of Artie, and Artie and Joanne, including one of them posing next to a beautiful marlin Artie had landed off Cabo San Lucas in the Baja. In the kitchen, there was a picture of Jim and Artie and their children that had accompanied a Sunday magazine story in the *Examiner*. Joanne had cut out a head shot of herself and inserted it in the center of the picture, next to Art.

"I'm not going to go through with this, Artie," Missy said, folding her arms.

"Neither am I," Joanne said, laying the gorilla head on her bed.

"The hell you're not!" Artie yelled. Then, turning to Joanne, he snarled, "Get me a drink!"

Joanne did not drink or use drugs, but she kept a bottle of Stolichnaya in the freezer for Artie.

For years, Joanne's dream had been to have Artie all to herself, but she did not mind his erratic behavior. She and Artie were play-ing an elaborate game only they fathomed, a game Joanne found deeply exciting.

But tonight Artie had gone too far. Joanne could handle the other dancers Artie had affairs with. They were passive women who went along for the ride and disappeared when it ended. But Missy, Artie's new girlfriend, was different. She was Artie's co-conspirator, and that made her a threat.

"Artie, how could you torture me with her?" Joanne asked plain-tively.

"Torture? Who said anything about torture?" Artie asked blithely. "This isn't about torture. This is a test. Let's see who's gonna pass."

A small, thin woman with big brown eyes, brown hair she wears in a Cleopatra cut, and a dancer's limber body, Joanne has a strange laugh that pops out at odd times. She is the only child of a lonely homemaker and an Army officer who was gone most of the time she was growing up. When Joanne's father was home, he was distant.

Joanne earned a master's degree in English literature at the Uni-versity of California in Davis and was enrolled in the Ph.D. program when she flunked Middle English and lost her teaching assistantship. A meanspirited adviser told Joanne he had never gotten the feeling she was brilliant and suggested she find something else to do. The insecure young woman dropped out of school and moved to San Francisco, where she got a job teaching part-time, which she found boring.

"I was after experience and adventure, not just a house in the suburbs," Joanne says.

Joanne quit to become a street artist who did pen-and-ink drawings on Fisherman's Wharf. Then she decided she wanted to take courses in art history, courses that met in the morning, so at age thirty-two she entered the Monday-night amateur contest at the O'Farrell and won a job.

"I found out I could do it," Joanne says. "I still had a certain amount of charm left; I thought: Why not make some money at it?"

Joanne holds the longevity record at the O'Farrell—she performed there for eight years—and because she was one of the older dancers, she had to be more creative than younger, more attractive women. For a while, she came onstage dressed as Dianne Feinstein and did an act with a dildo. The act she did in a gorilla suit was a favorite of Hunter Thompson's when he was "doing research" for a book about his experiences as a night manager at the theater.

Artie had come on to Joanne, as he did to most of the dancers, but while the other girls had had short, drug-filled flings, Joanne, as she repeats over and over again, "fell deeply in love with Art." The initial attraction was sex.

As time passed and Joanne's devotion became total and unquestioning, they developed their game, a game that, for Joanne, approximated love.

"What he played with was my loyalty," Joanne says. "If he did something really outrageous, would I take him back? It meant so much to him to get confirmation that I loved him over and over again."

Artie would bang on her door at 2 A.M. and disappear the next morning. Weeks would go by and then the phone would ring in the middle of the night. Joanne would wake up and say hello and whoever was on the other end would not answer. Joanne would ask, "Art? Is that you?" and the caller would hang up. Moments later, the phone would ring again. Joanne would ask if it was Art, and again the caller would hang up.

"I always knew it was him who was crank-calling me," Joanne

says. "It was kind of a teasing way of letting me know he was thinking about me. He was constantly keeping me aware he was around."

As the years went on, Joanne's relationship with Artie took on an S&M flavor.

"When Artie was very high and trying to get an erection, we'd use master-and-slave language," Joanne says. "He wanted me to call him master. That kind of sex talk heated him up. He very much wanted to be in charge."

The master/slave relationship went beyond sex talk. One night, Jim and Artie threw a birthday party for a fisherman who had become a good friend. A half dozen fishermen had arrived at the O'Farrell high on methamphetamine, which they, like long-distance truckers, took to work long, hard hours. Upstairs at the O'Farrell, the fishermen chased the crank with a variety of drinks and drugs. As the party was breaking up, Artie approached Joanne and told her he wanted her to accompany the fishermen back to their boat.

"Art set it up as a *Story of O* kind of thing, where the more he gives his lover to others, the more she belonged to him," Joanne recalls. "I didn't want to do it but I thought: Okay, I'll go out and be really outrageous, and I went out there and spent the night. I only messed around with one guy—the others were too sick from crank to do anything—and I felt okay about it because I knew the whole time I was out there because of Art.

"Two weeks later, the fishermen came in again, and this time Art wasn't around," Joanne continues. "They told Jim what a great time they'd had and Jim made me feel that if I wanted to keep my job, I had to go out with these guys again. This had nothing to do with Art and the *Story of O*. This was Jim intimidating me. If I did it, he'd have something on me and he'd have something on the fishermen. They'd owe him a favor. That kind of thing happened to a lot of dancers, I think."

Ending her "now he's here, now he's gone" relationship with Artie was not a possibility Joanne was willing to entertain, no matter what Art did. The game was far too exciting.

"Art kept my love for him going," Joanne says. "It's not a bad thing, really, because we reached an intensity few people get to. I experienced all the angles of love and loss and joy. If it hadn't been for all of those reversals, I'd have settled down with him in suburbia and the level of passion would have worn down. Playing the game that we did, loving him the way I did, I experienced something that almost no one goes through."

Artie was adamant about what he wanted Joanne and Missy to do that night. He had the whole thing scripted in his head and demanded that the two women play it exactly the way he had visualized it. Joanne and Missy did a girl-girl with Joanne in the gorilla suit, and then Artie had sex with both of them.

"When it was over, she and I were both upset and Artie took off his belt and started to whip us both for crying," Missy recalls. "And then he said, 'Come on, Missy, put your clothes on. We're going home,' and we left her there alone."

Thanks in large part to Artie's three younger children, Missy and Artie were able to develop a relationship that went beyond sex and drugs and the Grateful Dead. They found a lovely house in the Marina, one of the beautiful city's most desirable districts, and moved in together. They hired a Brazilian housekeeper, Missy made sure the house was full of flowers, and Artie's three younger children spent most weekends there.

Missy eventually became an important figure in the children's lives. Artie often referred to Karen as a slut or a dyke, a cunt, a sack of shit, or the slime of the earth in front of his children. Missy tried to get him to stop that, and did her best to get along with the children's mother. Missy and Jasmine, Artie's little girl, collected Hello Kitty toys, watches, and clothes, and made a regular pilgrimage to the Hello Kitty store every Saturday morning. Missy made a point of making French toast—his very favorite—for Caleb.

Missy and Artie and the kids camped out in a tent in the backyard and Missy told scary stories. They went fishing and took camping trips to Yellowstone and Bryce Canyon during the summer. Missy was very happy. Artie was turning her into an outlaw and she was providing him and his younger three children with a stability they had not had since Artie and their mother had split up.

Artie loved being with his younger children because he essentially had remained a child himself. He liked playing video games and baseball, and he especially enjoyed entering their fantasies, because —except for sex—the kids' fantasies weren't much different from his. Artie and Aaron would watch an old John Wayne Western, and at the end of the film, as John Wayne and a sidekick were riding into the sunset, Artie, eager as an eight-year-old, would say, "That's us, Ace! That's you and me ridin' off together! Can't you just see us on horses!"

When they did not have the children, Missy and Artie found ways to fulfill their longing for drama and intensity that did not involve sex or drugs. They even had a phrase for it: "Did you get your nut?"

The expression came from the Nut Tree, a large restaurant on Interstate 80 between San Francisco and Sacramento where Artie and Missy took the kids to rendezvous with Georgia Mae, who was living in a Sacramento suburb.

"Artie would ask, 'How many nuts did we get today?'" Missy recalls. "I'd say, 'We've had three nuts today. Let's get another one!' A nut could be going to dinner or seeing a movie or just going around seeing how happy we could be. We were getting our nuts and having a really good time doing it. It went on that way for a long time."

Once a month, Artie and Missy took a vacation. Sometimes they put Mr. T, a teacup poodle Artie had bought for Missy that accompanied them wherever they went, in the big Mercedes and drove out of San Francisco in a direction that seemed promising and just kept on driving. On one of those trips, they ended up in a tent pitched on a mesa in southern Utah. Outside, there was a terrific storm, with thunder and lightning and raindrops the size of Hershey's Kisses. Inside, Missy and Artie were tripping on acid. Awed by the elements, they exchanged vows in a spiritual ceremony that, to Missy, went beyond the vows that are said at a church altar.

"Only a person that loved me as deeply as Artie did could have said those things," Missy says.

Other times, Missy and Artie would go to the airport and get on the first plane bound for Mexico or any destination that happened to capture their imagination. If they struck up a conversation with a fellow passenger and the passenger asked what they did for a living, Artie said, "I'm a cabdriver," and Missy replied, "I'm a secretary."

But gathering nuts and escaping once a month was not enough for Artie. He could not escape his problems—ex-wives, his brother, too much cocaine, too much tequila, vodka, beer—and he could not escape his role as the renegade king of porn. He would tell some stiff on an airplane he was a cabdriver because he had long ago tired of debating the pros and cons of pornography, but he had no intention of abandoning his Party Artie, the King of the O'Farrell role because without it Artie was nothing, and he knew it. Artie had escaped the trap of Antioch only to end up in another trap.

Like Marilyn Chambers, his female counterpart, Artie was the prisoner of an image. Both Marilyn and Artie got into serious trouble because they tried to erase the line that separates reality from illusion and live the fantasy. Marilyn ended up with fists up her rectum. Artie came to believe he had extraordinary sexual powers.

"The girls call me the catnip man," Artie bragged to Missy. "They can't stay away from me."

"There are only ten real men left in America," he told Joanne Scott. "I'm one of them."

"Art felt his image was intrinsic to the success of the O'Farrell. It was his contribution to the business," Joanne says. "He always had to out-macho and get higher than everyone else. He had to be outrageous to impress some stockbroker with the fact that he had a sex slave. He had to date young dancers to impress other men. He was Hefneresque that way."

To prove his prowess, the "catnip man," the "master" of sex, came on to every dancer at the O'Farrell. Drunk and stoned, he'd wander back to the dressing room holding a joint and ask, "Who wants to get high?" If a dancer accepted the offer, Artie assumed she was ready to have sex.

Jim and Artie's management methods had not changed—they were still using a choke chain to control employees. Instead of paying dancers minimum wage, they had begun charging a $10 to $15 "stage fee," depending on what shift the dancers worked. DJs evaluated dancers on a scale of 1 to 10, with points given for punctuality, costumes, and performance. No matter how good the evaluations were, dancers were subject to summary firings.

"In a lot of cases, dancers were fired to let everybody know who was pulling the strings," says Joanne Scott. "It was a way of telling us, 'You're not valuable, no matter who you are.' Everybody who was there for any length of time realized that."

Some dancers begged for their jobs back and were rehired. Others ended up working in scuzzy joints in the Tenderloin. Artie kept upping the ante with the performers, just as he was with Missy and Joanne.

Dancers like Lisa Loring or Debi Sundahl who had known Artie for a long time could tell him to back off and he'd shrug and go on his way. But other dancers, for reasons no one understood, probably not even Artie, triggered a rage when they put him off. The more a woman denied him, the more the "master" wanted her.

"Women Artie thought were uppity really pushed his button," says Dave Patrick, the *Spectator* editor. "All a woman had to do was say, 'You can't do that, I won't tolerate it,' and it was war. From then on, he was like a shark who kept on coming."

One night, Artie got into a physical fight with a dancer named Lady T, who left deep scratches on his back. Another time, Artie grabbed the breast of a dancer who called herself Danielle from Hell. Danielle was a former street poet who knew how to handle herself, and she slugged him. Artie pushed her to the floor, and when the fight was over, he limped over to Joanne Scott's apartment with a gash down his leg that Danielle had inflicted with the heel of her shoe.

"He may have fired a shot back in the office after the fight with Danielle," Joanne recalls. "I know he got on the microphone and said, 'The whoremeister doesn't speak often, but when he does, the whores listen! That Market Street slut is finished!'

"It was part of his image," Joanne concludes. "When he said things like 'To work here you have to treat women like the cunts they are' and 'All women are cunts, they can all be bought,' he was keeping up the image of the most outrageous guy you can imagine."

One lesbian couple became an obsession with Artie, no doubt because they were committed to each other. Artie hounded them for months. One day, one of the women went into the bathroom. She was sitting on the toilet when Artie kicked in the door and burst into the stall with his pants down.

"They both quit and swore they'd never come back, but a couple of years later they did," Dave Patrick recalls. "I heard so many horror stories like that. I'd always say, 'Artie is a maniac, why don't you report him?' They'd say, 'I want to keep my job.'

"It wasn't just the money," Patrick continues. "It was the status. Women who perform at the O'Farrell feel they're better than the women who work in the other clubs. When a dancer goes from the O'Farrell to a place like the Lusty Lady, the other dancers really rub her nose in it."

When he took over the O'Farrell sound system to abuse Danielle from Hell, or went on a tirade about women, it wasn't just his image Artie was trying to uphold. After smoking a plantation of marijuana and snorting a planeload of cocaine, after having sex with enough women to fill the Great American Music Hall, after spending millions of dollars on adult toys and expensive vacations, Artie had emerged as a very angry man. And like many an angry man, he blamed women.

Meredith was to blame for the breakup of his first marriage, not him. He had missed seeing his older three children grow up because Meredith had turned them against him.

Artie got to know his older three children only after Liberty and Storm were old enough to drive and could travel to San Francisco to visit. Liberty and Missy became close friends, and Storm and his friends *loved* hanging out with Artie. Artie was Storm's coolest buddy. He turned Storm and his friends on to joints and beer. Storm played in a band, and Artie got band members backstage passes to Aerosmith, Mötley Crüe, and Red Hot Chili Peppers concerts.

Liberty and her little sister, Mariah, remained deeply ambivalent about their father. They loved him, but they despised him too. They could not pretend all the years their father had ignored them had not happened. And they hated the porn king role he played.

"My dad was an incredible egomaniac, he always had to be Mr. Macho," Liberty says. "A couple of times he told me, 'Your mother is the only woman I've ever loved,' and I always said to myself, 'Up yours!' He would never admit that my mom had hurt him. God forbid that 'Mr. Macho, the king' could be such a wimp as to really care. God forbid he should reform enough to withhold some of his manliness by not being able to screw every dancer at the O'Farrell. What would Jim think if he came crawling back to my mom? She crossed the Mitchell Brothers? Let her suffer! She did. We all did."

There were occasions when Liberty enjoyed her father. He was so exuberant, so full of energy that it was impossible not to get swept up in the excitement. She liked bringing her friends along and introducing them to her father—Artie was unlike any father they had ever encountered—but Liberty never really felt comfortable at the O'Farrell. Her father made sure of that.

"He'd say, 'I'm into beaver,' around my friends, particularly my male friends. It was a way of insulting me because I'm female," Liberty recalls, going on to describe the parties that were fun until the end, when drunk and stoned men began "leering at anyone who was female. I'd be sitting there saying, 'Go over to FeFe or whomever. I am not one of these fucking bimbos. I am not going to sit on your lap.' I was revolted by the whole thing and my dad held that against me. He'd try to make me feel bad by saying, 'You're such a prude' or 'You're so straight.' I'd say, 'Excuse me, but there are a lot of people who are not prudes who don't think having beaver everywhere is the greatest!' "

Artie's ultimate proof that all women are swine was, of course, his second wife. He and Karen separated in December 1983 and obtained a divorce in October 1985, but the dissolution brought them no peace. Kay filed motion after motion and took Artie back to court to increase her spousal and child support, which eventually reached $5,800 a month.

"Kay used the children as a club," says Eugene Seltzer, Artie's divorce attorney. "As soon as she got shot down in court on some issue—and I can hear her doing it—she'd turn around and say, 'You're not going to get the kids this weekend!' Just like that!"

But the real battles were fought outside the courtroom. The court records are loaded with descriptions of skirmishes.

"Respondent [Artie], after returning the children to Petitioner [Karen], used the automatic gate opener to gain access to the farm, and to accost and attempt to strangle Petitioner in front of the children."

"Artie Mitchell's dependencies on alcohol and drugs constitute an immediate danger to our children's health and safety. Artie is frequently under the influence when with the children. I have been at his house in order to pick up the children and have seen Artie drinking Stolichnaya vodka right out of the bottle. He frequently is up for days on cocaine. He has admitted to me his use of heroin, psilocybin mushrooms, and Valium. He has been dependent on marijuana for years and is always stoned."

Artie countered with petitions that said, "I am not alcohol or drug dependent, as petitioner [Karen] accuses. I believe the same accusation should be leveled at the petitioner. She is given to screaming, hysterical outbursts and often strikes our children."

To Artie's friends and apologists, Karen is the villain who was the cause of all of Artie's problems. They ridicule the claim that Artie used heroin—he was fond of saying the only drugs he had never tried were heroin and nicotine—and point out that Karen was once arrested for growing marijuana on the farm in Canyon (she claims that Artie set her up).

"I lay Art's drinking on Kay's constant torture," Meredith Bradford says. "[Georgia] Mae and I absolutely think that she tried to drive him crazy."

But that misses the point. Swords get sharper when they clash against each other. If Karen carried a gun, it was because Artie threatened her. He *was* frequently intoxicated and high on drugs. Any mother who cared about her children would be alarmed if they were in a car and Artie Mitchell was behind the wheel. And if Karen got some kind of twisted pleasure out of harassing Artie by summoning the police and filing motions for restraining orders, Artie did what he could to make life miserable too.

"I always thought that at some point two people finally adjust to one another," says Joanne Scott. "Karen and Art never did. They'd be on the phone and he'd be making cracks about her and she'd be furious at him. That constant struggle between them, that constant antagonism, that was their relationship."

Something else was eating away at Artie, something more caustic than Karen or drugs and alcohol. Artie Mitchell was scared of growing older.

All men are twenty-one, Chuck Traynor insists, and much of Artie's wild, self-destructive behavior was a desperate attempt to prove that when it came to the manly things that mattered, he was eternally twenty-one. If he drank and consumed outrageous amounts of drugs, if a dancer still in her teens was clinging to his arm, that was proof that Artie Mitchell, no matter what his age, was one helluva guy.

"My dad wanted to stay at that stage where life is a party forever," Liberty says. "That's why Storm and his friends just adored him. He'd hang out with them and drink beer all night. They all thought he was so cool. Of course he was cool. He got down to their level."

"Come and fucking get me, Ed Meese! Fucking come and get me! You fucker, Ed Meese! You can fucking come and fucking get me!"

It was August 7, 1986, the night of the premiere of *Behind the Green Door: The Sequel.* Inside, male sex performers in leather and dancers in G-strings were sampling smoked salmon, cracked crab, and tightly rolled joints and mingling with writers, cartoonists, politicians, publishers, lawyers, doctors, drug dealers, reporters, and fishermen. Outside, searchlights were roaming the sky in front of the theater. Vans equipped with banks of monitors were parked at the curb. And a slatternly Artie Mitchell, his black tie askew and his tuxedo shirt unbuttoned, was parading in front of the cameras, issuing his drunken challenges to Ed Meese, the right-wing Attorney General of the United States.

The Attorney General had appointed a panel, popularly known as the Meese Commission, to study the effects of pornography, an inquiry that Artie—and more sober critics—believed was more a witch-hunt than an honest, unbiased investigation.

"You fucker, Ed Meese! You fuckin' hear me? Come and fuckin' get me!" Artie shouted at the cameras.

Three O'Farrell employees standing on the sidewalk were watching the performance and grinning. "Nobody's crazier than Artie," said one admiringly. "Too bad they'll never be able to use this footage," added another. "There's no way you can edit out all those 'fucks.' "

The glass door to the theater flew open and Jim Mitchell appeared. The employees stiffened. Jim's eyes were blazing and his lips were stretched thin, revealing an effort to control his anger. He watched Artie for a few seconds, then walked up, put his arm around his brother's shoulders, and, without bothering to glance at the three employees, led Artie back into the theater.

The employees were not smiling now. Artie's antics no longer seemed funny. The Mitchell Brothers had spent more than $250,000 to produce the *Green Door Sequel*. This was to be the movie that would reestablish them as the leaders of the sexual pack. Jim and Rita Benton (wife of longtime sound man Alex Benton), who was in charge of the packaging, advertising, and public relations campaign for the film, had spent weeks and thousands of dollars planning this premiere. And on the big night, Artie was wasted and out of control.

For years, the Mitchell Brothers had kicked around ideas for a sequel to *Green Door*. They had finally gotten around to making it, but not because they needed the money or were desperate to recapture their biggest success. They made the sequel because they were bored.

Jim and Artie had done everything there was to do in pornography. Jeff Armstrong and Richard Mezzavilla were running the theater, so there really wasn't much for the brothers to do at the O'Farrell. The theater was a cash cow—it cost $15 to get in before noon, $20 from noon to six, and $25 after six—and according to the books, the theater was bringing in $3.3 to $3.6 million a year. Jim and Artie were paying themselves and their top employees annual salaries in the six figures, and the brothers were skimming cash.

One night after a particularly nasty fight with his brother, Artie had showed up at Joanne Scott's apartment, coked up and in a rage. Jim had punched him in the ribs, even though he knew Artie had a cracked rib, and while Artie was lying on the floor had picked up a tape dispenser and said, I could kill you, fucker, but I won't because I love you.

"Artie called the theater and said, 'Tell Jim I want ten thousand dollars in a paper bag or I'll Molotov-cocktail the lobby,'" Joanne recalls. "He wasn't going to do that, of course, but when I went down to the theater, Jim was there with a paper bag with five thousand dollars in it. Jim said, 'I'm tired of Art, he's a cocaine addict.' When I was leaving, he said, 'If you need more money, call.'

"We used the money in the bag to go to Cabo San Lucas," Joanne continues. "Art did everything on a cash basis. In the eight years I was with him, I never once saw him cash a check or go to an ATM machine. Once when he was about seven, I had Caleb with me and I stopped at a bank to cash a check. It was so novel to Caleb he asked why we had to stop. 'My dad always has hundred-dollar bills,' he said."

Jim and Artie were taking a great deal of money from the theater and investing it in Manteca, Inc., their commercial fishing business. With typical grandiosity, they had purchased an 82-foot boat called the *Graciosa*, which was twice the size of the *Bottom Feeder*. The brothers had also become serious about golf and were spending Fridays and many weekends out on the links. But most of the time the brothers could still be found upstairs at the O'Farrell, hanging out with their buddies.

At times, the boys' club upstairs at the O'Farrell felt like a living museum that preserved the best of the Merry Prankster spirit from the 1960s. The boys upstairs were always trying to figure out ways to put banana peels under the feet of the pompous and the arrogant. They pulled off one of their all-time best gambits in March 1983, when Queen Elizabeth II visited San Francisco.

Cartoonist Dan O'Neill, a longtime hater of the British, was drawing a strip about the Falkland Islands war that asked the provocative question "Is everybody out of their Falkland minds?" In the strip, O'Neill was sending the Irish Republican Navy, an imaginary branch of the IRA, off to do battle with the English.

Bob Callahan, author of *A Day in the Life of Ireland* and *The Big Book of Irish History,* was a Mitchell Brothers insider who, like O'Neill, was outraged that Americans were falling all over themselves to honor the queen, that symbol of monarchy and oppression. The more the boys upstairs talked about it, the more they decided the right thing to do was to bring the Irish Republican Navy to life.

Callahan invited the world's press—the BBC, the English tabloids, the wire services, and television reporters—to the deck of the Trident restaurant in Sausalito to witness the Irish Republican Navy on maneuvers. When the press arrived, they found Irish flags flying, hokey Irish music playing on boom boxes, and a Gaelic speaker named Paddy O. Furniture doing a running commentary into a microphone.

"What the hell is this?" the press wanted to know. "Be patient," Callahan counseled, "you are about to witness a demonstration of naval might." Around the bend came two tiny Boston Whalers; Jim and FM radio commentator Travis T. Hipp were in one boat, and Artie and Rocky Davidson, a Mitchell Brothers cousin and a custodian at the O'Farrell, were in the other. The sky above the boats was alive with hundreds of screeching sea gulls, who were competing for the mackerel that Jim and Artie were tossing into the air.

"You are witnessing the IRN's secret battle plan," Callahan told the press. "We are going to bloat every bird from here to Tierra del Fuego in the hope that one bird—and it will only take one—will get through and shit on the queen as she stands on the deck of the *Britannia.*"

"Guys almost fell off the dock, they were laughing so hard," Callahan recalls. "The next day, the queen wore a blue-and-white polka-dot dress and we claimed victory. There were headlines in the London tabs that said, 'San Francisco Pornographers Support IRA.' It was a wonderful way to say no in a world that doesn't have much of a sense of humor."

But plenty of things went on upstairs at the O'Farrell that were not this funny, at least to outsiders. To one degree or another, many of the insiders were mirror images of Artie, eternal adolescents with typically adolescent senses of humor.

"One of the things that was really bothering me when I left was the intense, complicated games that were going on all the time," says Denise Larson, co-founder of the Nickelettes. "It was very much male one-upmanship. Everybody played little tricks and took cheap shots and tried to make somebody look foolish so they could say, 'I got him!' "

Known as "rat fucking," the tricks could be Jim slipping a huge cockroach in an enchilada Hunter Thompson was about to eat in a Mexican restaurant in the Mission and watching with a poker face while Thompson devoured the meal. Or it could be telling a guy on his birthday that he was going to get laid, taking him down to the Ultra Room, and watching while four women proceeded to strip him naked and tie him up, and then waving goodbye and leaving him there for an hour or so.

The stars of the boys' club were Hunter S. Thompson and Warren Hinckle.

"My dad admired Hunter's craziness. Hunter was a big influence in my dad's life," Liberty says. "He talked about Hunter a lot, telling stories about what Hunter had done, or what he and Hunter had done. They were supposed to be friends, but they both had the same opinion of each other. My dad was always going, 'Stay away from Thompson. He's no good.' A friend of mine came up for a weekend, and at a party at the O'Farrell, Hunter took her aside and said, 'Stay away from Artie. He's no good.' "

Artie and Jim spent endless months making a documentary about Hunter Thompson called *The Dance of the Doomed* (the title was later changed to *The Crazy Never Die*), but with all the drugs and alcohol and the chaos, the project moved forward only in fits and starts, and the brothers were bored.

And then one day they were offered an opportunity to break out of their slump. Margo St. James and Priscilla Alexander, the founder and co-director of COYOTE, came up to the theater to talk to Jim and Artie about the scourge of AIDS. "You guys should do a safe-sex porn film," the women suggested. "People are dying out there. We've got to find some way to get the message to people who aren't listening."

The COYOTE women were convinced a safe-sex pornographic film would also help the sex-positive forces reclaim the initiative in the sex wars. Unbridled sex had become inextricably linked with death; anyone who behaved like a 1970s-style swinger in the 1980s had to have a death wish. But what if you made a film that showed safe-sex was erotic? A movie that proved that sex could be fun again, as long as you took the proper precautions?

The COYOTE women had appealed to Jim and Artie's best instincts, and the brothers decided to do it, and do it big by remaking *Green Door* as the world's first safe-sex pornographic film. Jim and Artie took a crash course in condoms, latex, spermicidal jellies, and dental dams. Rev. Ted McIlvenna had begun his career in sex by counseling paralyzed Vietnam vets (McIlvenna helped prepare Jon Voight for his role in *Coming Home*), and through him Jim and Artie had become interested in the sex lives of paraplegics. Anyone in a wheelchair was admitted to the O'Farrell free. In the *Green Door Sequel*, the brothers decided to cast a man confined to a wheelchair in a lead role.

The brothers placed an ad in *Variety* that announced they were casting the sequel for *Green Door* and were now auditioning fat ladies, midgets, two-headed people, and geeks. Geeks had to supply their own chickens.

"Putting an ad like that in a straight paper like *Variety* was their way of saying, 'We're just as big as you,' " Missy recalls. "All the DJs in L.A. were talking about it and people from all over came to audition."

Missy had decided she was the perfect successor to Marilyn Chambers and was dying to audition for the film. She was blond and pretty, just like Marilyn; she was fresh and had never appeared in a film, just like Marilyn. She would be Missy Manners, the Republican girl-next-door porn star!

Artie loved the idea; Jim hated it. Jim talked about how much heat Missy would bring, and how he didn't think it was a good idea for Missy and Artie to mix their personal and business lives. But Jim was just blowing smoke—since when was he worried about bringing "too much heat"? The real reason he didn't want Missy in the film was that she was his brother's girlfriend.

"Jim was a jerk to Missy," Liberty says. "Maybe he felt threatened by her, maybe he refused to take her seriously because she was my dad's girlfriend. But he wasn't nice to her, and they had a lot of problems."

Jim also didn't want Missy on the set because she and Artie had been running wild, interrupting shows in New York Live, disrupting business, drinking and doing drugs far into the night, and then curling up in the pool-table cover and falling asleep under the table. Missy knew that she and Artie were a problem to Jim—"To us, the things we did were funny. But I could see where they weren't that funny to Jim, who had a business to run and a lot of people working for him who were counting on him to keep it together"—but she decided to audition for the film anyway.

Missy went onstage and did a striptease and a masturbation scene. When the time came to simulate orgasm, Missy reached into her vagina for the small containers she had placed there and began pulling out a stream of colorful scarves, like the ones that magicians pull out of a hat.

The Mitchell Brothers had hired Sharon McKnight to direct the film, and when she heard about Missy's audition, she insisted on seeing it. Missy put the tape in the VCR upstairs in the office and McKnight and everyone else howled with laughter when the scarves appeared.

"That's a first-class audition. You could get a job anywhere in New York with that audition," McKnight told Missy.

"Do you think she should be in the movie?" Jim asked McKnight.

"I think she should be in the movie," McKnight replied.

"Well, yeah, okay," Jim said, turning to Missy. "I guess you can have a job."

Missy didn't just get a role; she got the lead as Gloria, the woman who fantasizes (instead of being kidnapped) being ravished in a secret club behind a green door. The sex club was going to have a classical motif, so the brothers commissioned three artists, including Mary Jane Mitchell, to cover the walls of the Green Door Room with replicas of Gustave Courbet's "Laziness and Sensuality (The Sleepers)," "Satyr and the Nymph," a sixteenth-century product of the Mannerists at L'Ecole Fontainebleau, and, from ancient Greece, "Polyphemus and Galatea."

The Mitchell Brothers shot *Behind the Green Door: The Sequel* in one sixteen-hour day in 1985 at the O'Farrell. Missy woke up that morning to find a note from Artie on her dresser: "Dear Missy: Your life will never be the same. What a wild ride. Artie."

Artie was right, Missy's life never was the same. Missy didn't just have sex that day with the Greek god Pan and with statues that came to life, she didn't just masturbate and have oral sex with a group of men, and she didn't just duplicate the trapeze scene from the original film. In that one long day, Missy became a spokesperson for pornography and safe sex.

Her Washington experience had served her well. Missy knew how to deal with the press at least as well as the Mitchell Brothers. She had called publications like the New York *Times, The Wall Street*

Journal, Playboy, and *USA Today* to tell them about a porn film that was also a cause. Because of the AIDS hook and her Republican background—a Bay Area TV station had broken the story—Missy and the film were good copy. Several of the big papers did stories, and talk shows began calling.

Unfortunately, Missy was much better at dealing with the press than she was at acting in the film. *Behind the Green Door: The Sequel* was another Mitchell Brothers disaster.

The film had the usual Mitchell Brothers hallmarks—garbled sound, an unintelligible or nonexistent plot, poor lighting, and amateurish camera work. It takes forever to get started—Missy plays Gloria, an airline stewardess, and there is a long, aimless scene where she is walking through an airport, jabbering with other stewardesses. On-camera, Missy appears leaden. The women in the audience at the sex club—O'Farrell dancers who were paid $125 for the day—are lethargic, the sex scenes with a fat lady are too grotesque to watch, the references to AIDS and safe sex are contrived and pedantic, and the use of condoms and latex gloves, however well-meaning, is so poorly handled that the sex comes across as absurd instead of sensible or erotic.

The best you can say for the *Green Door Sequel* is that it makes the viewer aware of how fundamentally ridiculous the sex act is. But, of course, the reviewers were not that kind.

"An orgy ensues, only it looks like open-heart surgery," wrote a reviewer from the *Chronicle.* "The film has a decidedly clinical flavor, what with all the squeaking rubber. . . . I've been more turned on at Walgreen's."

Nor did the *Green Door Sequel* do well at the box office. The safe-sex gesture was not taken seriously by the mainstream audience and it turned off the hard-core audience. *Hustler* named the film the most disappointing of the year.

"They put so much energy into the *Green Door Sequel,* it was going to be their magnum opus, it was going to put them in the forefront of the AIDS fight and show that they were comrades," Bob Callahan recalls. "When none of that happened, it increased Jim's desire to get out of the porn business. Jim kept saying, 'I need something more than this. I need to do something new.' Artie's position was 'Naw, we can't do that, we're just assholes, we'd just lose money. We should just take our money from the theater and fish.' "

In addition to growing old, Artie was haunted by another fear: he was afraid his brother was going to abandon him. He took the failure of the *Green Door Sequel* personally. His girlfriend, after all, had been the star and he did try to make this one work. But the film bombed, which proved that Artie didn't know how to make a good porn film anymore. No one at the theater took him seriously. Most of the dancers despised him or were afraid of him. And now Jim was talking about getting out of the business. That meant leaving him behind. Without Jim, what would he do?

Artie dealt with his fears the only way he knew how. He self-medicated, burying them under ever-increasing doses of drugs and alcohol. Some mornings, Artie greeted the day by filling a glass three-quarters full with tequila before adding orange juice.

"One time I asked Artie, 'What makes you drink so much? Do you think it helps you?' " Missy recalls. "Artie said, 'It doesn't matter if I go to work today or go golfing or if I stay home and get drunk. I'm going to make the same amount of money whether I go to work or not. So what the fuck?' "

While Artie was turning himself into a self-pitying drunk, Jim was talking to his journalist friends about starting a newspaper. For the first time in their lives, the Mitchell Brothers were headed in opposite directions.

12

"A Possible Multiple Drowning off Ocean Beach"

"I WANT TO CHANGE the theater, change the whole conception of the place," Jim was telling Bob Callahan over lunch at Maye's Original Oyster House, a few blocks up Polk Street from the theater. "What do you think I should do?"

"Clowns," Callahan replied.

"Clowns?"

"Send in the clowns," Callahan said with a straight face. "The city says the theater is dirty, you say it's a fun house, so go all the way. Hire some clowns, have them walk around with the girls."

Callahan watched Jim's usually impassive face and could tell he was intrigued. This was one of the things Callahan liked best about Jim, his friend for the past five years. Jim listened, he was willing to try things out. Callahan, a gregarious, warmhearted man, felt he was having an effect on Jim's life, and he liked that feeling. Everyone wants to matter to his friends.

"I think we should do the newspaper," Callahan said after they had discussed the clowns, which was more a way of making a statement than a serious business idea. "We could put out something we'd all be proud of, something that would follow in the San Francisco tradition of *Ramparts* and *Rolling Stone."*

"You know what?" Jim asked, his eyes widening. "I had an idea about that. We could bring back newsboys. Blacks, Hispanics, Vietnamese, we'd have one on every corner, hawking the paper. Who could pass one of those kids and not pick up a paper?"

"That's a great idea!" Callahan said. "We could have 'em wear floppy hats like old-time newsboys!"

Callahan, a fifty-year-old man with long, stringy hair and a bowling-pin body, wasn't spinning a fantasy. He was the founder of Turtle Island Press, once one of the finest small presses in America, and the editor of *The New Comics Anthology.* His friends included the writers Ishmael Reed and Barry Gifford and the Pulitzer Prize-winning cartoonist Art Spiegelman. Callahan knew from firsthand experience how much effort and insanity go into launching a new publication, and he was convinced Jim Mitchell had the intensity and drive to be a publisher.

Jim had always been fascinated by journalists; starting an alternative paper was his chance to become one. The paper would prove that Jim was a smart businessman who could succeed in a new world where ideas, politics, and style were what mattered. Best of all, becoming a publisher would take Jim out of pornography and establish him as a figure to be reckoned with in both the straight world and the counterculture.

"The difference between being a publisher and being a pornographer is that being a publisher is not a con," Callahan says. "Jim was coming into my world. He was ready to push beyond the boundaries of pornography and cast off that white-trash ball and chain he'd dragged with him from Antioch."

Jim had not undergone some miraculous conversion. He had simply hit middle age. In his quiet, subdued way, Jim had smoked almost as much grass, done almost as much coke, and had almost as many women as his theatrical younger brother. But Jim had the feeling that time was closing in on him. The 1960s were long gone and here he was approaching his fiftieth birthday. He longed to regain the feeling he'd had back in the 1960s, when his leftist friends were telling him that porn was going to transform America's sexual mores.

Now Jim could no longer use that rationalization. Thanks in large part to breakthroughs he and Art had made in San Francisco and

Behind the Green Door, porn had gone mainstream. Porn was an option in the consumer marketplace. All you had to do to rent a film was walk into the local video store and enter the section behind a curtain. Calvin Klein ads were hotter than the early movies Jim had made with Earl Shagley and Annie. But nothing had changed. Porn was still porn.

Being a Mitchell Brother had cost Jim two marriages. Adrienne had run off with a porn actor, and now Jim and Mary Jane were divorced. Mary Jane had begun a relationship with the children's swimming instructor. But she was not to blame for the breakup of their marriage; even Jim knew that.

"Jim told me that he'd gotten drunk one day and slapped her," says Jack Harvey. "He was fucking around and raising hell and one day he came up to her and gave her a slap. It really, really upset him that he'd lost control of himself and done that. It was totally against his makeup."

Jim and Mary Jane had separated in September 1986 and gone through a rocky divorce. On September 11, a judge issued a re-straining order against Jim, forbidding him from coming within fifty yards of Mary Jane's house, her parents' and sisters' houses, and the San Francisco Art Institute, where Mary Jane was a student. A year later, on August 26, 1987, Mary Jane asked for another restraining order.

"Respondent [Jim] has learned that Petitioner [Mary Jane] had started dating," a court document says. "He [Jim] has telephoned her several times since, and has threatened to kill her and her friend. His behavior has been violent, extremely irrational, abusive and out of control. Respondent has a history of physical violence. Petitioner is afraid for her safety and the welfare of her children."

Jim eventually got himself under control and he and Mary Jane came to terms, with Jim paying $5,867 per month in spousal and child support, plus school tuitions for two of the four children and therapy sessions for another. Despite all the troubles he was having with Artie, Artie was still his brother, and Jim had moved in with Missy and Artie in the Marina. Later, the brothers purchased a huge house that hung from a hill in the East Bay community of Moraga. The house was built long and low, had a pool in the back and wonderful views. Jim's four children and Artie's younger three children were there on weekends and for longer periods during the summer, and the Bradford children came by on occasion. Several live-in maids kept the house running and helped with the children.

In time, Jim began dating a longtime dancer at the O'Farrell named Lisa Adams. Under the name Lisa Thatcher, she had appeared in films with S&M porn star Jamie Gillis. A strikingly pretty WASPish blonde who was known for being cold and aloof onstage, Lisa was eager to get out of the sex business. After she began seeing Jim, she quit dancing and became a secretary at the theater. Eventually, Lisa quit the O'Farrell altogether, moved in with Jim, and dedicated herself to helping him care for his four children.

"Jim's children really adored Lisa," Liberty says. "He seemed to have a stability with her that he'd never had before."

Jim and Lisa eventually decided they wanted a place of their own and moved to 47th Avenue in San Francisco, a few blocks from Ocean Beach. Karen and the kids had moved from Canyon to a house on a hill in Marin, and Artie was becoming weary of hauling kids back and forth from Moraga to Marin. He had collected several Driving Under the Influence citations and had had his driving privileges restricted. It would be much easier if he moved closer to the kids in Marin, which is what he eventually decided to do.

Missy Manners had no idea that posing could be so strenuous. The *Playboy* photographer was a total perfectionist. Everything—the lights, the makeup, the backdrop—had to be impeccable before he would proceed, and then Missy had to hold a position for what seemed like hours while he took shot after shot, exploring different angles. Posing for *Playboy* is like doing Tai Chi, Missy had decided after the second day of shooting.

Missy was exhausted as she walked back to the Knickerbocker, the four-star hotel on Walton off Michigan in Chicago, where *Playboy* had rented a suite for her and Artie. But it was all worth it. She had become her own person, and she had done it her way.

Reviewers were saying nasty things about the *Green Door Sequel* and the film was dying at the box office, but that really hadn't mattered because the film's safe-sex message had raised Missy to a higher plateau than a porn star had ever ascended. Not even Marilyn Chambers had appeared in *Playboy*. Porn stars did not fit the magazine's formula. Playmates were innocents who were pictured doing things like cooking breakfast with a younger brother on one page and lying nude on satin sheets on the next.

Missy had appeared on *The Oprah Winfrey Show* and *Larry King Live* with Rona Barrett as hostess, and had proven herself to be an intelligent and sometimes flamboyant interview. On *Oprah,* she had enraged the panel's antiporn activists by passing out condoms to the audience. She was lecturing to college classes on safe sex, the BBC had interviewed her for a documentary on AIDS, and now *Playboy* was doing a story and a lavish photo spread.

Featuring Missy was a smart move on *Playboy*'s part. The magazine was under attack by the antiporn forces that had banded together under the banner of the Meese Commission. They had forced Southland, the giant corporation that owns 7-Eleven stores, to pull *Playboy* off its racks, and there was no telling where the pro-censorship movement would strike next. The Missy story was a way for *Playboy*'s editors to show their publication was solidly in the safe-sex camp.

"Artie! Artie! Are you here?" Missy yelled as she walked into the suite.

There was no answer. "Artie?" Missy called more tentatively as she walked into the bedroom. She came to a dead stop and stared at the bed. Missy felt like she had just been punched in the stomach.

The bed was torn apart, blankets and a sheet were crumpled on the floor, an ashtray was loaded with lipstick-stained, half-smoked joints, a pair of woman's silk panties was lying near a pillow and used condoms were on the floor.

Missy went into the bathroom, closed the door, and turned on the faucet to fill the tub. "I can't even . . . He won't even . . ." she said aloud, and began to cry.

Missy knew the scene in the bedroom was a fuck-you from Artie. It was his way of telling Missy that she meant nothing to him, that she and what she was doing were worthless. In a way, she wasn't surprised. Artie had been acting uncomfortable ever since she had begun doing interviews and appearing on talk shows. Part of him liked it; it was good publicity for the film and it had been fun passing out condoms on *Oprah.*

But Artie was also jealous. She had taken the spotlight away from him.

"Artie always competed with me," Missy says in retrospect. "He resented that I was doing something he didn't have control over. I think he felt that if I started feeling real good about myself, I might leave him, or someone might come after me, and that would be it.

"That was a fear Artie had, but he never expressed it. Artie couldn't express things like that. If he was in pain, he'd just drink it off, just cover it up. If he was angry, he'd hit someone."

Missy finished the *Playboy* shoot and forgave Artie, as she always did, and they went back to San Francisco. She found out whom Artie had been with, and when she heard "Phone call for Artie" and the woman's name come over the intercom at the O'Farrell, Missy picked up the phone and told the woman that if she ever called again, Missy would become her worst nightmare.

But Artie was not only using other women to humiliate Missy. He was using violence. Holidays have a way of bringing out the misery in unhappy people, and on Thanksgiving Day, a few weeks after he and Missy had returned from Chicago, Artie was in a rage, cursing Karen because they had argued over the kids. Missy, trying to make everything all right, said something that Artie didn't like and he erupted.

"Look, Artie, I've had it," Missy said. "I'm not going to take any more of your shit." Artie flew into a frenzy and clawed the left side of Missy's face.

Artie had beaten up Missy before. One night, they were arguing in the Mercedes and Artie opened the door and pushed her out of the moving car onto Scott Street in the Marina. On occasion, Missy had fought back, picking up a Coke bottle or a lamp and bashing him with it.

The claw marks bothered Missy more than the bruises and black eyes had, perhaps because they had come so soon after the *Playboy* shoot. Missy was building a career that was dependent on her looks, and Artie was trying to ruin that. Friends were telling her that if she didn't leave him, Artie would try to disfigure her. She had ignored them. This time, Missy listened.

Missy packed up her things and moved in with friends in Stinson Beach, a beautiful town north of San Francisco, behind Mount Tamalpais. Stinson was far enough away so that Artie could not drop in whenever he wanted, and Missy could not run back to him, which, more than anything, is what she wanted to do.

Leaving Artie was by far the hardest thing Missy had ever done. She stayed with her friends for four months, and then moved into a small house near Ed's Superette, the Stinson Beach store. Missy enrolled in a half dozen therapy programs—AA, Al-Anon, Women Who Love Too Much Therapy, counseling at the Marin Abused

Women's Services—in addition to sessions with a private therapist. The therapy kept her going, and she kept a journal to record her insights.

"I was a drama queen," Missy says. "I was hooked on chaos. There was a lot of chaos with Artie—an ex-wife would come over and beat down the door, girlfriends would call in the middle of the night, there was a Supreme Court case that could send him to jail. Growing up in Utah, my life had been boring. I wanted the chaos in my life, I wanted the drama."

While she was going through the breakup, Missy posted notes to herself all over her house—"Do not call Artie. He has not met your needs. He will never meet your needs." Some days, she put tape on the phone so she couldn't pick it up. When she found herself undoing the tape, she ripped the phone out of the wall and threw it through the window. Finally, she had her phone disconnected.

But every now and then, Missy broke down and allowed herself to see Artie. They would have lunch or dinner and see a movie, and sometimes they'd end up spending the night together. Artie would ask her to come back and assure her that things were going to be different, but Missy knew they wouldn't be.

Missy had stopped drinking, but when Jack Davis, a prominent San Francisco campaign manager and a close friend of both Missy and Artie, invited her to his birthday party at an Indian restaurant in San Francisco, Missy fell off the wagon. She made it back to Stinson Beach, but after putting on a pink flannel nightgown and climbing into bed with Mr. T, her little poodle, Missy couldn't sleep. She missed Artie. She wanted Artie. She had to have Artie.

Missy put on a pair of high heels, went back to her car, and drove thirty miles across the Bay Area to Moraga. When she arrived at the big house Artie was sharing with Jim, the first thing she noticed was Joanne Scott's car in the driveway. Furious, Missy rang the front doorbell over and over again. Artie finally woke up and opened the door, and when he saw Missy, he muttered "Oh shit!" and slammed it shut. Missy went through the bushes, trying to find a window that was open. When she got to the back of the house, she discovered the back door was unlocked and walked in.

Artie and Joanne heard Missy's high heels clicking down the hallway and locked the bedroom door. Missy took off a shoe and started pounding on the door.

"Get out of here! Get out of this house! We're calling the police!" Artie and Joanne yelled.

"Just you fucking go ahead!" Missy screamed back. She finally punctured the hollow-core door with her high heel and left the shoe sticking in the door.

Missy was turning off Highway 101 at the Mill Valley exit when she saw flashing red lights behind her.

"I got busted for drunk driving," Missy says. "And I had to go to my group therapy and confess that I'd needed a drama fix."

Time passed, Missy and Artie buried the incident, as they had so many others, and Artie began bringing his three younger children out to Stinson Beach on weekends. It was just like the old days, Artie, Missy, and the kids all having a good time together, and Artie seemed genuinely to want Missy back in his life. She kept her guard up, only seeing Artie in the presence of his children, until one night when she decided it would be okay to have dinner alone with him. Missy asked friends to babysit the children, and she and Artie went to a restaurant in Stinson Beach.

"Can I get you something to drink?" the waitress asked after they had sat down.

"I'll have a Heineken," Artie replied. "And do you give good head?"

Missy stood up. She had spent years listening to Artie call women cunts, dykes, whores, and pigs. She was not going to listen to him abuse women ever again.

"Fuck you, Artie," Missy said, throwing down her napkin.

Missy walked home and Artie caught up with her on her deck.

"Who the fuck do you think you are, walking out on me?" Artie demanded.

Before Missy could answer, Artie knocked her down and began banging her head into the deck. Missy was knocked unconscious. When she came to, she was bleeding and Artie was gone. She called a friend who was an EMT on the Stinson Beach Patrol, and he came over and took care of her. The friend wanted Missy to file charges, but she refused.

"At that point I knew Artie had the ability to kill me, because when he left, he didn't know whether I was dead or alive," Missy says. "At that point, I had to decide, 'Who do you like more? Yourself or Artie?' "

Missy decided in favor of herself, but therapy became harder after that, and she became more and more depressed. She would go to the home of some friends, sit down on the couch or lie down on their floor, and cry and cry.

It was not just her relationship with Artie that revolted Missy, it was her whole life. Her mother's alcoholism and her fear of abandonment after her parents had divorced and she had been sent to boarding school. Artie's problems with Karen and the way she had evolved into a co-alcoholic with Artie; the anger and the abuse, the unhappiness, it was all such a vicious cycle. Missy began to think the best way to end it was to commit suicide.

"A few people who lived at the beach had done it. Why couldn't I?" Missy says she asked herself.

But she kept going to therapy sessions and AA meetings and taking long walks up and down the fogbound beach. And then one day, Missy gave up.

"I thought: Oh, fuck it! This is really hard work. Let's party!" Missy recalls. "That was always Artie's solution: Let's party!"

Missy began drinking again and in one month she was arrested three times for Driving Under the Influence. The third time the cops pulled her over, Missy started sobbing.

"This is the saddest thing that has ever happened to me," Missy bawled to the cop. "Do you think that I could just have a hug?"

The cop couldn't believe what he had heard.

"Lady," he said, looking at Missy, "you are pathetic. You are a mess. And I am disgusted."

With that, he closed the door and drove Missy off to jail.

A judge looked at Missy's three DUI arrests, asked, "What is going on with you, young lady?" and sentenced her to thirty days in jail and a year in a court-supervised drug and alcohol program. Under an alternative sentencing plan, Missy was able to trade the thirty days for four days in jail and thirty days of community service. She served four days in the Marin County Jail with prostitutes and drug dealers and then returned to Stinson Beach, where she spent thirty days cleaning toilets, painting rest rooms, and picking up cigarette butts on the beach and in parking lots.

One afternoon, Missy was on her hands and knees, painting a red zone on the curb near a fire hydrant. A car drove slowly by. Missy glanced up to see Artie and his new girlfriend, Kristal, a dancer at the O'Farrell who was known as a Deadhead, a devoted follower of the Grateful Dead.

Artie parked the car and he and Kristal got out and walked toward Missy. Kristal was wearing a skimpy halter and a pair of very tight, very short shorts.

"Oh, hi, Missy," Artie said, faking nonchalance.

"Hi, Artie. Hi, Kristal," Missy said, doing her best to concentrate on her painting.

Artie and Kristal walked past Missy and sat down on a nearby bench. And then they started making out, exchanging long passionate kisses as their hands explored each other.

Missy finished painting the red zone and walked back into some bushes and hid until Artie and Kristal left.

It was Sunday, March 18, 1990, the birthday of Jim's oldest daughter, Meta. Liberty and Storm Bradford had joined their father and his three youngest children for a party at Jim's house on 47th Avenue. Early in the afternoon one of the kids said, "Let's go Boogie-boarding!" That sounded like a great idea, and the party moved to Ocean Beach, a few blocks from Jim's house.

The skies were blue, but it was a blustery day, with winds coming out of the west at 15 to 20 miles an hour. The surf was heavy and very disturbed, with treacherous, disorganized waves crashing in from the north and a violent rip tide carrying water through the surf and back to sea.

Rafe, Jim's oldest boy, and Aaron and Caleb, Artie's youngest, put on their wet suits, grabbed Boogie boards, and plunged into the surf. Jim and Artie and the other children spread out blankets and sat down on the sand. Everything was fine; the kids were getting knocked around in the surf, but they seemed to be enjoying it. And then Liberty noticed that they were farther away from the shore than they had been. And then she noticed that they had *really* moved out to sea.

Rafe came shooting through the surf on his Boogie board. He stood up and a wave knocked him down. He got up again, stumbled, and then ran to where everyone was sitting.

"It's really rough out there," Rafe said, panting and struggling to get his breath. "They can't get in."

"Storm," Artie said to his eighteen-year-old son, "go out there and get Aaron and Caleb."

Storm was an excellent surfer, but he did not have a wet suit and the water temperature was a bone-numbing 50 degrees. But without pausing to think twice, Storm stripped to his Jockey shorts, grabbed a Boogie board, and plunged into the surf.

As soon as Storm hit the water, Jim looked at Liberty.

"Call 911," Jim said, "now!"

Liberty leapt to her feet.

"Get Storm's surfboard!" Artie yelled as Liberty ran up the beach.

Liberty was screaming, "Help!" and "Call 911!" as loud as she could. Up on the street, a man jumped out of a van and cried, "I'll call!"

Liberty kept running until she reached her father's car. She grabbed Storm's surfboard and raced back to the beach. Artie had a Boogie board, Jim grabbed the surfboard, and they plunged into the angry surf.

By the time Storm reached Aaron and Caleb, Caleb had lost his Boogie board and was treading water, trembling with cold. Storm managed to get Caleb on his board, and was able to shoot him through the surf to the beach, Then Storm shot Aaron in. But after launching the boys toward the beach, Storm had no energy left. It was all he could do to tread water until his father and Jim arrived.

Aaron and Caleb's lips were blue, their teeth were chattering, and they were shaking so badly their knees were banging together. Liberty wrapped them in blankets and got them up to the car and drove them back to Jim's house. The whole time she was thinking: If anything happens to Storm, I'm going to fucking murder my father!

When the 911 call of a possible multiple drowning off Ocean Beach came in, Lieutenant Tilden Hansan of the San Francisco Fire Department grabbed his wet suit and headed for the beach. The organizer of the department's Surf Rescue Team, Hansan knew the waters around San Francisco as well as any man ever has. He had swum the length of the Golden Gate and had swum from Alcatraz to San Francisco.

But when Hansan reached Ocean Beach, he witnessed something he could not remember ever seeing: there were no surfers in the water. Surfers were human seals; if the conditions were too treacherous for them, who had been crazy enough to venture into the deadly surf?

Hansan had established protocol for the Surf Rescue Team. Going into the water was always voluntary, a decision that was left up to each member of the team. The lieutenant looked out to sea and saw three Coast Guard boats and two helicopters hovering above the boats and made a decision. Today, no member of the Surf Rescue Team would have the option of entering the water. He was going to order them to stay out.

But when Hansan fought his way through a crowd of 300 people that had gathered on the beach, he discovered that three of his men were already in the water. Captain Steve Freeman and firefighters Ralph Blanchard and Mark Evanoff were on surfboards, making their way to Jim, Artie, and Storm.

It took Steve Freeman twenty minutes to fight his way through the boiling white water and travel approximately 400 yards from shore to reach Jim, Artie, and Storm. Freeman reached Artie first; he was semiconscious and had a death grip on a Boogie board. Freeman was trained to engage a victim and try to get him talking. So the first thing he did was to ask, "How you doing?"

Artie was too far gone to respond, but someone said, "That's a rather silly question, isn't it?"

Freeman turned his head and saw Jim Mitchell looking at him and shaking his head. Jim and Storm were clinging to a surfboard.

Ralph Blanchard arrived and grabbed the surfboard Jim and Storm were hanging on to. "Oh God! Oh God!" Jim kept muttering over and over. Blanchard looked in Jim's eyes and saw he was terrified.

The rescuers now had to decide whether to go seaward, toward the Coast Guard ships, or to fight their way through the surf. The water between them and the ships was almost as treacherous as the surf. It is difficult to get victims into a boat in rough water and they were closer to shore than to the ships, so the rescuers resolved to head for the beach.

Evanoff got Freeman (who had been stunned by a blow to the head from a loose surfboard) and Artie onto a surfboard and began pushing them in a northerly direction, trying to make his way through the raging surf. Blanchard was behind him, pushing Storm and Jim. It took them twenty-five minutes to get to shore and the waiting ambulances.

"How's he doing?" Jim asked as the EMTs bundled up Artie.

Artie was not doing well. His body temperature was 86 degrees and he was suffering from severe hypothermia. Artie ended up spending four days in the University of California Medical Center. Captain Freeman spent more than a week recovering in San Francisco General Hospital.

"I was on my knees when they pulled them out of the surf," Liberty remembers. "There were all these people around and they were all saying, 'They're so stupid to be out there.' When I saw Storm was okay, I was so happy I started crying."

Months later, at the Washington Square Bar and Grill, Jim and Artie presented the Surf Rescue Team with a check for $10,000 and gave six members of the team lifetime passes to the O'Farrell. The incident at Ocean Beach became part of the Mitchell Brothers' lore: the firemen were heroes and Jim and Artie had rewarded them generously.

But the truth is, the spectators on the beach that day were right: Jim and Artie *were* stupid to let their kids go into a surf that wild. Despite the years they had spent hunting and their attempt to become commercial fishermen, Jim and Artie were still as reckless as adolescents. They had not learned that "Respect nature" is the first rule of the outdoors.

"I ran the fishing boats for a while," says Jack Harvey. "They'd go out in the *Bottom Feeder* with no tools, no compass, no radio, no knowledge, no brains."

It was cold on the boat, so the brothers had had Jack build a heated cabin. Everyone on the dock told Jack to install small, round windows with bulletproof glass to withstand the waves. But the brothers insisted on picture windows.

When Jim and Artie took the *Bottom Feeder* out to sea, "Boom! The first wave knocks the window out," Jack recalls. "The second wave sinks you, but luckily they got the boat turned and somehow got back in. So then I built little bitty windows."

"One time, Jim got the net caught on the bottom of the boat," recalls Richard Lackey, who, after spending years as a commercial fisherman in Alaska, was fishing out of San Francisco Bay. "The way you fix that is, you dive in and untangle it. But Jimmy decides to rip the net off with a winch.

"That's Jimmy, just jerk it off with power," Lackey concludes. To the Mitchell Brothers, there was only one way to do things: their way. "He ended up pulling the mast down."

13

Guns and
Threats

SOME DANCERS at the O'Farrell are as plain-looking off the stage as they are alluring on it. But not Julie Bajo. A beautiful woman in her mid-twenties with striking black eyes, lush brown hair that flowed down her back, and soft, rounded features, Julie had been raised in Miami and spoke with a Caribbean accent, a product of her Cuban ancestry. Her stage name was Gigi, and there was a sweetness about her, a certain vulnerability that was appealing in a business where most dancers, sooner or later, develop a hard, feline look.

"Gigi. I like that name, it really fits you," a bald man wearing blue jeans and a polo shirt told Julie as she was coming off the stage in New York Live. "You're probably one of the best dancers we've ever had."

"Thank you," Julie had replied. "Who are you?"

"One of the brothers," the bald man had answered.

Julie had been at the theater only a short time and did not know who "the brothers" were.

Later, Julie described her conversation to another dancer, and the dancer told her about Jim and Artie. Artie is trying to hit on you, the dancer warned. He tries to have sex with every new dancer, and he always uses the same come-on: you're the best dancer we've ever had.

Julie did not see Artie again until weeks later, when word circulated that the Mitchell Brothers were planning a gonzo road trip to Aspen to support Hunter Thompson in his hour of need. A former pornographer named Gail Palmer-Slater had charged Thompson with twisting her breast after she had refused to discuss the film rights to *Fear and Loathing in Las Vegas* in his hot tub. Investigators from the Pitkin County, Colorado, district attorney's office had spent eleven hours searching Thompson's house at Woody Creek, outside Aspen, and had reported finding quantities of cocaine, marijuana, LSD, pills that appeared to be Valium, plus four sticks of dynamite and three blasting caps. The DA had filed a sexual assault charge against Thompson, and had added four felony counts of possession of illegal drugs and dynamite.

Any dancer who wanted to make the journey to Aspen was invited to come along. Jim and Artie were planning to stage a rally for Hunter on the courthouse steps and to present him with the keys to a red Chrysler convertible—dubbed "the Sharkmobile"—and a huge buffalo head, in honor of the movie *Where the Buffalo Roam.* The more dancers they could muster, the better the rally.

Julie had signed on because a road trip to a place she had never been with lots of dope to smoke had sounded like fun. She was standing in the O'Farrell lobby the day they were scheduled to leave when Artie Mitchell came up and said, "Hey, I hear you're going to Aspen. Come outside and I'll show you the RV we're traveling in."

Before the RV had rolled out of California, Julie and Artie had left their seats and gone in the back, where they jumped into a bed and tore into each other. They were together the whole time in Aspen and they had fun, but Julie knew that Artie always had fun. She also knew that Artie went through women as fast as he drained fifths of Stolichnaya and Cuervo Gold tequila, and she was certain that when they got back to San Francisco, Artie would say, "Well, see you around."

To Julie's surprise, Artie didn't dump her. She and Artie had kept seeing each other, and she had ended up spending most of her nights in the dumpy little white house with blue shutters that he was renting at 23 Mohawk in Corte Madera, a commuter suburb just over the Golden Gate Bridge in Marin. The only signs of his formerly lavish lifestyle were a wall-sized television and a twelve-person hot tub in the backyard that had required a crane to install.

"I found the house in Corte Madera," says Joanne Scott. "I had the shelves half papered in the kitchen and my robe and shampoos in the bathroom and suddenly Artie takes up with a Deadhead [Kristal]," Joanne continues. "I moved back to my apartment. When he broke up with Kristal, I moved back to Corte Madera again and was there about three months. And then he met Julie Bajo. It was very, very hard to take, but that was Artie. He wanted to live all these simultaneous lives."

The house had quickly become kid central. Neighborhood kids were always there, playing ball in the backyard or Nintendo on the big screen. Artie threw terrific birthday parties, and up and down the block, moms and dads who knew all about Artie and the O'Farrell, but who had never been near the theater and wanted nothing to do with pornography, considered Artie Mitchell a great guy.

In December 1990, Julie slipped on the stage at the O'Farrell and damaged her left knee. She could not dance and was going to have to undergo surgery. Artie told Julie she could move in with him and offered to pay for the surgery. Julie thought: Wow, he really loves me! But Artie had an ulterior motive.

Karen had gone to court seeking to revoke their joint-custody agreement on the grounds that Artie was an alcoholic and a drug abuser and therefore an unfit parent. Julie's mother lived in the Bay Area, and they were both very good with children. If Artie could go into court and tell the judge he was living with Julie and that she and her mother were helping to look after the children, it might help his case.

Julie moved in with Artie on New Year's Day 1991. She was thrilled to be living with the one and only Artie Mitchell, and grateful that he was going to pay for her knee surgery. But she was worried too. By noon most days, Artie was a slobbering, word-slurring drunk. He would be sweet and attentive one moment and then, for reasons Julie could not decipher, turn into a maniac who growled like a rabid dog.

Artie's friends told Julie that Artie hadn't been the same since the near-drowning at Ocean Beach. Dr. Donald "Skip" Dossett, one of Artie's oldest friends and a longtime inhabitant of the O'Farrell, had been treating Artie for a hypothyroid condition that was caused by the hypothermia. People with a hypothyroid condition tend to put on weight, be mentally slower than they were previously, suffer from depression, and have trouble sleeping. The condition also reduces tolerance to drugs and alcohol.

But Julie could handle the drinking. She loved to smoke dope and get high, and when Artie got wild, she got out of his way. What worried her most was the guns. Artie had begun stuffing a pearl-handled 9mm pistol into a black fanny pack and taking it everywhere he went. Julie had heard stories about him pulling the gun at the theater and waving it around. Dancers and other employees were terrified when Artie walked in the door; sooner or later, intentionally or not, a drunken Artie was going to shoot someone.

In the middle of January, Artie had showed up for a party at Maye's Original Oyster House looking like a ragged, unshaven street person except for a brand-new $800 suit.

"You're a mess!" Jack Davis, the political consultant, said when he saw Artie. "I been up for three days," Artie replied, slurring his words.

Artie ordered a drink at the bar and a few minutes later, with no provocation, he unzipped his black fanny pack, pulled out his 9mm, and began waving it above his head. Davis and his friends ganged up on Artie and made him put the gun back in his pack. When Artie wasn't looking, Davis opened the pack and put the gun in his suitcoat pocket. As he was zipping the pack up, Davis noticed a bag of marijuana and what looked like a quantity of cocaine.

Davis went outside and locked the gun in his trunk and Artie did not miss it until after the lunch. Artie picked up his fanny pack and demanded, "Where's my fucking gun?" Everyone played dumb and Davis drove Artie back to the O'Farrell. Davis intended to give the gun to Jim, but when they were inside the theater, Artie jumped Davis from behind, got him in a choke hold, and screamed, "You got my gun, don't you, fucker! Gimme it!"

Davis admitted he had the weapon and walked out to his car, unlocked the trunk, and gave it to Artie. Artie stalked off.

At home in Corte Madera, Artie was using the 9mm to play a game he called "Mr. Peanut." He would take somebody out to the garage behind the house, produce the 9mm, and turn his back to a five-pound can of Planters peanuts that was punctured with bullet holes. The object of the game was to whirl and fire at the can as fast as possible after someone had shouted "Mr. Peanut." Artie had tried to coax one of the men who had helped Julie move into playing "Mr. Peanut," but the mover had fled in fear.

"Artie, listen, you don't have to do this. There's nothing in this for you guys. I called to *invite you*," Bob Callahan was saying into the telephone.

"No, this is where we have the parties," Artie insisted. "Just tell me how many people and what time and we'll be ready."

Callahan was touched. To him, Jim and Artie were the last true hippies left in San Francisco, the living embodiment of the old what's-mine-is-yours communal ethic.

Callahan had become friends with a boxing promoter who was attempting to found a boxing museum in San Francisco, and through the promoter had discovered a world of fascinating characters. The promoter, Callahan, and several boxing writers were planning to throw a party for an up-and-coming fighter in a tavern on Clement Street. He had called to invite Jim and Artie, and Artie had insisted Callahan hold the party at the O'Farrell, at no expense to himself.

When Callahan arrived upstairs at the O'Farrell, the refrigerator was stocked with beer and a spread of food was laid out on a table. Jim and Artie wouldn't let Callahan thank them. Things went smoothly, and Callahan was congratulating himself on having such great friends when he noticed that Artie had become very drunk and very belligerent.

"Hey, nigger," Artie suddenly snarled at the fighter. "You think you're a big fucking boxer? I'll kick your ass, nigger."

The fighter, who had been having a good time, looked around in disbelief. Who was this scrawny little bald-headed white guy? With one jab, he could take his head off.

"Hey, you! You, nigger!" Artie yelled. "You ain't nuthin'!"

Several people rushed up and grabbed Artie and dragged him away. Several others apologized to the fighter. Callahan glanced at Jim and saw that he looked like a man who had just seen his dog get run over. Callahan came up to him, and Jim clenched his fists, raised them to his eyes, brought them down to his waist, and stomped out of the room.

"My brother!" Jim wailed to Callahan. "He's raving like a Telegraph Avenue street person! [Telegraph is a street in Berkeley notorious for burnt-out acidheads and panhandlers.] After all we've been through, I've got to deal with this fucking shit!"

"Jim kept things hid, and that was the only time I saw his frustration with Artie," Callahan recalls. "He was very upset about what was happening to his brother. He couldn't control it, and that was getting him even more upset."

"War News," Jim said when Bob Callahan answered the phone. "What war news?" Callahan replied.

It was a week or so after the start of the Gulf war and Callahan assumed Jim was calling with news about President Bush's decision to unleash the U.S. arsenal against Saddam Hussein. The war had dominated everyone's thoughts since beginning on January 16, 1991. Jim and Callahan were opposed to the United States entering the war. So was Warren Hinckle, who had written a column for the *Examiner* comparing Bush to Tojo, the war minister of Imperial Japan. Editors at the *Examiner* had decided not to run it.

Hinckle and Will Hearst, the *Examiner* publisher, had been having trouble for years. Hinckle was writing a column about San Francisco from the Upper West Side of New York City, where he was living with his wife, Susan Cheever, the daughter of the great writer. Hearst wanted Hinckle back in San Francisco; Hinckle argued that he had to stay in New York because of a child-custody agreement his wife had with her former husband. Besides, he knew San Francisco so well he didn't have to live there to write about it.

Hinckle was furious when the *Examiner* pulled his column, and he and the paper parted company. The San Francisco Irish community was up in arms, and the boys who hung out at the O'Farrell picketed the *Examiner,* carrying signs with a caricature of Hinckle and his eye patch and the words "Stop Harassing the Visually Impaired."

"Not war news. *War News!* That's what we call the paper," Jim said. "We come out against the Gulf war. It's Vietnam all over again. The longer it lasts, the more people will come around to seeing we're right."

"Jim, this is great!" said the suddenly excited Callahan.

"And we don't end when the war ends!" Jim continued. "We keep doing special issues. The war on AIDS. The war on the homeless. The war on drugs. We do stories nobody else will do!"

"Let's do it!" Callahan said.

"We're gonna do it!" Jim replied. "Hinckle's in. He's gonna be editor. I already talked to Hunter. He's in too."

Callahan was going to function as the paper's managing editor. As he and Jim roughed out plans for *War News*, Callahan realized that Jim was already thinking like a publisher. "I don't care what Hinckle or Hunter contributes," Jim told Callahan. "All I need is their names. If I can get Warren and his dog in a limo and take them from talk show to talk show, that will be enough."

In his enthusiasm, Jim said, "You know, Bobby, this war is the best thing that ever happened to us!"

Both men paused to consider what Jim had said. And then both started to laugh. It was a politically incorrect thing to say, but completely honest. That was exactly the kind of honesty they wanted to get into the paper.

Even before war broke out in the Middle East, Jim was taking steps away from the porn business. He leased a lovely old building at 391 Broadway on the eastern edge of North Beach, where, with Dan O'Neill and several other investors, Jim was planning to open a restaurant—tentatively called Geezers—and nightclub that would offer cabaret singers, dancers, comics, and no sex. Jim had a former O'Farrell employee named Andy Finley scouting locations for a similar venture in Los Angeles. Finley was going to manage the club. Sharon McKnight was going to handle the floor show.

War News was started in the building. Callahan was calling friends from all over the country, friends who in the past had been too busy to write for whatever publication Callahan was trying to launch. This time, friends were saying yes, and writers Callahan did not know were calling from publications as different as *Time* magazine and *The San Francisco Bay Guardian* to say, I've got an antiwar piece I can't publish here; will you guys take it?

Starting a newspaper is an extremely difficult undertaking, especially when the editor, Warren Hinckle, was 3,000 miles away, sending instructions over the fax machine. The staff, particularly Jim and Callahan, worked brutal hours. There were fights between people who had different visions of what the paper should be—Dan O'Neill insisted it be humorous, but what was funny about a war? And what exactly was the "post-punk '90s look" everybody had agreed the paper should have?

But somehow the paper came together. The premiere issue had the Hinckle column the *Examiner* had refused to run, plus stories by Paul Krassner, the editor of *The Realist;* Daniel Ellsberg; Michael Kennedy; and Michael Moore, the producer-director of the film *Roger and Me.* Hunter Thompson sent a fax and Jim ran it. S. Clay Wilson, R. Crumb, and Gilbert Shelton contributed cartoons.

And that was just for starters. For issue number two, Callahan and Hinckle had lined up Ishmael Reed; Todd Gitlin, the Cal/Berkeley professor who had written an important book about the 1960s; the feminist writer Barbara Ehrenreich and the leftist journalist Andrew Kopkind; plus Representative Barbara Boxer and Art Spiegelman, the cartoonist famous for "Maus."

"We got a million-dollar staff for no money," Callahan says in amazement. "We re-created the 1960s. Jim had decided we were going to print 100,000 copies of the first issue, even though we didn't have a distributor. A whole bunch of guys showed up to help us take them off the truck and load them in a garage up the street from the theater. I looked around and music was playing and everybody was pitching in and I realized that we'd created a community."

The *War News* community did not include Artie Mitchell.

"It was probably the first project Jim had ever done without Artie," Callahan says. "He was doing it with a different set of brothers, and I think the message was coming through loud and clear to Artie. Artie was screaming at Jim, 'Don't you leave me! I'm not going to let you go, I'm dragging you back!' "

Things were going great for Liberty Bradford. She was sailing through acting classes at the University of Southern California, she had a boyfriend she really liked, and her dad was sober!

The last time Liberty had seen her father a month earlier, he had been in terrible shape. He seemed to be aging a year with every passing month. She, Jim, and Artie had been upstairs at the theater when Liberty had impulsively blurted out how worried she was about her father. Jim had listened, and had started explaining how he had bought the house on Cape Cod and had spent six months there kicking a coke habit.

"Liberty, I'm going to say this to you with your dad here," Jim said, looking her in the eye. "I think Artie should take six months to a year off. Go to Mexico, go to wherever and detox and get himself together. Porn is a tough business, it wears you down. I had a coke addiction, I had to get away from it, that's why I bought the house on the Cape. Now it's time for your dad to do the same."

"I agree! I agree!" Artie had kept saying.

Now it looked as if Artie was really serious about quitting drinking. When Liberty called to tell him she would be coming up to San Francisco for a weekend on Friday, February 22, her father's voice was crystal clear and full of hope. His court date in the custody battle with Karen was coming up and he had been sober for ten days! Artie was sure he was going to win. He wasn't drinking; he had Julie Bajo and her mother on his side; a Twin Cities Police Department detective had written a letter saying he was a responsible and competent father; and all the neighbors were behind him.

After years of being estranged, the custody case had brought Liberty's mother and father back together again. Three months earlier, in November, Art had called Meredith to ask her to represent him in his fight with Karen. Art had told both Meredith and Eugene Seltzer, his divorce attorney, that business was down at the O'Farrell. The recession was hurting them, nude dancing was not as fresh as it once was, and he could no longer afford Seltzer's services. Would Meredith take the case for $75 an hour?

It was a classic piece of theater from Artie Mitchell: who else would hire an ex-wife to defend him in a suit against another ex-wife? Artie was anticipating a nasty court fight, gleefully telling people that, next to him, nobody hated Karen as much as Meredith did.

A judge had disqualified Meredith, ruling that a wife who was getting child-support payments from an ex-husband could not defend him against an ex-wife to whom he was also paying child support. But that had hardly mattered. Liberty was thrilled her mother and father had reconnected.

When Liberty arrived in San Francisco that Friday, the first thing she did was to look up her father. She found him paying a rare visit to the *War News* office on Broadway in North Beach.

"Let's go get a drink," Artie said when he saw his oldest child walk in the door.

They went to a bar down the street and Liberty ordered a Coke. Artie ordered a shot of Cuervo tequila and a beer. Liberty's head dropped and she struggled to keep from breaking into tears.

"I've decided to start drinking again," Artie said when Liberty finally looked up at him. "I'm going to drink until I die!"

"That's really great, Dad," Liberty said. "Congratulations."

Artie had, he explained, a good reason. He had lost his court case to Karen. A judge had revoked joint custody and ruled that Artie could see his kids only eight hours a week on a Saturday or a Sunday, and only when a representative of the court was present. Artie had been enraged. How could the court believe that fucking witch Karen? Couldn't the judge see she was out to fuck him? It wasn't like he was a pervert or a child molester! Goddamnit, he loved his kids!

But once again, Karen had grounds. She had charged that Artie was frequently under the influence of drugs and alcohol when the children were present, and Artie was. She also charged that "Artie has taken the children to parties featuring X-rated film stars and exotic dancers from the O'Farrell Theatre." That may not have been true, but several times when the children were there, Julie Bajo had walked around the house in a thong bikini with no top.

The first court-supervised visit would be tomorrow, Artie told Liberty as he polished off another shot of tequila. Would she come over to the house in Corte Madera? They could all go fishing together.

Liberty said sure, she would love to see the three kids, and after saying goodbye, she left for Lafayette to visit her mother.

"It was really sad," Liberty says. "He really adored those kids. I had the definite feeling that he had been totally defeated, that he didn't want to live."

The next morning, Saturday, February 23, Liberty left Lafayette and drove across the Richmond Bridge to Corte Madera.

"Where are the kids? I thought we were going fishing?" Liberty asked as she walked into the small house at 23 Mohawk.

"The overseer called to say she couldn't make it, so everything is off," Artie glumly replied. His eyes were bleary and his head was swaying.

Liberty sat in a chair across from her father. There were so many things she wanted to say to him. He was really down, maybe this wasn't the right time, but she was going back to L.A. tomorrow and he was so unhappy, maybe she could get through to him.

She thought about bringing up his drinking. She had arrived in San Francisco expecting to find him sober and here he was, drunk the first thing in the morning. No, maybe she had better wait with that. Liberty made small talk before deciding to bring up the second of two volatile subjects.

"Dad, I need some money for school," Liberty said.

Her father looked up, suddenly interested.

"Tell you what: I'll pay all your debts if you move up here," Artie said. "I'll get you a job. You can go to work for *War News*. I've got lots of good contacts."

"Dad, I've got a life in L.A.," Liberty replied. "I don't want to work for the Mitchell Brothers. I want to make it on my own."

Her father's eyes turned hard and cold.

"All you want is money!" Artie snapped.

"All you want to do is control me!" Liberty snapped back. "Any woman you can't control you think is a threat!"

"You're all alike, you women! You're all sluts and whores! All you want is money!"

"You've never given me anything but money!" Liberty screamed, standing up. "The least you can do is give me some money so I can make something of myself!"

"You take after your fucking mother! You're a fucking Bradford!" Artie shot back, firing his biggest gun. "You're a WASP! A tight-assed WASP! Without the Mitchell Brothers, you're nothing! You'll never do a fucking thing on your own!"

Her father had called her names before. Usually, Liberty had ended up running home, throwing herself on her bed, and crying into her pillow. She had vowed never to do that again.

"You're wrong!" Liberty said, striding to the front door. "You're wrong! And fuck you!"

Liberty slammed the door and Artie spent the rest of the day drinking. That evening, he surprised Julie Bajo by suddenly announcing he was going to the O'Farrell. He went to a safe in the living room and took out the pearl-handled 9mm pistol. Julie listened while he methodically loaded the weapon and watched while he stuck the semiautomatic in his black fanny pack.

Julie was terrified. As soon as she saw Artie climb into a cab, she ran to the phone and called the theater to warn them Artie was on his way with a loaded gun. Hours passed and Julie heard nothing. And then the phone rang. Julie took a deep breath before picking it up, afraid that something had finally happened, but it was only Artie, calling to tell her to get in a cab, they were having a little party at the theater.

Julie did as she was told and found Artie and three friends upstairs, shooting pool on the full-size Brunswick Artie had had installed some years earlier. Julie was sitting down, concentrating on rolling a joint, when a BANG!!! went through her like an electric shock. She jumped up and saw Artie pointing the pistol at a poster in the corner of the room.

BANG!!! The sound vibrated against her ears, getting louder instead of softer. Julie covered her ears with her hands. She looked around the room, expecting to see terror in the eyes of the other men. Instead, they were laughing, like it was all a big joke.

An hour or so later, Julie and a friend poured Artie into a cab and she got him home and into bed.

"Me and Art have to get divorced," Jim told Jack Harvey one morning at the O'Farrell.

"Good luck," Jack replied. "You can divorce your wife, but how do you divorce your brother?"

Jim had a plan. If he made it *look* like he was serious about splitting up with Art, perhaps Art would get himself under control.

Jim had banned Artie from the theater after he shot up the poster. He had been having daily conversations with Rocky Davidson, his cousin and a custodian at the theater, and Dr. Skip Dossett, who worked in a clinic in downtown San Francisco. Rocky's job was to babysit Artie and report to Jim; Dr. Skip's was to try to figure a way to get Artie into an alcohol treatment program.

Jim called Dennis Roberts, a close friend and attorney who had handled many of the Mitchell Brothers' toughest cases, and asked him if, as a favor, he would put a little heat on Artie. Tell him he's running out of chances, Jim suggested. Tell him if he doesn't shape up, I'm going to have to go one way and he's going to have to go the other.

While Jim had no intention of buying Artie out, he was sending Artie a message. J.R. had always said that if two guys can't get along, it's better for them to go their separate ways. Artie would know that Jim was invoking J.R.'s memory. He would know that Jim was getting serious.

Roberts delivered the message, and Artie's response was fine, no problem, whatever Jim wants to do. When Artie told Meredith about Roberts's call, he said that as long as he got a fair shake, he didn't care what Jim did.

But inside, Artie was seething. The call was additional proof that Jim was deserting him. Jim wanted to take away everything Artie had worked for, everything he stood for. With the theater, Artie was a San Francisco character, a throwback to the Barbary Coast, a raffish entrepreneur and an icon from the 1960s. Without the O'Farrell, he was just another drunk.

The more Artie thought about it, the more he decided that Lisa Adams, Jim's girlfriend, had to be behind Roberts's call. If Jim bought Artie out, she could step in and take his place.

Artie picked up the phone and called the business office at the O'Farrell. Nancy Harrison, the theater's secretary, had been Lisa Adams's best friend since their school days in Redwood City. She and Lisa had just come in from lunch and were sorting through *War News* subscriptions when the phone rang and Nancy answered it. Lisa watched as the color drained out of Nancy's face.

"What's the matter? Nancy! What's the matter?" Lisa asked after Nancy had slowly placed the receiver back on its cradle.

"That was Artie. He was drunk," Nancy said.

"What'd he say?"

"He said, 'Tell that bitch Lisa if she has anything to do with the problems between my brother and me, I'll blow her fucking brains out.'"

Lisa slumped into a chair. In the more than three years she had lived with Jim, Artie had frequently slobbered drunken sincerity over her, telling her that this was the happiest he had ever seen Jim and how glad he was that they had found each other. And now he was threatening to kill her! That was how much he cared about his brother's happiness!

"Call Jim," Nancy urged. "Call him right away!"

"No, wait," Lisa said.

Lisa needed a moment to collect her thoughts. People were forever running to Jim with problems about Artie. Artie's doing this, Artie's doing that, you've got to deal with it, Jim. The pressure on Jim was incredible. People didn't see it, but Lisa did.

A few Sundays ago, Julie Bajo had called to say Artie was ready to check into a detox hospital. Jim had been elated. "I can't believe the nightmare is over!" he'd said over and over. Lisa had gotten the number of the hospital in Calistoga where dancers who had drinking problems went to dry out, and was ready to give it to Artie the next time he called.

But Artie had not been serious. He had called later that night, drunk and hostile as usual. When Jim heard that nasty voice, a look had come over his face that was so sad Lisa thought she was going to cry.

Lisa decided that this was one time Jim was not going to have to clean up after Artie. *She* was going to take care of it.

"I'm not asking you to do anything," Lisa said after she and Nancy had called Jim at *War News* to tell him about Artie's threat. "I'm going to call the police and swear out a warrant against Artie. I've got to do it. If he doesn't kill me, it's going to be some other innocent person, and I can't live with that."

Lisa may have meant well, but she was not lessening the pressure on Jim. She was escalating it.

"No, please, don't do that," Jim begged. "You don't understand what will happen! The cops will go over there to serve the warrant. There's a chance Art could get killed. There's a better chance he'll kill a cop."

"Everybody wants to just ignore Art's threats, but I'm not going to," Lisa insisted. "This can't go on."

"Hold off. Let me see what I can do," Jim pleaded.

Lisa finally agreed to give Jim until four o'clock to make some phone calls and try to do something about his brother.

Jim called Dennis Roberts and Tom Steel, but both attorneys were in meetings and could not take his call. He called Dana Fuller, an old and trusted friend, and asked his advice. And then he looked up a drug and alcohol hot line in the yellow pages and called the number.

"How can I get someone committed?" Jim asked.

"The first step is to bring everybody involved in for a counseling session," the crisis intervention worker explained.

Jim said thanks and hung up. Artie would never submit to that. Jim had once threatened to put him in a straitjacket and drag him to a hospital and Artie had said, "You'll never take me. I'll kill you first."

Jim was going to have to handle this his own way. But how? What was he going to do?

Lisa drove home and discovered she was terrified to be alone in her own home. Promptly at four o'clock, she called Jim.

"What have you come up with?" Lisa asked. "The time's up."

Jim told her that the lawyers had not returned his calls and begged Lisa to give him more time. Lisa insisted she was going to call the police, but finally relented and agreed to meet Jim at *War*

News at 7:30. They would go out to dinner and talk about it some more.

Lisa arrived upset, and when Jim wasn't at *War News*, she became even more agitated. She found him at Tosca's, a classic Italian bistro in North Beach, having a drink.

Lisa was too troubled to go to dinner, so she and Jim got into their new Ford Explorer and headed for home. They started discussing Artie's call, and Lisa began sobbing so hard that Jim made her pull over so he could take the wheel.

Jim had to do something about Artie. Things could not go on this way. Artie would not let Jim and Lisa live their own lives.

But what? What could he do?

14

Death in the Family

"ART'S OUT OF CONTROL," Rocky Davidson, Jim and Artie's cousin, was telling Jim on the morning of Wednesday, February 27, 1991, as he and Jim and Dan O'Neill were smoking a joint at the *War News* office. Rocky had been out to Corte Madera and was giving Jim a full report. Jim mentioned that he had been thinking of going over there and taking care of Artie himself.

"I don't think you should," Rocky said. "He's acting crazy. If you want me to, I'll go over there and sit on him or tie him up. Whatever you want me to do, I'll do."

Around 1:30 that afternoon, the phone on the bar rang and Dan O'Neill picked it up. Jim was on another phone, talking long-distance to a writer in New York about *War News*.

"Art's on the phone," O'Neill yelled.

"Tell him I'll call him back," Jim said.

O'Neill delivered the message and then hollered, "He says he's got to talk right now."

Jim told the writer he would get back to him, punched a button on the phone, and said hello to his brother.

"You are a chickenshit bastard!" Artie screamed in the tough, sarcastic tone of voice he used when he was angry. "If you want to talk to me, come and talk to me. If you want to see me, come and see me. Don't hide behind a fucking attorney."

With that, Artie slammed down the receiver.

Jim sat and stared straight ahead. Artie had just called him out, as if they were still kids on a playground in Antioch. If that was the way Art wanted it, fine, Jim would deal with him. In the end, he always did.

Jim got up and went to look for Rocky.

"I'm going over to Art's tonight," Jim said after telling his cousin about the call. "Can you go too?"

"I can be there," Rocky said.

"It'd be a really good idea if we got the guns out of his house," Jim said, and Rocky agreed.

"Let's meet a couple of blocks from his house," Jim suggested. "I don't want to drive up and have Art shoot at us through a window. I'm more scared of Art right now than I've ever been in my life."

They selected a spot around the corner from Art's house and agreed to meet at 9:30 that night. Rocky said he would try to have Dr. Skip Dossett there too.

In addition to Artie's hypothyroid condition, Dr. Dossett was treating Artie for a sinus infection. The medication was giving Artie indigestion, a common side effect, and on the afternoon of February 27 Artie called Dr. Skip and asked if the doctor would give him a shot so he could stop taking the pills. Dr. Skip had said yes and told Artie to come to the clinic in San Francisco. Artie said okay, and hung up.

Half an hour later, Artie called Dr. Skip to say he couldn't make it to San Francisco. Could Skip come to Corte Madera? The doctor had a waiting room full of patients and said he couldn't leave.

Artie started to growl.

"You son of a bitch! You motherfucker!"

Dr. Skip tried to reason with him, but Artie only became wilder. Finally, the doctor hung up.

Artie calmed down, as he always did after a fit of anger. He called Dr. Skip back and apologized and the doctor promised to stop by after office hours and give Artie a shot. And then he called the O'Farrell and spoke to Nancy Harrison.

Artie had called to say he was sorry about making the call threatening Lisa's life, but Nancy was having none of it.

"You can't threaten someone and then pretend it didn't happen," Nancy said, raising her voice to Artie for the first time. Artie tried to ignore her anger and asked her when she was going to come up to Corte Madera and hook up his fax machine. Artie had bought fax machines for himself and Jim and had been trying to get Nancy to come out and connect his. He had found the instructions bewildering.

"I am not coming to your house, Art. I am afraid of you," Nancy said firmly, and hung up.

Artie was furious. A woman, and an employee at that, had refused to do what he asked her to do. And he'd asked her nice!

Artie went to the kitchen to make himself a drink and returned to the living room just as eight-year-old Caleb came bouncing in the door. School had just let out and Caleb was looking for his baseball glove. Caleb didn't understand that he could no longer come over to his father's house whenever he wanted. All Caleb knew was that this was Wednesday, the first day of Little League tryouts. He had left his glove at his dad's house, and he had to have his glove.

The glove could not be found, so Artie gave Julie money to buy a new one and Julie and Caleb went out to the Dodge Colt minivan sitting in the driveway. Julie couldn't drive her burgundy 280Z because it had a stick shift and she was still recovering from surgery on her left knee. She drove Caleb to a sporting-goods store and helped him pick out a new glove. They went to the tryouts, but it had been raining, a rare and blessed event after five years of drought, and the ground was too wet to play ball. Caleb and Julie fooled around in the park for a while, and then Julie drove Caleb up the hill to his mother's house.

Half an hour later, Julie returned home and found Aaron, "Ace," Artie's twelve-year-old, munching on a cinnamon roll. Artie was frantic. When he saw Julie, he slapped himself on the forehead.

"All they need is one picture of him sitting here and they'll throw me in jail!" Artie said. "Get him home!"

Julie hobbled back to the Dodge Colt as fast as her sore knee would allow and chauffeured Aaron up the winding road to his mother's house. She dropped Aaron off and was on her way down the hill when Karen Mitchell's Jaguar appeared on the road beneath her. Karen was coming from Artie's house, where she had been looking for her children.

Karen slammed on the brakes and stopped her car in the middle of the narrow road so Julie could not pass. Throwing open the door, she bounded out of the car and ran at Julie. Julie didn't have time to be frightened. As fast as she could, she locked the doors and rolled up the window.

"If you ever kidnap my children again, I'll kill you, you slut!" Karen shouted.

Karen was holding a pistol. She banged it against the window and pointed it at Julie. Julie leaned back in the seat to get out of the line of fire and Karen adjusted her aim.

"I'll kill you, you slut!" Karen repeated. Her hands were shaking and her eyes were watering. "I'll kill you!"

Karen stomped back to her Jaguar and roared past Julie.

Julie took a deep breath, removed her foot from the brake, and devoted every ounce of concentration to driving back to 23 Mohawk. By the time she got there, the adrenaline had hit. Julie's hands were shaking. As soon as she told Artie what had happened, she was going to file charges against Karen.

"Artie! Artie! Karen just pulled a gun on me!" Julie yelled as she opened the door.

She ran through the entryway and into the living room and stopped in her tracks. There was Artie, glowering on the couch. The pearl-handled pistol was in his hand and the floor was covered with thousands of glass shards.

Artie didn't have to say a word, Julie knew what had happened. Karen had come by looking for the kids, she and Artie had yelled at each other, and Artie had gone into a black rage. He had grabbed the pistol and blown away the green-tinted glass coffee table. It was Julie's favorite thing in the whole house!

"Artie! Did you hear what I said? Karen pulled a gun on me!" Julie said.

"She what? Get out of here! Go find a cop right now!" Artie screamed after Julie told him what had happened.

Julie ran back to the Dodge Colt and drove around until she found a female officer, who took her complaint. Then she went back home and started to clean up the glass.

Dr. Dossett arrived around six o'clock and gave Artie a shot for his sinus condition, plus a shot of vitamin B_{12}. Artie seemed calm, so Dr. Skip decided to try one more time.

"Artie," the doctor said, "we've got to talk about getting you in a program."

"I'll only go through a hail of bullets," Artie snapped.

Julie cooked dinner. Artie kept drinking and finally passed out on a couch around 6:30. Julie was relieved and did not try to wake him.

Around 8:30, Georgia Mae called, upset as usual over her younger son. Julie was taking Mae through the events of the day when Artie woke up and grabbed the phone. He began screaming at his mother in a voice that sounded like it was coming from a coyote.

"CALL JIM!" Artie demanded. "TELL HIM HE'S KILLING HIMSELF. HE'S SMOKING THREE OR FOUR PACKS A DAY. I'M GOING TO LIVE TWENTY YEARS MORE THAN HIM. DO YOU HEAR ME! CALL HIM!"

Artie paused, out of breath.

"It's not Jim I'm concerned about," Artie's mother said. "I'm concerned about you."

"I KNOW HOW IT IS!" Artie shrieked. "I CAN DRINK A CAN OF BEER AND EVERYBODY'S ON MY CASE, BUT JIM CAN SMOKE THREE OR FOUR PACKS A DAY AND NOBODY SAYS ANYTHING!"

Mae was deeply shaken. The person on the other end was not her Artie. Artie, of course, took no notice. He demanded that his mother call Jim, and then, for an instant, he became Artie again.

"Bye, Mom. I love you. I'll call soon," Artie said, and hung up.

Mae called a hospital in Sacramento that specialized in chemical and alcohol dependency and told an intake worker that her youngest son was mentally deranged and dangerous. Could she have him committed? The counselor said they did not take involuntary commitments and gave Mae a number she could call and get help for herself. It's not me who needs help, it's Art, Mae thought as she hung up the phone. She did not call the number.

Moments after talking to his mother, Artie called Jim's house. He got the answering machine and, slurring his words, left a message. When the tape ran out, he hung up and immediately called again to leave another message.

"Hey, Mr. Perfect. It's your brother, Mr. Perfect," Artie said to the answering machine. "You're so bad I had to call Mother about you. You promised your girlfriend you were going to quit smoking but you haven't. Those cigarettes are going to take twenty years off your life.

"But don't worry, I'm going to kill you first, motherfucker!"

Artie hung up and Julie put dinner on the table. Artie picked at the veal and beans and then they tried to get interested in a television show. Halfway through Artie said, "Screw this, let's go to bed." Artie grabbed one last Heineken out of the refrigerator and he and Julie went back into the bedroom, crawled into bed, and turned off the lights.

"Don't go, please! Stay home with me! I want to be safe. I want you to be safe," Lisa was beseeching Jim as they drove home through the rain.

"There's nothing to worry about," Jim assured Lisa as they got out of the Explorer and walked into their house on 47th Avenue. "Rocky's going to be there and I think Dr. Skip will be too."

Jim had had a couple of margaritas earlier that evening and went straight to the bathroom to relieve himself. Lisa walked into the kitchen and noticed the little red light on the answering machine was flashing, indicating there were messages waiting. She hit the "play" button and Artie's drunken, growling voice filled the room.

Lisa slammed a hand down on the answering machine, hitting the "erase" button as hard as she could. She never wanted to hear that horrible voice again!

Lisa went to a cabinet, took out a bottle of cognac, and poured herself a drink. Her hand was shaking when she picked up the glass.

The answering machine was across the hall from the bathroom, only four or five feet away. The door was closed, but Jim had heard Artie's messages. He came out of the bathroom and walked toward the garage. Alarmed, Lisa put down her cognac and followed him.

Jim took a key from above a paint locker and unlocked it. He opened the cabinet and took out a Winchester lever-action .22. The rifle had been a present to Storm on his twelfth birthday, but Meredith didn't want it in the house, so Jim had kept it. He got out a box of ammunition and loaded the gun with fifteen .22 long-rifle bullets.

"Jim, don't! I beg you! Don't do this!" Lisa sobbed.

Jim took a shoulder holster that held a .38 Smith & Wesson Chief's Special out of the cabinet and strapped it on. Lisa got down on her hands and knees, as if the garage were a church and the paint cabinet was an altar.

"Don't, Jim! Please! Don't go! Stay with me!"

"Everything is going to be okay," Jim said, trying to calm Lisa down. "This is just bluffing power. I'm going to go over there and get Art's guns out of his house."

Jim went back into the house and put on an Ivy League cap and an expensive custom-made leather jacket that Lisa had given him.

"If the doorbell rings, don't answer it," Jim warned as he was leaving. "Go to the back of the house. Stay out of the living room and stay away from the windows."

After Jim drove away, Lisa turned off the lights and sat down on the kitchen floor with her dog and her glass of cognac.

Jim drove up Geary Boulevard and stopped for gas at a Chevron station. It was drizzling and foggy when he crossed the Golden Gate Bridge. He turned off Highway 101 at Paradise Drive, made a left on Mohawk, and cruised slowly past the small white house with the blue shutters that Artie was renting.

Jim couldn't believe the house was dark. When Artie was drinking and doping, he stayed up for days at a time. Jim had been absolutely certain Artie would be sitting inside on the couch, a joint in one hand and a shot of tequila in the other.

Then it hit him: What if Artie really intended to carry out his threats? What if he was on his way to 47th Avenue, looking for Lisa? What if he was going to shoot up the O'Farrell, as he had vowed to do so many times?

Jim turned off Mohawk and spotted Rocky's pickup truck up the street. He parked the Explorer, got out, opened the back door, and took out the rifle. In all the years he had gone hunting, this was the first time Jim had ever traveled with a loaded weapon.

Rocky climbed out of his pickup and told Jim that Dr. Skip wasn't home when he called. When Jim pulled the rifle out of the Explorer, Rocky said, "Jesus, Jim, we won't even get to Artie's house with you carrying that rifle. Every one of these houses has a 'Neighborhood Watch' sign in the window."

Jim took a large red-and-white-striped umbrella out of the Explorer and concealed the rifle next to the umbrella. He and Rocky walked back to Mohawk and approached Artie's house from the sidewalk across the street. They gazed at the silent house, and when they had decided that Artie wasn't crouched behind a window, waiting in the dark to pick them off, they walked across the street and up the driveway.

Jim tried the door handle. It was locked.

"Go around the back and see if there are any lights on in the bedroom," Jim whispered to Rocky. Rocky went to the back of the house and came back moments later to report that it was dark too.

"Go call Lisa and make sure she's staying away from the windows," Jim instructed Rocky. "Call the theater and find out if Art's been there."

Rocky left to search for a phone in a huge shopping center that was only two blocks away. Jim stood outside the house, getting more and more uncomfortable as the moments passed. The first neighbor who happened to peek out the window would take him for a prowler.

Jim sat down on the front bumper of the Dodge Colt minivan and lit a cigarette. As he would recount later at his trial, Jim decided that car was a perfect example of what an unappreciative son of a bitch Art was.

Art had called one day to say he had to have a van right away because he was going to take the kids on a trip. Jim had called around and picked up the Dodge Colt. Art had so many DUIs he could not register a car in his name. The Colt minivan was registered in Jim's name. Because Art was driving the car, the insurance was an astounding $18,000 a year. The O'Farrell was picking up the tab.

Had Art said thanks for all Jim had done to get him the van? Like hell he had! The day it was delivered, Art had called Jim and told him the minivan was no good because it did not have automatic door locks.

Jim pulled out his pocketknife and punctured the front passenger tire. It made Jim feel good to hear air whooshing out, and he walked to the back of the car and stabbed the rear passenger tire.

That will keep him home for a while, Jim thought as he put away the knife. There's no way he should be driving.

There was another reason why Jim had flattened the tires. "Artie can't change a flat tire" had been a running joke in the family for as long as Jim could remember.

Artie could not change a tire. He could not direct a film. He could not write a decent script. He could not handle a camera. And he sure as hell could not run a business.

Jim had been changing tires for Artie all his life. Jim directed the films, Jim established the O'Farrell, Jim changed it from a movie house to a live sex venue. Artie had gone through millions and millions of dollars, he had smoked a forest of marijuana and done a planeload of coke, all because Jim had been a damn good brother. He had carried Art the whole way. And in every damn interview, he had made sure Art got half the credit.

And what did he get for it? He got Artie cussing him out because the car he'd bought didn't have automatic door locks. He got Art threatening to kill Lisa. He got Artie shooting up the O'Farrell.

Artie had even screwed up tonight! Jim and Rocky had come all the way over the Golden Gate Bridge on a miserable, rainy night to settle him down and take away his guns, and Art wasn't even home!

Angry and frustrated, Jim walked over and kicked the front door. The door popped open. Jim went into the foyer, not sure what he was going to do.

If Art wasn't there, maybe he would leave a calling card by shooting up the house. Art had shot up the theater; let him see how he liked having his house shot up. Art would know Jim had done it. It would show him how angry Jim had become.

If Art was inside, which Jim doubted—Art hadn't gone to bed at ten o'clock since they were kids in school—Jim would scare the shit out of him. That would make the trip across the bridge worthwhile.

"You speak Spanish, so we'll get the best rates," Artie Mitchell was telling Julie.

Artie was naked and was lying on his back in bed. Julie had a leg draped over Artie and was idly playing with the hair on his chest. Artie had resurrected the Mexico trip. He was going to call Jim first thing in the morning and tell him that he and Julie were going to spend the next six months in Cabo San Lucas. He would come back tanned and strong and off the bottle. He'd be ready to go to work at the theater and back into court to try to regain joint custody of his kids.

"We'll fly to San Diego and visit Storm," Artie said. Storm was a freshman at San Diego State. "Then we'll take a taxi to Tijuana and make all the arrangements there."

Julie sighed and let herself imagine a sparkling new condo right on the beach with nothing to do but snorkel and sunbathe and make sure Artie ate well enough to get his health back. Artie should really be checking into a room at the Betty Ford Center, but Julie knew he would never do that. She knew that going to Mexico to dry out was like going to Tangier to stop smoking dope. But it was worth a try. The craziness had to stop.

Julie scrunched up closer to Artie and was stroking the hair on his chest when the front door opened and slammed shut. Julie knew it was the front door because it had a distinctive creak. She and Artie sat up to listen, but neither was alarmed. Artie almost always left the door unlocked. He was always inviting people over, always telling someone, "The door is always open."

Another door opened and slammed shut. They couldn't tell if it was the door that led from the front entry to the kitchen or the door that led from the front entry to the living room. But the second slam had an ominous sound and Julie and Artie threw off the bedcovers and jumped out of bed. Artie turned on a light and opened a closet door.

Bang!!

Bang!!

The shots were not loud like the reports that had followed Artie's pistol shots at the O'Farrell. Julie thought they sounded like BB-gun shots. Two bullets whistled through the air and Julie heard them crunch into wood.

"Give me something to wear!" Artie whispered. Julie handed him a pair of green sweat pants and Artie ducked into a closet and struggled into them.

Bang!! Another shot crunched into wood.

"What's going on? Who's out there?" Artie yelled.

No one answered, but Julie heard someone running through the house, bumping into things. Terrified, she ran toward the other closet, but stopped long enough to snatch the phone off the night table and take it with her.

Julie and Artie leaned out of their closets and looked at each other, confused, unable to tell where the shots were coming from. One or two of the shots had rattled the Levolor blinds. Were they being fired from inside the house, or were they being fired from the outside, through the window? Was this a drive-by shooting?

"Is there a bat around?" Artie asked, thinking that perhaps Caleb had left a baseball bat in the room. Julie looked around but did not see one.

"Never mind, I've got something," Artie said.

Julie dialed 911 and said "23 Mohawk" when the dispatcher, Sherri Tompkins, came on the line.

"What's the problem?" Tompkins asked.

"I'm in the bedroom and we hear noises, like gun noises, outside the door," Julie said.

"You hear shots?"

"I think so."

Tompkins advised officers of a shooting in progress and told Julie to hold on, units were on their way.

Artie picked up a Heineken bottle and headed toward the bedroom door. He was probably on his way to the living room, where the 9mm was locked in the safe.

Julie started to sob, then screamed, "ARTIE, DON'T GO OUT THERE! ARTIE, DON'T GO OUT THERE!"

"What's going on?" Tompkins asked.

"I think somebody's sho—" Julie said through her sobs. "ARTIE, OH MY GOD! ARTIE, DON'T GO OUT THERE!"

"Can you, can you see anything?" Tompkins asked.

"I'm in the closet."

"Okay."

Bang! . . . Bang! . . . Bang!

"ARTIE, GET DOWN!"

Julie heard a scream, a low, painful scream.

Seconds that seemed to last longer than minutes went by. Tompkins kept a running conversation going with Julie, who remained in the closet.

Bang! Bang!

More seconds passed.

"Can you hear anything, Julie? . . . You don't hear any of my units or anything?" Tompkins asked.

Julie did not answer immediately. She had put the phone down and sneaked across the bedroom to peek down the hallway.

"Oh my God!" Julie replied when she got back on the phone. "I went to the hall and I saw . . . saw a beer bottle. It's knocked over in the hall."

Seconds later, Julie said, "I heard one siren! I heard one siren!"

Tompkins told her to stay in the closet and suggested she put some clothes on.

"Are there any weapons in the house, Julie?" Tompkins asked.

"Hell no!" Julie replied. "He told me to give him a bat and I didn't even have that."

Seconds later, Tompkins informed Julie that officers were at the front door and told her to let them in.

Half a mile away, police sergeant Tom Paraspolo had pulled over a drunk-driving suspect. Officer Kent Haas had been assigned to patrol for drunk drivers on the three-to-eleven shift, and the sergeant had radioed Haas for assistance. But when Haas arrived, the sergeant had waved him off. The sergeant had stopped a little old lady whose nose was level with the top of the steering wheel. She was lost and had been weaving because she was trying to read street signs in the dark and was not paying attention to the road.

Julie Bajo's 911 call came in just as Haas was passing the sergeant. Haas immediately went code three—flashing lights and siren —and stomped on the accelerator.

Haas was blasting up Mohawk when Officer Bonnie Page came on the radio to say she had taken an assault complaint from a woman who lived at 23 Mohawk earlier in the day. Page told the officers that the assault charges had been filed against a woman and advised them to be on the lookout for a female leaving the scene.

An acoustics expert would later determine that 55.9 seconds had elapsed from the time the first shot was heard on the 911 tape to the time the last shot was fired. When Haas arrived on Mohawk, he cut his lights and siren. He was slowly approaching 23 Mohawk, looking for a female suspect, when a man stepped onto the sidewalk almost even with his patrol car. The dark figure walked down the street away from Haas with a stiff-legged gait. He was wearing a tweed Ivy League hat, a dark leather jacket, and stone-washed jeans.

This wasn't the woman Haas had been warned to expect, but he thought it was strange that the man had his umbrella up. The rain had decreased to a drizzle. Could this dark figure be using the umbrella to conceal himself? Could he be a witness?

Haas got out of his car and yelled at the man to stop.

The man increased the pace of his stiff-legged walk. Haas jumped out of the car and drew his revolver but did not aim it.

"Stop! Police!" Haas yelled.

The man hopped along even faster. If he didn't have a stiff leg, he would be running. Haas took off after him and had closed to within ten yards when the man ducked behind a car parked in a driveway.

Haas spotted a rifle stock and saw the man try to jerk a rifle out of his pants. Twice he tried to yank the rifle free but it would not come out. A sight shroud on the barrel of the lever-action Winchester .22 was caught in his pants.

"Stop what you're doing or I'll have to shoot!" Haas yelled, bringing his .38 up level with the man's chest.

The dark figure looked up for the first time. Haas would later tell a grand jury he had "the most desperate look I've ever seen on a human being."

In the split second Haas had to decide whether to fire or yell another warning, a squad car driven by Tom Paraspolo, the sergeant who had stopped the old lady, screamed to a stop at the curb. The bright lights on the side of the car's roof rack fully illuminated the figure. The sergeant leapt out of the car, pulled his revolver, crouched behind the door, and yelled, "Put your fucking hands up or I'll blow your fucking head off."

The dark figure looked at Haas for a moment, then said, "Okay," and raised his hands.

As the officers approached, the suspect said he was carrying a .38. The officers found it under his jacket.

Haas handcuffed the suspect and put him in the back of the sergeant's squad car.

The radio was crackling with traffic, and Jim Mitchell, sitting with his hands cuffed behind his back, began listening. He heard a female dispatcher call the fire department and request an ambulance and paramedics. A few minutes passed. The dispatcher came on the air and canceled the call for the paramedics.

That was the moment it hit him. Jim Mitchell had killed his little brother.

Epilogue

The Trial

WHEN FRANK LLOYD WRIGHT studied the site that had been selected for the Marin County Civic Center, he must have decided to do an enlarged California version of his famous Prairie House. Like the Prairie House, the Civic Center in San Rafael is long and distinguished by sharp angles, with a mission-style tile roof that is turquoise instead of the traditional burnt orange.

Inside the courtrooms, the blue fabric on the spectator seats reflects the big blue roof, and large circular lights contrast with the endless linear hallways. Sliding-glass doors along the hallways open onto a balcony, and during a recess on January 15, 1992, the first day of testimony in the Jim Mitchell murder trial, George McDonald walked past the television cameras that were set up in the hallway, slid open a door, and ducked outside for a smoke.

George was definitely looking middle-aged, with a receding hairline and teeth that had yellowed from years of smoking. He was out there alone, looking over a vast parking lot, grounds that winter rains had turned a lush green, and traffic streaming north on Highway 101, when the door slid open and Jim Mitchell walked onto the balcony.

After spending a month in custody, Jim had been released on April 30 on $500,000 bail. He was heavy and looked like an aging accountant in his brown slacks, an English-style tweed jacket with leather patches on the elbows, a V-neck sweater over a tie and button-down shirt, and red tortoiseshell glasses. Jim lit a cigarette and stared straight ahead. George didn't know what to say, but he figured he had to say something.

"Hey, Jim, how you doin'?" George said as he was turning to go back inside. Then he smiled and said, "Isn't that a stupid question on a day like today?"

Jim laughed and put out his cigarette. He walked up to George, grinned, rubbed the top of George's head, and walked back toward Courtroom D of the Marin Superior Court.

George had decided to attend the trial because, like everyone else who had known the Mitchell Brothers, George wanted to know why Jim had killed Artie, and because he knew people would be asking him about it for the rest of his life. But as he watched Jim walk away, George realized there was another, deeper reason that had drawn him to the trial.

Jim had always been the director, the guy who controlled things from behind the camera. George had been the guy who took his clothes off and went in front of the camera. Now the tables had finally turned. Jim was the show. He was going to be stripped naked. And he had no control over the production.

George liked that. Jim had always been contemptuous of people who had exposed themselves in front of the camera. This time Jim's life was going to be exposed. He couldn't hide out in his clubhouse upstairs at the O'Farrell.

I wonder how he likes it under the lights, George thought as Jim walked away.

The drama that McDonald and the spectators who filled the seats in Courtroom D had come to watch pitted Michael Kennedy against Marin County deputy district attorney John Posey. Kennedy had aged well. He was tall and erect, his face was long and deeply lined, and his mane of graying blond hair was combed straight back so that it flowed over the collar of his beautifully tailored suits. Since leaving San Francisco for a Park Avenue office in New York, Kennedy had established a high-profile practice that featured clients like Jean Harris, the spurned lover who had murdered Dr. Herman Tarnower, the Scarsdale diet doctor, and Ivana Trump, when she was divorcing her husband, Donald.

Kennedy's legal team included the lawyerly-looking Dennis Riordan, an expert in legal procedure and appellate court work. Riordan had won national attention, including a long piece in *Esquire,* for a fifteen-year legal battle he fought to overturn the murder conviction of a black man named Johnny Spain, a case that went to the U.S. Supreme Court twice before Riordan won.

Jim's legal team went on the attack early and won several major battles. The trial was supposed to have begun on August 16, but Riordan had discovered the grand jury that had indicted Jim Mitchell for murder had made procedural errors, and a judge had overturned the indictment. That forced the Marin DA to take the case before another grand jury, which also indicted Jim for murder, in addition to the lesser charges of discharging a firearm in a grossly negligent manner and brandishing a deadly weapon in the presence of a police officer.

Nanci Clarence, a partner in the law firm of Tom Steel, Jim Mitchell's friend and longtime attorney, assisted Kennedy during the trial. A tough-minded former federal public defender, Clarence played the bad cop to Kennedy's good cop several times during the trial, asking prosecution witnesses hardball questions and attacking their answers.

A few minutes before the trial began each morning, deputy DA John Posey pushed a cart into the courtroom that groaned under the weight of volumes containing grand jury testimony, police reports, and reports filed by expert witnesses. Part Cherokee Indian, Posey had thick graying black hair, prominent cheekbones, pockmarked skin, and resembled the actor Richard Crenna. Dressed in conservative charcoal or dark blue suits, Posey often walked away from a witness with his brow furrowed, deep in thought. Suddenly, he would dive for one of his evidence books and turn to a colorcoded page.

Posey's reputation as a pit bull of a prosecutor was based largely on the four years he had devoted to the David Carpenter case. Known as the Trailside Killer, Carpenter was a monstrous psychopath who had killed five hikers on beaches in Marin and on trails leading up Mount Tamalpais. Carpenter had also killed two hikers in Santa Cruz County, down the coast from Marin. Posey won convictions on all five murders that had occurred in Marin, but they were overturned after a judge discovered the jury forewoman knew that Carpenter had previously been convicted of the two murders in Santa Cruz County.

From the first day on, it was apparent that it made no difference to Posey who was opposing him, a famous and very expensive attorney from New York City or a public defender who had just passed the bar. Once Posey had mastered the facts and put his case together, he was like a freight train. Anyone who stepped out onto the tracks in front of him was going to get run over.

Presiding over the case was Marin Superior Court judge Richard Breiner. A handsome, suntanned, gray-haired man in his mid-fifties, Breiner had a reputation as the best judge in Marin. Smart and blessed with a wit that was as quick as a professional comic's, Breiner was known for making fast, crisp rulings and keeping trials moving along.

The jury of eight men and four women (late in the trial, one of the women got sick and a male alternate replaced her) looked more like it had been drawn from a pool in Milwaukee, Wisconsin, than in Marin County, home of the hot tub and Werner Erhard's est. The women appeared to be overweight homemakers; the older, gray-haired men dressed casually in sweaters, and the younger men had the bleached-out look of computer technicians who spend long days hovering over circuit boards. Jury members got comfortable with each other early, smiling and sharing asides during breaks in testimony, and they paid attention, taking notes diligently during five weeks of testimony.

In his opening statement, Michael Kennedy told the jury that if Jim Mitchell had wanted to see his brother dead, he would have left him alone. Artie was killing himself with drugs and alcohol. Kennedy pointed out that legally there is a difference between killing, which Jim did do, and murder, which his client did not do. Sometimes speaking in a stage whisper that people had to strain to hear, Kennedy reconstructed the near-drowning at Ocean Beach to make Jim a hero who had gone into the water to save his little brother.

"Just as sure as Artie Mitchell was drowning in the surf off Ocean Beach [on March 18, 1990], Artie Mitchell was drowning in alcohol on February 27, 1991," Kennedy told the jury. Jim was "willing to go through a hail of bullets . . . to save Artie from himself."

"Jim Mitchell will answer the biblical question 'Am I my brother's keeper?' with a resounding yes," Kennedy concluded. "If anything, he is too much his brother's keeper. If he erred, he erred because he cared too much. He couldn't let Artie go."

In his opening statement, John Posey rose to suggest that Jim had a motive for the killing. Artie had taken out a $1 million life insurance policy and named Jim the beneficiary. Jim would become sole owner of the O'Farrell and the Mitchell Brothers' films. He would also free himself of a drunken, dangerous, humiliating brother.

But Posey did not work very hard to convince the jury that Jim had killed Artie for financial gain. Posey based his case on a state-of-the-art crime-scene reconstruction that, he promised, would leave no doubt in the jurors' minds that Jim had committed premeditated, first-degree murder. To make the night of the killing come alive in the jurors' minds, Posey played the tape of Julie Bajo's 911 call. Throughout the trial, the prosecutor played it every time he could.

Posey's case was built around the testimony of two expert witnesses, Dr. Harry Hollien, a professor of linguistic speech and criminal justice at the University of Florida, and Lucien Haag, a crime-scene reconstruction specialist with twenty-six years of experience who has a consulting business in Phoenix, Arizona.

Before Professor Hollien took the stand, it was widely believed that Artie had been struck three times: once in the upper arm; once in the abdomen; the fatal shot was believed to have ricocheted off his wrist and into his right eye. Hollien determined that five of the eight shots Jim fired could be heard on the 911 tape, and used oscilloscope and spectroscope graphs to determine exactly when the shots were fired. His study showed that Jim had fired the first shot on the tape 5.5 seconds after Julie Bajo had contacted the emergency dispatcher. The second shot came 4.8 seconds later; the third, 15.5 seconds after that; the fourth, 28.3 seconds after the third; and the final shot, 2 seconds later.

The fourth shot was the kill shot, the shot that had hit Artie in the right eye. Already struck twice, Artie had fallen into the bathroom. He had picked himself up, realized he was hit, and stuck his head back into the hallway. Jim was standing approximately thirty-three feet away with a rifle at his shoulder that was accurate at several hundred yards. He had waited 28 *seconds,* an eternity in a situation like that, for Artie to peek into the hallway. When he did, Jim, an expert shot, had drilled his brother through the right eye.

To bolster his case that Jim had killed Artie in cold blood, Posey called Lucien Haag, an imperturbable lantern-jawed veteran who had testified in more than 300 trials. Haag used lasers to trace the trajectory of the shots, and used phrases like "solid mass pattern, three-feet nine inches from the ground" to describe the cluster of bullets found in the bedroom door. Haag emphasized that the man who had fired the shots was an expert marksman.

Employing a novel technique, Posey had a computer-generated animation called "The Death of Artie Mitchell" made to re-create the crime. Computer animations had been used before in civil cases, such as those involving car crashes, and were once used in a criminal drunk-driving trial in New Jersey, but a cartoon reenactment of a killing had never before been used in a trial. Over Kennedy's strenuous objections, Judge Breiner allowed the video to be shown after it was modified to remove illustrations the defense believed were based on speculation rather than evidence.

The animation resembled a video game. Artie Mitchell was shown in the bedroom of a three-dimensional blueprint of the house at 23 Mohawk. He walked robotlike out of the bedroom and into the hallway. Three red bursts, representing bullets, pierced the animated figure that was Artie, which ended up crumpled on the bathroom floor.

Lucien Haag and the animation underscored the points Professor Hollien had made: the shot that killed Artie was fired after a 28-second wait. The kill shot was not a ricochet; it had been fired directly into Artie's right eye. The shooter had probably dropped to one knee to steady his aim when he fired it.

Kennedy contested Hollien and Haag's testimony—the debate over whether the jury should be allowed to see the computer animation was particularly heated—and called his own expert witnesses to refute their testimony. Kennedy's experts were not as impressive as the prosecution's, but they did raise questions about the validity of crime reconstructions in general and Professor Hollien's work in particular.

In the preface to one of his books, Hollien had written that, to be accurate, acoustic re-creations had to be done in an environment that replicated the setting of the original event. But the professor had re-created the acoustics of 23 Mohawk in a laboratory far away in Florida. Hollien explained that, because of advances in equipment, exact replications were no longer necessary. The professor said he was rewriting his book—Judge Breiner wryly observed, "He's rewriting it now"—but Kennedy had scored a point. The prosecution's expert witness had contradicted his own book.

After eight days of testimony by a parade of prosecution witnesses had ended, the defense began presenting its case, and it quickly became clear that the defendant Michael Kennedy wanted to put on trial was not Jim Mitchell. It was his dead brother, Artie.

A telling moment occurred shortly after Kennedy called Georgia Mae Mitchell. Georgia Mae took the stand dressed in a gray suit with a light orange turtleneck accented with a green-and-yellow scarf. She testified about how close her boys always were, how she and her husband, J.R., had raised Jim to look after Artie, and how proud she was of her boys because they had gone to court to fight for people's right to see what they wanted to see. Georgia Mae said that Jim had always been a fighter, and when she illustrated the point by saying that he had refused to cross a picket line to attend classes as a student at San Francisco State, Posey rose to object.

"Posey wants to block anything about fundamental humanity because he's a high technician," Kennedy told Judge Breiner. "But I've got to establish the character of the man. . . . How can we draw a human portrait in the courtroom except by getting information from those who knew him best?"

"How is refusing to cross a picket line in the 1960s relevant to firing eight shots on February 27?" Posey asked the judge.

Judge Breiner overruled the objection.

Each witness Kennedy called—Georgia Mae, Liberty Bradford, Lisa Adams, the campaign manager Jack Davis, Charlie Benton, an assistant manager who had worked at the O'Farrell for nineteen years—testified to how out of control Artie had been; how close Artie and Jim had always been; how concerned Jim was about his brother. Everyone had a horror story to tell about Artie's drinking, right down to the last night of his life. Artie's blood alcohol count was .25 the night he was killed. (The legal limit in California is .08.)

Jim rarely looked up at a witness, even when his mother was testifying. Each morning, he opened a notebook, laid out two pens, and spent the day taking notes. One of the few times he showed any emotion was when Liberty was on the stand, describing what had happened at Ocean Beach. Jim took off his glasses and began crying.

The moment that the five television cameramen, three still pho-

tographers, courtroom artists, reporters, writers, friends of Jim
Mitchell, and curious spectators were all waiting for occurred when
Michael Kennedy said softly, "I now call the accused and brother of
the victim, Jim Mitchell."

"On the day your brother died, did you love him?" Kennedy
asked.

"Yes, I did," Jim replied in a flat voice. Only his quivering lips
betrayed emotion.

"We've had evidence that Artie was abusive and out of control.
Are you telling us you still loved him?"

"Yes, I loved Art," Jim said in a level voice.

"Did you ever give up on him?"

"No."

Kennedy took Jim step by step through the events of the day. He
had taken the rifle along "for show. Maybe it made me feel better, I
don't know." After he had entered the house, he had yelled, "Hey,
killer! Get your skinny ass out here!" Artie had appeared in the
hallway, crouched in a menacing position. Jim thought the
Heineken bottle he was carrying was a pistol. Art yelled, "Okay,
motherfucker! I'm going to blow your fucking brains out!"

At that point, Jim fired his rifle. He heard another shot and
thought he had been hit. And then he went into temporary amnesia.
The next thing Jim remembered was bright lights shining in his face
and somebody screaming, "Put your fucking hands up or I'll blow
your fucking head off."

"I don't know how I got out there," Jim testified. But after sitting
through the trial, he now knew that Artie had been holding a beer
bottle that night, not a pistol.

"I now know what I did in that house," Jim said.

"What'd you do?"

"Killed Art," Jim said, choking on the words.

"Did you intend to kill your brother?"

"No."

"How do you feel?"

"I'm sorry," Jim said in a hushed voice. "I wish it could have been
me instead of him," he added, wiping away tears.

Calling the claim of amnesia a last-minute fabrication, John
Posey tore into Jim in a cross-examination that lasted three hours.
He tried to portray Jim as an imperious older brother who had killed
his younger brother because he could no longer control him.

"Did the thought of calling the police cross your mind?" Posey asked.

"No," Jim replied.

"You wanted to control the situation yourself, didn't you?"

"We were hoping to."

"You wanted to be in charge, didn't you?"

"I didn't have a choice."

"You weren't able to control Art, were you?"

"I never controlled Art."

"He was an embarrassment, wasn't he," Posey said in a voice that made clear he was stating a fact, not asking a question.

"I was beyond being embarrassed by Art. He was my brother and he was having trouble," Jim replied.

At one point, Posey turned on his heel and strode purposefully across the courtroom. He picked up the Winchester .22 and carried it back to the witness stand. The prosecutor presented the gun to Jim and asked him to demonstrate how he had loaded it on the night he'd killed Artie.

Jim stared at the rifle. The court reporter froze with her hands above the keys. No one in the courtroom moved. Slowly, Jim began shaking his head.

"I don't want to touch that," Jim said.

Posey walked back to the evidence exhibits and picked up the .38 in the shoulder holster. He carried it back to the witness stand and asked Jim to demonstrate how he had put it on. Jim refused.

"You didn't have any trouble putting it on that night," Posey remarked as he took the .38 back to the evidence cart.

"You said you yelled when you went into Artie's house that night. Could you show us how loud you screamed?" Posey asked.

Jim refused, and Kennedy jumped to his feet, red with anger.

"Your honor, this is sadistic! He doesn't have to answer these questions."

Judge Breiner allowed Posey to continue, and the prosecutor went on with his cross-examination. But Kennedy was boiling, and after court adjourned for the day, he snarled, "Don't you glare at me, you little shit!" as Posey passed on his way out of the courtroom. Posey allowed himself a small grin and kept walking.

After Jim got off the stand, it was apparent that there were important contradictions in the testimony given by witnesses presented by the prosecution and witnesses called by the defense. Georgia Mae testified that during the phone conversation she had with Artie a few hours before he was killed, Artie had said, "I'd like to put a gun between Jim's eyes and pull the trigger." Julie Bajo, who was standing next to Artie at the time, testified that Artie had said no such thing. Julie also testified that Artie had not threatened to kill Jim when he left the two drunken messages on his brother's answering machine.

Jim Mitchell, Lisa Adams, and Nancy Harrison, the O'Farrell secretary, all testified that Artie had made the call threatening Lisa's life on February 27. But Posey produced Artie's phone logs and showed that Artie had called the theater only once that day, in the afternoon, to apologize to Nancy. The threatening call was made a day or two earlier.

Jim testified that he knocked on the front door and that it was locked when he tried it. Jim also said on the stand that he had kicked the door open. Julie testified that she heard no one knocking on the door, and that the door had been left unlocked. A detective who had examined the door testified that the lock and its bolt appeared to be unharmed, and that the door showed no evidence of being kicked. Jim also said that when he went into the house, he yelled, "Hey, killer! Get your skinny ass out here!" Julie testified that she did not hear anything but doors slamming.

But Julie Bajo had a tough time on the stand. Because he knew the defense would do it if he didn't, Posey impeached his own witness, pinpointing inconsistencies in interviews Julie gave shortly after the shooting and versions she related to reporters months later. Most of the contradictions related to the fact that Julie had decided over time that another man had entered the house that night. There were so many sounds, so many bumps and bangs in the house that night, Julie had come to the conclusion another man had been in the house with Jim. Neither the prosecution nor the defense believed her. Both sides were certain Jim had acted alone.

Posey also brought out the fact that Julie had accepted $5,000 for an interview on the tabloid television show *Hard Copy,* $1,500 for an interview on *Inside Edition,* and had posed barely clothed on a pool table for a photo that accompanied a story in *People* magazine. None of these disclosures helped her credibility with the jury.

After Jim's testimony, the defense called a psychiatrist who said that Jim Mitchell could indeed have been suffering from psychogenic amnesia. As often happens in criminal trials, the prosecution immediately called a psychiatrist who took the stand to say that the defense psychiatrist had no idea what he was talking about, and that a far more detailed study would have to be done to determine what had gone on in Jim Mitchell's mind that night. But neither side seemed interested in pursuing the psychiatric argument. Forty-seven witnesses had been called—22 for the defense, 25 for the prosecution—and both sides were spent.

In his closing argument, Posey stood before a ten-foot flow chart that illustrated events on the night of the shooting. Jim Mitchell was not on a mission of mercy that night, Posey told the jury. He was "ready to go to war." He had killed his brother "in cold blood . . . with malice aforethought." Jim had parked his car three blocks away so he could make a clean getaway. He had lain in wait for his brother behind a cabinet in the kitchen. When Artie appeared in the hallway, Jim had shot to kill.

"Those bullets were like a magnet following him down the hallway," Posey said.

Jim himself had testified that the only time he had ever had a loaded weapon in a car was that night. Didn't that show that he planned to kill his brother? Didn't that show the killing was willful and intentional? Jim had tried to conceal the rifle in his pants and had tried to draw the weapon on a police officer. Does that sound like a man suffering from temporary amnesia? Jim had testified that he was afraid to call the police because his brother might harm them, or they might harm him. But the police had been to Artie's house many times to help settle disputes between him and Karen, and nothing had ever happened. Jim had not armed himself because he was afraid of his brother that night. He had armed himself to go to war. If Jim had really been convinced his brother was a raving maniac, he would have stayed home and protected Lisa Adams.

What if Julie Bajo had not had the presence of mind to call 911? What if Officer Kent Haas didn't happen to be only a few blocks away? Jim would be playing the grieving brother and the police would be questioning Karen Mitchell, who had pulled a gun on Julie Bajo earlier that day. The theater would be Jim's, he would be rid of the brother he could no longer control, and, as a bonus, he would inherit $1 million in life insurance money.

"If I could just have your attention for a moment," Posey asked in conclusion. And then he began to count "1,001 . . . 1,002 . . .

1,003 . . ." The prosecutor counted up to 1,028, told the jury they had just witnessed the last 28 seconds of Artie Mitchell's life, and sat down.

In his summation, Michael Kennedy went back to the themes he had presented in his opening statement. Jim Mitchell was his brother Artie's keeper. He had gone to Corte Madera that night armed "for defensive purposes, for lifesaving, life-helping purposes. That can go awry, but going awry is not the same as premeditated, cold-blooded murder."

Jim may have been stupid to go into his brother's home with two loaded weapons, but "it's not a crime to be stupid . . . it's not a crime to try to save your brother's life," Kennedy told the jury and asked that they acquit Jim on all charges.

The jury began deliberations on Tuesday, February 18. They had the option of finding Jim guilty of first-degree murder. First degree is premeditated murder carried out with express malice. It carries a penalty of twenty-five years to life.

Second-degree murder is a killing that is deliberate and done with express malice but is not premeditated. The penalty is fifteen years to life.

Voluntary manslaughter is a killing that is willful but is committed in the heat of passion while a defendant mistakenly but honestly believes his own life is in danger. A conviction on voluntary manslaughter can send a person to prison for as few as three or as many as eleven years.

Jim Mitchell was also charged with the grossly negligent discharge of a firearm and with brandishing a weapon in the presence of police officers. Each charge carries a possible prison term of sixteen months to three years.

Under a California law popularly known as "enhancement," a felon who uses a firearm during the commission of a crime can have five years added to any sentence a judge imposes. Posey asked that the enhancement provision be applied in Jim Mitchell's case.

After thirteen hours of deliberation, the jury came in with a verdict on Wednesday, February 19. Jim Mitchell was guilty of voluntary manslaughter committed "in the heat of passion."

Jim stared straight ahead, as if he was stunned. He had won. It was the best verdict he could have reasonably hoped for. He stood up and embraced Michael Kennedy and Nanci Clarence, and then he hugged a tearful Lisa Adams.

"This is more than a partial victory," a jubilant Michael Kennedy said outside the courtroom. "It's a great victory to be found not guilty of murder."

Kennedy said he would appeal the decision—the appeal would concentrate on the use of the "prejudicial" computer animation—but quickly added, "The Mitchell family is very happy. We are not disturbed by the manslaughter conviction. If he is obliged to go to prison, he'll be fine."

Kennedy had briefed the press every day after trial. Posey had refused to answer questions. When he finally faced the cameras, microphones, and tape recorders, the prosecutor said he was not disappointed by the verdict.

"That's the way the system works," Posey said. "I argued for what I believed the facts showed. I believe in our system of justice, and that's what the jury decided."

There were three major reasons why the jury came in with a lighter verdict than the prosecutor had demanded. Jurors want to understand *why* someone commits a crime, and Posey had never really explained Jim's actions. Instead, they accepted Jim's and Michael Kennedy's version of what had happened that night. Jim had flipped out. The DA should never have prosecuted him for first-degree murder.

"I am extremely comfortable with the decision," Juror Kentner Scott, a retired banker, told the *Examiner* after the trial. "I think [voluntary manslaughter] is what the prosecutor—had he had his head screwed on straight—should have charged [Mitchell] with initially. . . . I hope the outcome of this will be that the district attorney's office will look more carefully at the big picture next time."

John Posey's presentation was far too technical. He buried the jurors under an avalanche of scientific information. When it came down to a choice between scientific evidence and evidence based on human emotion, the jury chose the latter.

"Posey's mechanistic dedication to pure science lost me midpoint in the trial," Kentner Scott told the *Examiner*. "I was not hearing anything about the man Jim Mitchell. All I was hearing was the prosecutorial mind ticking and ticking."

Finally, the jurors did not like John Posey. They found him to be rude and badgering, particularly when he was questioning Lisa Adams. The prosecutor's attempts to make Jim handle the rifle and the

.38 backfired badly, creating sympathy for Jim Mitchell and antipathy for John Posey.

"It absolutely infuriated me," juror Scott said in the *Examiner*. "I was so glad that Jim Mitchell had the presence of mind to say, 'I don't want to.' I thought that was one of the cheap things that really made me go back and question everything that Posey had done."

The trial did not end after the jury reached its verdict. It entered an intense phase that was conducted out of the public's view. Twenty-one years earlier in the *Reckless Claudia* case, a poll conducted by the Field Research Corporation showing that pornography was not a pressing concern to 1,050 people had helped Jim and Artie Mitchell beat an obscenity charge. Now Jim Mitchell's defense team tried the tactic again.

The Marin DA's office had sent a sentencing memorandum to Judge Breiner stating that "public outrage exists in Marin County" over the Jim Mitchell case and that Jim, therefore, must be sentenced to a term in state prison. The defense team believed there was no "outrage" in Marin, and conducted a poll of 507 Marin residents. Seventy-two percent of the respondents rejected the prosecutor's claim that the public was outraged. Ninety-six percent of the people who were polled knew about the case. Eighty-eight percent thought the verdict was appropriate or were neutral on the case.

At the same time the poll was being conducted, the boys who hung out upstairs at the O'Farrell were pulling strings to help Jim. Jack Davis had masterminded the mayoral campaign of dark-horse candidate Frank Jordan, a former San Francisco chief of police. Warren Hinckle had played an important role in the campaign, blasting the incumbent, Art Agnos, in a series of columns that ran in a small weekly newspaper. Davis and Hinckle had collected some political chits, and they called them in for Jim Mitchell.

The letter-writing campaign Davis and Hinckle organized resulted in Judge Breiner receiving more than a hundred letters calling for leniency for Jim Mitchell. Among them were letters from Mayor Frank Jordan, San Francisco police chief Richard Hongisto, San Francisco sheriff Mike Hennessey, and Supervisor Terence Hallinan. The letters caused quite a stir when they hit the papers.

"There's nothing illegal or unethical about this, but it stinks," the *Examiner* said in a lead editorial. "There is a line between personal and official business. Hongisto, Jordan and Hennessey crossed it."

Jim appeared before Judge Breiner for sentencing on Friday, April 24, 1992. John Posey asked Breiner to impose the maximum eleven-year sentence. A probation officer read from a report written by Bruce Pither, a court-appointed psychologist. Pither said what had happened on the night of February 27, 1991, had been an aberration and that Jim Mitchell did not pose a danger to the community. But Pither also discovered that Jim exhibited "strong antisocial, paranoid and narcissistic personality features."

Judge Breiner took note of the letters he had received, but said that "I cannot make my decision in this case as if it were a popularity contest. It is the judge, not the public, who has the responsibility to determine the sentence."

Gazing down at the defendant standing before him, Judge Breiner said that the gravity of the case, the taking of a human life, required him to impose a prison sentence.

"You became Travis Bickle," Breiner told Jim, referring to *Taxi Driver,* the 1976 movie in which a deeply troubled cabbie played by Robert De Niro wreaked vengeance on the pimps who controlled a teenage prostitute played by Jodie Foster. "As a result, Artie is dead. Despite his faults, Artie did not deserve to die. His children did not deserve to be orphans."

Breiner sentenced Jim to six years in state prison. The sentence included three years for voluntary manslaughter and a consecutive three-year term for using a firearm.

Jim also received a sixteen-month sentence for exhibiting a firearm to a police officer in a threatening manner, but it will run concurrently with the manslaughter and firearms convictions. A four-and-one-third-year sentence for discharging a firearm in a grossly negligent manner will be dropped as soon as Jim serves his time for the manslaughter conviction.

The bottom line is: Jim Mitchell will be eligible for parole three years after he enters prison.

THE FAMILY

JIM MITCHELL has appealed his sentence and is free on $500,000 bail. The appeal process is expected to take six to twelve months.

"Mr. Mitchell indicated to me that he understands the sentence, he accepts it, he will do it," Michael Kennedy said after the hearing. "But he also believes that he will be vindicated on appeal."

ARTIE MITCHELL was buried next to his father in a cemetery in Lodi, California, where he had been born forty-five years earlier.

GEORGIA MAE MITCHELL is living in a suburb of Sacramento and is pursuing her avid interest in psychic phenomena. She remembers waking up in a bedroom in Jim's house a day after the shooting. What am I going to do? Georgia Mae asked herself. Artie's dead and Jim's in jail for shooting him. She looked at the door and saw an eye gazing at her. As she watched, the eye swirled toward her, growing larger and larger. When it was right next to her, the eye turned into Artie. Georgia Mae says that her son radiated happiness and was so at peace he gave her the strength to carry on.

META, RAFE, JUSTIN, and JENNY, Jim's four children, divide their time between their mother, MARY JANE's home in Marin and Jim and LISA ADAMS's home in San Francisco.

AARON, CALEB, and JASMINE, Artie's youngest three children, are living with KAREN MITCHELL, their mother, in Marin.

LIBERTY BRADFORD is studying acting in Los Angeles. STORM BRADFORD is a sophomore at San Diego State University. MARIAH BRADFORD is a freshman at Syracuse University. All three have filed wrongful-death suits against their uncle, Jim Mitchell.

MEREDITH BRADFORD is practicing law in Lafayette, California. She is hoping to wrap up her practice soon and move back East to Cape Cod. Meredith still believes that Jim committed first-degree murder that night in 23 Mohawk. She is still troubled that the bullet holes in the door were chest high and closely grouped.

ROCKY DAVIDSON, the cousin and O'Farrell custodian who was with Jim outside 23 Mohawk shortly before Jim killed Artie, was named to replace Art on the O'Farrell Theatre board of directors.

FRIENDS, REPORTERS, AND FORMER EMPLOYEES

BILL BOYER is a devoted family man who owns a bar and a comedy club in Contra Costa County. He delivered a eulogy at a memorial service held in Antioch for Artie Mitchell. Paraphrasing Dan Aykroyd at John Belushi's service, Boyer said when Artie was good, he was very, very good, and when he was bad, he was very, very bad.

MARK BRADFORD is an executive with the Minolta Company.

MIKE BRADFORD is the president of the Lakeside Inn, a casino-motel complex in South Lake Tahoe, Nevada. Mike is married and the father of two young daughters. He still loves fast cars and is an avid glider pilot.

Bob Callahan is working with the cartoonist Art Spiegelman on a series of books that will turn works by writers like William Kennedy and Elmore Leonard into lavishly illustrated comic books. "One more sign of postliterate America," Callahan says.

Bob Cecchini, Jim's friend from high school and a former Mitchell Brothers employee, lives in Stinson Beach, where he does carpentry and works in video and film.

Dr. "Skip" Dossett, Artie and Jim's close friend, is practicing medicine at a clinic in downtown San Francisco.

Herb Gold, the writer, is working on a book about bohemias—"I see them as islands"—around the world.

Jack Harvey is still working at the O'Farrell, where he recently completed the Turkish Bath Room. The room was a pet project of Jim Mitchell. While he was in jail waiting to make bail, Jim kept calling Jack to get progress reports on the Turkish Bath Room.

Phil Heffernan, the former art director at the O'Farrell, has a computer design firm in New York City. He created the cover shot of a pregnant Bruce Willis for *Spy* magazine. "My goal," he says, "is to make the camera obsolete."

Warren Hinckle and his wife, Susan Cheever, are at work on a book about . . . the Mitchell Brothers.

Richard Lackey, Jim's high school friend, owns a construction equipment leasing firm in Marin.

Denise Larson, the inspired co-founder of the Nickelettes, is married and has a daughter. She works for Macy's. In June 1992 the Nickelettes regrouped to celebrate their twentieth anniversary with an encore production of *Anarchy in High Heels*.

Deborah Marinoff, the former art director of the O'Farrell, co-founder of the Nickelettes, and Jim Mitchell's former girlfriend, recently moved back to the Bay Area from Los Angeles. She is working as an artist.

Dan O'Neill is trying to open a bar, restaurant, and nightclub at 391 Broadway in North Beach.

Dave Patrick is the Renegade Editor of *The Spectator*.

Earl Shagley is selling real estate in San Francisco.

Vince Stanich runs Dancers Guild International, the company that hires and books the dancers at the O'Farrell. Vince is married to a former dancer, and they have two sons.

JERRY WARD operates a courier service in San Francisco.

MAITLAND "SANDY" ZANE is a reporter for the San Francisco *Chronicle*.

PORNOGRAPHERS AND FORMER PORNOGRAPHERS

ALEX DE RENZY, the groundbreaking pornographer, still lives in Marin and still makes an occasional sex film.

ARLENE ELSTER, one of San Francisco's leading pornographers in the early 1970s, has a commercial plant nursery in Santa Rosa, California.

LOWELL PICKETT, the former beat turned highbrow pornographer, has a small service business in Oakland.

CHUCK TRAYNOR is the proprietor of the Survival Store in Las Vegas. To open the store, Traynor had to sign an agreement with Nevada authorities promising that he would not work in the pornography business in the United States. The female dancers, most prominently his young wife, Bo, who work for Charles Traynor Enterprises work the Canadian circuit.

POLICE, PROSECUTORS, AND ANTIPORN POLITICIANS

JEROME BENSON, who prosecuted the Mitchell Brothers for obscenity in the early 1970s, is a judge in San Francisco Municipal Court.

DIANNE FEINSTEIN, the former mayor of San Francisco, who was detested by members of the Mitchell Brothers fan club, is now a member of the *ultimate* boys' club: the United States Senate.

DENNIS MARTEL, the captain in charge of the vice squad during the Marilyn Chambers raid, is now a lieutenant in charge of the Traffic Division of the San Francisco Police Department.

JOHN POSEY is trying cases in Marin County.

BERNARD WALTER, the determined DA who opposed the Mitchell Brothers, is a private attorney working out of an office in his beautiful home on Ashbury Street. Walter was involved in an important case in which a minor was repeatedly calling a 900 sex-talk line. The case resulted in important modifications to the laws that govern phone sex across the country.

THE ATTORNEYS

NANCI CLARENCE is practicing law in San Francisco. Shortly after the verdict came in in the Mitchell case, she and DENNIS RIORDAN made a presentation to the Criminal Trial Lawyers Association of Northern California entitled "Mitchell Brothers Murder Trial: Defeating Darth Vader"—i.e., John Posey, the "Robo-prosecutor."

MICHAEL KENNEDY is practicing law in New York City. He and his wife, ELEANORE, divide their time between New York, a beach house in the Hamptons, and an estate in Ireland.

DENNIS ROBERTS is practicing law in Oakland.

THE PERFORMERS

JULIE BAJO is dancing on the club circuit, appearing in cities like Boston, Kansas City, and San Diego, where she is frequently introduced as Artie Mitchell's last lover. The wrongful-death and reckless-endangerment suits she has filed against Jim Mitchell did not keep her from calling the O'Farrell and asking permission to perform a love dance for Artie at Artie Mitchell's wake. She has signed a film deal with a television producer.

MARILYN CHAMBERS is happily married and has a beautiful newborn baby. Marilyn was on her way to an early grave, consuming massive amounts of alcohol and cocaine daily, when she met her husband-to-be. They had a great first date, but then he called to say he couldn't see her again. He was a recovering heroin addict and had taken a vow not to associate with anyone who was using drugs. Marilyn got so angry she kicked a wall and broke her leg. Her husband-to-be came to visit her in the hospital and Marilyn ended up in Narcotics Anonymous. Today, Marilyn drives a black Lexus with the license LUV NA and wears a large gold Roman numeral V around her neck. She has been clean and sober in Narcotics Anonymous for five years.

"What am I gonna tell her when she's old enough to know what I've done?" Marilyn asks, gazing lovingly at little Mckenna, who is lying on a blanket on the floor. "Oh hell, I'll just tell her the truth!" Marilyn says in her rough voice. Then she pauses for a moment. "Would I want her to do what I've done? To go through what I did?" Marilyn thinks for a while, then she says, "No!" and starts to laugh.

LISA LORING, the former O'Farrell dancer, is happily married to one of the Bay Area's leading sound technicians. She lives in a spacious apartment high above Lake Merritt in Oakland.

MISSY MANNERS married a successful entrepreneur. They have two small sons and divide their time between homes in the San Francisco area and the Southwest.

JOANNE SCOTT is a secretary in an attorney's office and is working on a memoir of Artie Mitchell.

GEORGE MCDONALD turned out to be a true bohemian. Married for seventeen years to a wife he sees on weekends and holidays, George lives in the same apartment in Sausalito he first rented in the early 1970s. He works on road crews or washes dishes just often enough to pay the rent and buy groceries. Most of the time, George can be found reading in the Sausalito library or helping his favorite widow polish an epic poem she has been working on for years. Every evening in a downtown bar, he attempts to answer the "final question" on *Jeopardy!* The bartender keeps score on a board behind the bar. George enjoys putting matchbooks, fortunes from fortune cookies, and whatever else he finds on the street into a collage, encasing it in plastic to make a postcard, and mailing it to a friend.

George has never had an AIDS test. He is afraid to take one.

Index

ABC (American Broadcasting Company), 111

ABCs of Sex, The (film), 85

Acid. *See* LSD

Adams, Lisa (Lisa Thatcher), 10, 343, 365–67, 373–75, 387, 390, 391, 392, 393, 396

Adult Film Association, 61

Aerosmith (band), 329

Against Our Will (book), 281

Agnos, Art, 394

Ah Toy, 81

AIDS, 338, 358

Alioto, Joseph, 82, 93

Alpert, Hollis, 56, 116

American Civil Liberties Union (ACLU), 94, 275

Amsterdam (Holland), 258, 264

Anarchy in High Heels (show), 233, 397

Annie (Jim's girlfriend), 50, 51–52, 77–78, 85–86, 98, 103–4, 108, 112, 122–23, 147, 152, 159, 160, 175, 214

Antioch (California), 4, 15–21, 27–36, 38–40, 45–46, 47, 62, 188, 251, 396
  description of, 17–19

Antioch *Ledger,* 67

Armon, Matthew, 200

Armstrong, Jeff, 262, 332

Arnold, Matthew, 203

Ashby, Hal, 290

Aspen (Colorado), 354

Autobiography of a Flea (film), 249, 298

Aykroyd, Dan, 396

Bajo, Julie, 11, 353–56, 361, 362, 363–64, 365, 370–73, 399
  on night Artie was killed, 11, 376–79, 385, 391
  testifies at Jim's trial for murder, 390–91

Bangkok (Thailand), 264

Barr, Candy, 56

Barrett, Rona, 344

Bath (New York), 65–66

BBC (British Broadcasting Corporation), 334, 344

Beardsley, Aubrey, 121

Beatles, the, 137

Beaver houses, 77, 81, 82–84, 90. *See also* O'Farrell Theatre

Beavers (softball team), 252

Behind the Green Door (film), 5, 162–71, 176–99, 202, 205, 208–9, 218–20, 242, 249

Behind the Green Door: The Sequel (film), 9, 331–32, 336–39

Belushi, John, 396

Benson, Jerome, 91, 98, 113, 118–19, 398

Benton, Alex, 151, 273

Benton, Charlie, 308, 387

Benton, Rita, 332

Berkeley (California), Mitchell Brothers theater in, 198

Berkeley, University of California at, 43, 315
  seminary of, 108–10

Berkeley Barb, The (weekly newspaper), 102, 155, 285

Bestiality, 85, 90

Big Book of Irish History, The, 334

Big Brother and the Holding Company, 42

Black, John Davies, 118

Black Panther Party, 43, 97

Blacks
  in Black Panther Party, 43
  at San Francisco State, 44, 46

Blake, William, 49

Blanchard, Ralph, 351

Blinder, Martin, 62, 63, 118, 203

Blue Light Cafe, 317
Bottom Feeder (fishing boat), 8, 223, 333, 352
Bourbon Street Irregulars, 227
Boxer, Barbara, 360
Boyer, Bill, 18, 27, 31–34, 36, 40, 67, 103, 151, 176, 186, 245, 248, 396
    leaves Mitchell Brothers, 249
Bradford, Jennifer, 83, 106, 123–26
Bradford, Liberty (Artie's daughter; Liberty Mitchell), x, 152, 213, 223, 292, 300–4, 329–31, 335, 349–50, 352, 360–63, 387
Bradford, Mariah (Artie's daughter; Mariah Mitchell), 217, 292, 300–2, 329
Bradford, Mark, 87, 123, 186–87, 216, 396
Bradford, Meredith (Artie's wife; Meredith Mitchell), ix
    Adrienne's "pregnancy" and, 211–12, 216–17
    as Artie's girlfriend, 73, 75–80, 83–87, 92, 99–100
    assaulted by Artie, 254
    background of, 73–75
    in Cannes, 217–19
    children of, 152, 213, 217, 218, 223, 253, 292, 297, 298, 300–3
    divorce of, 252–54, 289, 297, 329
    filmmaking by, 83–84, 85, 103–4, 122–23
    judgment against Mitchell Brothers won by, 302
    as Mitchell Brothers' attorney, 288–89, 295–98
    on murder of Artie, 11–13, 396
    in O'Farrell Theatre, 87, 93, 97, 101–4, 205
    as proposed divorce lawyer for Artie, 361–62
    at trials of Mitchell Brothers, 113–15, 120, 157
    wedding of, 124–26
Bradford, Mike, 147–51, 153, 154, 175, 176, 181–82, 186–87, 190, 206, 221, 222, 232, 233, 396–97
    leaves Mitchell Brothers, 249
    in Nickelettes show, 226–27
Bradford, Storm (Artie's son; Storm Mitchell), 213, 218, 223, 292, 300, 302, 329, 331, 373, 376
    in surf accident, 349–51

Bradford, William, 73–74
Bradford family, 74, 106–7, 124, 289, 292–95
Brando, Marlon, 136
Breiner, Richard, 384, 386, 387, 389, 394, 395
Brennan, William J., 121
Bricken, Gordon, 296
Bridge, The (film), 122–23
Bridges, Harry, 6
Briggs, Marilyn. *See* Chambers, Marilyn
Brown, Ira, 277–78
Brown, Jerry, 275
Brownmiller, Susan, 281
Bruce, Lenny, 104
Bruckheimer and Simpson, 111
Burger, Warren, 207
Burlesque, 58
Bush, George, 358

Caen, Herb, 85, 321
Cahill, Thomas, 82
Callahan, Bob, x, 334, 338, 340–41, 357–60, 397
Campbell, Joseph, 221
Cannes festival, 218–20
Cannon, H. Leroy, 94
Canyon (California), 300–1, 343
Carpenter, David, 383–84
Carson, Johnny, 201
Cassavetes, John, 52
Cassidy, David, 291
Castle Air Force Base (California), 129–31, 133
Catholic Church, 69, 153–54
Cavett, Dick, 111
CB Mamas (film), 248
Cecchini, Bob, 30, 45, 53–54, 136–38, 173, 195–96, 209, 397
Censorship, 97, 207–8, 281–85
Chambers, Marilyn, x
    arrest of, 310–13
    Artie as similar to, 327
    background of, 179–81
    in *Behind the Green Door*, 5, 162–71, 177–81, 183–85, 189–93, 205, 218, 219
    husbands of, 165, 178, 199, 219, 240–41, 264, 282, 305–9
    Inside Marilyn Chambers, 241
    on Ivory Snow box, 200–1
    later life of, 399–400

leaves Mitchell Brothers, 237–38, 240–41, 242
as live act for Mitchell Brothers, 305, 308–9
Mitchell Brothers described by, 223, 240–41
in *The Resurrection of Eve*, 199, 236
Charles, Robert, 157
Chicago Seven, 91
Chico State College (California), 40
Choctaw Indian Reservation (Oklahoma), 22
Cinema 7, 150, 153, 297
Citizens for Decency Through Law, 296
Citizens for Decent Literature (CDL), 116, 296
Clancy, James J., 296
Clarence, Nanci, 383, 392, 399
Cleaver, Eldridge, 43
Cleaver, Ward, 21
Cocaine, 150, 194, 232, 243, 273, 276, 291, 293, 306, 308, 314, 316, 319, 321, 326, 330, 333, 354, 360
Cochran, Eddie, 33
Colma (California), 101–3
Coming Home (film), 336
Communism, 38, 42
Community standards, 115, 119, 156, 207–8
Computer animation at Jim's trial, 386
Condor Club (San Francisco), 58–59, 230
Copenhagen (Denmark), 258
Coppola, Francis Ford, 251
Cora, Belle, 81
Corte Madera (California), 354–55, 356, 362, 368–80
Courbet, Gustave, 337
COYOTE, 152, 279, 335
Crazy Never Die, The (documentary), 335
Crown Theatre (San Francisco), 90
Crumb, R., 153, 360

Daly, Jo, 312
Dance of the Doomed, The (documentary), 335
Dancers Guild International, 397
Dancing
bottomless, 165
lap, 7, 270
nude, 8
topless, 58–59, 230, 239
Danielle from Hell, 328

D'Apice, Bobby, 307–8, 310, 313
Davidson, Ben, 193–94
Davidson, Rocky, 334, 364, 368, 369, 373–76, 396
Davis, Jack, 346, 356, 387, 394
Davis, Sammy, Jr., 240, 277, 307
Day, Doris, 52
Day in the Life of Ireland, A (book), 334
Dean, James, 136
Deep Throat (film), 201, 209, 238, 239
De Mille, Cecil B., 242
De Niro, Robert, 395
Denmark, abolition of laws on pornography in, 105–6, 117
de Renzy, Alex, 78–79, 91, 94–95, 105–6, 110, 172, 398
DeSalvo, Robert, 205–6, 209
Devil in Miss Jones, The (film), 237
Diablo Valley College (DVC), 28, 36–41, 154, 174
Diary of Anaïs Nin, The (play), 229
Dick Cavett Show, The (TV show), 111
Doda, Carol, 58, 230
Dossett, Donald "Skip," 355, 364, 369, 371–72, 374, 397
Douglas, Michael, 146
Draft protesters, 43
Drugs, 232, 233, 245. *See also specific drugs*
Dworkin, Andrea, 281–82, 284–85
Dylan, Bob, 159

Ecstasy (drug), 321
Ehrenreich, Barbara, 360
Elizabeth II (Queen of England), 2–3, 333
Ellsberg, Daniel, 149, 360
Elster, Arlene, 59, 61, 90, 105, 110, 111, 172, 207, 208, 398
Enhancement law, 392–93
Eno, Freaky Ralph, 227
Ephron, Nora, 281
Erhard, Werner, 384
Erotic Neurotic, The (play), 229
Evanoff, Mark, 351–52

Falkland Islands war, 333
Fat Larry (attorney), 195
FBI (Federal Bureau of Investigation), 57, 82, 209
Fear and Loathing in Las Vegas (film), 354
Feinstein, Dianne, 3, 81, 82, 156, 260, 274, 323, 398

Fellini, Federico, 49
Feminists, "pro-censorship" vs. "sex
    positive," 281, 335
Ferdon, John J., 82
Ferguson, Dianne, 295
Field Research Corporation, 158, 394
Fighting Sullivans, The (film), 144
Film
    Jim's college experience in, 40–41, 45,
        48–49
    by Mitchell Brothers. *See* Mitchell
        Brothers—films by
Finley, Andy, ix, 359
First International Erotic Film Festival, 111
Fishing, commercial, 8, 223, 333, 352
Flaherty, Robert, 106
Florez, Elisa. *See* Manners, Missy
Florez, John, 314–15
Fog City Diner (San Francisco), 320
Fonda, Jane, 131, 212
Fontana, Jon, 135, 139–42, 143, 151,
        154–55, 184, 185, 217, 273
Ford, Phil, 305
Fornelli, Gina, 242
Fort Holabird (Maryland), 64
Foster, Jodie, 395
Free love, 60–61
Freeman, Steve, 351
Free Speech Movement, 43
Freitas, Joseph, 276
Fuller, Dana, 366

Galante, Carmine, 210
Gambling, 19–21, 24–27, 41, 46–47, 68
Garner, James, 19
Gays
    Mitchell Brothers' attacks on, 279–80
    police raid on club of, 312–13. *See also*
        Lesbians
Gentry, Curt, 81
Gifford, Barry, 341
Gillis, Jamie, 343
Ginsberg, Allen, 42, 45, 96
Gish, Jim, 185
Gitlin, Todd, 360
Glowy Flesh (film), 119–22, 157
Godard, Jean-Luc, 45, 159
Gold, Herb, 1–8, 153, 260, 397
Golden Gate Bridge (San Francisco), 122–
        23
Golden Gate Park (San Francisco), 42, 45,
        76, 86, 90, 103

Goldner, James, 49
Goldstein, Al, 277
Gould, Elliott, 128, 135
Graciosa (fishing boat), 333
Grafenberg Girls Go Fishing, The (film),
        249
Grafenberg Spot, The (film), 249
Graham, Bill, 42
Grateful Dead, 42, 45, 314, 348
Great American Music Hall (San
        Francisco), 267, 298
Greenland, Harold, 51, 58, 59
Gulf war (1991), 358–60
Gunilla (nursing student), 194

Haag, Lucien, 385, 386
Haas, Kent, 379–80, 391
Haggard, Merle, 38
Haight-Ashbury Free Medical Clinic, 90
Haight district, 42, 76, 82, 85, 90, 103,
        105
Hair (musical), 72, 94, 169
Hallinan, Terence, 10, 394
Hallinan, Vincent, 10–11
Halvonik, Paul, 94, 275, 277
Hansan, Tilden, 350–51
Hard Copy (TV show), 390
Hardcore (film), 306
Harris, Jean, 383
Harrison, Nancy, 365–66, 369–70, 390
Hart, Frank E., 120
Harvey, Jack, 187, 206–7, 243, 247, 249,
        256, 261–63, 299, 304–5, 342, 352,
        364, 397
Hashish, 232
Hassall, Karen. *See* Mitchell, Karen
Hatch, Orrin, 315
Hayden, Tom, 212
Hayman, Jessie, 81
Haywire (band), 305
Hayworth, Rita, 291
Hearst, Will, 358
Heffernan, Phil, 187, 213, 250, 397
Hefner, Hugh, 110
Helper, Hinton, 55
Hennessey, Mike, 394
Hermosa Beach (California), 75
Heroin, 232, 330–31, 399
Hicklin decision, 121
Hill, Morton, 117
Hinckle, Warren, 42, 150, 311–13, 335,
        358–59, 394, 397

Hipp, Travis T., 334
Hippies, 39, 42, 48, 75, 82, 90, 135, 165–66
History of Sex in the Cinema, The (book), 56, 116
Hollien, Harry, 385–86
Holmes, John, 259
Honeymooners, The (TV series), 305
Hongisto, Richard, 394
Hoover, J. Edgar, 57, 116
Hoppity Goes to Town (film), 303
Horner-Greenberg, Joy, 245–46
Hot Nazis (film), 248
House Un-American Affairs Committee (HUAC), 43
Hudson, Rock, 52
Hurley, Gerald, 40–41
Hurricane Express (film), 227
Hustler magazine, 338

I Am Curious (Yellow) (film), 105–6
Indianapolis (Indiana), 282
Inside Edition (TV show), 390
Inside Marilyn Chambers (film), 241
Inside the Flesh Factory (film), 172–74
Institute for the Advanced Study of Human Sexuality, x, 279, 281, 283
Ivory Snow, 200–1

Jackson, George, 92
Jack Tar Hotel (San Francisco), 288
James, Henry, 220
Jana (porn star), 211
Japanese tourists, 234–36 255, 267, 320
Jefferson Airplane, 42, 125
Jimmy's Billiards (Antioch, California), 31
John Fitzgerald Kennedy Law School (Orinda, California), 288
Johnny Concho (film), 33
Johnson, Lyndon Baines, 116, 135
Joplin, Janis, 90
Jordan, Frank, 394
Jules and Jim (film), 41

Kean, Jane, 305
Keating, Charles, 116 –17, 203, 296
Kennedy, Biff, 91
Kennedy, Eleanore, 113, 212, 218, 399
Kennedy, Michael, 6, 11, 153, 157–58, 218, 275, 288, 360, 399
  background of, 91

as defense lawyer in obscenity cases, 92–94, 99, 112–15, 118–20
  at Jim's murder trial, 382–84, 386–90, 392–93, 395
Kennedy, William, 397
Kerouac, Jack, 3, 136
Kesey, Ken, 42, 45
Keyes, Johnny, 189–90, 200
Kinsey Institute, 116, 283
Klein, Calvin, 342
Knievel, Evel, 226
Knight, Arthur, 56, 111, 116, 198
Kopkind, Andrew, 360
Kopp, Quentin, 6
KQED auction, 148–49
Krassner, Paul, 360
Kristal (Artie's girlfriend), 348, 349, 355
Kunstler, William, 91

Lackey, Richard, 17, 18, 29, 31, 32, 35–38, 41, 62, 352, 397
  at San Francisco State and after, 41, 44–48
Lady Chatterley's Lover (book), 120
Lady T (dancer), 328
Lafayette (California), 152, 232, 297
Land of Gold (book), 55
Lansky, Meyer, 209
Lap-sitting, 268–71
Larry King Live (TV show), 344
Larson, Denise, 226, 229, 231–33, 246, 334, 397
Last of the Red Hot Lovers (play), 305
Last Tango in Paris (film), 170, 208
Las Vegas (Nevada), 67–73, 147
Lee, Gypsy Rose, 59
Leibovitz, Annie, 111
Leigh, Megan, 286
Lelania (performer), 140–45
Leonard, Elmore, 397
Lesbians
  in film, 120, 189
  hounded by Artie, 327–28
  in live show, 7, 255–56, 261, 264, 266, 267, 309
  among O'Farrell dancers, 284
Lessons in Love (film), 88
Let My People Come (musical), 265
Life with Father (film), 144
Lincoln Savings and Loan debacle, 116
Lockett, Ralph, 119
Loops, definition of, 58

Lord Jim's (San Francisco club), 312
Loring, Lisa, 265–71, 283, 292, 298–99,
    327, 399–400
Los Angeles *Times,* 296
Lovelace, Linda, 236–40, 282, 283
LSD (acid), 9, 42, 46, 195, 231, 319, 326,
    354
Lucas, George, 251
Luttinger, Ben, 115

McCarthy, Eugene, 75
McDonald, George, ix–x, 127–46
    background of, 128–32, 133
    as celebrity, 202–3
    description of, 7
    at Jim's trial for murder, 381–82
    later life of, 400
    as pornographic actor, 139–46, 154–56,
        172–75, 242
        Behind the Green Door, 182–85, 189–
            90, 191–92, 194–98
    retirement of, 249
McIlvenna, Ted, x, 279, 283–84, 336
MacKinnon, Catharine A., 282
McKnight, Sharon, 8, 152, 249, 337, 359
McWilliams, Carey, 17
Madams of San Francisco, The (book), 81
Madonna, 233
Mafia, pornography and, 207–11
Malden, Karl, 146
Maloney, Pete, 96–98
Manners, Missy, x, 314–16, 336–39, 343–
    49, 400
    Jim's attitude toward, 336–37
    public nudity by, 320–21
    at wake for Artie, 8–10
Mansfield, Jayne, 51, 230,
Marijuana (pot; joints; grass), 42, 46, 60,
    76, 82–83, 88, 101, 112, 150, 155,
    165, 191, 194, 225, 262, 273, 275,
    306, 319, 330, 354
Marin County Civic Center, 381
Marinoff, Deborah (Debbie), 173, 188,
    228–29, 231–36, 247, 290–92, 397
Mark Hopkins hotel, 231
Martel, Dennis, 82, 310–11, 398
Martin, Judith, 318
Mayflower (ship), 73–74
Meese, Edward, 331–32, 344
Melody (New York City club), 256, 262
Mescaline, 232
Methamphetamine, 82, 195, 324

Mezzavilla, Richard, 262, 332
Mickey Mouse Club, The (TV show), 109
Milk, Harvey, 274
Miller v. *California,* 207–9
Mind with a Dirty Man (play), 305
Minneapolis (Minnesota), 282
Mission Coalition Organization (San
    Francisco), 90
Miss Nude America, 315–16
Mr. T (poodle), 8, 10, 326, 346
Mitchell, Aaron (Artie's son), 300, 349–50,
    370, 396
Mitchell, Adrienne (Jim's wife), 152, 159,
    184, 211–17, 219, 245–47, 289
Mitchell, Artie Jay
    Adrienne and, 211–12
    Army service of, 40, 63–67
    birth of, 27
    boyhood of, 15–16, 27–36
    burial of and memorial to, 396
    child molestation case against, 303–4
    children of, 10, 152, 212–13, 217, 218,
        223, 253, 292, 298, 300–3, 325–26,
        329–31, 347, 361–63, 396
    surfing accident, 349–52, 355–56, 384
    declining physical and mental health of,
        355–56, 357–58, 360–61, 363–73
    divorces of, 252–54, 289, 297, 329, 330
    first wife of. *See* Bradford, Meredith
    on giving freedom to women, 138
    hypothyroid condition of, 355–56
    at Institute for the Advanced Study of
        Human Sexuality, x
    killing of, 10–13, 376–80
    personal characteristics of
        alcoholism, 326, 330–31, 339, 343,
            348, 355–56, 357, 360–67, 387
        carrying loaded gun, 356–57, 363–64
        center of attention, 232
        drug use, 9, 73, 232, 316, 330, 333,
            355, 360–61, 362
        fear of aging, 331, 339
        fear of losing brother, 339, 360, 364–
            65
        gambling, 68
        hates "halfway guys," 150
        leering grin, 168
        love of father, 223–24
        love of vehicles, 221–22
        methods of control, 232, 319, 327–28
        nebbish charm, 73
        pool-playing, 31, 223, 363

prankster, 2–3, 274, 333
razor-tongued, 1, 31, 32, 148, 317
sexual mania, 9, 246, 299–300, 304,
    320, 324, 327–29, 344–45
television-watching, 148
violence against lovers, 254, 345, 347–
    48
in pornography business
    acts in soft-core films, 106–7
    Behind the Green Door, 184–86, 188–
        89
    joins Jim, 63, 69–70
    See also Mitchell Brothers—films by
in surf accident, 349–52, 384
wake for, 1–2, 5–11, 399
Mitchell, Bessie (aunt), 22
Mitchell, Caleb (Artie's son), 325, 333,
    349–50, 370, 396
Mitchell, Charles (uncle), 21–24
Mitchell, Georgia Mae (mother), 15–17,
    20, 21, 25–30, 67, 114–15, 217,
    223, 326, 331
    rebirth of, 302–3
    seeks involuntary commitment of Artie,
        372
    after shooting of Artie, 7, 396
    on son's payroll, 302
    testifies at Jim's trial for murder, 387,
        389–90
Mitchell, James Lowell (Jim)
    Army service of, 36, 38
    Artie's death threats against, 373, 390
    Artie killed by, 10–13, 376–80
    at Artie's wake, 5, 9–11
    at Artie's wedding, 125
    birth of, 27
    boyhood of, 15–16, 28–36
    children of, 10, 292, 342–43, 396
        surfing accident, 349–52, 384–85
    college education of, 37–42, 44–49
    description of, 5–6
    divorces of, 246–47, 342–43
    first filmmaking by, 48–56
    first nudie and pornographic photographs
        by, 49–54
    at Institute for the Advanced Study of
        Human Sexuality, x
    murder trial of, 381–95
        appeal, 395
        his testimony, 388–90
        sentence, 395
    personal characteristics of

attitude to women, 290
courage, 50
drug use, 46, 232, 291, 293, 360
generosity, 32, 50
leadership and control, 32, 41, 233,
    327, 388–89
love of father, 223–24
love of vehicles and boats, 221–22,
    262
outsider-outlaw feeling, 62
paranoia, 207, 395
pool-playing by, 31, 223
prankster, 2–3, 35, 274, 334, 335
sex as exercise of power, 245–46
in pornography business
    as director, 139–44, 146
    first nudies, 54, 71–72
    political motivations, 61, 62–63
    See also Mitchell Brothers—films by
restaurant proposed by, 359
in salary dispute with Shagley, 158–61
as summons server, 50
in surf accident, 349–52, 384–85
as survivalist, 206–7
War News of, 358–60, 361, 363
Mitchell, James Robert (father), 15–17,
    28–31, 62, 86, 93, 364
    boyhood of, 21–24
    death of, 223–24
    as professional gambler, 19–21, 24–28,
        41, 46
    sons' way of life supported by, 114–15
    supposed prison term of, 24–25
Mitchell, Jasmine (Artie's daughter), 325,
    396
Mitchell, Jenny (Jim's daughter), 396
Mitchell, Justin (Jim's son), 396
Mitchell, Karen (Artie's wife), x, 298–301,
    303–4, 325, 330–31, 345, 355,
    361–62, 370–71, 391, 396
Mitchell, Liberty (Artie's daughter). *See*
    Bradford, Liberty
Mitchell, Mariah (Artie's daughter). *See*
    Bradford, Mariah
Mitchell, Mary Jane (Jim's wife), 291–95,
    298–99, 337, 342, 396
Mitchell, Meredith (Artie's wife). *See*
    Bradford, Meredith
Mitchell, Meta (Jim's daughter), 292, 349,
    396
Mitchell, Rafe (Jim's son), 349, 396
Mitchell, Robert Lewis (brother), 27

Mitchell, Storm (Artie's son). *See* Bradford, Storm
Mitchell Brothers
  arguments and power struggle between, 88–89, 185–88, 214–16, 243–44, 331–32, 333, 369
  authority hated by, 236
  "Bob" as mutual nickname of, 78
  commercial fishing by, 8, 223, 333, 352
  decision-making by, 83
  embezzlement against, 220–21
  films by
    Behind the Green Door, 5, 162–71, 176–99, 201, 202, 205, 208–9, 218–20, 242, 249
    Behind the Green Door: The Sequel, 9, 331–32, 336–39
    first insertion, 99–100, 108–10, 113
    first sound camera, 139
    first use of a man, 106–7
    Inside Marilyn Chambers, 241
    masturbation films, 79–80, 104
    music for, 102, 104
    political messages, 173–75
    Requiem, 103–5, 120
    Resurrection of Eve, The, 199, 233, 236, 242, 249
    Sacramento Salami, 84
    Sodom and Gomorrah, 242–45, 247–48, 296
    films after *Sodom and Gomorrah,* 248–52
    split beaver, 79–80
    story lines mandated, 121–22, 123
    titles, 77, 85, 102
    weekly schedule for, 151
    See also specific titles
  first pornography seen by, 34–35
  fund raisers by, 228
  male actors for, 137–38. *See also* McDonald, George
  obscenity cases against, 4, 6, 11, 88–99, 112
    conviction and appeal, 119–20
    first trial, 113–20
    live-sex cases, 274–80, 308–9
    Reckless Claudia trial, 157–58, 394
    Santa Ana lawsuits, 296–97
  porn film business abandoned by, 251–52
  resemblance of, 5–6
  softball team of, 252

theaters owned by, 198, 208, 210
Ward as Las Vegas distributor for, 70–72
See also O'Farrell Theatre
Monroe, Marilyn, 169, 201
Moore, Michael, 360
Moraga (California), 342–43, 346
Morgan, Mimi, 199
Moscone, George, 260, 274
Motion Picture Association of America, 208
Mötley Crüe (band), 329
Movement, the, 42, 60, 61
Movies. *See* Film
Murphy, Cornelius, 312

Nader, Ralph, 63
National Organization for Women (NOW), 281
New Comics Anthology, The (book), 341
New Follies (San Francisco burlesque house), 51, 54, 63
Newton, Huey P., 43, 92, 150, 153, 212
New York City
  Melody club in, 256, 262
  Nicks and Madonna in, 233
  pornography in, 5, 55, 207, 208
New York Supreme Court, 242
New York *Times,* 80, 208, 337
Nickelettes and Nickelodeon, 225–33, 236, 397
Nixon, Richard M., 116, 117
Noltimier, Louis, 118
North Palm Beach (Florida), 239
Novello, Don, 227
Nudism, 58, 62
Nun, The (film), 34–35
Nut Tree (California restaurant), 326

Oakland (California), 43
Oakland Raiders, 193–94
O'Farrell Theatre (*later* O'Farrell Eros Center)
  Adrienne's role at, 159, 213
  amateur night at, 315–16, 323
  boxing party at, 357
  Cine Stage, 7, 263, 268
  clowns proposed for, 350
  as clubhouse, 150–53, 299, 333, 335
  couples in audience of, 172, 235, 248
  description of, 4–5, 132
  Green Door Room, 7–10, 264
  hard-core films first at, 110–11

J. R. Mitchell Lo-Ball Tournament at, 224
after killing of Artie, 396, 397
Kopenhagen Intimate Lounge, 7, 260–62, 267, 269, 270, 309
lap-sitting at, 7, 268–71
live sex shows at, 7, 244–45, 265–86, 321–22
prostitution charged, 276–80, 310–11
mayor's telephone number on marquee of, 3
murals on outside walls of, 228
new film every two weeks at, 176
New York Live, 8, 263–64, 268, 269, 270–71, 277, 308, 336
Nickelettes and Nickelodeon at, 225–33, 236, 397
opening of, 11, 87–88
at opening of *Behind the Green Door*, 193–98
police raids on, 88–90, 91, 258–60, 272–75, 310–11
porn magazines sold at, 234
Pyramid Room (planned), 263
Shower Room (planned), 263
Streets of Paris room (planned), 263
Turkish Bath Room, 397
Ultra Room, 255, 257–60, 266–67, 269, 278, 298, 309, 335
wake for Artie at, 1–2, 5–11, 399
women picketing against, 280, 283
Oh! Calcutta! (revue), 204
Okies, 17, 38, 46, 48, 151, 177, 291, 294
O'Neill, Dan, 153, 233–35, 333–34, 359, 397
On Our Backs (periodical), 284
Oprah Winfrey Show, The (TV show), 344
Oracle (underground publication), 102
Orgies, 60–61, 86, 130, 137, 145–46, 172, 320
Osborne, John, 136
Our Bodies, Ourselves (book), 281
Owl and the Pussycat, The (film), 163–65, 171, 180–81
Ozzie and Harriet, 52

Page, Bonnie, 379
Palmer-Slater, Gail, 354
Paraspolo, Tom, 379
Patrick, Dave, x, 285–87, 328, 397
Peerless Theatre (San Francisco), 91
Pentagon Papers, The, 149

People magazine, 390
Peraino, Lou, 207
Peraino, Tony, 207
Performance art, 230
Peter Pan (show), 233
Peyote, 232
Physicians for Good Government, 118
Pickett, Lowell, 59–61, 81–82, 86, 90, 105, 110–11, 145, 172, 251, 398
Pither, Bruce, 395
Pitkin County (Colorado), 2
Pittsburg (California), 19, 33
Plainfield (New Jersey), 65–67
Playboy magazine, 110, 198, 338, 343–45
Plays, experimental, 229
Poland, Jefferson, 61
Police
called in killing of Artie, 11, 378–80
infrared cameras of, 97–98
live sex shows raided by, 258–60, 272–73, 310–12
Mitchell Brothers' father and, 29–30, 62
pornography and, 75, 82, 88–99, 118–19
patrons arrested and harassed, 91, 94, 95
prostitution at party of, 312
at San Francisco State, 46–48
theater permits to be issued by, 156–57
Polk Street (San Francisco), 3–4
Polls
on outrage in murder case, 394
on pornography, 158
Pornography
attempted civil rights laws vs., 282
community standards on, 115, 119, 156, 207–8
copyright protection of, 210
as dehumanizing by the powerful, 276, 282
as expression of women's freedom, 75, 105, 138, 284
history of, 55–59
industrial films compared to, 147–48
interstate shipping of, 70, 111–12, 209–10
Jim's still pictures, 53
Johnson Commission on, 116–17
mainstreaming of, 201–3, 251–52, 342
masturbation and criticism of, 204
Meese Commission on, 332, 344
mob's interest in, 207

in New York City, 5, 55–56, 207, 208,
    256, 262
in old San Francisco, 80–82
picketing of, 90
recruiting women for, 53–54, 103–5,
    134–38, 149
as reflection of society, 34, 280–81
San Francisco's DA and, 82, 90–91, 113,
    118–19, 248, 258–59, 276–79, 308,
    311–13
as sexual outlet, 77–78
Sontag's analysis of, 203–4
spoof of, 229–32
subversive nature of, 61–62, 79–80, 153
as totalitarian assault on individual, 206
VCR revolution in, 251–52
vile types of, 172–73
"wet" shots in, 173
whether linked to sex crimes, 105, 116–
    19, 260, 281–82
as "without redeeming social
    importance," 121, 140, 156, 161
See also Mitchell Brothers—films by
Pornography in Denmark (film), 105–6, 172
Posey, John, 382–87, 389–95, 398, 399
Presant, Beatrice, 87
Priscilla (Nickelette), 230, 233
Prostitution
    definition of, 277
    Mitchell Brothers charged with, 276–80,
        310–13
    in old San Francisco, 80–82
    at police party, 312–13
psilocybin mushrooms, 330

Quicksilver Messenger Service (band), 42

Rabbit Redux (book), 210
Rajneesh, Bhagwan Shree, 284, 317
Rampaging Nurses (film), 86
Ramparts magazine, 42, 311–12
Rand, Al, 226–27
Rand, Sally, 59
Raye, Martha, 98
Reagan, Ronald, 42–43, 134, 296, 315
Reckless Claudia (film), 153–58, 172, 394
Redball (film), 110
Red Hot Chili Peppers (band), 329
Reed, Ishmael, 341, 360
Reed, Jimmy, 3
Reefer Madness (film), 60, 228
Requiem (film), 103–5, 120

Resurrection of Eve, The (film), 199, 233,
    236, 242, 249
Rhine, Joe, 91, 157–58, 288
Richmond (California), 198
Riordan, Dennis, 383, 399
Roberts, Dennis, 152, 212, 278, 364–65,
    366, 399
Roff, Hadley, 93
Roger and Me (film), 360
Rolling Stones, 3
Rosenberg, David, 58–59
Roth v. *The United States of America,* 120,
    123
Rowe, John, 64–66
Roxie Theatre (San Francisco), 51, 54, 59,
    63
Rubenstein, Maggie, 281
Rydell, Bobby, 33

S&M, 257, 266, 309, 324, 343
Sacramento River, 18
Sacramento Salami (film), 84
Saddam Hussein, 358
Safe sex, 335–36, 338, 344
St. James, Margo, 152, 279, 335
Salt Lake City (Utah), 208
Samuel, James (grandfather), 21, 23
Samuel, Minnie Lee (grandmother), 21–23
San Francisco (California)
    history of sex in, 54–55, 59–62
        prostitution, 81
    in 1960s, 42–43
    pornography in, 80–82, 115
        porn theater cases, 89–99, 274–80,
            310–13
San Francisco Bay Guardian, The, 102, 359
San Francisco *Chronicle,* 42, 61, 80, 85,
    93, 95, 102, 119, 163, 166, 247–
    48, 258, 265, 277, 280, 338, 398
San Francisco *Examiner,* 111, 278, 312,
    322, 358, 394
San Francisco Mime Troupe, 42
San Francisco Opera, 231
San Francisco State College (SFS), 28, 38,
    41, 153, 227, 265
San Joaquin Valley (California), 26
San Rafael (California), 381
Santa Ana (California), 296–97
Santana (band), 42
Saturday Night Live (TV show), 227
Saturday Review (magazine), 198

Scott, Joanne, x, 257, 321–25, 327–28, 331, 333, 346–47, 355, 400
Scott, Kentner, 393–94
Screening Room, 92, 95, 105–6, 110, 255
Screw magazine, 277
Seduction (film), 113, 121
Segal, George, 164
Seger, Bob, 107
Sellers, Peter, 65
Seltzer, Eugene, 330, 361
7-Eleven stores, 344
Sex industry, profile of women in, 285–87
Sex parties. *See* Orgies
Sex Surrogate, The (play), 305
Sexual Freedom League, 61, 145
Sexual revolution, 105, 161, 280
SFS. *See* San Francisco State College
Shagley, Earl, 49–54, 63, 87–88, 93, 101, 108–10, 112, 135, 137, 139, 141, 175, 397
  dispute with Mitchell Brothers, 158–61
  quits Mitchell Brothers, 160, 188
Shagley, Maureen, 50, 85, 158–60
Shampoo (film), 170
Shaughnessy, Gerald, 95, 119–20
Shaw, Frank, 279–80
Shelton, Gilbert, 360
Shepherd, Cybill, 162
Sherill, Peter N., 158
Silva, Lou, 228
Simpson, Don, 111
Sinatra, Frank, 33
Sip the Wine (film), 250
Skaggs, Boz, 317
Slick, Grace, 125
Smart Aleck (film), 56
Smith, Arlo, 276
Smokey (sound man), 195
Sodom and Gomorrah: The Last Seven Days (film), 242–45, 247–48, 296
Soft (film), 113, 121
Sontag, Susan, 203–4
Southland (corporation), 344
Spain, Johnny, 383
Spectator, The (weekly newspaper), 285, 328, 397
Spelvin, Georgina, 236–37
Spiegelman, Art, 341, 360, 397
Spy magazine, 397
Stage A (San Francisco sound studio), 150–51, 162, 166, 170
Stag films, 56–58, 99

Stanich, Vince, 88, 150, 196, 198, 235, 246–47, 397
  Nickelodeon created by, 227–29, 233
Steel, Tom, 302, 366, 383
Steinbeck, John, 21
Steinem, Gloria, 281–83, 284
Steiner, George, 204–5
Stratford (California), 26
Streets of San Francisco, The (TV show), 146
Streisand, Barbra, 164, 181
Summer of Laura (film), 107
Sundahl, Debi, 284, 327
Sunshine & Health (magazine), 58
Surf Rescue Team (San Francisco), 350–52
Sutter Cinema (San Francisco), 90, 110, 172
Sweeney, Micheal, 20, 31
Swingers, 136
Syufy Enterprises, 93

Tanya (performer), 286, 304–5, 309
Tarnower, Herman, 383
Taxi Driver (film), 395
Telegraph Avenue (Berkeley, California), 357
Thatcher, Lisa. *See* Adams, Lisa
Thompson, Hunter S., 2, 150, 323, 335, 354, 359–60
Time magazine, 359
Tompkins, Sherri, 378–79
Topless dancing, 58–59, 230, 239
Traynor, Chuck, 237–41, 264, 282, 305–9, 331, 398
Trident restaurant (Sausalito, California), 334
Truffaut, François, 45, 49, 250
Trump, Ivana, 383
Tubes (band), 227
Turner, Tina, 309
Turtle Island Press, 341
Tynan, Kenneth, 204

Ultrakore (film series), 248, 262
Ulysses (book), 121
University of California at Berkeley. *See* Berkeley, University of California at
Up Against the Wall (film), 113, 119, 121
Updike, John, 210
USA Today, 338

Valenti, Jack, 208

Valium, 330, 354
VCR revolution, 251–52
Vee, Bobby, 33
Vietnam War, 37–38, 42, 55, 60–61, 66,
    80, 129–31, 134, 158, 336, 358
Vincent, Gene, 33
Vinton, Bobby, 33
Voight, Jon, 336
Von Daniken, Erich, 247

Wall, Tessie, 81
Wall Street Journal, The, 337–38
Walnut Creek (California), 317
Walter, Bernard, 275–79, 293, 311, 398
Ward, Jerry, 64–73, 147, 176–77, 185,
    187, 213, 220, 234, 262, 398
  lawsuit of, 249–50
War News, 358–60, 361, 363, 368
Washington *Post,* 318
Wasserman, John, 42, 247, 258
Wayne, John, 34–35, 227, 247, 296, 325
Weathermen, 82

Weiner, Sol, 96, 97, 115–16, 117–18
Welles, Orson, 291
Weston, Rusty, x
Where the Buffalo Roam (film), 2, 354
White, Dan, 274
Whitty, Mary Jane. *See* Mitchell, Mary
    Jane
Wild Campus (film), 154, 174–75
Willis, Bruce, 397
Wilson, S. Clay, 360
Winchester, Sarah, 262
Women Against Pornography (WAP), 280–
    81, 283
Women Who Love Too Much Therapy, 345
Wood, Natalie, 238
World War II, 55, 176
Wright, Frank Lloyd, 381
Wright, Lillian, 271–73, 283

Zaffarano, Michael "Mickey," 210–11
Zane, Maitland "Sandy," xi, 61, 95–97, 398
Zirpoli, Alfonso J., 93–94, 97

JOHN HUBNER, winner of several prestigious journalistic prizes and staff writer for the San Jose *Mercury News*, is the author of the best-selling *Monkey on a Stick: Murder, Madness, and the Hare Krishnas*. He lives in San Jose, California.